# SMALL POWERS IN ALIGNMENT

Catholic University of Leuven
Department of Political Science
Studies in International Relations Number 2
Under the Editorial Direction of Prof. Dr. O. De Raeymaeker

# SMALL POWERS IN ALIGNMENT

by   Omer DE RAEYMAEKER
     Willy ANDRIES
     Luc CROLLEN
     Herman DE FRAYE
     Frans GOVAERTS

LEUVEN UNIVERSITY PRESS
1974

© 1974 by Leuven University Press

Krakenstraat 3, B-3000 Leuven/Louvain (Belgium)

Wettelijk Depot Nummer: D/ 1974/ 1869/ 3
ISBN-nummer: 90 6186 014 8

# ACKNOWLEDGMENTS

*Although the authors are solely responsible for the views and opinions expressed in this book, they are gratefully indebted to the following persons for their advice, encouragement and stimulating criticism.*

*Luc Crollen's contribution is to a certain extent the result of a series of interviews carried out during the month of June 1968 and involving diplomats, politicians, and civil servants responsible for the elaboration and execution of Portuguese foreign policy. These interviews have been made possible thanks to a Fellowship granted by the North Atlantic Treaty Organization in 1968. His gratitude for this financial and administrative assistance goes therefore to this Organization and its Cultural Relations Officer Mr. J. Vernon.*

*Willy Andries is grateful to the Belgian National Foundation of Scientific Research for assisting him with a grant which made it possible to do research in Turkey. He had interviews and contacts with several Turkish politicians, civil servants and diplomats and he is especially indebted to Mr. Ariman, Turkish official at NATO, who was extremely helpful in selecting the Turkish officials to be interviewed. Finally, he wants to express his gratitude for the help and assistance rendered by the Belgian Consulate in Istanbul and the staff of the Belgian Embassy in Ankara.*

*Herman De Fraye expresses his special thanks to the Belgian Ministry of Education, whose generous allowance enabled him to make a prolonged study trip to Denmark in the autumn of 1969 where the Danish Atlantic Association proved most helpful in making contacts with politicians, scholars, and journalists. Thanks are also due to the Royal Library of Copenhagen and Aarhus.*

*Finally, Frans Govaerts is obliged to the following people for their critical comments on his contribution: Ambassador L. Schaus, A. van Staden, J.H. Leurdijk, Dr. L.G.M. Jacquet, Professor E.H. van der Beugel, Major R. Schal-*

5

broeck. He owes a word of thanks to Mrs. B. Leliaert, who aided him in the initial research on Dutch foreign policy.


The authors are especially indebted to Professor L. Daugherty, Director of the Institute of Modern Languages and Communication (Brussels) who made the necessary arrangements with the authorities of Boston University to correct language and style errors. Our thanks go to Professor E. Bustin and especially Miss P. Horn. We would also like to thank the Commission for Publications of Leuven University Press for its financial assistance which made the publication possible. The authors are indebted to Mr. L. Van Depoele, assistant in the research-group "International Relations" of the K.U.L., who contributed by his valuable advice to the thinking that has gone into this book.

Finally, our thanks go to Mrs. M. Niclaes and Mrs. J. Nackaerts who took care with both grace and effectiveness of the typographical work.

# TABLE OF CONTENTS

# THE AUTHORS

**Omer De Raeymaeker** is Dr. jur., Dr. rer. pol. et diplom., ordinary professor at the Faculty of Social Sciences of the Catholic University of Leuven (K.U.L.). He is chairman of the Department of Political Science, director of the research-group "International Relations" of the K.U.L., ex-chairman of the Institute for Political and Social Sciences, professor at the Université Catholique de Louvain, ex-vice-president of the Belgian National Foundation for Scientific Research, member of the Board of Directors of the Belgian Institute of International Relations, member of the International Law Association, member of the Board of Directors of the Belgian Institute of Political Science, deputy-chairman of the Belgian-Luxembourg-American Studies Association.
He was also visiting professor at the Department of History of Kent State University (Ohio, U.S.A.) in 1967, and at the Department of International Relations of the Hebrew University of Jerusalem and the universities of Algiers and Oran in 1972. He received a Fulbright travel grant in 1967 and is ex-representative of Belgium in the Economic and Social Council of the United Nations.

**Luc Crollen** is Research Fellow at the Department of Political Science (Catholic University of Leuven) and Lecturer at the College of Europe - SUNY programme (Bruges). A graduate of Leuven University *(Licentiaat in de Pol. en Sociale Wet.)*, he has been granted a NATO research Fellowship in 1968. He has studied both in Italy (Bologna Center, SAIS) and in the U.S. and holds a Master's Degree from the Johns Hopkins University School of Advanced International Studies. He has written a number of articles on NATO problems and a book under the title, *Portugal, the U.S. and NATO* (Leuven: Leuven University Press, 1973). His Ph. D. thesis is on *Small Powers in International Systems* (Leuven: Acco, 1974). He teaches courses in Strategic Studies and Contemporary U.S.-European Relations.

11

**Willy Andries** is Research Fellow at the Department of Political Science at the Catholic University of Leuven. After graduating at Leuven University (Licentiaat in de politieke en sociale wetenschappen), he studied as a fellow of the Belgian American Educational Foundation at Columbia University in New York and obtained the Master of Arts degree in 1969. He teaches a course on "International Politics since 1945" at the K.U.L. and "Comparative Politics" and "International Organization" at the Katholieke Vlaamse Hogeschool in Antwerp. He is presently preparing a Ph. D. thesis on "U.S. Policy towards the Establishment of the State of Israel."


**Herman De Fraye** studied political science at the Catholic University of Leuven and contemporary history at Kent State University, Kent, Ohio.
He was research assistant in the political science department at Leuven and at the College of Europe, Bruges. He prepares a doctoral dissertation on Yugoslavia and integration in East and West Europe under Professor J. Lukaszewski, rector at the College of Europe, and Professor O. De Raeymaeker, Leuven.


**Frans Govaerts** is Research Fellow of the National Foundation for Scientific Research at the Department of Political Science of the Catholic University of Leuven. He studied Germanic Philology and Political Science at Leuven University and is preparing a Ph. D. thesis on "Switzerland and the Common Market." A publication on "The Impact of the Cold War on Belgium" is in print.

# INTRODUCTION

by Omer DE RAEYMAEKER

For almost a quarter of a century, political scientists and specialists in international relations consistently have forsaken the subject of small states. However, the recent publication of two books and numerous articles which attempt to define the small-power phenomenon and formulate theoretical rules concerning small-power behavior are evidence of a remarkable revival of the subject. With the exception of Annette Baker Fox's pioneering investigation into the behavior of five small neutral European states in World War II *(1)*, very little systematic work had been done on small states' foreign policies previous to Robert Rothstein's *Alliances and Small Powers (2)* and David Vital's *The Inequality of States. (3)* The latter two works are welcome contributions to knowledge about the historical behavior of small nations within alliances (Rothstein) and to the precarious situation of the isolated "maverick, unaligned power, the small power alone" in the contemporary world (Vital). None of these studies exhausts all aspects of the topic, however. Additional investigations of small-power capabilities, determinants, motivations, and behavioral patterns during the Cold War and the era of peaceful coexistence seem useful, even necessary.

One of the most striking features of contemporary international politics has been the rise of the lesser states, if not in power at least in numbers. There are as of now 135 states in the U.N., of which at least 120 are labelled simply *small powers* or *small states* both by foreign-policy makers and foreign-policy scholars. Certainly the increment of the number of small states in the international arena has by no means changed the traditional proposition that the great powers have always possessed both the substance and the form of power, whereas the small states have possessed merely the accidental attributes of power. International politics being quintessentially power politics (we define the

1 Annette Baker Fox, *The Power of Small States* (Chicago, 1959).
2 (New York, 1968).
3 (London, 1967).

15

phrase without pejorative or purely *Realpolitik* connotation), the majority of scholars in the field quite naturally are primarily interested in the behavioral patterns of the so-called essential units of the international systems, namely, the great powers. The very structure of the international systems has always been defined in terms of the number of great powers in them, without any reference to the power political situation of the lesser states. The great powers are the very core around which international politics evolve. They continue to seek and to possess what R. Aron calls an offensive capacity. They continue "to take the initiative, make alliances, stand at the head of coalitions." *(4)* The states of the first rank still consider the maintenance of their power position of primary political value. They continue to subordinate considerations of welfare, of political tradition, and of national ideals to the diplomatic and military requirements of power. As Quincy Wright once put it, "the great powers have been the great fighters not only because power has made for belligerency and successful belligerency has made for power, but also because the great powers have had a better chance of surviving war than have the little powers." *(5)* In short, the great powers have always been and still are system dominant. It is only natural then that the scholars of power and power relationships are most often lured into the study of intragreat-power rivalry and cooperation.

Nevertheless, despite the traditional theory that the influence of the small states remains weak in a world of power politics, one cannot ignore them altogether. We will never reach a well ordered world "by ignoring the differences between the elephants and the squirrels of international politics." *(6)* As the concept itself reveals, a small power is not entirely powerless. It may exert influence not only on the even weaker members of the international hierarchy, but also on the power permeated segment of the international system. And even if one ascertains that in a world of power relations one does not compensate one's own weakness with the weakness of others but rather with countervailing power, the source of which cannot be with the weaker but with the more powerful members of the international community, it still seems useful that at least some scholars -- particularly those raised in a small country -- devote some time and energy to the study of the latter mechanisms.

The purpose of the present study is to contribute to the efforts of those aiming at a better understanding of the position and role of the weak in a world

4  R. Aron, *Peace and War. A Theory of International Relations* (New York, 1966), p. 83.
5  Q. Wright, *A Study of War* (Chicago, 1942), p. 268.
6  W.T.R. Fox, *The Superpowers – The United States, Britain and the Soviet Union: Their Responsability for Peace* (New York, 1944), p. 3.

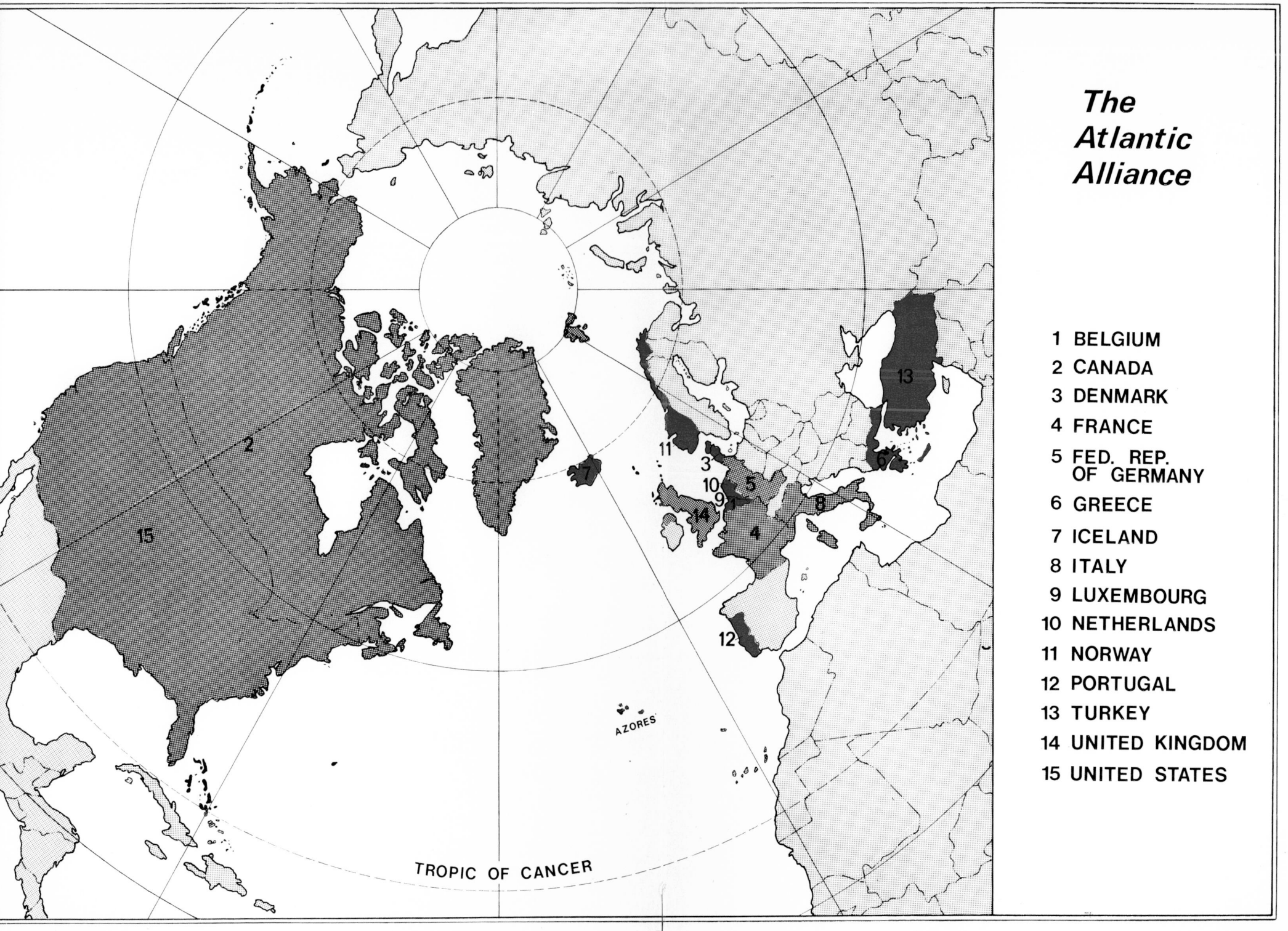

## The Atlantic Alliance

1 BELGIUM
2 CANADA
3 DENMARK
4 FRANCE
5 FED. REP. OF GERMANY
6 GREECE
7 ICELAND
8 ITALY
9 LUXEMBOURG
10 NETHERLANDS
11 NORWAY
12 PORTUGAL
13 TURKEY
14 UNITED KINGDOM
15 UNITED STATES

AZORES

TROPIC OF CANCER

dominated by the strong, more particularly to small-power behavior toward and within alliance systems. The authors' concern is with the smaller West European NATO members. Before selecting the major issues upon which this study focuses, however, two questions need consideration. Although it may not be possible to comprehensively and finally define the concepts *small power (7)* and *alignment*, we must at least state what both mean to us.

## On the Definition of the Concept of Small Power (8)

A clear-cut definition of a small power is hard to reach, because the smallness or the greatness of a country is a relative thing. Still, the attempt has to be made, because the very act of defining will show the lack of maneuverability and of choice in the formulation of a small power's basic strategic orientation. The

---

7  Until now there have been almost as many definitions as authors. See, for instance, Annette Baker Fox: "We cannot avoid some definition of small states. On a world scale of powers these might include all those below the well-recognized rank occupied by Great Britain, France, Germany, and China, but not necessarily those often ranked as middle powers, such as Canada, Italy or India. The definition depends upon the use, and in different domains the classification will differ. Thus some states, not all of them small, are more influential in determining economic issues than military questions (Germany and Holland, for example). Since our concern is with the whole international system we can think of small states as those whose leaders (as well as those of other powers) recognize that their own state's political weight is limited to a local arena rather than a global one, that they are dependent upon outside political forces for much of their security, and that their particular state's interests may be dispensable in the eyes of one or more great powers" (Annette Baker Fox, "The Small States in the International System, 1919-1969," *International Journal*, XXIV, 4 (1969), pp. 751-752); R. Rothstein: "A small power is a state which recognizes that it cannot obtain security primarily by use of its own capabilities and that it must rely fundamentally on the aid of other states, institutions, processes or developments to do so; the small powers belief in its ability to rely on its own means must also be recognized by the other states in international politics." (R. Rothstein, *op. cit.*, p. 29). A more complex but perhaps more accurate definition can be found in R. Keohane's "Lilliputians' Dilemmas: Small States in International Politics", *International Organization*, XXIII, 2 (1969), p. 296: "A Great Power is a state whose leaders consider that it can, alone, exercise a large, perhaps decisive, impact on the international system; a secondary power is a state whose leaders consider that alone it can exercise some impact, although never in itself decisive, on that system; a middle power is a state whose leaders consider that it cannot act alone effectively but may be able to have a systemic impact in a small group or through an international institution; a small power is a state whose leaders consider that it can never, acting alone or in a small group, make a significant impact on the system".

8  See O. De Raeymaeker, "Signification de l'appartenance à une alliance pour les petits pays", *Chronique de Politique Etrangère*, XXIV, 1 (January, 1971), pp. 5-35. From the same author: "Betekenis van de alliantie-oplossing voor de kleine landen", *Congres Defensiepolitiek der Kleine Mogendheden, Eeuwfeest – Krijgsschool* (Brussel, 1971), pp. 128-166.

authors agree completely with R. Aron, who writes in his *Peace and War*: "The states called 'small powers' generally have -- can only have -- defensive ambitions. They seek to survive as such, as seats of free decisions." *(9)* Another author, David Vital, thinks in the same terms: "The measure of State Power is the capacity of a government to induce other states -- or governments -- to follow lines of conduct or policy which they might otherwise not pursue; alternatively it is the capacity to withstand the pressure of other states -- or governments -- which are intent on deflecting it from a course which the national interest -- or the interests of its leaders -- would appear to require." *(10)* Vital adds: "But in fact all nations or governments may be in situations where the non-customary posture dominates; small states may seek to pursue an active policy." *(11)*

Indeed, many examples exist of small nations that have the ambition to act as if they were great or that on occasion took on offensive postures, refusing to restrict themselves to a status quo policy or a purely defensive stand. At the Paris Peace Conference of 1919, for example, Belgium attempted the adaptation of the boundaries determined by the treaties of 1839, or at least the creation of international servitudes at Dutch cost. Another example is the expansionist policy of Israel after 1948, of Greece in the 1920s ("Greater Greece"), and of Egypt in the 1960s (union with Syria). It seems clear, however, that small countries lack both the capacity and the political will to act offensively and to exert a decisive influence on other nations. Small countries usually hold to the status quo; they never nourished imperial dreams (Luxembourg) or gave them up (Holland, Sweden).

*The foreign policy of small states therefore aims at withstanding pressure from the great powers, at safeguarding their territorial integrity and independence, and at insuring the continued adhesion to national values and ideals. A small power is a state on the defensive, a state that thirsts for security.*

Accepting this definition does not diminish the obligation to search out criteria to classify the countries in various categories. When one understands the concept of power as essentially the capacity to use violence, that is, military power or force, only two countries belong to the category of superpowers: the United States of America and the Soviet Union. But as J. Boyesen states in his

---

9   R. Aron, *op. cit.*, p. 83.
10   D. Vital, *op. cit.*, p. 87.
11   *Ibid.*

study, "Contributions of Small Powers to the Alliance" *(12)*: "in view of their histories and traditions, population and economic strength, it would hardly occur to anyone to call countries like Britain and France or Germany or Italy Small Powers". Nobody will deny that France, the United Kingdom, and Germany have the capacity and the political will to influence other countries through the threat or actual use of military, political, and/or economic coercion. Indeed, international politics cannot be reduced to the possession and use of an efficient military instrument. *Wars occur, politics endure. (13)* A whole range of categories, from the superpowers -- the U.S. and the U.S.S.R. -- down to the so-called micropowers *(14)* of West Samoa and the Barbados Islands, are needed to reflect this situation. Besides Imperial America *(15)* and the Soviet Union, other large powers exist, such as China, Great Britain, and France. Examples of the middle powers are Italy, India, and Mexico. Such countries as the Benelux and the Scandinavian countries, the countries of Central and Eastern Europe, Greece, Turkey, and most countries in Latin America, Africa, and Asia belong to the category of small powers.

Unlike D. Vital, *(16)* we do not believe it possible to find appropriate definitions for the concepts of small powers and great powers based on purely quantitative criteria. *(17)* He describes the category of small powers as including all economically advanced countries with a population of ten to fifteen million maximum, and all developing countries as those with a population of twenty to thirty million maximum. However, he does not provide a clear framework for distinguishing between developed and less developed nations. In addition, Soviet satellites such as Poland or Czechoslovakia, which have a relatively large population and cannot be labelled *less* developed, have lost so much of their independence and room to maneuver since World War II that it is difficult to include them in the category of middle powers.

Hence we want to stress that:
1) There is no definite and well-defined hierarchy of states. Small states may in

---

12  J. Boyesen, "Contributions of Small Powers to the Alliance", E.S. Furniss, (ed.), *The Western Alliance. Its Status and Prospects* (Athens, Ohio, 1965), p. 117.

13  C.B. Marshall, "The Nature of Foreign Policy", *Department of State Bulletin*, XXVI, 664, p. 420.

14  J. Van der Steen, "De V.N. en de micro-staten. Problemen omtrent de toetreding van micro-staten tot de V.N.", *Revue belge de droit international*, VII, 2 (1971), pp. 578-618.

15  See R. Aron, *La République impériale. Les Etats-Unis dans le monde 1945-1972* (Paris, 1973), and G. Liska, *Imperial America. The International Politics of Primacy* (Baltimore, 1968).

16  D. Vital, *op. cit.*, p. 8.

17  A much more sophisticated quantitative study is the memoir of G. Tegenbos, *De machtshiërarchie der staten* (Louvain, 1972).

certain circumstances behave as if they were great and vice versa. Whether a state can be considered small, great, or medium depends on the level of analysis. Thus, a state great or medium on the regional level can be small on the global level. For instance, Egypt may be a great power in relation to its direct environment; compared to the Soviet Union it is definitely a small state.

2) The greatness or smallness of states is also related to the issues under investigation. Undoubtedly Belgium or Holland are relatively weak with reference to the global strategic balance and in terms of military manpower. Yet in international trade and international monetary matters both nations rank highly.

3) A rigid division of all nation-states into great and small powers seems too simplistic. A varied and flexible set of categories is more tenable and more useful.

For our purposes, however, in view of both the kinds of issues investigated -- diplomatic and strategic problems -- and the level of analysis -- the NATO framework -- it seems reasonable to put Portugal, Greece, Turkey, Denmark, Norway, Iceland, Belgium, Holland, and Luxembourg into the category of small European powers.

### Alignment, Nonalignment, and the International Political System

The concepts of alignment and nonalignment will be analyzed here in the light of the balance-of-power theory in international politics. This theory draws on the equilibrium model used by many disciplines, such as economics. It postulates either a bipolar or a multipolar international system. The actors on the stage of international politics -- principally states -- are supposed to have the natural tendency to consciously or unconsciously oppose excessive concentrations of power in one nation or group of nations. Under conditions of the possible use of force, the increment in the coercion capacity of one power unit will lead to a more or less proportionate growth of the means of coercion of at least one other unit in the system. Great disturbances in the equilibrium of the system, for instance, through the rise of an hegemonial power, will generally lead the other actors to augment their coercive capacities and/or to join together for the purpose of containment. This leads to equilibrium or stalemate, situations which may then be provisional or permanent, partial or total. Change is not impossible. Equilibrium may be disturbed and eventually end up in a new equilibrium on a different level. *(18)*

18 See H. Morgenthau, *Politics among Nations. The Struggle for Power and Peace* (New York, 1948), and G. Liska, *International Equilibrium* (Cambridge, Mass., 1957). From the same author: *Nations in Alignment. The Limits of Interdependence* (Baltimore, 1962).

Alliances are regulators in the equilibrium mechanism. They are as old as the spear and as modern as strategic nuclear weapons, and tribes, city-states, peoples, and states have sought various kinds to fulfill their respective security needs. Nowadays entire continents are entrenched in alliances. Yet even the permanent ones seldom last. They fail and fall apart; they are successful but may experience a disintegrative process. Today's ally may be a neutral tomorrow and an adversary the day after, and in fact alliances perform their various functions through movement as well as through their existence. The principal movements include joining an alliance (alignment), leaving an alliance (dealignment), or returning to an alliance (realignment). Conflicts are the first although not the only determinants of such movements, the process of which starts whenever a state or a grouping of different states is perceived as a threat. In economic terms one could say that an alliance aims at maximizing the profits and sharing the burdens. Hence, the North Atlantic pact is an equilibrium regulator in the bipolar world structure. The rationale of its creation was Soviet expansionism. During the sixties a limited disintegrative process occured; some political leaders were convinced that the alliance had completely fulfilled its task, the successful containment of the Soviet Union. Yet no country chose to withdraw when the twenty-years membership period lapsed.

Since small states are essentially defensive, they have few alternatives in a world which, because of alliances, aims at equilibrium. Only two fundamental options are possible:

1 *Alignment:*
A small state can decide to ally itself with one or more states in order to deter a potential aggressor. This can be done on either a bilateral or a multilateral basis.

2 *Nonalignment:*
A small state may decide to provide its security outside alliance systems. Various kinds of nonalliance policies range from neutralization or permanent neutrality to neutralism, nonalignment, and noninvolvment.

At present the world structure is still bipolar on the strategic and nuclear level, but on the political level shows a tendency toward new power centers. This may be the case in the short run with China and Japan for example, and in the long run with Europe. Within this structure a strategically-located small state seems to have only two alternatives: integration in one of the two power blocs, or the risky nonalignment option that hopes for no conflict, or if conflict happens, hopes for uninvolvement.

For our purposes two series of questions are relevant. A first is related to the security alternatives of small powers caught in the middle of great power rivalry and conflict. Which range of policies is open to them, once confronted with the rise of an hegemonial power within a particular international system, in this case the post-World War II bipolar system? Should they achieve security through an alliance or a nonalliance policy? What is the rationale behind alignment, nonalignment, or dealignment? Is the quest for survival but one of a wide gamut of motives for choosing an alliance or a nonalliance policy?

A second series of questions is related to the posture and behavior of small powers within an alliance, in this case the North Atlantic alliance, once the decision to join has been taken. What does smallness denote? Does it mean lack of influence within the alliance? How do small states derive advantages and share responsibilities with reference to their own national interests? How does the influence of small powers contribute to or detract from the cohesion of the alliance system?

Four studies dealing with Portugal, Greece, and Turkey, Norway, Denmark, and Iceland, and Holland, Belgium, and Luxembourg will allow us to offer some tentative answers. All contributions are built on a more or less similar structure. They all endeavor to concentrate on the motives which led the concerned powers to become part of the North Atlantic treaty in 1949 or later, and led at least some of them to question the validity of staying members during the period between 1966 and 1972, although eventually none of them withdrew after the twenty-years period which was set by the treaty.

In addition to concentrating on the motives of alignment or possible dealignment, clearly the very core of this study, the four contributions all touch upon the question of how these small states have sought to exercise some influence on the formulation and/or implementation of NATO policies and continued to seek a balance between their national interests and the exigencies of intra-allied solidarity and cooperation. For the study of the latter problem area we have set up no general scheme or framework of analysis proper to the four contributions. Concern for this type of question grew a posteriori out of the dynamics of the individual contributions themselves. Each essay, initially only interested in the hows of the process of alignment and dealignment, later became entangled in a whole range of sui generis questions related both to the behavior of the small powers within the alliance and to the specifics of each country's geographical location and particular political experience. Thus, Portugal's entanglement in a protracted conflict in Africa, the Greek and Turkish rivalry over Cyprus, the Scandinavian NATO allies' conflict between Nordic cooperation and the Common Market, and the Benelux's middle

posture on the European Europe–Atlantic partnership dilemma, are all problems discussed in the individual contributions somewhere between the analysis of the alignment and quasi-dealignment phases. Conclusions on these types
of questions occur within the closing remarks of the various contributions.

In discussing the core of this study, we have tried to set up an unpretentious
yet operational framework of analysis useful throughout and dealt with more
thoroughly in the final conclusions. We have assumed that a small power élite
making decisions about alignment, nonalignment, and dealignment, seeks to
maintain or improve its position in the international, regional, or domestic
arena. In theory, decisions about such kind of movements are made with
reference to the national interest. However, no abstract criterion for defining a
state's national interest exists. To supply reliable guidance in analyzing alignment and nonalignment motives, we have found it necessary to refer to "concrete conditions and conflicts, and to particular objectives" *(19)* in matters of
security, the status of states and regimes in the international community,
domestic stability, economic aid and military assistance, and ideology.

Each of these small power motives for adhering to or possibly withdrawing
from alliances will be discussed below:

### 1. *Security in Relation to the Geographical Situation*
The first and most vital motive determining a small power's basic strategic
choice is the quest of survival as an independent and sovereign entity. To
survive, a small power élite must defend its national sovereignty and territorial
integrity. Yet the security of a small nation depends heavily on variables within
the international system and on its geographic and topographic location
within the system. Much will also depend on the small nation's historical
experience, on its perceptions concerning the attitudes of foes and friends alike,
on the military capabilities of enemies, on its own industrial-military potential,
on the quality of its leaderships, its morale, its political cohesion, and similar
characteristics.

### 2. *Prestige in the International Community*
A nation's relative rank in the international hierarchy of prestige, thus of its
estimation in the eyes of other countries' decision makers, is not altogether
insignificant. An alliance or nonalliance policy may enhance or diminish a
small power's status. Superior recognition will accord it wider influence in the
international community, and by the same token the prestige of its ruling élite

*19*  Liska, *Nations in Alliance*, p. 26.

will augment or decrease. Prestige is also a kind of first defense line of a country's security. Its erosion may induce other nations to consider pressure or even attack.

### 3. Domestic Stability

Domestic stability may be threatened by "material and political burdens and strains flowing from alliance" (20) or nonalliance. Whether small states' decision makers decide to join or reject a coalition is very much related to their quest for the security of tenure. Some governments may stay or fall by their identification with a great power or a coalition. Particularly in democratic nations the government's choices may be narrowly limited by pressure from the press, public opinion, various interest groups, or the legislature.

### 4. Economic Aid and Military Assistance

In the eyes of the ruling élite, even in the eyes of the peoples concerned, alliances may result favorably in the pooling of resources and the material support of allies. As G. Liska argues: "On the economic plane, alliance promotes internal stability most commonly when pooling of resources and division of roles among members enables a regime to stop short of mobilizing disaffected groups and interests; beyond that, alliances may entail outright subsidy or other forms of material support." (21) But this attraction that a stronger state holds for the weaker aware of its trade and economic needs is only provisional. "Resentment of economic dependence and an opportunity to draw on alternative sources and outlets" (22) may set off a political reaction.

### 5. Ideology

Ideology, which may or may not be tied to cultural affinity, is definitely related to the ruling élite's quest for both external and internal security. For instance, in the West the fear of Russian expansionism was probably augmented by the fear of Communist ideology and totalitarian political structure.

Almost certainly, then, the movement toward or away from an alliance is a function of these five motives, and any assessment of a basic strategic choice involves a comparison of the hypothetical gains and liabilities of either move. Whether interstate or intergroup conflicts determine a country's position depends on their relative intensity. This question will be also discussed in the various contributions.

20   Ibid., p. 30.
21   Ibid. p. 37.
22   Ibid., p 14.

24

Part I considers Portugal, a special case in the series because of its insistence on empire in an age of anti-imperialism. We then turn to NATO's flank nations, in the first instance to Greece and Turkey (Part II). The Truman Doctrine made the two quasi-allies of the U.S. even before the North Atlantic alliance was set up. Enthusiastic in the beginning, they turned more and more critical because of the ambiguous attitude of both the U.S. and NATO in the Cyprus affair. The northern flank nations, Norway, Denmark, and Iceland (Part III) are considered next. Never enthusiastic and sometimes reluctant, they continue to dream about great schemes of Nordic cooperation, but at the same time they are forced to rely on NATO for their defense and on the Common Market for their economic survival. Finally, Part IV is devoted to the faithful. The Benelux nations have been among the first and most consistent supporters of the Western defense coalition. In the forefront of the fight for defense, then for deterrence, and now for détente, they have probably had more influence on NATO policies than their small size might suggest.

\*   \*   \*

As the research for the various contributions ended by the end of 1972, *(23)* the reader may notice that recent developments were consequently not covered. These new events (e.g., the military coup in Portugal, the Greek-Turkish feud about oil resources in the Aegean Sea, a strong anti-NATO tendency in one of the governmental parties in Holland, the military coup in Cyprus, the Greek and Turkish interventions in this country, the changes of regime in Greece, the Greek-Turkish conflict, the decision of Greece to leave the NATO-Organization), however, are not derogatory to the analysis of the alignment and dealignment processes which constitute the central theme of the book.

---

*23* The contribution by H. De Fraye on "Denmark, Norway, and Iceland" ended, however, somewhat later.

# Part I
# PORTUGAL

By Luc Crollen

# INTRODUCTION

Portugal, for some a tiny, underdeveloped, and poor republic of south-western Europe, for others a commenwealth of huge dimensions extending far into Africa and Asia, is at present both a European and an Afro-Asian power. Sharing the Iberian Peninsula with Spain, metropolitan Portugal covers 35,553 square miles – 92,082 square kilometers – (including the Azores and the Madeira islands in the Atlantic), with a population of roughly 9.78 million. Overseas Portugal at present consists of Angola and Portuguese Guinea in West Africa, Mozambique in East Africa, the Cape Verde Islands of São Tomé and Principe, Macão in China, Timor in the Indonesian archipelago. In addition it still claims the Indian provinces of Goa, Diu, and Damão, although they have been under Indian occupation since 1961. Is Portugal, then, a small nation or an empire?

In reaction to the eruption of rebellion in three of his overseas possessions, Antonio de Oliveira Salazar, prime minister of Portugal, tenaciously defended Portugal's centuries-old, vast, multiracial, pluricontinental, Christian, Lusitanian community. As his action shows, Portugal continues to think of itself as a world empire; in the Atlantic alliance, however, the emphasis clearly has always been on Portugal's European role as a small NATO member rather than on its universal mission.

In addition to looking for the factors which determined Portugal's alignment with the Atlantic powers and for the rationale behind its possible dealignment, this contribution also explains how much almost every aspect of Portuguese political life, particularly of contemporary Portuguese foreign policy, has consistently been a function of Portugal's obstinate efforts to hold the line in Africa.

# Chapter I

# PORTUGAL ENTERS THE ATLANTIC ALLIANCE

Flanking the western side of the Iberian Peninsula and bordering the Atlantic Ocean, Portugal is first an Atlantic nation. The great oceans, the great spaces were the source of its power. There was a time when Portugal ranked first in navigation, in the race for discoveries, conquests and empire building. Since then other Atlantic nations have asserted their maritime primacy, yet the sea remained Portugal's highest calling and continues to explain much of Portuguese contemporary political behavior and foreign policy. For some, Portugal's adherence to the North Atlantic Treaty has been an incomprehensible departure from traditional political wisdom, diverting Lusitanian energies from wide global civilizing missions to narrow inextricable problems in the heart of continental Europe. To a certain point one may argue that Portugal's need for empire compelled its friendly relations with the dominating powers in the Atlantic, Great Britain and the U.S. Yet did this necessarily require Portugal's entrance into a western alliance, the main task of which is to hold the line in Central Europe? Other factors had a bearing on Portugal's entry into NATO. Some, such as the compulsion of the international system itself, the quest for security and survival as an independent nation, and the search for increasing prestige abroad, were international. Others, for example the security of tenure of the political élite, were national.

## FROM NEUTRAL NEUTRALITY TO BENEVOLENT NEUTRAL

After relying for many centuries on an English alliance for protection of its overseas possessions and as a check against possible Spanish ambitions, Portugal sought to broaden its foreign policy base and reach out for new international friendships. *(1)* In the years before the second world war, the country emphasized its kinship with Brazil, its growing understanding with Franco's Spain, its reconciliation with the Holy See, and its sympathy for Mussolini's

1  H. Kay, *Salazar and Modern Portugal* (London, 1970), p. 121.

Italy. It was as if Portugal wanted to make it clear that it had grown up and could function without British guardianship. Daring enough to show its independence of the British, it was prudent enough not to sever ties with Geat Britain altogether. Anglo-Portuguese trade was affected by the plans for economic self-sufficiency of Salazar's Estado Novo and by a decrease of exports to Britain, particularly port wine. German and Italian propaganda and influence were allowed to flourish in Lisbon. Yet there can be no doubt that Prime Minister Salazar remained fundamentally loyal to the alliance. Some evidence indicates that in sharp contrast to Franco's scepticism he kept believing that England would stand undefeated, that the U.S. would join the war effort, and that eventually victory would go to the Allied powers. *(2)*

Hence, Salazar clearly wanted to do what had almost never succeeded in the past: to insulate Portugal from the coming cataclysms of World War II. His was a minor European power whose mainland and dependent Atlantic islands were so strategic that great wisdom, patience, and statesmanship were needed to avoid the dangers of war, at least to a tolerable degree. The matter was even more complex because Salazar was equally afraid of a war ending with a complete Axis victory. Such a victory would encourage the realization of the Falangists' dreams of Iberian unification, and would mean a long, exhausting war leading to the complete collapse of Germany accompanied by Soviet Russian expansion and the spread of Communism. In fact, without believing it possible, Salazar hoped for a short war, the conclusion of which should be some kind of stalemate or equipoise. Moreover, at the start of the war Salazar was as apprehensive of being pushed into English arms as he was of being cut off from them. He feared German covetousness of his country's colonies and he suspected American economic and even territorial ambitions in the Azores. To be sure, most of those suspicions turned out to be unjustified or unduly stressed. But this is perhaps partly due "to a six-year piece of tightrope diplomacy" *(3)* and to Salazar's brilliant efforts at equilibrium, which at first consisted of a well-balanced position of neutrality announced before Geat Britain and France had declared war on Germany. The basic principles of this policy were foreshadowed by Salazar's speech before the National Assembly on the 22 May 1939, and

---

2   In the *Milwaukee Sentinel* of 2 October 1968, the American journalist H.J. Taylor revealed that "as early as Hitler's attack on Poland, in 1939, and even after France fell", Salazar told him privately "that he foresaw a very long struggle and the war ending in an Allied victory, instead of a short war and a German peace". In February 1942 "when the Allied fortunes were still at a low ebb, Salazar insisted at his Seville meeting with Franco that the Allies would win in the end". (Kay, *op. cit.*, p. 123).

3   Kay, *op. cit.*, p. 122.

set forth in a statement on 1 September 1939. His policy contained three major points:

*1* Portugal's friendship with Great Britain and its loyalty to the English alliance were reaffirmed;
*2* Portugal would maintain the status of neutrality until its honor, interests or diplomatic commitments compelled the nation to abandon it;
*3* Each European state was duty bound to help create and consolidate peace, if necessary through the establishment of peace zones. Portugal and Spain would be part of an Iberian peace zone. *(4)*

From then on, Salazar played skillfully at the double role of neutral and ally, particularly in the economic sphere. In selling raw materials (notably wool, skins, tin, sardines, and olive oil) and even strategic goods such as wolfram (a vital component of modern weapons) to some belligerents of both sides, he believed that his desire to maintain "a sufficient and indeed a prosperous level of wartime trade" with both the Allies and the Axis was at least as much an assertion of "the rights and dignity of a neutral as a matter of expedient profiteering." *(5)* In the political and military spheres he at once took measures to check German penetration, which had extended deeply during the Spanish Civil War, *(6)* and to strengthen the defense of the Atlantic islands the latter on British advice and with American consent. If attacked by Germany, he would stage a token resistance and move his government to the Azores under the protection of British or American naval and air forces. With this idea in

4   K. Duff, "The War and the Neutrals", Arnold and Veronica Toynbee (eds.), *Survey of International Affairs*, (London, 1956) pp. 319-320. The original text in Antonio de Oliveira Salazar, *Discursos e notas Politicas* (Coimbra, 1944), III, pp. 173-174.
5   W.N. Medlicott, *The Economic Blockade* (London, 1952), II, p. 608. This fascinating book tells the story of Allied negotiations with Portugal concerning the economic blockade and the preemption campaign, and shows how "with considerable subtlety and some genuine passion" Salazar "maintained the rightness of a neutrality which extracted abundant profits from both sets of belligerents" (p. 582). Nevertheless, the record of Portugal's economic cooperation with Great Britain in the economic and financial fields is not all that gloomy. In July 1940, Portugal supported Great Britain's policy of assistance for Spain by supplying Spain with products from her colonies. Payment for this was to be made through Anglo-Spanish clearance. And in October of the same year Salazar agreed to supply Great Britain with escudos for the duration of the war in exchange for sterling credits. This behavior contrasted sharply with that of other neutrals, who only sold their currencies in exchange for gold. See Kay, *op. cit.*, p. 155.
6   During the Spanish Civil War the Germans gained considerable influence in Lisbon, particularly with the upper classes, the youth movement, the press, the universities, and the paramilitary legion. Also, the Portuguese security police were initially trained in Germany.

mind, he doubled the strength of the Portuguese army to 80,000 between 1940 and 1941 and deployed half of those troops in the Azores and Cape Verde Islands. *(7)* All this did not mean that Salazar renounced his plans for neutrality at this early stage of the war. A number of other Allied requests were rebuffed with vigor and as late as January 1943 he impounded and interned the crews of eleven American fighter aircraft which had been forced to land in Lisbon.

In time, however, Salazar felt he had to abandon too strict an interpretation of his rights and duties as a neutral for a more benevolent neutrality favoring the Allies. The turning point of this about-face was the Allied landings in North Africa. With the Battle of Alamein and the success of Operation Torch the Allies' chances of winning the war improved significantly and this meant that their "needs of mid-Atlantic bases" would grow "greater rather than less." *(8)* The Azores were thus bound to become a major issue in Allied Portuguese relations.

The Azores is the name given for an archipelago of nine islands comprising part of metropolitan Portugal and lying a "third of the way from Lisbon to New York." *(9)* The archipelago is divided into three widely scattered groups: the southeastern one consists of São Miguel, Santa Maria and Formigas. The central group includes Faial, Pico, Terceira, and Graciosa, and the north-eastern cluster comprises Flores and Corvo. The largest island is São Miguel. Its capital, Ponta Delgada (20,000 residents), is the largest port of the archipelago.

In the beginning, the strategic importance of the Azores was essentially related to antisubmarine warfare. It was from near the Azores that from 1942 on German U-boats ravaged the American and British Atlantic convoys, obliging them to follow the impracticable, icy northern route under bad weather conditions, particularly in the winter, without air cover. The staging of Allied bombers with a radius of 800 miles on Terceira Island would give air protection to Allied convoys and would allow them to chase and attack the U-boats, which met their supply submarines near the Azores or at the Bay of Biscay, and rested, refuelled, or recharged their batteries. An efficient anti-U-boat operation would permit greater variation of convoy routes. Allied shipping would be routed farther south, particularly when the U-boats concentrated in the north, and vise versa. Refuelling facilities at either San Miguel

---

7 *The Times*, 17 April 1943, reported that by the spring of 1943, eleven battalions of infantry and anti-aircraft batteries had been stationed in the Cape Verde Islands.
8 Duff, *op. cit.*, p. 336.
9 Kay, *op. cit.*, p. 160.

or Fayal would permit an increase in the carrying power of the convoys. At any rate, the greater the security of the convoys, the less the number of naval escorts needed to protect them. Bases in the Azores "could also be used for meteorological observations, navigational aid, and air-sea rescue." *(10)*

Later, with the lessening of U-boat pressure, the expansion of the theater of operations, notably in the Far East, and the increasing importance of air-supply on the Allied side, the Azores gained in importance as staging posts for the air-ferry route. At that time experts estimated that the occupation of the islands might save the Allies one million tons of shipping, thousands of lives, and 100 million gallons of aviation fuel a year. From a military point of view, the case for a swift Allied occupation of Portugal's Atlantic islands was over-whelming. But as long as there was any chance that Germany would retaliate by marching on Portugal through Spain, Salazar was very reluctant to grant such bases. Negotiations were extremely tough, lengthy, and unpleasant. Nevertheless, when Salazar realized that the Allies would seize those bases with or without Portuguese consent, he finally yielded to their pressure and on August 1943 entered into an agreement with the British on the basis of the Anglo-Portuguese alliance. *(11)* He was given explicit guarantees for Portu-guese sovereignty in the post war world, not only over the metropolitan area but over the entire Portuguese empire. *(12)* And notwithstanding all the talks and all the pressure, the facilities Portugal granted to the Allies were still narrowly limited. *(13)* They included: 1) the use of Lagens airfield on the

---

10  Duff, *op. cit.*, pp. 331-336. See also W. Churchill, *The Second World War* (London, 1950), III, pp. 388-389; IV, pp. 705, 716.
A. Eden, *The Reckoning* (London, 1965), pp. 390-400; Kay, *op. cit.*, pp. 165-170; F.L. Wood-ward, *British Foreign Policy in the Second World War* (London, 1952), pp. 375-376, 379-382.
11  On 12 October 1943, W. Churchill reported the agreement to Parliament in the following terms: "I have an announcement to make to the House arising out of the Treaty signed between this country and Portugal in the year 1373 between His Majesty King Edward III and King Ferdinand and Queen Eleanor of Portugal". Churchill, *op. cit.*, V, p. 146.
12  Eden, *op. cit.*, p. 393.
13  Salazar wanted to remain technically neutral. As a consequence, he wanted to restrict facilities to the British and Commonwealth members, that is, only to those who could have a claim under a treaty. He made it plain that he wanted no other than British troops on the island and even those should be limited in numbers. The Americans had no rights in Portugal whatsoever and should understand that "Portugal was not a country from which they could get everything by threats or bribes". In practice, however, Salazar himself agreed that it was very difficult to discriminate between British and American vessels, as the Allied convoys were mixed, and he "quickly allowed the refuelling facilities to be extended to American warships and merchant vessels" Kay, *op. cit.*, pp. 168-169. The regular use of the Lagens airfield by American transport aircraft began in November 1943. See G.F. Kennan, *Memoirs, 1925-1950* (Boston, 1967), pp. 158-159.

island of Terceira by all members of the British Commonwealth, with the possible use of facilities at Rabo de Peixa on São Miguel in emergencies; 2) the right to refuel, provision, and repair ships at the port of Horta on Fayal. In return, Salazar was promised fighter aircraft, anti-aircraft guns, and other material valued at fifteen million pounds sterling, together with the protection of his navy, merchant fleet, and deep-sea fishing vessels in the case of Axis retaliation.

This arrangement, satisfying to the British, left the Americans less than content. The Lagens airfield on Terceira island was considered by some members of the Joint Chiefs of Staff as nothing "but a goddam swamp", *(14)* not at all fit for the important role these men intended the archipelago to play in their overall strategy for the reconquest of Europe. The American armed forces demanded a list of facilities much more pretentious "than all that the British, even involving their ancient alliance, had ever dreamed of requesting: a naval base, a seaplane base, bases for landbased aircraft on three different islands, cable and communications systems, observation posts, radar, facilities for accomodation of American naval vessels" in each of the Azores ports with "unrestricted port facilities and shore accommodations for necessary personnel", and so on. *(15)* The American military wanted the Azores to offer those facilities which would permit the ferrying of a great number of landbased aircraft to Europe for participation in the Normandy invasion and later to support the Allied advances on the continent. *(16)*

Salazar was very suspicious of American intentions *(17)* and unwilling to

14   G.F. Kennan quoted General Henry H. Arnold, chief of staff of the United States Air Force (Kennan, *op. cit.*, p. 158).
15   *Ibid.*, p. 151.
16   The American Joint Chiefs of Staff estimated at that time that the use of the Azores "would permit a saving of about 51.5 million gallons of high octane aviation fuel. It would also release a great number of transport aircraft and ground personnel which otherwise would have been tied up in the effort to move those planes by a more costly and less direct northern route". U.S. Department of State, *Foreign Relations of the United States*, 1943, Europe, Vol. II, (Washington, D.C., 1964), pp. 547-548.
17   In sharp contrast with A. Eden's remarkable understanding of Salazar's mind and the Portuguese national character, American statesmen had been less patient with the Portuguese prime minister. At the start, both the president of the U.S. and the secretary of state, Cordell Hull, felt they should not occupy the Azores unless the Germans seized them or moved against continental Portugal or Spain. But in the spring 1941, negotiations between Darlan and Hitler opened the prospect of German aircraft and vessels at Dakar and even of a German attempt to set up bases in the Azores. American public opinion and the press became very restless. Some, for example Senator Pepper, recommended that the Azores should be seized without delay and if necessary without Lisbon's permission. And while the U.S. government agreed to leave negotiations concerning the archipelago to the British, President Roosevelt ordered

negotiate without receiving a prior American guarantee to respect Portuguese sovereignty in all Portuguese colonies. This was eventually extended to him on 23 October 1943 by the U.S. chargé d'affaires in Lisbon, G.F. Kennan. *(18)* But not until 28 November 1944 was a final agreement reached over a U.S. airbase on Santa Maria, of use only in the Far Eastern campaign. The agreement was concluded on the basis of Portugal's indirect participation in the operations of the Pacific, which was justified by the Japanese occupation of the Portuguese colony of Timor on 20 February 1942. *(19)* The covenant provided for an airdrome on Santa Maria to serve as an airbase (Art. Ia); stipulated that all construction, once in serviceable condition, was to be considered the property of the Portuguese state (Ib), and that the agreement would end six months after the termination of hostilities or the signing of an armistice with the power with which the U.S. was at war in the Far East. *(20)*

The Azores agreements, concluded with the British in 1943 and with the Americans in 1944, came in time to be of great value to the Allies in the Battle of the Atlantic and in the struggle for mastery of the Pacific. Throughout the

a force of 25,000 to be ready for action against the Azores. In a radio fireside chat on 27 May 1941, he again stressed his government's intention to guard against any German move toward the islands, in which case preemptive measures would be taken. All this aroused the indignation of Portuguese public opinion and a state of unease persisted between the two countries until the end of 1944. Salazar particularly feared that once the Americans had succeeded in worming their way in, they might very easily take over. They might even wish to stay after the war without Portuguese consent. Kay, *op. cit.*, pp. 161-163.

*18* G.F. Kennan served as counselor of legation and later as the American chargé d'affaires in Lisbon from the fall of 1942 to the winter of 1943. According to his memoirs he played a key role in persuading President Roosevelt to temporize with the Portuguese prime minister. He also reduced the exhorbitant demands of the Joint Chiefs of Staff to something more acceptable to the Portuguese, for instance, the temporary use by the Americans of facilities already enjoyed by the British at Lagens. He even went as far as extending a guarantee to the Portuguese without having been properly and formally instructed to do so. The guarantee reads as follows: "in connection with the agreement recently concluded between Portugal and Great Britain the U.S. of America undertakes to respect Portuguese sovereignty in all Portuguese colonies". See Kennan, *op. cit.*, p. 155.

*19* The island of Timor in the Malay Archipelago lies midway between New Guinea and Java. Half of it has belonged to the Portuguese since the sixteenth century; in 1941 half belonged to the Dutch. It was attacked in the night of the 19-20 February 1942 and defended by some Portuguese troops, together with 350 Dutch and Australians; the latter participated in the defense of Timor without being formally invited. Salazar protested to the Allies but accepted the situation. A guerilla war dragged on until the end of the war, when Timor was restored to full Portuguese sovereignty.

*20* Appendix 1, "Santa Maria agreement of 28 November 1944", in "Agreement on Transit Use of the Azores Airfield", *Department of State Bulletin*, XIV, 364 (1946).

bargaining process Salazar kept in mind that under no circumstances should he compromise his neutrality as long as Germany was in a position to retaliate. Negotiations were therefore protracted, particularly with the U.S., which had willfully withheld the guarantees Portugal demanded in order to influence the discussions to its own advantage. When the Americans finally yielded, the obstacle disappeared and negotiations were eventually concluded. In patiently and stubbornly delaying his consent to Allied use of the Azores, Salazar scored many points:

1 He was able to resist American pressure until late in 1944. By then all fears of possible German retaliation had completely vanished.

2 He succeeded in limiting the dimensions and the numbers of facilities the American War Department requested. In this way he avoided the danger that huge facilities might sink the economy and the administration of the archipelago under their weight, and diminished the likelihood that the still primitive "economy of the islands would be debauched by the amount of money brought in and expended." *(21)*

3 Portugal's sovereignty overseas was guaranteed by both the British and the Americans, and he recovered Portuguese Timor without doing any real fighting.

4 He now possessed certain trump cards for use in the imminent postwar period. Without major risk, without severe war damage, Portugal somehow felt that it was among the victors rather than associated with the vanquished, as was the case with Spain.

5 And finally, Salazar could from then on reckon on British and American gratitude and solicitude. The Estado Novo was saved. Great Britain and the United States would not interfere in the internal affairs of his country and his own security of tenure was thereby increased.

Portugal's gradual evolution from neutral neutrality to benevolent neutral has no doubt been a major event in the process of its association with the great Atlantic and democratic nations. Unlike many other small and medium states, Portugal came out of the war strengthened rather than weakened. Under the most able guardianship of its prime minister, it broke out of its isolation by surrendering some limited real estate for a limited time and with limited use without suffering much from German retaliation. Salazar's switch from traditional British ally with slight pro-Axis sympathies to all out supporter of the Allied cause came at the right time and over the right issues. But above all for the Allies Portugal would from then on remain a desirable partner. An impressive British empire still had vital need for safe maritime routes and communication lines. And the U.S. tragically and unwillingly entangling itself in Europe

21  Kennan, *op. cit.*, p. 151.

and in an anti-Soviet containment policy, would continue to rate Portugal's services highly. Atlantic Portugal was to become a strategic asset in the Atlantic alliance.

## PORTUGAL AND WESTERN CONTAINMENT POLICY

Even before the war Salazar was apprehensive of the postwar emergence of a new power balance which would favor the Soviet Union. He was convinced that one of the most disastrous consequences of the Western alliance with Russia would be the spread of Communism, and he hoped for a short war in which neither side would lose. His hopes were deceived but his forecasts materialized. Before the Allies could achieve victory in Europe their unity withered away, engendering a Cold War between East and West while the fighting was still going on.

Salazar subsequently was most critical of the policies of the Western allies. He particularly deplored the total defeat and partition of Germany, which to his mind was the only natural barrier against Russian Communism and Slavic expansion: "the goal which was given to the war", he said, "was to prevent the creation of a strong hegemony in the center of Europe and for this reason – according to a determination which we denounced as very dangerous – it was decided to crush Germany"; hence "a strong and well established Russian hegemony in Europe and in Asia has been substituted for the simple scheme of German hegemony." *(22)* According to Salazar, the Western Allies misunderstood the real nature of what was at stake and were so naive that they let themselves be doublecrossed by the Soviet Union. They reaped the honors, not the real, tangible benefits of victory, "After all", Salazar continued,

> what is victory? It is without any doubt a disequilibrium of forces which occurs and which permits one of the parties concerned to impose its will upon the opponent within the limits of relativity and within the bounds imposed by the very nature of things themselves. In this war, however, not only have many victors paradoxically been ranged amongst the vanquished, but neither the U.S.A. nor Britain nor France – to speak only about the biggest – have been able to impose their wills upon those nations they had been fighting; they are reduced to preventing the intermeddling of a foreign will in the Western zones of Germany. For her part, Russia imposes her sovereign and exclusive will in the north, in the east, in the southeast of Europe and penetrates into Asia... . In such conditions one is perfectly authorized to affirm that if the glory belongs to some, victory effectively reverted to others. *(23)*

In his view the Allies' biggest mistakes were two: they exacted the unconditio-

22  J. Ploncard d'Assac, *Dictionnaire politique de Salazar* (Lisbon, 1964), pp. 241-242.
23  *Ibid.*

nal surrender of the Third Reich, and they accepted Germany's division into separate parts. *(24)*

The unconditional surrender of Germany left a power vacuum at the periphery of the Soviet Union. Clearly it would be filled not by statements of goodwill and commitments to friendly behavior made at international conferences, but by that party which had a relative advantage in terms of political power and military force in the area. At Yalta the Big Three agreed on the future of Germany and Eastern Europe, on the organization of the U.N., and on the ending of the war in the Far East, but their conclusions were immediately interpreted differently by the parties concerned. And at Potsdam, London, Paris, and Moscow suspicion and misunderstanding were bound to grow.

Fear and tension spread all over Europe with a series of takeovers in Central and Eastern Europe. Minority Communist parties, assisted by Soviet secret agents and police and backed by Red armies, set out to establish so-called friendly governments under Soviet control in Poland, Bulgaria, Rumania, and Hungary. Europe feared subversion from within and trembled before the power and strength of well-organized Communist parties in France and Italy. Moreover, anxiety was magnified in Western Europe and the U.S. by a series of Communist-inspired revolutionary movements in Southeast Asia and in China, by the Communist-led guerilla's in Greece, by the Soviet claims on the Dardanelles, Kars, and Ardahan which brought heavy pressure on the Turkish government, by the Soviet reluctance to evacuate Iran, by the recurrent Soviet vetoes in the U.N., but above all, by the Berlin blockade and the Communist coup in Czechoslovakia in February 1948, under which the democratic Benes government suddenly succumbed.

This was the atmosphere and the international situation which Salazar had foreseen. He had hoped that Europe could avoid it; on the other hand it could only strengthen Portugal's position in the Western camp and help end its isolation. Portugal would again be courted and esteemed by the great Western leaders. Indeed, disruption in Big Three unity and a power vacuum and disequilibrium in Central Europe could only underscore the need for a permanent commitment of Western maritime powers in the affairs of Europe.

24  In an interview with *Le Figaro* (September 2, 1958) Salazar said: "The Western Allies, one should say, bear their part of responsibility in this dangerous situation. First, because they demanded the unconditional surrender of the Third Reich. Second, because they accepted the division into two parts of a partitioned Germany. A unified Germany would have been an insuperable rampart. If Germany did not exist, one would have to invent her. The German is traditionally the shield of Europe in the face of Slavic pressures".

40

The importance of the Atlantic would grow again. Atlantic islands and the Portuguese coast and ports would continue to be valued highly.

Salazar understood very quickly that the Cold War would increase Portugal's prestige and influence abroad while strengthening his own position at home. The Estado Novo, the Corporate State, had been engendered by a strong, doctrinaire anti-Communism. To Portugal's Catholic right-wing leader, "atheistic Communism" was "the synthesis of all traditional revolts of the matter against the spirit, of barbarism against civilization"; (25) it was the great heresy of the epoch; it had assumed aspects of a worldwide, monolithic conspiracy of evil forces against the political and moral values he felt the West should stand for. Salazar believed the promises of Communism to be valueless, its methods to be violent and mendacious and, above all, its victories to be irreversible. No wonder that he adopted anti-Communism wholeheartedly, and that the Cold War took on a deeper intensity in Portugal than enywhere else. The Communist menace, a concept in Salazarism before the Cold War, now despite its oversimplification and emotionalism was allowed to override all previous Portuguese efforts at aloofness, nonentanglement, and noninvolvement. Portugal slid inexorably into alliance with the greatest anti-Communist leader since the end of World War II, the U.S.

For the reasons I have already mentioned above, the U.S. government explicitly requested Portugal's adhesion to the Atlantic pact. Prof. Caeiro da Matta, Portugal's foreign minister, was present at the creation of what was later to become NATO. With the other eleven original signatories, he signed the North Atlantic treaty in Washington on the 4 April 1949. In Portugal, the process of ratification began with the consultation of the Corporative Chamber, which advised "that the North Atlantic Treaty must be ratified by Portugal without any hesitation." (26) On the 26 July the National Assembly approved the pact by an eighty to three vote. The negative votes were cast in protest against Spain's exclusion from the alliance. On the 28th, the *Diário do Governo* published the text of the assembly's decision, and the instrument of ratification was deposited with the U.S. Department of State on 24 August 1949. (27)

However, the main question, what real reasons convinced Salazar to join the Atlantic alliance, remains unresolved. After all, some Portuguese argued, Portugal was an Atlantic nation. Its interests spread over several continents

---

25 Ploncard d'Assac, *op. cit.*, p. 104.
26 *Câmara Corporativa*, parecer, 39 (20 June 1949).
27 See *NATO Bibliography* (Paris, 1967), p. 19, and *Diário da Sessões*, 201 (1949), pp. 742-751 and *Diário de Governo*, N. 165 (1949).

and it was hard to believe that events in Europe offered an immediate or important threat to them at the time. Undeniably, both logically and historically

> Portugal turns her back to Europe as soon as a peninsular entente ensures her a convenient safeguard of her independence and national integrity. NATO thus turned Portugal towards problems which are not hers, the defense of remote lines (a whole range of very complex questions, where not even the Balkans, the Mediterranean and the Near East were missing). And on the other hand, while forcign Portugal to accept a share of responsibilities in those sectors, the Pact gave it little assurance about other sectors, which in fact are vital to the country. *(28)*

In the minds of its critics, Portugal's participation in the Atlantic alliance was an absurd departure from traditional Portuguese foreign policy. Portugal did not and could not perceive the Soviet military buildup in Central Europe as an immediate and direct threat to its own independence and territorial integrity; if the menace was real, and almost every Portuguese agreed that it was, it touched mainly the future of Western Germany and other West European nations such as the Brussels Pact powers, rather than Portugal, which lay thousands of miles from Moscow. The Pact by no means protected Portugal's colonies and overseas territories, yet some of these possessions were most vulnerable because of their location near some Communist power, for instance, Macão.

Nevertheless, one of the reasons for Portugal's entrance into the Atlantic alliance undoubtedly was its quest for security. Salazar, and most other European and American statesmen of that period agreed that, with the German bulwark dismantled, Slavic Communism would spread all over Europe if nothing were done to stop it. The danger was seen as imminent, and a free Europe, could survive only if united. Solidarity and the pooling of Euro-American resources and manpower were the only ways to contain the Soviet Union. Portugal should not undermine this collective defense effort by refusing participation.

Although Portugal's colonial possessions in fact were not explicitly included in the geographic area covered and protected by the Atlantic pact, Salazar thought that somehow the overseas territories would profit from it. He did not foresee the West's hasty withdrawal from Africa and America's ambiguous and often hostile attitude toward European colonial policies, but on balance Portugal's presence in NATO was beneficial rather than detrimental to his country's defense efforts in Africa throughout the 1960s. Commenting upon the Atlantic treaty in the National Assembly, the Portuguese prime minister said:

> The pact does not cover in a direct manner the defense of Colonial Territories, more

28  H.M. de Carvalho, *Portugal e o Pacto do Atlântico* (Lisboa, 1953), p. 46.

42

particularly of our Overseas Territories. Yet complications which might result from difficulties in those territories might create weighty problems with serious consequences. It is therefore likely that the procedure of consultations, which is provided for by Article 4 of the Pact, and which is only applicable to a well defined region, might be extended to all other regions where difficulties are of a nature to create troubles. *(29)*

However, security, one of the major factors of alignment in general, does not seem on the whole to have been an overriding one in the Portuguese case. To be sure, it is one of a fund of possible explanations for Portugal's early commitment to the alliance. Other policy choices, ranging from a continuation of neutralism or nonalignment to full-scale alignment with the U.S. on a bilateral basis, could also have been adopted. Dr. Henrique Martins de Carvalho, a former Portuguese minister of public health, thought a bilateral agreement with the U.S. would have been the perfect solution, *a solução perfeita*: on the one hand, it would provide the Americans with the bases, ports, and Atlantic islands necessary to a conventional defense of Western Europe; on the other, it would leave Portugal free from involvement in the complex division of Germany. But Dr. de Carvalho immediately added that, if this was the best of all theoretical solutions, in practice it was unfeasible. Other nations, such as Denmark and Norway, would ask for the same privileges, and the idea of a collective effort, the only real hope for effective containment of Communist expansionism would be undermined. *(30)* That the Danes and the Norwegians would have followed this hypothetical Portuguese example in asking for bilateral rather than for multilateral arrangements is not certain, however. *(31)* The Scandinavian political leaders were clearly of the opposite view in the late 1940s. A bilateral treaty, they thought, would benefit the greater instead of the lesser powers; it would imply the lease of some national territory to the U.S. armed forces, which in the Scandinavian view was hardly acceptable; moreover, they were convinced that small powers can be heard more properly in an international setting.

29 Ploncard d'Assac, *op. cit.*, p. 237.
30 See De Carvalho, *op. cit.*, pp. 49-54. In an interview with the author in June 1968, Dr. de Carvalho once more stressed that his views on this issue were only theoretical and that they were not to be considered a critique of the policies pursued by the Portuguese government in that period.
31 In a series of interviews with foreign policy research fellows, critics and decision-makers in both Denmark and Norway (in August-September and October 1968 respectively) the author was told that a bilateral arrangement with the U.S. would have been the worst possible solution to the Scandinavian security problem. Among the personalities interviewed were Tim Greve, Petter Graver of the Norwegian Foreign Affairs ministry, Gram Victor, former minister of defense, and Erik Kragh, former chief of staff in Denmark.

## PORTUGAL IN QUEST OF PRESTIGE AND DOMESTIC STABILITY

Security, although important, was not then the major reason for Portugal's decision to join the Atlantic pact. The prestige factor was also important. Indeed, one of the advantages of alignment with the U.S. and other great Western powers has been a strengthening of Portugal's status in Western Europe and in the international community as a whole.

Salazar's Portugal and Franco's Spain, ideologically akin, politically allied, and close friends since the latter part of the 1930s, both favored a new order in Western Europe that was close to Italian fascism. Initially they followed similar neutrality policies aimed at the establishment of an Iberian peace zone. They favored the Allied powers slightly once it was overwhelmingly clear they would win. Yet, when the war ended the concert of European nations treated each country differently. Although Salazar's Portugal was definitely counted among the authoritarian régimes of the interwar era, many people felt that Salazar's dictatorship was not of the Nazi-fascist type. Rightly or wrongly, "Portugal was generally regarded as less obnoxious than Franco's Spain." (32)

Respectability Salazar got from the old alliance with Great Britain. His country's purely Atlantic posture and age-old ties with England saved it, if not from disaster, at least from the unpleasant experience of ostracism. Drawing Portugal out of the fascist clique, reinvigorating her preferential ties with England, helping her to lease bases to Great Britain and the U.S. without Axis retaliation, and finally seeing her admitted to the community of Western democratic nations were Salazar's major successes, acts of great statesmanship. Once invited to become one of the original founding members of the North Atlantic Treaty Organization, Salazar proudly told his fellow citizens that Portuguese diplomacy had succeeded where Spain's failed. Admission to NATO gave his régime a new and fresh outlook abroad.

The concept of prestige in international relations is a very loose one perhaps difficult to grasp. Even more difficult is getting Portuguese officials to admit that it played a role in Portugal's decision to join the Western alliance. On the other hand, the same officials will not hesitate to assure that Spain and Portugal could not be compared, since Portugal had been honored with an invitation to join the democratic alliance while Spain had been left outside. (33)

---

32  A.P. Whitaker, *Spain and the Defense of the West* (New York, 1961), p. 268.
33  Many non-Portuguese residents in Lisbon interviewed in the same period accepted the prestige thesis. They thought that both Iberian nations had at some point in the late forties or early fifties wanted to join the community of Western nations for prestige reasons.

Another important factor influenced Portugal's decision to become a NATO member. Not only did the move increase Portugal's prestige abroad, it also did much to improve the government's position at home *(34)*: "What better argument against the liberal opposition could the government produce than the admission of Portugal to the community of democratic nations." *(35)* Membership in NATO gave Salazar unlimited tenure, virtually guaranteeing that any revolution sponsored by the Communist party or other leftist organizations would provoke the wrath of his new military allies. Moreover, the Portuguese prime minister "evidently reckoned that the cachet which membership in NATO and the U.N. would give his régime outweighed the attendant danger of external interference with Portuguese sovereignty; and the introduction into Portugal of ideas that were modern, foreign and from his point of view subversive." *(36)*

And again, as time went on events proved Salazar's foresight. From the very beginning Salazar understood that the weakness of the treaty's preamble would secure the primacy of anti-Communist ideology over the principles of liberty, equality, and democratic government. Salazar's security of tenure, as he explained in the National Assembly on 15 July 1949, would not be endangered by democratic phraseology and the unfortunate wording of the preamble of the pact. On the contrary, he believed that the only ideological content common to all signators would be, had to be, anti-Communism:

> The definition of the ideology [of the North Atlantic treaty] in the preamble of the Pact is doubtless anything but happy. It is sullied by emptiness and the vagueness of certain hackneyed and vain formulas which are used everywhere with most different meanings.... . Their first fault is in not limiting the Pact to a negative content, i.e. anti-Communism but instead in asserting principles of a civilization it was thought necessary to defend. *(37)*

Salazar never felt he had committed his country to the defense of Western democracy and the implementation of the most basic human rights, such as privacy, due process of law, freedom of opinion and thought, freedom of speech, press, and other forms of communications, freedom of assembly and association, and the right to participate in the government directly or through freely-chosen institutions. As a matter of fact, one of the most peculiar and characteristic features of Portugal's entry into NATO is that the highest poli-

---

34 This argument was similarly invalidated by official Portuguese informants in Lisbon while mostly confirmed by foreign observers.

35 P. Fryer and P. McGowan Pinheiro, *Oldest Ally: A Portrait of Salazar's Portugal* (London, 1961), p. 153.

36 *Ibid.*, p. 154.

37 Ploncard d'Assac, *op. cit.*, p. 237.

tical authority in the nation publicly denounced the ethical principles underpinning the preamble of a treaty which he asked his parliament to ratify.
Salazar left no doubt about his contempt for democratic government. He
made no secret of his profoundly reactionary views, his hatred of Communism,
parliamentary government, democracy and equality, universal suffrage, and
up to a certain point even progress.

Although Portuguese corporatism can by no means be compared to Italian-
style fascism or to Nazism, the fascist nature of Portugal's political institutions
and particularly of Salazar's political creed cannot easily be denied. *(38)*
Basic to the philosophy of the Estado Novo is Salazar's strong belief that the
very foundation of public power or the source of sovereignty is to be found in
God *(non est potestas nisi a Deo)*, *(39)* and that Christianity and Christian
principles imply "that society should not be based on equality but on hierarchy." *(40)* From this, of course, it follows that "people have less need of
being sovereign than of being governed." *(41)* In an interview granted to
Le Figaro on 3 September 1958, Salazar stated bluntly:

> I do not believe in universal suffrage, because the individual vote does not take into
> account human differentiation... Man, in my opinion, should be equal before the law,
> but I believe it dangerous to attribute to all the same political rights. *(42)*

Between 1930 and 1935 the basic principles of the Estado Novo were laid

---

38 "The Portuguese dictatorship, then, is a fascist régime with specific features arising from
the way it came into existence, from Portugal's internal class structure and from her international relations. But the label is hardly the most important thing. In common with different
régimes, elsewhere in the world, Portuguese fascism practices censorship, the denial of free
speech, arbitrary imprisonment and torture. Even if he were innocent of these crimes, Salazar
would stand condemned by this: that after a third of a century of power nearly half the population is still illiterate, there is widespread and crushing poverty and the figures for diseases of
poverty and infant mortality are practically the highest in Europe". Fryer and Pinheiro, *op.
cit.*, p. 138.
39 On the foundation of political power in Salazar's political theory, see Ploncard d'Assac,
*op. cit.*, pp. 26-30.
40 A.O. Salazar, in an interview with *Le Figaro*, 3 September 1958.
41 A.O. Salazar, quoted in S.E. Ayling, "Antonio de Oliveira Salazar", *Portraits of Power*
(New York, 1963), p. 327.
42 On Salazar's political thought and the philosophy of the Estado Novo see among others,
A. Ferro, *Salazar: Portugal and Her Leader*, H. de Barros Gomes and G. Gibbons, transl.
(London, 1939); Fryer and Pinheiro, *op. cit.*, pp. 132-142; *Le Figaro*, 3 September 1958; *La
pensée de Salazar* (Lisbon, 1941); *Observer*, 24 August 1954; Ploncard d'Assac, *op. cit.*;
H. Massis, *Salazar face à face: Trois dialogues politiques* (Paris, 1961); *The Times*, 21 May
1959.

out – strength, authoritarianism, unity, nationalism, and corporateness – and although the constitution of 1933 guaranteed fundamental human rights to all citizens, it equally gave the government the powers to override these rights in the name or cause of order. The politics of the new state are by no means as ruthless and brutal as either Nazism or fascism, and Portugal is evidently less ostracized by the community of Western nations than Franco's Spain. The fact remains, however, that present-day Portugal cannot be reckoned among the democratic NATO members. To a more than negligible fraction of European public opinion, particularly for such allies as Denmark and Norway, Portugal's political régime is undoubtedly authoritarian even dictatoral. Some feel that the Atlantic alliance need not be concerned with the political régimes of the member countries; for others, it is definitely important that the alliance lives up to its democratic image of a group of states determined "to safeguard the freedom, common heritage and civilization of their peoples, founded on the principles of democracy, individual liberty and the rule of law." *(43)* Where the emphasis is on image-building rather than on military strength, Portugal is a liability rather than an asset.

## AMERICAN AID AND THE PORTUGUESE ECONOMY

Salazar regarded foreign investments with suspicion, and in the early postwar years he tended to discourage them. He was by no means eager to receive foreign assistance, since he understood that no government gives economic or military help to another government without one day demanding a political price for it. Official Portugal, therefore, refused to ask a broad U.S. aid program; the country was determined to leave the bulk of the money to the nations which had suffered most from the war and were sustaining internal threats. Its concern with the chaotic state of Western Europe's economy and the political liability this situation represented in the face of recurring Communist subversion was genuine. At any rate, it is unlikely that the prospect of American aid lured Portugal into alliance with the U.S. and NATO. The basic reasons for Portugal's adhesion to the Atlantic pact in the late forties were political rather than economic.

Portugal, together with Spain, was among the few Western European countries that did not receive economic aid or military assistance in the postwar relief period (1946-1948). That Salazar refused to exact his share of the American dollars streaming into Europe in exchange for the extension of American

43 Preamble, the North Atlantic Treaty.

use of the Azores is remarkable. The only real economic benefit the Azores agreements promised was an improved infrastructure in the islands. The Americans would leave this to the Portuguese when and if they should leave. Portugal's approach to this question contrasted sharply with Spain's a few years later. During the negotiations for the Pact of Madrid (1952-1953), Spain pressed hard for substantial U.S. economic and military aid in exchange for the naval and air facilities it would lend to the U.S. navy and air force. *(44)* Apart from the costs of the base construction program, borne almost entirely by the U.S., Spain managed to receive U.S. $ 719.2 million, in loans and grants in the period between 1953 and 1957, and by the end of 1960 American aid to Spain had grown to nearly $ 977.6 million. In the Marshall Plan Period (1949 and 1952), when Portugal was already officially aligned with the U.S. and NATO, U.S. assistance to Portugal was still remarkably slight: U.S. $ 61.8 million in comparison with $ 1,056.9 million for Greece, $ 461.0 million for Turkey, or even with the Belgian or Danish figures of $ 740.9 and $ 346.7 million, respectively. *(45)*

During the Mutual Security Act period (1953-1961) this pattern was to continue. Again Greece, Turkey, Italy, and now Spain received the lion's share with $ 273.6, $ 457.8, $ 435.6 and 494.8 million respectively, compared with only $ 12.4 million for Portugal. In this period, Portugal received a more impressive amount of military assistance ($ 228.8 million), but even this does not rank favorably with the military assistance received by other small NATO members. Belgium, for example, received $ 890.4 million, the Netherlands $ 828.7, Greece $ 433.7, even the Scandinavian figures were higher. The decision to step up military assistance to Portugal was connected with the NATO Council of Ministers decision in Lisbon in 1952 to build up a conventional shield in Europe. Portugal was given a limited part in the rearmament program. Yet even a modest participation imposed great sacrifices on the poverty stricken country. An important part of its military equipment from the pre-World War II period was completely outmoded, and Portugal had good reason to claim a fraction of the huge amounts of military assistance the U.S. was pouring into Europe at the time.

Overall U.S. economic and military assistance to Portugal over the period

44 Whitaker, *op. cit.*, pp. 239-242.
45 See *U.S. Overseas Loans and Grants and Assistance from International Organizations* (1 July 1945 - 30 June 1965), Special Report prepared for the House Foreign Affairs Committee (Washington, D.C.).
46 *Ibid.*

from 1946 to 1965, although important, cannot be considered excessive in the light of that received by many other countries with a more or less equal and in some cases smaller population.

TABLE I

Total U.S. Economic Aid and Military Assistance 1946-1965

(In Millions of U.S. dollars)

| | Total 1946-1945 | Repayments and Interests 1946-1965 | Total less Repayments and Interests |
|---|---|---|---|
| Belgium | 1,986.7 | 229.3 | 1,757.4 |
| Denmark | 923.1 | 39.4 | 883.7 |
| Greece | 3,669.9 | 156.9 | 3,513.0 |
| Italy | 6,053.7 | 673.4 | 5,380.3 |
| Netherlands | 2,472.3 | 414.9 | 2,057.4 |
| Norway | 1,254.4 | 113.2 | 1,141.2 |
| Portugal | 516.7 | 28.8 | 487.9 |
| Spain | 1,863.9 | 147.2 | 1,716.7 |
| Turkey | 4,755.2 | 121.0 | 4,634.2 |
| Europe (*) total | 46,732.9 | 7,229.2 | 39,503.7 |

(*) The total for Europe does not include the Greek and Turkish figures but includes aid given to other European states, such as Great Britain and France.
Source: U.S. Overseas Loans and Grants, op. cit.

Total aid to Portugal, less repayments and interest, reached $ 487.5 million in this period, in Greece it attained $ 3,513 million, in Belgium $ 1,757.4, in Norway $ 1,141.2, and in Denmark $ 883.7. That this was so was probably due on the one hand, to Portugal's own restraints, and on the other to the American belief that Portugal remained politically secure despite its comparative poverty. The Communist party was outlawed, opposition to the regime weak, and social unrest very easily contained through the corporate state's channels of control and suppression. As long as the Salazarian government remained in power, Portugal was a perfect ally, strongly anti-Communist, a rampart of Western civilization, faithful and above all inexpensive. Moreover, the Joint Chiefs of Staff valued not its military contributions but its geographic location, its air and naval bases and facilities.

The thesis that, contrary to the Spanish case, economic aid had not been a major issue in Portugal's leasing of bases in the late forties and early fifties and in its decision to join the North Atlantic alliance is substantiated by the fact that U.S. non-military assistance to Portugal from 1946 to 1966 amounted to only $ 186.3 million. In a much shorter period (1951-1959) Spain received a total of $ 929 million. *(47)*

The U.S. has extended Portuguese aid chiefly through a United States Operations Mission (from 1950 to November 1956), the American Embassy in Lisbon, the Export-Import Bank, and the U.S. Mission to the European Regional Organization in Paris. For the most part the money was used in the building of hydroelectric facilities and power distribution lines, in the establishment of paper industries, in agricultural development schemes (ranging from irrigation projects to chemical fertilizer production), and in the preparation of international administration reporting requirements such as analysis of payment reviews. *(48)*

The military assistance programs were controlled from Washington, with the military assistance and advisory group (M.A.A.G.) acting as an agent on the spot. In the mid-1950s M.A.A.G. involved about fifty-six U.S. personnel.

Though the bulk of U.S. military assistance to Portugal was extended in the fifties (of a total of $ 333.9 million covering the period between 1946 and 1966, $ 288.5 million was granted between 1949 and 1961), funding continued on a less massive scale throughout the sixties, involving small amounts at the end of this period: $ 2.2 million in 1967, $ 3.2 in 1968, and $ 2.7 in 1969. *(49)* As a later chapter will discuss in more detail, the scaling down of U.S. military assistance at a moment when because of its military involvement in Africa, Portuguese needs were greatest, did by no means imply that the U.S. had abandoned Portugal altogether. Numerous marks of U.S. moral, political, and even material support have appeared during the last decade. Moreover, simultaneously with the decrease of military assistance the U.S. has escalated its economic and financial aid. Although the total of U.S. economic aid to Portugal from 1946 was only $ 69.6 million, it reached $ 109.9 million from 1960 to 1965, a much shorter period. Evidently, Portugal's determination not to be drawn into alliance with the U.S. and NATO by the prospect of receiving massive economic aid has been shaken since its costly military entanglement in

47 Whitaker, *op. cit.*, p. 241.
48 U.S. Congress, Senate. *Foreign Aid program: Compilation of studies.* Special Committee to Study the Foreign Aid Program; Compilation of Studies and Survey presented by Theodore Francis Green, Chairman (Washington, 1957), pp. 1335-1339.
49 *Military Assistance and Foreign Military Sales Acts* (Washington, D.C.: 1970), p. 12.

Africa. It is well known that each negotiation extending the base agreements in the sixties had included or been followed by additional Portuguese claims for loans; those claims were never completely rebuffed. *(50)* This kind of aid was clearly as important as strict military assistance, as it allowed Portugal to divert important fractions of its own national resources to the military.

Portugal's alignment with NATO did not happen overnight. Its association with the leading Western powers dated back centuries in the case of Great Britain, and from the latter part of World War II in the case of the U.S.. Which factor was eventually decisive in pushing Portugal into the Atlantic alliance is still not completely clear. Yet Salazar's strong fear of international Communism and Russian expansion, his belief that without a common defense line post-World War II Europe was at the mercy of the Soviets, and his need to improve Portugal's image abroad and to strenghten the corporate state at home have all determined his shift from neutrality toward full alignment. American economic and military assistance was probably not the main factor in Portugal's decision to align with the U.S. and NATO. In fact, Salazar's economic philosophy of the late forties left little room for foreign aid and investments in his country's development. During the Cold War, some U.S. military assistance allowed Portugal to modernize its armed forces and to play its part in the alliance, but in the sixties events in Africa compelled the Portuguese government to appeal to whatever source of funding was available.

---

50 This was particarly the case in the fall of 1962. See S. Bosgra and C. Van Krimpen, *Portugal en de NATO* (Amsterdam), p. 35. And *Frankfurter Allgemeine Zeitung*, 29 June 1962.

# Chapter II

# NATO COMMITMENTS vs. WAR EFFORTS OVERSEAS

Present-day Portuguese defense efforts support two main foreign policy goals, each of which the nation considers essential for survival:

1 The maintenance of Portuguese overseas provinces within the Portuguese community;
2 The defense of metropolitan territory and Western civilization against the threat of world Communism, whether from inside or outside the country.

Although the Stalin menace necessitated the emphasis of the latter in the late forties and early fifties, the former became Portugal's major concern with the initiation of rebellion in Angola in 1961 and its spread to other African provinces, Guinea in 1963 and Mozambique in 1964. The Portuguese government believes that both efforts are complementary, part of Portugal's share in a Western strategy of global containment of world Communism. In the Portuguese view containment must be organized on a world-wide scale. Lisbon is aware, of course, of the balance of terror established in Europe since the Soviet Union achieved nuclear parity with the U.S. Each side is in a position to destroy important areas of the enemy's territory or annihilate a substantial proportion of the enemy's population and industrial output capacity, even after receiving a first strike. In fact, the costs of general war inevitably involving strategic nuclear attack would be so great on both sides that initiation of a major offensive in Central Europe almost equals suicide. No responsible political leader is prepared to commit suicide. The genuine fear of reciprocal extermination has led to nuclear stalemate and relative security in Europe. But such a stalemate is not peace. Communist peaceful coexistence and Western détente are not quite the same thing. In Portugal's estimation, international Communism has not abandoned conquest and expansion altogether. It is now prepared to outflank Western nations by striking in Asia, Africa, and Latin America through the stimulation and organization of wars of national liberation and subversion. In this protracted conflict, this gigantic struggle for mastery in

Europe and in the world, Portugal knows it stands almost alone in the Western camp. It thinks of itself as the only Western nation to understand the true nature of the Communist menace. All the more reason to continue its resistance. Therefore, although it tries to keep up with its NATO commitments, Portugal has definitely given priority to its overseas war preparedness as its most efficient contribution to the defense of the West. But before we enter the debate on Portugal's NATO commitments versus its war efforts overseas elaborating on the importance of the Azores as a transit zone for NATO may be useful.

## THE AZORES: IMPORTANT TRANSIT ZONE

Earlier this essay argued that the strategic value of the Azores was so paramount in the second world war that by 1943 the Western Allies were prepared to possess them with or without Salazar's permission.

In those days, civilian and military air transit between Europe and America was no longer an adventure; still, an air voyage from one side of the Atlantic to the other was quite an expedition. The civilian air trip from Portugal to the American east coast was performed by the Pan-American Boeing seaplanes, commonly called the Pan-American clippers, which were not "normally capable of flying the Atlantic west-bound". The "voyage from Lisbon to New York went via Africa, the east coast of South America, the Caribbean, and Bermuda. The trip took five days and nights." *(1)* The performance of the Boeing 747 of the Galaxy C-5A were part of the future. *(2)* The Lagens and Santa Maria airfields were therefore very important steps in the communications system linking the European theater of war with the U.S. and the U.S. with the Far East. The facilities Portugal granted to the American and British governments were of invaluable assistance in the prosecution of the war.

Technological breakthroughs in civilian and military transport aircraft (from the C-54 to the C-141 to the Galaxy jet) saw the decline in value of such airfields over time, but it was still fairly great in the late 1940s and in the 1950s. For this reason the Pentagon was very anxious that the American government enter into new agreements with Portugal and in addition secure its entry into

---

1  Kennan, *op. cit.*, p. 156.
2  The range of a C-5A Galaxy is more than 6,300 miles with fifty-six tons of cargo, versus the war performance of a C-47 with a 1,500 miles range and a cargo capacity of 2,045-2,270 kg (twenty-eight fully-armed troops) or of a C-54 Douglas Skymaster with a range beyond 2,000 miles (*Nato's Fifteen Nations*, XIV, 2 (April-May, 1969), p. 61).

the North Atlantic alliance. On 2 February 1948, the two governments signed an agreement on the continuation of facilities for the transit of American military aircraft through Lagens airfield on Terceira Island. It took the place of the one finalized in May 1946, which in turn followed the one made during the second world war that permitted the construction and operation of a military airfield on Santa Maria Island. *(3)* In June 1947, the Santa Maria airfield was returned to the full control of the Portuguese government to become a keystone in the network of international civil aviation, while steps were taken to improve military facilities at Lagens on Terceira Island.

The consecutive agreements saw a great variation in the official rationale for the extension of Portuguese bases to the U.S. In 1944, the document established the form of Portugal's indirect participation in the operations in the Pacific. The U.S. government,

> conscious of the legitimate desire of the Portuguese Government to put an end to the Japanese occupation of Timor and recognizing that this Portuguese territory lies within the large area of operations undertaken in the Pacific... agrees to the participation of Portugal in such operations as may be conducted eventually to expel the Japanese from Portuguese Timor in order that the territory may be restored to full Portuguese sovereignty. *(4)*

It further recognized that such participation could be effected either directly or indirectly, the latter by conceding to the Americans facilities for the construction, use, and control of an airbase on Santa Maria Island. In 1946, the Portuguese government officially extended the use of the Lagens airfield to the U.S. in order that it might maintain "safe and efficient lines of communication with the American forces of occupation in Germany and Japan". This was done in a spirit of international cooperation and in view of the great worldwide responsibilities with which the U.S. was burdened at the moment. *(5)* In 1948, the agreement reads as follows: the U.S. and Portuguese governments had "in mind the advantages which those facilities will achieve for the security

---

3  See "Agreement on Transit use of Azores Airfields", *Department of State Bulletin*, XIV, 364 (1946), pp. 1080-1081 and Appendix 1: "Santa Maria Agreement of November 28, 1944"; Appendix 2: "The American Ambassador to the Portuguese Minister of Foreign Affairs, Lisbon, May 30, 1946". On the 1948 agreement see: "Air Transit Agreement with Portugal", *Department of State Bulletin*, XVIII, 450 (15 February 1948), p. 231 and "Air Transit Agreement with Portugal", in *Department of State Bulletin*, I, 454 (March 1948), which includes "A note from the American Ambassador to the Portuguese Foreign Minister (2 February, 1948)", p. 359 and "A note from the Portuguese Minister for Foreign Affairs to Ambassador Wiley, 2 February, 1948", pp. 358-359.

4  Appendix 1, "Santa Maria Agreement of 28 November, 1944", *loc. cit.*

5  "Agreement on Transit use of Azores airfield", *loc. cit.*

of Europe and for the establishment and consolidation of world peace as well as the indirect value which the same may bring about for the common defense and security." *(6)* Over a period of four years the rationale behind the agreements shifted from defeat of Germany and Japan to the need to maintain U.S. troops in both defeated countries to the desire to increase security in Europe and to strengthen the common defense.

By 1951 the whole thing was called "Defense Agreement between Portugal and the U.S.", *(7)* and its preamble referred to the obligations arising from Articles III and IV of the North Atlantic Treaty, implying the necessity of a common defense. The 1951 contract deserves some attention since it has remained the basis of American-Portuguese relations to the present time. With this accord, the Portuguese government grants to the government of the U.S. the of use facilities in the Azores during the life of the North Atlantic treaty in case of war in which they are both involved (Art. I). Both governments agreed to construct new installations and to enlarge and improve the existing ones. Renovation of the bases at Lagens were to include facilities for the storage of oil, munitions, spare parts, and other equipment (Art. II). The term of execution of the works was 1 September 1956, with a four-month grace period (Art. III). The construction and the materials of the soil were property of the Portuguese government (Art. III), which undertook to maintain them after the withdrawal of American personnel (Art. IV). The American government agreed to carry on the apprenticeship and training of Portuguese personnel (Art. V). During the period of the preparation of the base, "the transit of American aircraft through the Lagens Airdrome continues to be permitted and there will be authorized on that base, during the same period, the training of U.S. aviation and naval personnel and U.S. military and civilian personnel" (Art. VII). The American government may renounce the concessions at any moment (Art. VIII). In case of war, the facilities granted to the U.S. may be utilized by the other NATO members; the conditions of utilization are to be established in negotiations between the interested governments (Art. IX). And finally, Article X provides that after the period of evacuation fixed by Article VII, transit through Lagens of U.S. military aircraft carrying out missions within the framework of NATO was permisable provided such operations were controlled and serviced by Portuguese personnel. From time to time the Portu-

6 "Note from the Portuguese Minister for Foreign Affairs to Ambassador Wiley, 2 February, 1948", *loc. cit.*, pp. 358-359.
7 "Defense Agreement between Portugal and the U.S.", *U.S. Treaties and other International Agreements*, 3087 (Washington, D.C.), pp. 2263-2268.

guese government could also permit the training of NATO forces on those bases.

The 1951 agreement fully authorized American and other NATO forces to use the Azores in times of war as long as NATO continues in existence, or even in certain circumstances in times of peace. Clearly the Azores bases must have been a cornerstone in NATO strategy in the early fifties, when the situation in the Far East (Korea) heightened fear of an all-out conventional Soviet attack. At the time NATO members still hoped to build up an integrated conventional force capable of holding the line in Central Europe, at least until massive aid from the other side of the Atlantic could reach them.

Articles II and VII are also worthy of attention. These articles permit the use of the Lagens airdrome for the training of U.S. aviation and other person- nel and for transit of American aircraft until completion of the construction projects theoretically scheduled for 1956. A supplementary defense agreement, signed at Lisbon on 15 November 1957 provided for a new extension of Ameri- can use of the base until the 31 December 1962. Both governments recognized that some of the preparatory works provided by Article V, which were abso- lutely essential to the fulfillment of the defense mission in the Azores, had not been completed. In fact, as the following chapters will explain, the Azores agreement has been extended beyond December 1962 and is still active today. In spite of the present emphasis in strategic thought on deterrence rather than on defense, the technological breakthrough in military transport aircraft, and the climate of détente Portugal's most efficient and important contribution to the U.S. and to NATO clearly remains those bases in the Azores.

## PORTUGAL'S WAR POTENTIAL AND NATO COMMITMENTS

Prime Minister Salazar determined the present structure of the Portuguese armed forces in the mid-thirties when he implemented a series of basic reforms aimed at the rejuvenation of the defense force. By 1939 and 1940 an army of 40 000 men transported on Portuguese ships was ready to protect Portugal's territorial integrity overseas. During the course of the war this figure was doubled. In 1944 a period of mechanization began, followed by very profound reforms in organization, instruction, equipment, and infrastructure. These efforts were carried through with even more vigor after Portugal's membership in NATO, and have widened in scope since the beginning of rebellion in Angola in February 1961. The total strength of the armed forces shifted from 80,000 in 1961 to 148,000 in 1966 and even jumped to 218,000 in 1972 and 1973. The percentage of regular armed forces to men of military age, 11.2 percent in 1972, was the highest in Europe, surpassing even the American figure of 6.1 percent.

## TABLE II

### Portuguese Military Manpower, 1961-1973

| | 1961-1962 | 1962-1963 | 1963-1964 | 1964-1965 | 1965-1966 | 1966-1967 | 1967-1968 | 1968-1969 | 1969-1970 | 1970-1971 | 1971-1972 | 1972-1973 |
|---|---|---|---|---|---|---|---|---|---|---|---|---|
| Length of military service (in number of months) | Army: 18-24<br>Air Force: 36<br>Navy: 48 | 18-24<br>36<br>48 | 18-25<br>36<br>48 | 18-24<br>36<br>48 | 18-24<br>18<br>48 | 18-24<br>18<br>48 | 18-24<br>18<br>48 | 18-24<br>18-24<br>48 | 18-48<br>18-48<br>48 | 18-48<br>18-48<br>48 | 24<br>36<br>48 | 24<br>36<br>48 |
| Total Armed Forces | 80,000 | 80,000 | 102,000 | 108,500 | 148,000 | 148,000 | 148,500 | 182,500 | 182,000 | 185,500 | 218,000 | 218,000 |
| Army | 58,000 | 58,000 | 80,000 | 120,000 | 120,000 | 120,000 | 120,000 | 150,000 | 148,000 | 150,000 | 179,000 | 179,000 |
| Air Force (including Parachute Troops) | 12,500 | 12,500 | 12,500 | 14,000 | 13,500 | 13,500 | 13,500 | 17,500 | 17,500 | 17,500 | 21,000 | 21,000 |
| Navy (including Marines) | 9,500 | 9,800 | 10,200 | 14,500 | 14,500 | 14,500 | 14,500 | 15,000 | 16,500 | 18,000 | 18,000 | 18,000 |

Source: Institute for Strategic Studies, *The Military Balance* (London, 1961-1973).

The total strenght of the army increased from 58,000 in 1961 to 179,000 in 1972 *(8)*, and the vast majority of this impressive fighting force is assigned to the defense of the overseas provinces. In 1961, 30,000 out of the 58,000 troops served in Angola; only one division remained at NATO's disposal in the metropolitan area. By 1969, the ratio of metropolitan troops to overseas troops increased sharply; out of 79,000 men, 55,000 were sent to Angola, 60,000 to Mozambique, and 27,000 to Guinea. Elements of two infantry divisions are still stationed in metropolitan Portugal, one of which is earmarked for assignment to NATO and is only fifty percent complete. The other division, assigned to Joint Iberian Defense through the Spanish-Portuguese Mutual Security Treaty, is said to be even lower in numbers. *(9)* The NATO division carries some M 41 and M 47 tanks, and both divisions are equipped with 105 mm and 140 mm Howitzers. *(10)* Much of Portugal's heavy equipment, for example, jeeps, trucks, and artillery, needs replacement. Mortars, grenades, mines, and munitions of all kinds are homemade. The old Mauser rifle has been gradually handed over to the indigenous population of some African provinces for the implementation of self-defense schemes, and has been replaced by the German G-3 automatic rifle manufactured under license in Portuguese factories.

In 1952 the air force entered a new period of expansion and modernization during the period of the American Mutual Assistance Act program and under NATO influence. Since then it has acquired new aircraft, particularly jets and radar units, and a center for air defense has been organized. In 1961, Portuguese air policy could not but follow the general reorientation of military policy from a Euro-Atlantic and NATO course toward an Euro-African orientation. Thus, air policy is conditioned by the exigencies of the antiguerilla wars in Africa. Portugal's NATO obligations notwithstanding, requirements overseas continue to receive high priority. The once-cherished dream of a completely independent and articulated air force able to carry out independent operations without subservience to the army, had to be abandoned for two reasons. The

---

8   *The Military Balance 1972-1973* (London, 1972), p. 72.

9   According to R. Warning, Portugal's wartime military commitment, in addition to a full-strength NATO division, is two divisions to come under a unified Iberian command, for use in the defense of the Pyrenees and the whole Iberian Peninsula (R. Warning, "Portugal as a NATO Ally", *Nato's Fifteen Nations*, XVIII, 1 (1963), p. 107). See also *The Military Balance 1972-1973, op. cit.*, pp. 21-22.

10   See Major E. O'Ballance, "Portugal's War Potential", *Military Review*, XLIV, 8 (1964), pp. 84-90.

first is the ever increasing needs of the wars overseas and the difficulty of finding credit to augment the number and quality of aircraft; the other is the U.N. embargo on the supply of aircraft capable of use overseas. In 1972 and 1973, the total strength of the air force reached some 21,000 men, 150 combat aircraft, 110 transport and reconnaissance aircraft numerous trainers and liaison aircraft, some of which have been armed for light strike missions in Africa and helicopters. *(11)* A paratroop regiment of 4,000, contrary to the common usage operates under the air force and not the army. Three battalions of this regiment are serving in each of the three African provinces. The mission of the Portuguese air force includes: (1) the defense of national airspace metropolitan and overseas; (2) cooperation with the army and navy in the tactical realm and logistic support of the antiguerilla combat action; (3) cooperation with foreign air forces in the framework of international agreements.

NATO has assigned the Portuguese air force anti-submarine reconnaissance tasks and the patrolling of a fraction of the Iberian Atlantic. A squadron of P2V5 Neptunes has been earmarked for this mission. To carry out such varied responsibilities, the Portuguese air force has only a small number of troops and few aircraft at its disposal. This is especially difficult considering the vastness of territories to be protected and the great distances which separate Portuguese possessions. The operational value of the air force is therefore modest. Material is often deficient, air defense inadequate, and the recruitment of competent personnel particularly difficult owing to the absence of technical and professional training facilities. The diversity of the types of aircraft in service, often purchased secondhand in many countries, together with the U.N. embargo all present debilitating obstacles. It is not uncommon for the air force to encounter major problems when in search of spare parts. Nevertheless, it is trying to do the utmost with the means at its disposal and has been active from the beginning of the counterinsurgency campaign in Africa. Portugal has used air power extensively for strikes in Guinea, Angola, and Mozambique, for the landing, supply, and recovery of combat units, battle casualty evacuation, the tactical redeployment of ground forces, and reconnaissance and detection of enemy forces.

Of all the Portuguese armed forces, the navy is greatest in tradition and in prestige. Following its major role in the centuries of discovery, Portuguese naval power declined in the nineteenth century. Although it regained some strength after the first world war, in 1926 the navy still only possessed forty-

---

11  *The Military Balance 1972-1973, op. cit.,* p. 23.

six ships with a total tonnage of 30,000. But from then on it grew steadily and in 1967 reached a total tonnage of 90,000 in 155 vessels. In 1972 and 1973, the fleet included four submarines, eleven frigates, sixteen coastal escorts, four oceanic minesweepers, twelve coastal minesweepers, thirty-seven patrol launches, five LTC-type landing craft. The total strength of the navy's manpower reached 18,000 men, including 3,300 marines. *(12)* Despite this limited potential, the Portuguese navy has been and still is expected to accomplish a great number of difficult and varied missions: it (1) ensures free communications between the different provinces (after all, metropolitan Portugal represents only four percent of national territory and thirty nine percent of the total population); (2) guarantees the integrity of those territories by helping to subdue subversions (the navy has been of special value in Guinea, where the deep estuaries provide easy communications with parts of the interior, and on the rivers and lakes of Angola and Mozambique); (3) fights exterior threats, protects national harbors (overseas ports included), and the vast territorial waters; (4) collaborates with NATO in an effort to retain Western supremacy in Atlantic maritime communications.

The Portuguese navy is not completely operational, particularly in relation to ships of gross tonnage and in everything that touches upon infrastructure and logistics on the ground. Yet the training of personnel is said to be excellent. Portuguese sailors and marines are conscious of belonging to a nation with great maritime traditions and they want to live up to the celebrated past. Foreign observers have recurrently praised the services rendered by some special units, such as the coastal patrols and marines, in active combat overseas. The U.S. Military and Advisory Group in Lisbon (M.A.A.G.) has consistently felt that the Portuguese navy ought to be given large responsibilities for the defense of the Iberian Atlantic frontier and encouraged by meaningful assistance programs, consisting of technical advice, loans of U.S. vessels and gifts. *(13)*

Oriented toward the Atlantic, Portugal has taken little interest in commiting major forces to the defense of Central Europe. Instead it contributes to the

---

12  *Ibid.*

13  U.S. aid to the Portuguese navy has included:

– the loan of two frigates (the *Corte Real* and the *Dio Cão* in 1957)

– one A.S.W. frigate of 1,600 tons, the *Pero Escobar*, constructed in Italy upon a U.S. order (1957);

– four minesweepers of 790 tons, each constructed in the U.S. on a U.S. order (1955);

– a fifty percent (15 million dollars) participation in the construction in Portuguese yards of three frigates of the Dealy type.

defense of the Iberian Atlantic zone, which falls under the NATO Atlantic Command. Nothwithstanding its dislike of major responsibilities to the battle-field of continental Europe, Portugal's army is required to maintain one classic, NATO-type infantry division trained to operate under nuclear conditions, which in times of war or serious threat of war should be ready in M+30 (mobilization day plus thirty days) at the north of the Pyrenees for use anywhere in Europe. The headquarters of this NATO division is Camp Margarida. The division is supposed to be organized on NATO patterns, with three infantry regiments of 3,000 men each, three battalions to the regiment, plus the necessary artillery, staff, and engineering services – altogether between 15,000 and 18,000 men. It is commonly known that this division is only at half strength, is badly equipped, and is incapable of preparing for war on the continent in one month. Moreover, the units which presently constitute the bulk of the division are mainly trained for antiguerilla warfare, sent overseas after a brief training period, and replaced by new conscripts. The navy and air force are expected to assign six oceanic escorts and eighteen ASW reconnaissance aircraft to the Commander Iberian Atlantic Area (COMIBERLANT, which is part of SACLANT). In fact, only three oceanic escorts and twelve P2V5 Neptunes were at NATO's disposal in 1969 and 1970.

Portugal's main contribution to NATO is the use of its ports, air, and naval bases on the continent or in the Atlantic islands. Among the facilities available to NATO are: (1) the whole infrastructure of a naval base in Lisbon, (2) an operational center for traffic control run by the naval staff in Lisbon, and (3) the operational center for traffic control at Ponta Delgada (Azores). In addition, some infrastructure has been constructed and equipped with NATO aid: (1) an ammunition dump at Lisbon, (2) fuel depots at Trafaria and Ponta Delgada, (3) radiostations at Sagres, P. Santo Madeira, and Santa Maria. Portugal also promised NATO that it would equip a certain number of bases for NATO use, including an airbase at Espinho, a naval air base at Montijo (AB 6), and hydrocarbon depots. The time schedule for the realization of those works and the imposed norms have all been respected. Moreover, Portugal has granted facilities to three important NATO members:

1) The airbase at Lajes on Terceira Island is theoretically under Portuguese authority but is to a certain extent an American-operated base. The 1951 agreement provides that all NATO members may use Lajes in times of war and crises, and in certain cases and with Portugal's explicit permission for exercises in times of peace. Extended in 1957 for a period of five years, this agreement expired in November 1962. On 4 January 1963, it was provisionally extended

with a revocation term of six months. *(14)* Under these conditions, the Portuguese could renounce this arrangement whenever it suited them. This has provided them an excellent means of pressuring the American government for more U.S. aid in support of their African wars.

2) As a consequence of a series of secret agreements between the Federal Republic of Germany and the Portuguese government (14 October 1963), the national air base No. 11 at Beja was to be constructed jointly by both countries (West Germany would bear up to seventy-five percent of the costs) and was to serve as a training area for the West German Luftwaffe. The Beja base located in the Alentejo was to consist of training grounds, airstrips, barracks, schools, churches, and hospitals. *(15)*

3) On 7 April 1964, France and Portugal signed a cooperation agreement. It provided for the installation of a French base on the island of Flores, to be used as an observation post and as a tracking station for France's ballistic experiments. The station was officially activated by the French General Fourquet on 6 October 1966. *(16)*

In addition to the leasing of facilities to the major NATO allies, Portugal also extended its hospitality to the new NATO command IBERLANT, inaugurated on 22 February 1967 in the presence of Admiral Moorer (SACLANT), General Gomes de Araujo, Portuguese minister of national defense, and General Lemnitzer. IBERLANT is under the command of SACLANT (the Allied Command Atlantic), which extends from the coastal waters of North America to those of Europe and Africa. In wartime, SACLANT's main duty is to ensure safe communication lines in the Atlantic Ocean, to conduct conventional and nuclear operations against enemy naval bases and airfields, and to support operations carried out by other NATO commands. The IBERLANT area, "extending from the Tropic of Cancer to Portugal's northern border and

---

14 The 1962-1963 negotiations for prolongation of the use of Lajes by the U.S. armed forces have been extremely lengthy and difficult. The Portuguese exacted complete support for their Africa policies and additional financial assistance and military aid. On this episode, see: The *New York Times*, 29 June 1962; the *West German* D.P.A. press release of 25 June 1962, and the *Christian Science Monitor* of 8 January 1963. On the further development concerning the Azores leave see pp. 86-88.

15 A full description of those facilities can be found in the German military review "Wehrkunde" (1965, p. 692).

16 See *Le Monde*, 10 April 1964 and 1 October 1966. The French station at Flores comprises a technical base at *Ponta Delgado* and a fourteen km. road to Cedros; a hydroelectric station; harbor installations; radar, radio and other communications systems, and a life base.

stretching 700 nautical miles westward from the Straits of Gibraltar into the Atlantic" is a key focal point "where all the ships moving in and out of the Mediterranean meet the vessels plying between north-west Europe and South America, Western and Southern Africa, the Persian Gulf and the Far East." *(17)* IBERLANT comprises the island command of Madeira, the naval command of Gibraltar, and is responsible, "in cooperation with Portuguese military authorities, for the defense of continental Portugal." *(18)* Initially, headquarters were established at Mem-Martins near Sintra. In the fall of 1971, however, they were to be transferred to Oeiras, very near to the famous fort of São Julião da Barra. When fully operational IBERLANT will have a staff of 206 people drawn mostly from Portugal, the United Kingdom and the United States.

On the whole, then, with its valuable, strategically located islands, its Atlantic ports, and its communications facilities, Portugal has certainly been a most welcome NATO partner; certainly also, in terms of manpower, training, and equipment the Portuguese armed forces have been unable to live up to their NATO commitments, since their main defense efforts lie overseas.

## METROPOLITAN DEFENSE VERSUS OVERSEAS WAR COSTS

Although Portugal was largely succesful in staying out of World War II, neutrality required a vigilant military attitude, and necessitated extraordinary defense disbursements to safeguard Portugal's colonies and guarantee national integrity.

Expenditure on defense and security, which reached its maximum in 1943 and fell to 684.7 million escudos in 1945, has shown little reduction since then. In 1947 the figure totaled 649 million escudos. In that year the category "exceptional military expenditure" was limited to commitments made earlier, that is to reconstruction works in Timor. The necessity of rearming for the Cold War prevented a lessening of expenditure in the immediate post-World War II period, however. At that time, the government hoped that maintenance and replacement costs could be transferred to ordinary expenditures once the rearmament plans had been carried out. But those hopes did not materialize. The

---

17  P. Jenner, "Iberian Atlantic Command Watches over Crossroads of the Seas", *NATO Review*, XIX (1971), pp. 6-7.
18  *Ibid.*, p. 7.

Communist coup in Prague, the Berlin blockade, and above all the events in Korea prevented a steady decrease in Portugal's defense expenditures, which remained at fairly high levels throughout the fifties. Between 1950 and 1960, the average defense expenditure as a percentage of the G.N.P. was 4.3, which represented a substantial fraction of the state budget (29.5 percent in the period

TABLE III

Portuguese State Budget: Extraordinary Expenditures
(In Thousands of Contos*)

|  | 1939 | 1943 | 1945 | 1946 | 1947 |
|---|---|---|---|---|---|
| Defense and Security | 177.7 | 1,210.4 | 684.7 | 674.7 | 649.1 |
| Other Categories i.e. economic development, social welfare and public health, etc. | 291.8 | 181.5 | 456.2 | 718.9 | 1,605.3 |
| Totals | 469.5 | 1,391.4 | 1,140.9 | 1,393.6 | 2,234.4 |

* 1 Conto = 100 Escudos

Source: *Overseas Economic Surveys: Portugal*, (London, 1949), p. 5.

between 1952 and 1960. *(19)* As in most NATO countries, the Korean affair generated great fears in Portugal and, faithful to its commitments to the NATO

19  Defense expenditure as a percentage of the state budget and of G.N.P. varies greatly according to the definitions used. Figures from the NATO Information Service differ from the figures published by the Institute of Strategic Studies, the former are generally higher than the latter.

## TABLE IV

### Portugal: Defense Efforts and Economic Data

| | 1950 | 1951 | 1952 | 1953 | 1954 | 1955 | 1956 | 1957 | 1958 | 1959 | 1960 | 1961 |
|---|---|---|---|---|---|---|---|---|---|---|---|---|
| Gross National Product (at factor costs - current prices. In millions of escudos) * | 37,250 ,, | 40,630 ,, | 41,460 ,, | 43,420 ,, | 44,760 ,, | 47,220 ,, | 50,970 53,634 | 56,146 | 57,600 | 61,427 | 67,368 | 71,395 |
| Gross National Product (at factor costs - current prices. In millions of U.S. dollars) | 1,290 | 1,408 | 1,436 | 1,503 | 1,550 | 1,635 | 1,857 | 1,944 | 1,994 | 2,127 | 2,333 | 2,472 |
| Defense Expenditure as a % of Gross National Product (at factor costs - current prices) | 4.1 | 3.8 | 4.1 | 4.6 | 4.7 | 4.7 | 4.3 | 4.3 | 4.3 | 4.6 | 4.5 | 6.9 |
| Military or Defense expenditure. In millions of escudos. | 1,516 | 1,553 | 1,691 | 1,975 | 2,100 | 2,224 | 2,297 | 2,391 | 2,485 | 2,820 | 3,023 | 4,922 |
| Budgetary expenditure (overall-in millions of escudos | ,, | ,, | 5,852 | 6,406 | 6,683 | 7,330 | 7,671 | 7,997 | 8,690 | 9,751 | 11,336 | 13,941 |
| Defense expenditure as a % of budgetary expenditure | ,, | ,, | 28.9 | 30.8 | 31.4 | 30.3 | 29.9 | 29.9 | 28.6 | 28.9 | 26.7 | 35.3 |
| Population ooo | 8,405 | 8,477 | 8,596 | 8,534 | 8,570 | 8,610 | 8,647 | 8,680 | 8,725 | 8,776 | 8,865 | 9,932 |

* Note: The definition of G.N.P. having been changed in 1956, the two series are not completely comparable.

Source: *Documentation OTAN* (Brussels, 1969), pp. 247-253, and information personally provided to the author by the NATO Division of Economic Affairs.

## TABLE IV

### Portugal: Defense Efforts and Economic Data

|  | 1962 | 1963 | 1964 | 1965 | 1966 | 1967 | 1968 | 1969 | 1970 | 1971 | 1972 (forecasts) |
|---|---|---|---|---|---|---|---|---|---|---|---|
| Gross National Product (at factor costs - current prices. In millions of escudos) * | 76,317 | 82,188 | 89,735 | 99,265 | 108,162 | 121,410 | 133,808 | 145,658 | 163,101 | 177,170 | 199,050 |
| Gross National Product (at factor costs - current prices. In millions of U.S. dollars) | 2,643 | 2,846 | 3,107 | 3,437 | 3,745 | 4,204 | 4,654 | 5,066 | 5,673 | 6,163 | 7,305 |
| Defense Expenditure as a % of Gross National Product (at factor costs - current prices) | 7.5 | 7.0 | 7.2 | 6.7 | 6.9 | 7.4 | 8.0 | 7.4 | 7.7 | 8.3 | 8.3 |
| Military or Defense expenditure. In millions of escudos. | 5,744 | 5,724 | 6,451 | 6,680 | 7,393 | 9,575 | 10,693 | 10,779 | 12,538 | 14,699 | 16,559 |
| Budgetary expenditure (overall- in millions of escudos | 15,181 | 15,850 | 17,497 | 18,055 | 19,621 | 23,359 | 25,913 | 27,713 | 31,735 | 32,050 | 36,875 |
| Defense expenditure as a % of budgetary expenditure | 37.8 | 36.1 | 36.7 | 37.0 | 37.7 | 41 | 41.3 | 38.9 | 39.5 | 45.9 | 44.9 |
| Population ooo | 9,008 | 9,074 | 9,143 | 9,234 | 9,335 | 9,415 | 9,497 | 9,582 | 9,669 | 9,730 | 9,780 |

* Note: The definition of G.N.P. having been changed in 1956, the two series are not completely comparable.

Source: *Documentation OTAN* (Brussels, 1969), pp. 247-253, and information personally provided to the author by the NATO Division of Economic Affairs.

Lisbon Council of Ministers of 20 February 1952, it embarked upon a serious rearmament program during 1953, 1954, and 1955. In this it paralleled the great majority of NATO members.

Once the virulence of the Cold War began to subside, some people again hoped that the extraordinary expenditure needed for the rearmament and equipment of Portugal's NATO-assigned troops and for its military infrastructure, logistics, naval, and air bases could gradually be transferred to productive investments, which would generate a faster growth rate of the national economy and improve the Portuguese standard of living. Yet Portugal would be spared no sacrifices. At a moment when defense disbursements slackened or even dropped in a great number of smaller NATO countries, they increased in Portugal. Between 1960 and 1969 the average Portuguese defense expenditure as a percentage of the Gross National Product was 6.7 and as a percentage of the national budget 36.7. In the Western camp those figures were second only to the American ones. By 1971 Portuguese defense expenses as a percentage of the Gross National Product and of the general budget reached peaks of 8.3 and 45.9 respectively (See table IV). Since the beginning of the colonial wars overseas, additional amounts have systematically swelled the normal budgetary credits; without doubt Portugal spent even more on defense throughout the sixties than is shown by the regular defense budget. The Ministry of Finance has provided part of the added funds from the budgets of the overseas provinces, from other departments which had not expended their own allocations in previous years, and from other sources. *(20)*

In the narrow sense, the relatively high defense expenditure figures undeniably had almost nothing to do with Portugal's NATO commitments. The bulk of defense disbursements is attributable entirely to the Department of National Defense and not to the forces, and is part of the extraordinary budget devoted to the build-up of military infrastructures overseas and to the maintenance and logistic support of the Portuguese forces engaged in battle abroad.

20 In some interviews, particularly with foreign diplomats posted in Lisbon, some reference has been made to Gulbenkian funds.

## TABLE V

Portuguese National Defense Budget: Extraordinary Expenditure 1960-1968
(In Millions of escudos)

| | 1960 | 1961 | 1962 | 1963 | 1964 | 1965 | 1966 | 1967 | 1968 |
|---|---|---|---|---|---|---|---|---|---|
| a) Military expenditure by virtue of international agreement | 260 | 260 | 260 | 260 | 260 | 260 | 260 | 257 | 260 |
| b) Extraordinary expenditure on military overseas forces | 280 | 950 | 1,500 | 1,700 | 1,750 | 2,000 | 2,500 | 3,500 | 4,000 |
| c) Acquisition of four naval escorts and four submarines | — | — | — | — | — | 25 | 100 | 500 | 500 |
| d) Acquisition of four corvettes | — | — | — | — | — | — | — | 45 | 87 |
| e) Development of naval infrastructure, workshops, arsenals, and schools for the navy | — | — | — | — | — | — | — | — | 125 |
| f) NATO infrastructure | 237 | 274.6 | 264.9 | 230 | 220 | 180 | 130 | 90 | 90 |
| g) Expenses of first urgency concerning the storage, functioning, and surveillance of NATO installations | — | — | 34.1 | 34.1 | 30 | 30 | 15 | 15 | 30 |
| h) Construction of naval escorts | — | 50 | 100 | 100 | 100 | — | 100 | 85 | 60 |
| i) Aerial Base Nº 11 (Beja) | 2 | 1 | 50 | 210.8 | 221.5 | 400 | 400 | 400 | 250 |
| j) Aerial Base Nº 11 (Beja residential district) | — | — | — | — | 19.3 | 200 | 200 | 200 | 50 |
| k) Military constructions to be carried out in the Troian Peninsula | — | — | — | — | — | 25 | 25 | 14 | — |
| l) Development of establishments for aeronautical equipment | — | — | — | — | — | 200 | 150 | 100 | 100 |
| m) Expenditure resulting from the execution of Decree Law Nº 45.885 of 24 August, 1964 (Agreements with France on a base in the Azores | — | — | — | — | — | 35 | 60 | 50 | 40 |
| n) Military hospital at Beja | — | — | — | — | — | 25 | 25 | 30 | — |
| o) Materiel depot at Casteloes | — | — | — | — | — | 25 | 35 | 40 | — |
| p) Communications Center at Evora | — | — | — | — | — | — | 5 | 15 | 15 |
| q) Offshore Procurement | 20 | 20 | 12 | — | — | — | — | — | — |
| TOTAL | 811.5 | 1,670.6 | 2,109.0 | 2,593.4 | 2,609.3 | 3,515 | 4,005 | 5,341 | 5,607 (*) |

* To reach the 1967 extraordinary expenditure figure, add 6 million escudos expended on infrastructure for public security.
Source: Portuguese Department of Defense.

A breakdown of the extraordinary defense budgets indicates plainly that the major effort in Portuguese defense extraordinary expenditure has been the colonial wars rather than NATO. Over eight years, item b has swelled from 280 million escudos in 1960 to 4,000 in 1968, while the disbursements directly related to NATO programs either diminished (item f) or stagnated (items a + g). A great many headings, such as c, d, e, h and l, can of course be useful for both the war overseas and for NATO commitments.

During the last decade the Portuguese defense expenditure has been among the highest in Europe; in the NATO framework it ranks second only to the American performance. Yet only a small part of the effort has been employed for Portugal's NATO commitments almost all has been used to wage war in Africa.

# Chapter III

# PORTUGAL : UNHAPPY ALLY ?

Portugal was unhappy in the early and mid-sixties. It believed it was one of the few NATO members to understand the real nature of the Communist menace, and to act accordingly by resisting three African movements of national liberation. Soon it realized that many allies were not very much concerned with its heroic resistance overseas. The government objected very strongly to the initial aloofness of some of the smaller NATO members and the perfidy of Great Britain, its oldest ally. On every occasion it communicated its growing discontent threatening withdrawal from the alliance at the end of the twenty-year membership period unless NATO drastically altered its attitudes toward the African situation. The threat of dealignment is an old and well-known tactic to convince the larger partners to yield to the smaller. In fact, whatever Portugal felt about the attitudes of its friends, it knew quite well staying in the alliance offered more than leaving it. The Americans, the Germans, the French, and the British were more valuable as difficult and uneasy friends than as outspoken enemies.

## DISENCHANTMENT WITH THE U.S.

Portuguese disenchantment with the U.S. grew out of the American attitude toward the debate on colonial emancipation that took place in the early sixties. The United States attempted to balance "those American interests which imply a pro-Portuguese policy – NATO commitments and the Azores military base – with those which call for a pro-African orientation – leadership in the U.N. and the effort to prevent Communist penetration and racial conflict in Southern Africa." (1)

The historic United Nations debate on emancipation that culminated in the Fifteenth General Assembly's adoption of an Afro-Asian-sponsored Declara-

1 D. Wainhouse, *Remnants of Empire: The United Nations and the End of Colonialism* (New York, 1964), pp. 40-41.

tion on Colonialism marked a crisis point in Portuguese-American relations. *(2)* The old dilemma, whether to support an ally on what was not strictly a NATO matter, thereby suffering a heavy loss of prestige in the U.N., or disregard faithful partners in an attempt to court emerging nations ,grew sharper when it became apparent that the Declaration on Colonialism would be applied to Portugal's African possessions during the U.N. debate on Angola in the spring and summer of 1961.

Although the U.S. delegation abstained from voting on a declaration in the General Assembly, it did so exclusively because Prime Minister Harold Macmillan pressed President Dwight D. Eisenhower to avoid embarassing the United Kingdom. "But for the pressure from the British government the U.S. would have voted in favor of the Resolution thereby following its nominal commitment to anti-colonialism which had become part of American policy ever since the time of Franklin Roosevelt." *(3)*

When J. F. Kennedy was elected to the presidency, the alteration in political atmosphere and the change in policy makers also saw a new interpretation of the national interest. The Kennedy administration, including Secretary of State Dean Rusk, was determined to give more weight to the Africanists in the State Department, to alter traditional U.S. attitudes toward the Third World, and to evince more empathy to the emerging peoples in the U.N. America wanted to be placed on record as sympathetic to self-determination.

Then revolt broke out in Angola. Reports reaching U.N. headquarters described in full detail the increasing intensity of rebel attacks and the ruthless Portuguese countermeasures. Liberia placed a resolution before the Security Council, urgently calling on Portugal to consider reforms which would allow the Angolan people to evolve toward self-determination. The resolution also proposed a subcommittee to report on the situation. The measure was defeated

2   This resolution on the granting of independence to colonial countries and peoples declared that "all peoples have the right of self-determination", that "inadequacy of political, economic, social or educational preparedness should never serve as a pretext to delaying independence" and that "immediate steps shall be taken" in the remaining self-governing territories to transfer all powers to the peoples of those territories, without any conditions or reservations, in accordance with their freely expressed will. After a long debate, the General Assembly adopted the resolution on 14 December 1960 by a vote of ninety to zero. Nine countries abstained: Australia, Belgium, the Dominican Republic, France, Portugal, Spain, the Union of South Africa, the United Kingdom and the U.S. (U.N. General Assembly, *Official Records*, *A/PV 947* (14 December 1960, p. 21).

3   *The United States in the United Nations: 1960 – A Turning Point*, Supplementary Report to the Committee on Foreign Relations, United States Senate, by Senator Wayne Morse, Oregon (Washington, D.C., 1961), pp. 20-21.

by the abstentions of Chile, China, Ecuador, Turkey, and Britain. This time, however the U.S. joined the Soviet Union to vote in its favor, and the statement made by the U.S. representative, Ambassador Adlai Stevenson was, even more important than the vote because it affirmed American support for the self-determination of colonial peoples: "The U.S. would be remiss in its duties as a friend of Portugal", Ambassador Stevenson said

> if it failed to express honestly its conviction that step-by-step planning within Portuguese territories and its acceleration is now imperative for the succesful political, social and economic advancement of all inhabitants under Portuguese administration – advancement, in brief, toward full self determination. *(4)*

Following the failure of the Angola resolution in the Security Council, the debate was pursued in the Fifteenth General Assembly, where America reiterated its support of a policy which urged Portugal to consider the necessary institutional reforms, to promote self-determination, and to cooperate with the U.N. On 20 April 1961, the General Assembly adopted the Angola resolution by a vote of seventy-three to two, with nine abstentions. The American vote was acclaimed throughout the Third World, where President Kennedy increasingly was seen as a friend to oppressed peoples. It also resulted in anti-American riots in Lisbon and a surge of criticism of U.S. foreign policy in Washington and New York, particularly among the Europeanists, who feared that Kennedy had opened a gap in the Atlantic alliance. It also caused growing restlessness and bad temper in the Portuguese government. Salazar had been informed of the American intentions a week before the vote, and Ambassador Stevenson had taken great care to debate the matter politely, with due concern for the Portuguese feelings. Despite his efforts, the American position was considered deeply inimical to Portugal, and contrary to the interests of a close and faithful ally. The vote on the Angola resolution of March and April 1961 "had liberated the U.S. from its position of systematic deference" to the colonial interest in NATO, and the Africa people in the State Department were very pleased. The price for their pleasure was alienation among NATO allies, in the Bureau of European Affairs of the State Department, and in the Pentagon.

In the General Assembly, the debate on colonialism and emancipation continued, and on 25 September 1961 President Kennedy set out to make U.S. policy clear. He stressed particularly that the U.S. continued to support the growing tide of self-determination, and he called for the application of free choice and free plebiscites in every corner of the world. *(5)*

---

4  U.N., Security Council, *Official Records*, S/PV 946 (15 March 1961), p. 21.
5  The latter part of Kennedy's statement was aimed at the Communist empire and was just

The Sixteenth General Assembly opened its session in January 1962 with a plenary debate on Angola. Throughout the discussion Stevenson continued to press for self-determination. He urged Portugal to improve economic and social conditions in Angola and to seek peaceful solutions to the conflict. And in his view, the best hope for a settlement was Portuguese cooperation. American policy on the matter, he added, rests not on trivial or accidental circumstances but on fundamental and long-range considerations of our national tradition of anti-colonialism, our friendship with Portugal and our fidelity to the Charter." (6) In addition, Stevenson disclosed that the U.S. had encouraged Portugal to move toward "a constructive and harmonious solution embracing full self-determination". The American government had informed the Portuguese that any diversion of military equipment supplied for NATO purposes to the African war theater would be considered a serious violation of the U.S.-Portuguese military defense agreement; in return it had received assurances that the Portuguese armed forces would employ no NATO equipment in Angola. Finally, he revealed that measures had been taken to prevent the sale of arms by U.S. firms to Portugal for use in the Angolan conflict. (7) These were the limits of the U.S. delegation's support of self-determination for Africa; they were consistent with Kennedy's policy of moderation and persuasion. They attempted to balance America's "traditional anticolonialism and relations with its ally, Portugal" (8), in an effort to promote "realistic resolutions which could help lay the economic, educational, and institutional foundations for self-government" rather than "mistrusted U.N. resolutions which promised big things but could not be carried out." (9) Other more hard-line paragraphs of the Afro-Asian resolution of January 1962, including a call for the speedy independence of the Angolan people, were succesfully opposed by the U.S. delegation, so that the forty-five Afro-Asian nation draft, minus two paragraphs could be approved by a substantial majority, the U.S. included. The measure was passed by ninety-nine votes. South Africa and Spain opposed it, and France abstained.

In the meantime Kennedy's moderate Angola policy had come under serious fire from Europeanists in the executive branch itself, and Lisbon was using every opportunity to oppose America's Africa policy, making it clear that the U.S. could only expect understanding and support in matters of American

for the record. The former was based partly on the president's deep convictions on self-determination and partly on fear that the Soviet Union would press the colonialism issue. (See Wainhouse, *op. cit.*, pp. 14-15).

6 A/PV 1097, 25 January 1962, p. 1279.

7 Wainhouse, *op. cit.*, pp. 20-23.

8 *Ibid.*, p. 21.

9 *Ibid.*

interest "in exchange for American solidarity in the defense of Portugal's legitimate interests" *(10)* Portuguese Foreign Minister Dr. Franco Nogueira voiced this opinion on every possible occasion, through traditional diplomatic channels, at a meeting of a NATO Council of Ministers, to visiting Americans with influence in Washington, and even during a press conference. "It is no secret", he said "and it has been made public by American attitudes and statements" *(11)*, that the colonial issues in the U.N. "have created differences between the two countries [Portugal and the U.S.]. It will not be in the interest of either party that those differences endure and damage the relations between the two peoples." *(12)* Nogueira cleverly linked the Angolan problem to other American-Portuguese issues "of an exclusively bilateral scope, such as that of economic cooperation between the United States and Portugal in the execution of Portuguese projects and that of the utilization of the base of Lajes." *(13)* The U.S. government would have liked to extend the Azores lease beyond its expiration date, 31 December, 1962. In this atmosphere the Portuguese foreign minister was able to exhort the American decision makers to more temperateness, skillfully playing off the Europeanists in the Pentagon and the State Department against the newer Africa advocates.

*A Thousand Days*, by A. Schlesinger, provides an excellent description of the debates generated by Portuguese pressure. Schlesinger stresses particularly that the American ability to help Angola, Mozambique, and Portuguese Guinea was limited by U.S. "dependence, or alleged dependence, on the military and naval installations which Portugal made available to us in the Azores." *(14)* The problem "led to continuous wrangling in Washington – the Bureau of European Affairs vs. the Bureau of African Affairs; the Mission to the U.N. vs. the Pentagon – with occasional interventions by such kibitzers as J.K. Galbraith, who angered the Europeanists by suggesting that they were trading off Africa for a few acres of asphalt in the Atlantic" *(15)*, and by Dean Acheson, who enraged the Africanists by recommending that the United States stop

---

10　The foreign minister Dr. Franco Nogueira talked to visiting American congressmen, in Lisbon, on 30 November 1962, Ministry of Foreign Affairs (eds.), *Portuguese Foreign Policy* (Lisbon, 1965), p. 29.
11　Press conference by the Minister of Foreign Affairs held in Lisbon, on 13 July, 1962, *Portuguese Foreign Policy, op. cit.*
12　*Ibid.*
13　*Ibid.*
14　"In the summer of 1961, for example, the Joint Chiefs of Staff declared the Azores base essential to American security in case of trouble, over Berlin". A. Schlesinger, *A Thousand Days* (London, 1965), p. 490.
15　*Ibid.*

helping draft resolutions on Angola." *(16)* Without the Azores complication, Kennedy policy toward the Portuguese colonies would unquestionably have been stronger. But the Portuguese had carefully joined the Azores to the Angolan issue, and the U.S. felt itself unable to do more than to press the Portuguese to make self-determination the ultimate goal in Africa, using "private suasion in Lisbon as well as public argument in the U.N. in a constant effort to induce Portugal to reform its colonial methods." *(17)*

At the General Assembly's seventeenth session in the fall of 1962, the Afro-Asian delegations and Yugoslavia introduced a resolution requesting the Security Council to "take appropriate measures, including sanctions to secure Portugal's compliance" with former U.N. resolutions calling for freely elected and representative political institutions in the Portuguese overseas territories. The measure, which stipulated an arms embargo against the Portuguese nation, carried by a fifty-seven to fourteen vote, with eighteen abstentions. The U.S. and most colonial powers voted against it, arguing that neither the arms embargo nor the sanction provisions were consistent with the U.S. policy of persuasion and moderation. In fact, the Pentagon's fear of jeopardizing the Azores base had actually determined the limits of Kennedy's Africa policy.

Under the Johnson and Nixon administrations, U.S. attitudes toward Portugal and the African situation has followed a much more traditional, even prudently pro-Portuguese, course. Both in the General Assembly and in the Security Council the U.S. recurrently abstained on resolutions concerning the Portuguese colonies. Although the American delegates have accepted the essential substance of those resolutions, a call for self-determination for the peoples of Portuguese territories in Africa, they have refused such provisions as an arms embargo or the cessation of economic and financial assistance as long as Portugal repudiates U.N. resolutions. *(18)*

On the whole, then, the influence of State Department officials concerned with the welfare of the Portuguese African territories has been extremely short-

16  *Ibid.*
17  *Ibid.*
18  See Security Council Resolutions of 31 July 1963 and 23 November 1965 and the General Assembly Resolutions of 13 November 1963; 21 December 1965; 12 December 1966; 17 November 1967; 29 November 1968; 21 November 1969. On all these resolutions the U.S., France, and the U.K. abstained. However, the U.S. and the U.K. were in favor of a Security Council resolution of 11 December 1963, referring to the need for negotiations between the nationalist leaders under Portuguese rule and the Portuguese themselves.

lived – their tenure ran from the spring of 1961 to the summer of 1962 – and during almost the entire following decade the U.S. has been careful not to prejudice vital Portuguese interests. Portuguese disenchantment with the U.S., greatest in the early sixties, has been reduced considerably since the U.S. stopped favoring resolutions which Portugal interpreted as extremely inimical to its interests.

## THE END OF THE ANGLO–PORTUGUESE ALLIANCE?

As early as the 1930s, Dr. Salazar defined clearly the foundations upon which the Anglo-Portuguese alliance had been built, indicating at the same time the conditions of its possible disintegration. "The Alliance between Great Britain and Portugal would only lose its appeal if and when the British empire will come to an end or if a cataclysm would have removed England's insular nature." *(19)* Certainly the Portuguese prime minister did not foresee either of those events at that point, yet by the early sixties the "most ancient of European treaties" was experiencing difficult times. The most important reason for the ill feeling between the old friends was Britain's gradual decline as a major naval, colonial, and world power. Although Britain did not lose its insularity, it nevertheless lost its empire and both sides were bound to question the validity of the old treaties as a result, especially the one which saw its colonial and maritime support collapsing. The end of the British empire naturally augured the end of the Anglo-Portuguese alliance.

The fact that both maritime nations possessed numerous colonies, depencies, and interests all over the world had kept them closer than any other covenant or written agreement. England assisted Portugal in maintaining its sovereignty overseas; in exchange Portugal bolstered Britain's attempts to defend its colonies and dominions, mainly by providing the facilities and logistic support based in the Portuguese ports and territories. Portugal has never failed to respond to British appeals. In the second world war, for example, Britain requested that Portugal extend use of the Azores to the royal navy and air force and the privilege was granted without question.

When Portuguese India was threatened by the young Indian Republic, the Portuguese government notified Her Majesty's government to these events without formally invoking the treaties, and Winston Churchill intervened forcefully with the New Delhi government. Britain's strong attitude clearly had some moderating influence on Indian ambitions at that time *(20)*, but the

19  Ploncard d'Assac, *op. cit.*, p. 142.
20  In addition, John F. Dulles pressured the New Delhi government heavily to stop the acquisition of Portuguese India by the force of arms.

incident was probably the last striking example of British support for Portuguese colonial interests.

Since then Great Britain has conceded the nationalist revolution in Afro-Asia, while Portugal has stubbornly resisted it. The division has led to considerable misunderstandings between the allies. In British judgment, the conditions on which the Anglo-Portuguese alliance had been based had changed by the early sixties. Political and strategic circumstances had altered dramatically, and the nature of British obligations toward Lisbon had to be revised in light of them. The emergency of the two superpowers after World War II, the decline of British influence and the rise of Imperial America, the Atlantic pact the United Nations, the process of decolonization, and Britain's increasing attraction to the Common Market and continental Europe all changed the international environment. The concept of British national interest, including the obligation to defend the Portuguese overseas terrirories, changed with it. *(21)*

When the Indian government occupied the Portuguese enclaves at Goa, Damão, and Diu in the early days of 1961, the Portuguese government called upon Great Britain for assistance and was flatly refused. Even though the alliance had been formally invoked, the British withheld support on the grounds that the alliance had clear limitations and that it could not take action on an issue involving a member of the Commonwealth.

At a NATO meeting in Paris held on the eve of the Indian attack, the Portuguese minister of foreign affairs warned the British and the Americans that the Goanese would fight bitterly and were prepared to die, but not without killing ten Indians for each of them. On December 17, the Indian army supported by naval and air forces, entered the contested area. The invasion was over in twenty-four hours; sixty-seven people, including forty-four Portuguese and twenty-two Indians, had been killed. *(22)* Neither Great Britain, the U.S., or any other NATO ally had provided the Portuguese with material aid or moral support, and this created great bitterness in Lisbon. Dr. Nogueira accused the British government of even refusing the utilization of some airdromes vitally necessary for smooth Portuguese communications between Lisbon and Goa.

In addition to the Goan affair, the Portuguese had accumulated other grievances against Great Britain. A great many Commonwealth members had evinced great hostility toward Portuguese activities in the early sixties. In the

21  See M. Caetano, "L'alliance Anglo-Portugaise: histoire et situation actuelle", *Chronique de politique étrangère*, XX, 6 (1967), pp. 695-708.
22  See Kay, *op. cit.*, pp. 294-328, and L. Lawrence, *Nehru Seizes Goa* (New York, 1962).

U.N., many draft resolutions against Portugal had been introduced with the assistance of one or more of these countries and the enthusiastic support of most of them. In the Security Council and in the General Assembly, Great Britain had almost never dared to take an explicitly pro-Portuguese attitude, although the Portuguese recognized that, unlike the U.S., the British never voted against them.

The Rhodesian crisis only deepened misunderstandings. From the British point of view, treating Ian Smith's unilateral declaration of independence of 11 November 1965 as an act of rebellion was reasonable, and in line with the practice of successive governments not to concede independence to any former colony or dominion without substantial guarantees for the advancement and representation of the indigenous inhabitants. But once Mr. Wilson had ruled out force and failed to affirm London's authority over its colony, Rhodesia's neighbors, particularly one so close and friendly as Portugal, were confronted with a difficult situation. Bringing the issue before the Security Council, the British government attempted to minimize the rebellion with an economic and financial blockade in which all U.N. members were invited to join. Economic blockades of this kind have seldom proved the best means to break the resistance of an unlawful government, particularly if the isolated state is surrounded by countries not hostile to their cause. The blockade failed.

Then oil shipments to Rhodesia were cancelled in the hope that this would stop the rebels, but Portugal unconditionally refused to apply any embargo or sanction against Rhodesia. It considered the question an exclusively British concern and not within the realm of the United Nations. "We would admit the illegality of the Rhodesian government", Mr. Nogueira said, "but that illegality only existed in the face of the legal and constitutional structure of the British." *(23)* Mr. Nogueira made many more statements on this issue, arguing either that international peace in that area was not threatened, making debate in the Security Council senseless, or that many international treaties between Portugal and the former Federation of Rhodesia and Nyasaland (the Beira Convention, for example) were, in Portugal's view still valid with the successor states. Mr. Nogueira stressed that Portugal would "not carry out any positive act aimed at supplying fuel oil to Rhodesia" and would abstain from diverting to Rhodesia any fuel arriving in Mozambique and destined for Mozambique, Malawi, or Zambia *(24)*, but that Portugal considered it a right and

---

23  Mr. F. Nogueira, Comment on Portugal's position on the Rhodesian Affair (Press Conference held in Lisbon on 3 May, 1966), *Ministry of Foreign Affairs* (eds.), (Lisbon, 1967), p. 58.
24  *Ibid.*, p. 57.

duty "to ensure freedom of transit through its territory and ports without conditioning it on political considerations." *(25)*

His position was "repeated by and officially communicated to the British government", which, according to Mr. Nogueira, labeled it as "correct, clever, prudent and impeccable". Britain nevertheless concentrated a powerful air and naval force in the international waters of the Mozambique Channel, allowing them to interfere with merchant shipping of various nationalities not only on the high seas, but in some cases within Portuguese territorial waters and air space. The Portuguese protested these infringements on their sovereignty, although they hoped that no ships would break the naval blockade and embarrass them by witnessing the arrival in their ports of oil tankers bound for Rhodesia. They were extremely irritated when the powerful British force let through a Greek-manned tanker flying the Panamian flag, the *Johanna V*, which the Smith government in alliance with a South African company and some Greek speculators had dispatched to force the blockade. Moreover, at this stage the Foreign Office dispatched Minister of State Lord Watson to Lisbon for assurances from Dr. Nogueira that the oil would not be pumped from Beira to Umtali in Rhodesia.

In the meantime, however, the British government introduced a resolution in the Security Council which singled out Portugal. It called upon the Portuguese not to permit the oil transfer and not to receive oil at Beira consigned for Rhodesia. "To the Portuguese it was a case of extremely bad manners on the part of an ally to take this hostile action while conversations were in progress. Tempers rose. The British were accused of doing a Pearl Harbour on the Portuguese." *(26)* Resentment against the United Kingdom was high. Lisbon felt particularly that the British lacked the courage to settle the rebellion clearly. They had found it easier "and ingratiating" with their "Pan-African friends to humiliate a smaller country which is the object of their hatred." *(27)*

By 1965 not much was left of the "true, faithful, constant, mutual and perpetual" friendship which once characterized relations between England and Portugal. Great Britain's refusal to assist Portugal in the defense of Goa, even more its refusal to permit Portugal the use of "some airfields necessary for connec-

---

25   F. Nogueira, Portugal and the Transit Problem of Landlocked Countries (Press Conference held in Lisbon on 12 July 1966), *Portuguese Foreign Policy, 1965-1967, op. cit.,* p. 63.
26   "The Anglo-Portuguese Alliance. Past, Present and Future", *British Survey,* XXVIII, 207 (1966), p. 5.
27   *Ibid.,* p. 5.

tions with Goa" *(28)*, had come as a shock to Salazar, and he never quite got over it. The Rhodesian affair merely turned a bitter disappointment into violent anger. And although Salazar himself had foreseen that the Anglo-Portuguese alliance would end with the British empire the realization of this prediction in his lifetime, and particularly the crude and brutal way it came about, deeply wounded him. Moreover, Portugal's disenchantment with the U.S. and with Great Britain happened at a moment when the disintegration process in NATO begun by the French government climaxed. Exactly at that moment, Portugal chose to warn the major NATO allies that if no substantial solutions could be found in the near future Portugal would be one of the first to leave.

## PORTUGAL'S COMPLAINT

At the beginning of the 1960s Portugal was evidently NATO's unhappiest member. At times angrily, at times pathetically, the Lisbon government complained about the allies' lack of sympathy and support. Portugal was above all disenchanted. Colonial war had become the ugly reality with which most of Portuguese youth were confronted daily, and war imposed setbacks in economic advancement and social welfare on the entire nation. In this enterprise Portugal stood pretty much alone, at least in the beginning. Singled out and stigmatized as one of the most reactionary among Western nations, ostracized by the Afro-Asian majority in the U.N., where initially even NATO allies such as Denmark and Norway and sometimes the U.S., opposed its policies, Portugal was obliged to struggle patiently, skillfully, and relentlessly, on a bilateral and on a multilateral basis, in the U.N. as well as in NATO.

For twelve years now, Portuguese diplomacy has endeavored to explain and to defend its overseas policies in the hope of avoiding complete isolation in NATO and embargoes on weapon deliveries from Western Europe and the U.S.. It has done so with great proficiency. It never failed to express its discontent with the initial anticolonial bias of the Kennedy administration, Britain's infidelity to the Anglo-Portuguese alliance, groundless Scandinavian moral judgments, Italian and Benelux coolness, and Greek and Turkish aloofness.

---

28  Salazar later recalled that when the Portuguese asked the British for the use of some of those airfields, the British Government waited a week before responding negatively. "Had it not been for this delay we should certainly have found alternative routes, and we could have rushed to India reinforcements in men and material for a longer sustained defense of the territory" (Salazar's address to the National Union, 3 April 1962). H. Kay has pointed out that if Britain had responded favorably, "it would not have made much difference to the outcome, but it was the silence that hurt" (Kay, *op. cit.*, p. 321).

Salazar took the lead in this national, international, and transnational campaign for moral and material support of Portugal's African crusade. "I am not at all satisfied with the support of other [other than the Federal Republic of Germany] European states to Portugal", he said,

> they do not seem to understand that their own essential interests are at stake here... Moreover, this is not an issue which concerns Portugal in the first place. What is at stake is Europe, all of us. Who attacks Portugal from behind betrays Europe and denies our right to live. Only Western Germany, France and Spain are exceptions to this. With them we find the required understanding and support. This strengthens my confidence in Europe. *(29)*

This kind of statement is typical of every official declaration on this matter, and sets the tone of relations between Portugal and its allies.

Until the mid-1960s, Portugal's recriminations and its insistence on a change in attitudes among NATO members aroused only hostility or silent sympathy. Answering a parliamentary question on the attitudes of the NATO members toward Portuguese overseas policies, the Dutch minister of foreign affairs, Mr. J. Luns, said that an atmosphere of disapproval was maintained mainly by Portugal who attacked the hostility and indifference of its allies, rather than by other NATO members, who were accused of voicing their disagreement with Portuguese policies. *(30)* Indeed, at the first meeting of the NATO Council of Ministers following the beginning of rebellion in Angola in Oslo on 8 May 1961, the Portuguese foreign minister complained that some NATO members had been outspokenly critical of Portuguese colonialism in the U.N. General Assembly. Citing the French precedent in Algeria, he affirmed that Portugal had the right to send NATO-assigned troops with NATO equipment to Angola, and although he was not able to convince all delegations at the time, many of them did try to erase the bad impressions their U.N. intervention had created. On the other hand, in July 1961 a NATO mission headed by Admiral Evans went to Lisbon to see out what effects the Portuguese war effort was having on Portugal's NATO contribution. *(31)* The relatively unfriendly U.S. attitude, underscored by the hostile silence of some smaller NATO allies continued at least until January 1962, giving rise to more resentment and bitter disappointment: "The truth however, is", said Dr. Nogueira to visiting congressmen in Lisbon on 30 November 1962 "that the United States expects a solidarity from

29 Dr. Salazar in an interview with the *Deutsch National- und Soldatenzeitung*, 15 November 1963.
30 This question was put by Mrs. de Vink (KVP-Catholic People's Party) on 9 December 1964. See Bosgra and Dijk, *op. cit.*, p. 150.
31 *Neue Zürcher Zeitung*, 29 July 1961.

its allies, which at times goes beyond the geographical limits of the Atlantic alliance." *(32)* For instance, European support was expected unconditionally during the Cuban crisis, when the security of the Western Hemisphere, a matter of the utmost importance to the U.S. was at stake. "Granting that this may be so, what is beyond understanding is that the United States should seek to invoke the geographical limits of NATO, when the interests of European nations are at stake in areas outside the alliance." *(33)* In Dr. Nogueira's opinion, the security of Africa is no less important to Western Europe than that of the Western Hemisphere is to the U.S. "Portuguese solidarity in problems of American interests" can therefore "only be guaranteed in exchange for American solidarity in the defense of Portugal's legitimate interests." *(34)* And those interests were still in Africa.

The African theme remained the leitmotiv of Portuguese foreign policy throughout the sixties and early seventies. What Portuguese diplomats were instructed to tell the allies was that Portugal's African struggle was not so much for mastery in Africa as for survival in Europe. As Dr. Salazar put it, "no security in the Atlantic, without security in Africa". Africa was the greatest, perhaps the last, of Europe's chances.

Changes in technology and nuclear strategy, changes in East-West relations and their bearing on the European security issue, and the approaching reconsideration of NATO membership as provided by Article XIII, all gave Portuguese diplomacy splendid opportunities to argue the Euro-African case again and to press once more for the need for a global strategy.

Time and again, year after year, the Portuguese delegation in NATO has pleaded the cause of globalism. According to the Portuguese, Article VI unjustifiably limits the alliance to the Atlantic area north of the Tropic of Cancer, and they have pressed for its nullification as well. Mr. Nogueira himself has reiterated this theory numerous times, specifically in a press conference held in Lisbon on 2 July 1964. The delimitation of a precise geographical area, "confining and facing the Soviet World and threatened by it", and in which "a collective defense was established, automatic and indivisible in its solidarity before any attack coming from the outside", had been an effective answer to the Soviet threat in the days following World War II. "Before this organized barrier

---

32  F. Nogueira, Rights and Obligations of the U.S. in Relation to its Allies (F. Nogueira talks to visiting American congressmen in Lisbon, on 30 November 1962), *Portuguese Foreign Policy, op. cit.*, p. 29.
33  *Ibid.*
34  *Ibid.*

the Soviet Union stopped and waited". For fifteen years no attack had come, and "throughout this period the conviction took root among some of the bigger allied powers that, should the Communist world not unleash the attack, it would remain immobilized at the frontiers of the Alliance, without seeking any other objectives and without attempts in any other region." *(35)* Clearly such a massive assault, which would have unleashed all the conventional and nuclear power of the U.S., had not occurred, but at the same time the Soviet Union had not been immobilized by the American deterrent. Quite the contrary, "Moscow was penetrating in limited areas through subversion and revolution; these were large enough to represent a profit to the Soviet Union, but restricted enough not to justify in public opinion a massive retaliation bringing on a general war". Soviet imperialism was not "motionless at the doors of the free world, it only diverted its attack to other places, leading it through other methods, maybe, without softening its virulence or changing its objectives." *(36)* In Dr. Nogueira's opinion, Communist domination of non-European areas, particularly of Africa, accompanied by nuclear parity would be fatal to the West. "In this new and challenging situation NATO waits, perplexed and motionless, though with growing nervousness at the decline, one after the other, of all the positions favorable to the West." *(37)* This is the origin of Portugal's major crisis of confidence. Some Western countries believed expansionism could be stopped merely by ensuring

> a solidarity limited to the framework of the Pact; and so, outside it, they felt free to abandon or even to oppose their own allies. And when these appealed to the solidarity they supposed should be observed, they were answered with the clauses and cold terms of the treaty, and it was suggested that they should comply with and obey what were said to be the inevitable winds of freedom. *(38)*

For Portugal, however, there can be no solidarity in Europe, Latin America, or Asia, where some big power interests are at stake, without the mutual support of those major allies with the smaller members fighting not only for their own survival but for the security of the Atlantic area as a whole. Dr. Nogueira concluded that the aims of the alliance must be reconsidered and new political objectives assigned to it:

> Because of all this, for many years we have tenaciously, indefatigably, stubbornly defended the criterion of universal and global solidarity as the only means to face succesfully

---

*35* F. Nogueira, NATO's Present Crisis (Press Conference held in Lisbon on 2 July1964) *Portuguese Foreign Policy 1965, op. cit.*, p. 77.
*36* *Ibid.*, p. 78.
*37* *Ibid.*
*38* *Ibid.*

a global and universal offensive. NATO will only escape dissolution and be saved as an effective instrument of policy, if it is reoriented in the sense indicated above. *(39)*

The French withdrawal from the organization in 1966 and the subsequent grave crisis within NATO was therefore not seen as springing from the French decision itself; rather the decision was a "consequence or reflection of a long-standing crisis that has been steadily worsening." *(40)* The occasion was an excellent one for recalling that for years, in the NATO Council and elsewhere, the Portuguese government had drawn attention to the urgent need to review the alliance, improve its political framework, and adapt it to the realities of the day. Even if it could not "give complete support to the individual policy of each member country, [the alliance] should at least give them all the feeling that the dangers they run as members of the Alliance are at any rate compensated for or extenuated by the advantages they gain from membership." *(41)* Without this the treaty organization risked dissolution in 1969.

Notwithstanding the statements and interventions of the Portuguese foreign minister and other diplomats, Portugal's impatience with the attitudes of some allies and the alliance never went beyond vocal opposition. Although at one point Dr. Salazar threatened withdrawal, Lisbon has never seriously considered dealignment. The truth is that U.S. and NATO disapprobation of Portugal's African designs has been extremely short-lived and not very harsh. Without economic and financial aid, military assistance and arms sales from the major NATO allies, Portugal would have found it impossible to carry on the war, or at least to carry it on vigorously.

## NATO AND PORTUGAL: A JANUS-FACED RELATIONSHIP

Official Portugal has lost no opportunity to communicate its growing discontent to its allies; a great many of them have officially expressed their disapproval of Portugal's overseas policies, specifically in the early sixties. The fact is, however, that in order to secure the use of air and naval bases on Portuguese continental territory or on the Atlantic islands; to strengthen their hold on the raw materials and strategic goods (ranging from sugar and cotton to iron ore, manganese, mica, oil, diamonds, and wolfram) of continental and overseas Portugal; to defend the freedom of the seas and to improve the military control over the southern Atlantic and the Cape route, which

---

39   *Ibid.*, p. 79.
40   F. Nogueira, On the NATO Crisis – Its Reflexes in France (Press Conference held in Lisbon on 12 July 1966), *Portuguese Foreign Policy 1965-1967, op. cit.*, p. 65.
41   *Ibid.* p. 65.

gained in commercial and strategic importance after the closing of the Suez Canal in July 1967; to protect their ever-increasing investments and financial interests in Angola and Mozambique; and to frustrate every attempt, whether Chinese or Russian, to increase Communist influence in Africa south of the Sahara the NATO allies do whatever they can to strengthen the already strong ties which link them together.

By the end of the Kennedy era the anticolonial bias in American foreign policy had been replaced by an attitude of tacit understanding. Kennedy succumbed to Portuguese pressure. The Lajes facilities, which the Pentagon still claimed to be of utmost importance in any confrontation between East and West, served as a powerful argument, and the Portuguese used it skillfully. In fact, they made it clear to the Americans that continued use of the island bases and the Radio Free Europe station in Portugal were dependent upon America's solicitous concern for Portugal's problems. By then, the Americans had spent about 96.2 million dollars *(42)* in the Azores, and most advisers felt that to abandon that investment was foolish. Negotiations on the extension of the arrangements began early in 1962, and Washington was confronted with some hard bargaining. Not only did Portugal exact complete political support of its policy in Africa, it also asked for concrete material help. According to the West German Press Agency (D.P.A.) *(43)* the Portuguese government in particular demanded increased financial aid, warships, and other military equipment of various types. The *Frankfurter Allgemeine Zeitung* of 29 June 1962 reported that the Portuguese went so far as to insist on a sum of $ 82.5 million a year.

The period of negotiations shows a slow but clear reversal of the downward trend of American assistance to Portugal. In fact, although planned U.S. military assistance for 1961 had been cut back from $ 24.75 million to $ 2.75 by the Kennedy administration *(44)* and all arms sales to Portugal had been forbidden in order to prevent the use of U.S. weapons in Africa, the American Import and Export Bank had extended an important loan of $ 48.75 million during the negotiating period. *(45)* An agreement providing for the construction of one warship, half of which the U.S. would subsidize, was enlarged to three ships. This amounted to a gift of $ 13.75 million. *(46)* On 4 January 1963, the Azores lease was extended and American military assistance

---

42   *New York Times*, 29 February 1962.

43   D.P.A., 21 March 1962.

44   U.S. Department of Commerce, *Statistical Abstracts of the United States 1961*, 82nd ed. (Washington, 1961), p. 879, and 83d ed., (Washington, 1962), p. 251.

45   D.P.A., 25 June, 1962.

46   Bosgra and Van Krimpen, *op. cit.*, p. 35.

and arms deliveries regained momentum. In the same month an announcement reported the delivery of thirty T-37 C fighter aircraft, and on 16 May a Portuguese newspaper, the *Diario de Lisboa*, described the recent arrival of American military aircraft engines in Portugal. *(47)* In 1965 a decision to construct three more destroyers under the same conditions as in 1962 was finalized and at the end of the same year the Central Intelligence Agency attempted to deliver 20 B-26 bombers to Portugal. The Federal Bureau of Investigation, which had not been informed of the secret transaction, thought it had discovered a case of arms traffic and arrested the pilot while he was attempting to fly in his seventh aircraft. Despite a formal American request to return the bombers, the aircraft remained in Portuguese hands. *(48)* In these ways official American military assistance, added to assistance earmarked defense support, reached $ 30.25 million in the period between 1962 and 1968. *(49)*

At the beginning of 1963 the U.S. assistant secretary of state for African affairs, G. Mennen Williams, tried to convince journalists that his promise of unconditional U.S. support to the liberation movements in Angola had been misinterpreted and that the Portuguese government was doing its best to improve conditions in its colony. Half a year later he stated openly: "It is not in our interest to see the Portuguese leaving Africa, neither do we want to reduce their influence there." *(50)* According to F. Koeppen-Schomerus, official support to the American Committee on Africa stopped when a P.I.D.E. agent proved that it had contributed substantial aid to Holden Roberto's G.R.A.E.; in the final analysis Roberto's group was receiving money belonging to the American taxpayer. *(51)*

After Professor Caetano came to power in Lisbon in September 1968 *(52)*, negotiations extending the Azores lease further resumed at the request of the

---

47  *Ibid.*, p. 35.
48  Bosgra and Dijk, *op. cit.*, p. 159.
49  *U.S. Overseas Loans and Grants and Assistance from International Organizations July 1, 1945 - June 30, 1968*, prepared by the Statistics and Reports division of AID.
50  *Neue Zürcher Zeitung*, 1 September 1963.
51  F. Koeppen-Schomerus, *Angola 1966-1967* (Bonn), p. 205.
52  Prof. Marcello Caetano das Neves Alves, Salazar's successor, was appointed new premier in September 1968 at the age of 62. He was one of the first of Salazar's companions in the early thirties and had also been one of the architects of the New State legislation. Since the early sixties he has departed somewhat from the official Salazarian line and became known for his more liberal attitudes. Once appointed premier, he made moves toward political liberalization, yet those moves practically ceased in 1970. On 25 April 1974 a military rebellion put an end to his rule and to the Corporate State.

Portuguese, since Caetano understood that Portugal could remain in Africa only with American backing. *(53)* In the meantime, U.S. interest in Portuguese bases increased when Spain seemed to be considering demanding the highest possible price for continuation of the Spanish-American base agreements. If necessary, the Spanish Polaris submarine base at Rota could be replaced by a base in Portugal at Vila da Prai da Victoria. *(54)* According to *Newsweek* (25 August 1969) the Portuguese would have exacted arms deliveries of a total of U.S. $ 192.5 million over a period of five years.

Without doubt the U.S. military continues to value Portuguese real estate highly. The Azores and other U.S. bases in continental Portugal remain a major political weapon in the hands of the Lisbon government, a weapon which they apparently still use skillfully. The highest level of U.S. decisionmakers have acknowledged this fact. Secretary of Defense Robert MacNamara stated in April 1967 that in Europe only Spain and Portugal still received military aid, and that this was entirely justified in the Portuguese case by the great importance of the U.S. military bases in Portugal. *(55)*

Moreover, American interest in the air and naval base at Lajes is likely to continue in coming years. On the eve of the Nixon-Pompidou talks of December 1971, William Rogers, the American secretary of state, and Mr. Rui Patricio, Portuguese foreign minister, concluded a new agreement extending the Lajes lease. This agreement was signed in Brussels on 9 December 1971. On 16 December, Newsweek commented:

> Before flying off to his mid-Atlantic rendez-vous, Mr. Nixon announced a major international agreement: in return for the use of military bases on the Portuguese-controlled island, Washington pledged to give Lisbon $ 435 million in economic aid over the next three years. Portugal can use the money. For the Portuguese Government is currently spending almost half of its annual budget in an effort to put down rebellions in its African territories. *(56)*

French-Portuguese relations have been almost entirely influenced by Gaullist dreams of grandeur in which there is no greatness without independence, no

---

53 Portugal had previously refused to renew the agreement, mainly because Salazar was displeased with the lack of U.S. support for Portuguese Africa.
54 Report of Walter Hackett in the U.S. Congressional Record, Senate, 5 June 1969.
55 Bosgra and Dijk, *op. cit.,* p. 157.
56 See also the *International Herald Tribune,* 13 December 1971 and *Le Monde,* 19-20 December 1971. *Le Monde* mentions that the extension of the Lajes lease should continue until 1974. In exchange Portugal would receive loans up to $ 500 million, of which $ 400 million would be used for various development projects; $ 30 million would affect other projects of an economic and social nature; $ 1 million was marked for educational purposes, and $ 5 million for the purchase of equipment of a non-military nature. According to the same newspaper Mr. Caetano was not very happy with this amount and thought the Portuguese should have received more.

independence without military strength, no strong defense without an efficient national armament industry, no such industry without a highly developed technology, and no highly developed economy without a sales market extending far beyond the too narrow national boundaries of France. The dream is one reason for France's tolerant attitude toward South Africa and Portugal. A second is its need of a tracking station for ballistic missiles launched at Riscarone in southwestern France. French arms are delivered to Portugal for a set of less tangible explanations as well. These include de Gaulle's sympathy for Franco and Salazar, the still strong ties of the French navy with NATO, the near-obsession of Western naval staffs with the idea of controlling and defending the western gates of the Mediterranean and the route around the Cape, and so on.

France thus became one of the most important furnishers of war material to Portugal, delivering warships, helicopters, tanks, rifles, guns, and ammunition in great numbers. *(57)*

Among the major NATO countries, the Federal Republic of Germany is clearly one of Portugal's most loyal allies. In turn, Portugal's former Premier has always been one of the warmest supporters of Germany. On 3 May 1945 the Portuguese government was among the very few to decree that "all official flags would be flown half-mast until noon on May 4, in mourning for the death of Adolf Hitler." *(58)* Since then, relations between the two nations have remained cordial. The Portuguese are proud that Salazar's minister of defense, Santos Costa, was the first representative of a NATO country to officially re-

---

57 For instance, in September 1968 Portugal ordered Alouette III helicopters valued at U.S. $ 3.15 million for counterinsurgency action in Mozambique and Guinea. The Alouette III is equipped with French air-surface rockets with a 6 km range, produced by Nord-Aviation. The French firm, Barbier, Bernard and Turenne, S.A., delivered electronic equipment and illumination for military airfields overseas. Portuguese warships have been built on the French dockyards at St Nazaire and Nantes. On 24 September 1964, a Franco-Portuguese agreement arranged for the construction of twenty warships, including four frigates of the Nantes class. By 1968 two of them had been delivered for use in the African war theater. The French long-term loans (ten to twenty years) with an interest rate of six percent financed these orders. The contracts were concluded with the cooperation of the French government, which guaranteed the loans. Since June 1965, forty percent of the trucks used by the Portuguese army are build by the Portuguese firm of *Metalurgica Duarte Ferreira*, working closely with the French firm, Berliet. The other sixty percent comes from France (Berliet) or West Germany (Mercedes Benz). See Bosgra and Van Krimpen, *op. cit.*, p. 43 and Bosgra and Dijk, *op. cit.*, p. 156.
58 Fryer and McGowan Pinheiro, *op. cit.*, p. 119. Perhaps this gesture was only meant to show the international community how faithful Portugal had been to the concept of neutrality. Yet the only neutral to do likewise was Iceland.

quest Bonn's admission to the alliance in 1952. Portugal's foreign minister, Da Cunha, offered similar support, and when Bonn joined NATO as a full member in 1955 the National Assembly in Lisbon extended a surprisingly warm welcome. *(59)* Portugal's friendliness toward West Germany is not only a function of similarities in the political experience of both, but arises from a necessary cooperation imposed by Western strategy. Moreover, it rests on solid business arrangements. Portugal supplies the German steel industry with the required raw material, and Germany provides the Portuguese armaments industry with the machinery, technology, and financing it needs to keep up with the ever-growing demands of the Portuguese armed forced overseas. *(60)*

Immediately after the beginning of the Angolan insurgency West Germany delivered tanks, machine guns, and broadcasting equipment worth $ 55 million to Portugal. *(61)* In 1961 and 1962 West Germany sold Portugal about thirty-two Dornier 27 aircraft and 10,000 Israeli UZI submachine guns.

A series of arrangements further strengthened cooperation between Bonn and Lisbon. Secret agreements concluded in October 1963 parts of which were made public in June 1964, finalized the basic structures. A permanent West German military mission was installed in Lisbon under the command of Brigadier General Herbert Becker to oversee the execution of the agreements, in which the federal republic was given the use of a military base in Portugal in exchange for its support of Portugal's war efforts overseas. Additional training facilities were extended to the Bundeswehr at Santa Margarida, and subsequently armories and warehouses at Castelo and a center of telecommunications at Evora were added. In exchange Germany contributed a certain number of field hospitals with 9000 beds to Portugal for the lodging of soldiers wounded in Africa. Serious cases would be treated in a German military hospital at Hamburg. *(62)* German military personnel would help train Portuguese pilots and soldiers, and the costs of both the medical program and the military training were to be supported by Germany. Finally, the West Germans agreed to sell a great number of arms and new weapons systems to Portugal, to be partially financed by German orders for minor military equipment such as ammunition from Portugal.

Between 1965 and 1967 the federal republic again delivered training, transport, and combat aircraft: 50 Dornier 23, 60 Dornier 27, four Noratlas, 60 Sabre F-86 (constructed under Canadian licence), 40 Fiat-G-91, and a fraction

59  *Münchner Merkur*, 27 October 1956; *Der Kurier*, 20 November 1956.
60  Bosgra and Dijk, *op. cit.*, pp. 154-155.
61  *Ibid.*, p. 155.
62  *Ibid.*

of an order of 400 Fouga Magisters. The Portuguese air force has not been the sole beneficiary of the German arms deliveries. Germany further furnished a certain amount of Unimogs, heavy Mercedes Benz trucks, and rockets. The Portuguese navy has ordered three corvettes of 1400 tons to be built by Blohm and Voss of Hamburg. Their completion date was set for 1970, but delivery has been delayed somewhat because of West German fears that they would be used in the overseas provinces. *(63)*

In addition to military equipment, most of which ends up in Africa, the federal republic has made substantial financial loans to Portugal (U.S. $ 41.25 million in 1961, 37.12 million in 1962, 15.95 million in 1963, and so on). This has been an important kind of assistance, since it allowed Portugal to allocate a considerable fraction of its own savings rather than productive investments to colonial warfare.

In 1968, however, West German interest in Beja diminished, as did German eagerness to extend aid and trade heavy weapons. Beja's usefulness had been marred by various difficulties, ranging from the numerous Starfighter crashes to the reductions of the federal defense budget and problems with Spain over overflight rights (*Financial Times*, 24 October 1968). Portuguese technicians were said to lack the necessary skills to recondition the aircraft engines (*Frankfurter Allgemeine Zeitung*, 8 October 1969). Conditions such as these lessened the cordiality of relations between Bonn and Lisbon. In its commentary on this affair, the *Frankfurter Allgemeine Zeitung* (18 August 1968) wrote that the German Luftwaffe would never be able to use the military airfield; for this reason a project involving more than 100 million D.M. had become an absurd scandal. The Portuguese, the German newspaper argued, are anything but hospitable. They want more aid, more money, always more money. Eventually a new agreement between Bonn and Lisbon in 1969 arranged for the use of the Beja facilities by the West German civil aviation company Lufthansa. Despite the difficulties with Beja and the increasing unwillingness of W. Brandt's Social Democratic government to sell heavy arms to the Portuguese armed forces, Luso-German cooperation is still viable. Bonn remains one of the surest and strongest of Portugal's friends in the Atlantic alliance.

British military assistance and arms deliveries, though appreciable during the war years and into the fifties (from 1949 to 1963 they amounted to $ 330 mil-

---

63 According to the *Johannesburg Star* (19 September, 1970), a first corvette ordered at the Hamburg dockyards, the *João Coutinho*, was delivered at the end of 1970. Although the Social Democratic government in Bonn has repeatedly stated that this ship was to be used in a NATO capacity only, various Portuguese military reviews made it clear that it would be sent overseas.

lion) has lessened during the sixties. Cooperation has been greatest in the maritime field. Many Portuguese naval officers have been trained by the royal navy and a great number of Portuguese warships have been constructed in Britain. In November 1952 a treaty was concluded that granted the same rights in the Azores to the British as to the Americans. And Britain enjoys the use of a naval and air base at Montijo in metropolitan Portugal to the present day. Since war broke out in overseas Portugal, Great Britain has officially refused to sell any military equipment to Portugal that was likely to be used overseas. The *D. Francisco de Almeida* and the *Vasco da Gamma* are examples of this policy. *(64)* However, between 1961 and 1965 140 light aircraft of the Auster type *(65)* and 200 Austin jeeps *(66)* have been sold to the Portuguese armed forces. Holland and Belgium have also been sources of arms procurement. Light transport aircraft have been produced by Fokker of Holland and the F.A.L. automatic rifle was supplied by the F.N. factory in Belgium.

Thus, although Portugal on the one hand and the NATO allies on the other have publicly disagreed and disapproved of each other, in fact all major and some minor allies have helped sustain the colonial war. And moral support has come from others beside NATO governments. High ranking NATO officers and military personnel of member countries have been outspoken defenders of Portugal's grand design, either in statements or in articles in leading military journals. General Lemnitzer, at the time supreme allied commander Europe, has clearly shown his admiration for Portuguese troops in the overseas provinces. The Portuguese soldiers, he said, defend raw materials, territory, and bases in Angola which are not only indispensable for the defense of Western Europe but for the whole Western world. *(67)* The *General Military Review* and particularly *NATO's Fifteen Nations*, both close to NATO military and civilian top-ranking officers, have carried numerous articles in defense of Portugal.

Since the latter half of the 1960s, then, Portugal's image abroad particularly in the Atlantic alliance, improved significantly. During 1968 and 1969 a great many newspapers and reviews indicated the change of attitudes in NATO circles, whose tone was set by an article in *U.S. News and World Report* (4 April

64 Bought by Portugal in the U.K. shortly after the outbreak of violence in Angola, they were, according to the British admiralty and Prime Minister McMillan, specifically to be used in the framework of Portugal's NATO commitments (*The Times*, 23 June 1961, *The Sunday Times*, 18 June 1961). Yet they have recurrently served in Angola and Mozambique.
65 *Air Pictorial* (1967), p. 270.
66 *The Times*, 15 February, 1965.
67 See Bosgra and Van Krimpen, *op. cit.*, p. 46.

1969): "For years, the Portuguese complained that the U.S., their ally in Europe, worked against them in Africa. There is less talk about it now, and the Portuguese expect that the relations will even improve under Nixon." *(68)* During the early seventies Portuguese relations with the principal NATO allies continued to improve. Indeed, since September 1968 the Portuguese government has placed less emphasis on its dissatisfaction with NATO support for its policies overseas, and given more attention to attempt at reducing Portuguese isolation.

The less dogmatic foreign policy pursued during Mr. Caetano's rule has shown concrete results. In October 1970 the Portuguese secretary of industry, R. Martins, went to London, in the first official ministerial visit in some years. *(69)* He was followed by British Foreign Secretary Sir Alec Douglas-Home, who was in Lisbon in the summer of 1971. *(70)* U.S. Secretary of State William Rogers and Vice-President Spiro T. Agnew also visited Lisbon, in May 1970 and summer 1971 respectively *(71)*, and when Richard Nixon met with French Premier Georges Pompidou, on the Azores in December 1971 *(72)* both men expressed their understanding of Portugal's problems to Premier Caetano, who hosted the conference.

In November 1970 Portugal formally announced its intention to seek association with the European Economic Community. French Foreign Minister Maurice Schumann used the occasion to declare his country's appreciation of this Portuguese move toward Europe, and to pledge France's support for whatever effort Portugal might make to become part of the European communities.

With the notable exception of Denmark and Norway, NATO members seemed amenable to the policy of rapprochement initiated by the U.S., the U.K., and France. One of the most remarkable evidences of increased Portuguese acceptance was the decision of the NATO Council of Ministers of Foreign Affairs to hold its 1971 spring session in Lisbon, despite objections from the secretary general of the Organization of African Unity, Mr. Diallo

---

68 See also *Deutsche Tagespost*, 4 August 1967; *Der Tagespiegel*, 18 November 1968; *Süddeutsche Zeitung*, 22 April 1969, and General J. Marchand, "l'Empire Luso-Africain", *Revue de la défense nationale* (1968), p. 1.635: "The U.S. are currently more conciliatory with their NATO ally [Portugal]. They do not care much about the accusations of international and African organizations concerning the arms that they deliver via NATO and which are allegedly used against liberation movements".

69 *Britannica Book of the Year 1971* (Chicago, 1971), p. 608.

70 *Britannica Book of the Year* (Chicago, 1972), p. 573.

71 *Ibid.*

72 *Keesings Historisch Archief*, 2 January 1971, p. 75.

Telli, who called the choice a provocation of African goodwill. *(73)* A great many action committees in European countries also denounced the arrangement, arguing that the meeting place implied open NATO support for Portugal's overseas policies. *(74)* In December 1970 the Norwegian representative to the NATO Council of Ministers, sustained by Denmark, publicly objected to the measure. Yet the majority of the NATO members seemed not to concur, saying that the choice of a meeting place was a purely technical matter. *(75)*

The meeting was held according to original plans, and in the midst of its deliberations bombing attempts were directed at telegraph and telephone offices in Lisbon and Sacaven. As a result communications between the NATO press center and the outside were blocked for a few hours. The aggression was believed to have originated with the A.R.A., the Portuguese Revolutionary Army, known to oppose Portugal's war in Africa. In this climate the Norwegian minister of foreign affairs, Andreas Capellen, made an unexpected direct attack against the colonial policies of the host country. *(76)* He told his allies that Portuguese policies were contrary to the purpose and principles of the charter of the United Nations, and that they undermined public support for NATO in the member countries. The then secretary general of NATO, Manlio Brosio, declared the Norwegian intervention misplaced and no reference was made to the incident in the subsequent press conference. Despite such setbacks, Portugal's relations with most NATO members and with the organization itself improved significantly during the early seventies. Norway and Denmark may still officially question Portugal's Africa policies, but other NATO members seem to have abandoned such a course.

However maligned Portugal might have felt during the first months of the Kennedy administration and after the clashes with Great Britain over Goa and Rhodesia, the country has developed powerful friends in most of NATO's senior members and has profited greatly from economic, financial, and, to a certain point, even from military assistance from its four major partners. Furthermore, its assignments in the alliance have provided an excellent excuse to purchase from its allies the huge amounts of arms and equipment needed so desperately for the African wars. If only one nation is presently committed to association in the North Atlantic alliance, that nation is Portugal.

73  *Ibid.*, 18 June 1971, p. 388.
74  *Ibid.*
75  *Ibid.*
76  *Ibid.*

94

# CONCLUSION

During the second world war Portugal's position on the edge of the Atlantic prevented its association with the fascist powers, and kept it neutral in the first phase of the war. An Atlantic orientation obliged it to grant base facilities in the Azores to the major Western powers, Great Britain and the U.S., at the very moment the Axis's Atlantic and Mediterranean power position had weakened considerably.

With the emergence of the Cold War and the increasing fear of a major conventional Soviet attack on Western Europe in the late forties and early fifties, the strategic importance of Portugal's Atlantic islands and continental coast increased tremendously. Portugal became a vital component in Western containment policy and in the Pentagon's plans for an aerial encirclement of the Soviet Union, and Salazar saw changing circumstances as signifying an end to Portugal's neutrality. After a very brief interlude of splendid isolation, Portugal reverted to the Atlantic and democratic nations. Invited and even pressed to join the Atlantic alliance, Portugal accepted enthusiastically, although the democratic overtones of the treaty's preamble did -- at least in Salazar's eyes -- cast some shadows on the attractiveness of the pact. But the Portuguese prime minister brushed away those objections; not the principles of liberty, equality, and the rule of law but a virulent anti-Communism would hold the members of the Atlantic alliance together. Beyond that, Portugal was genuinely concerned over the failure to extend the guarantees of the Atlantic treaty to the overseas territories south of the Tropic of Cancer. On the other hand, participation in an alliance, the major rationale of which was the protection of Central Europe from Soviet aggression, risked diverting Portuguese energies from the vital responsibility of defending the overseas territories to a whole range of remote and complex questions such as Berlin, the Dardanelles, and the Danish Straits.

If Salazar felt compelled to align with the major Western powers, it was because basically his political philosophy was violently anti-Communist. In his view, a crushed and dismantled Germany would allow Slavic Communism and Russian expansionism to threaten all of Europe. Traditional power political thinking persuaded him to accept a diversion from Lusitanian and global designs for the sake of maintaining order and holding the European balance of power, however. On the other hand, participation in a great democratic Western alliance would give Portugal a democratic reputation abroad, in turn providing Salazar with excellent arguments against his liberal opposition and significantly increasing his security of tenure. It is also important to note that the financial, economic, and military assistance of major allies generally so attractive to a small country was not very important to Portugal at the end of the forties. At that time Salazar still believed that Portugal could develop its own economy, and in fact was afraid of the political consequences of economic dependence on one or more great powers.

Since the initiation of rebellions in the overseas territories, the whole of Portugal's defense and diplomatic effort clearly has been oriented toward the preservation of the colonial structure. Militarily this has meant a costly anti-guerilla war. Diplomatically, it involved a relentless fight against ostracism in the General Assembly of the U.N. and against apathy, if not enmity, among some of Portugal's allies in the NATO council. Together with South Africa, Portugal was treated as a pariah by the majority of U.N. members, most particularly the Afro-Asian bloc. And when in the early sixties the Kennedy administration set out to promote an image of a progressive and liberal America by supporting some Afro-Asian resolutions calling for self-determination in its African territories, the Portuguese felt increasingly unhappy. Frustration with NATO allies grew greater when British diplomatic support, hitherto correct but unenthusiastic, declined notably after the Goan disaster and recurrent Rhodesian crises. In those years Portugal's feelings of isolation led to increasing diplomatic criticism of allied support. Time and again the Portuguese foreign minister and representatives to the NATO council pleaded for global solidarity and the abrogation of Article VI, which limits the Atlantic pact to the area north of the Tropic of Cancer. Whether great or small, allies must be friendly toward each other in NATO and elsewhere. If this was impossible, the Portuguese argued, the alliance risked dispersion, and they would not be among the last to leave.

Yet Portugal's criticism of NATO never went beyond vocal opposition. And in its relations with the U.S., Portugal never did more than threaten to refuse further extensions of the Azores bases to U.S. military forces. However reluctant it was to deal with outspokenly critical or apathetic allies, Lisbon soon realized that if Portugal was to stay in Africa, it could do so only with the implicit moral, economic, and financial support, as well as arms sales, of the major NATO allies and military assistance from the U.S.

# Part II

# GREECE AND TURKEY

### By Willy Andries

# INTRODUCTION

Modern Turkey emerged from the ruins of the six-century old Ottoman Empire after four years of bitter struggles. In 1923 the Republic of Turkey entered the international arena as a secular state, determined to become part of the European civilization without, however, abandoning its Islamic heritage. Following Atatürk's "Peace at home, peace abroad" concept, Turkey followed for almost twenty years a neutral foreign policy course which enabled it to foster friendly relations with the traditional enemies of the Ottoman Empire, especially Soviet Russia.

Greece on the other hand, owed its independence in 1830 to the direct intervention of the European powers. Consequently, its geographic and strategic location in the Mediterranean were detrimental for Greece's participation in numerous alliances with Western European countries. While Greece had a record of military links with the West, Turkey stubbornly refused to engage in entangling alliances.

World War II and its immediate aftermath brought home such a shocking experience for Turkey that alignment with the West became the only feasible answer for the preservation of the country's national independence and territorial integrity. The threatening posture of the Soviet Union and the global confrontation between the U.S. and the U.S.S.R. opened the way for exclusive alignment with the West. Soviet policies, however, were not the only factor to explain Greece's and Turkey's unyielding persistence to become members of NATO. This study, then, focuses on the many complex factors that motivated Turkish and Greek decision-makers to seek exclusive military ties with the West.

# Chapter I

# THE ALIGNMENT PROCESS
# IN GREECE AND TURKEY

## THE AMERICAN RESPONSE TO SOVIET EXPANSIONISM:
## THE TRUMAN DOCTRINE

As the second world war drew to a close, observers saw clearly that the American dream of a world order based on active cooperation among wartime allies was undergoing shattering blows. In Eastern Europe the Soviets gradaully laid down their new pattern ef expansion. Yalta or no Yalta, the U.S.S.R. indisputably wanted friendly regimes along its borders, and by the end of 1946 firm Soviet control of the Balkans was established beyond any czar's imagination. With the Allied victory in Europe, Stalin embarked on a fantastic gamble to seize, perhaps in one thrust, all the advantages czarist Russia had so frenetically sought: major breakthroughs in the eastern Mediterranean and the Middle East.

John Spanier has observed that every would-be conqueror -- Napoleon, Kaiser Wilhelm II, Hitler -- has tried to control the vital area comprising Iran, Greece, and Turkey. *(1)* In early 1946 the Soviet Union began its offensive in this traditionally British sphere of influence by refusing to withdraw the Red Army in Iran. In 1942 both the Soviet Union and Great Britain had placed troops in northern and southern Iran to forestall an already increasing German influence and control Iranian oil resources. The Tripartite Treaty of Alliance signed in early 1942 among the Soviet Union, Iran, and Geat Britain provided that all Allied forces were to withdraw six months after the end of the hostilities. In compliance with the treaty provisions, American and British troops left Iran. The Soviet army not only remained but was reinforced. *(2)* In addition the Soviet government began to pressure the shah, demanding exclusive mineral and

---

1   J. Spanier, *American Foreign Policy since World War II* (New York, 1965), p. 23.
2   The American troops were stationed in Iran under the auspices of British treaty arrangements. See J. M. Jones, *The Fifteen Weeks* (New York, 1955), p. 49.

oil rights in northern Iran. Faced with his strong negative response, the U.S.S.R. provided arms to the separatist Tudeh party, which revolted against the shah in November 1945 and installed a separatist government in Azerbaijan. These developments catapulted the Iranian situation onto the international stage. The Western powers especially feared that if the Teheran government acquiesced to Soviet demands, Iran would gradually become an effective Soviet satellite. The words of Secretary of State Byrnes must have sounded almost like an ultimatum in Moscow. Defining the American position, Byrnes said:

> We have joined with our allies in the United Nations to put an end to war. We intend to live up to that covenant. But as a great power and as a permanent member of the Security Council we have a responsibility to use our influence to see that other powers live up to their covenant. And that responsibility we also intend to meet. *(3)*

President Truman also instructed Byrnes to contact Stalin directly. Although he fails to mention the incident explicitly in his memoirs, the president described his communication in an article in the *New York Times*:

> The Soviet Union persisted in its occupation until I personally saw to it that Stalin was informed that I had given orders to our military chiefs to prepare for the movement of our ground, sea and air forces. *(4)*

His strong words had an effect on Kremlin leaders. *(5)* The Soviets evacuated their troops from northern Iran, and the Azerbaijan government collapsed a few months later.

But Iran was only one pawn on the Soviet chessboard. His design to secure a foothold in the eastern Mediterranean made Greece and Turkey the most natural targets of Stalin's foreign policy. Let a broad outline of the situation in both countries suffice here. Beginning in June 1945 the Soviet Union exerted considerable pressure on Turkey; it claimed large parts of Turkish territory and, more importantly, it demanded a revision of the 1936 Montreux Convention which vested in Turkey final authority for managing naval traffic through the straits. And as if that were not enough, the Soviet Union called for an end of Turkish ties with Britain, proposing a treaty similar to those Moscow had just concluded with Bulgaria and Rumania. Throughout 1945 and 1946

---

3  *Ibid.*, p. 54.
4  Quoted in *New York Times*, 25 August 1957.
5  Mr. Churchill's Fulton speech (3 March 1945), in which he described the methods and continuing expansionist efforts of the Soviet Union, should also be noted here. Some scholars argue that this had a restraining effect on Soviet policies toward Iran. See A. Ulam, *Expansion and Coexistence. The History of Soviet Foreign Policy 1917-1967* (New York, 1968), p. 425.

Ankara stated clearly that Turkey would allow no encroachment on its territory. With or without the help of the United Nations, the Turks would fight to retain their present territory and sovereignty. *(6)*

Divisive and debilitating civil war made the Greek situation entirely different. The end of the second world war saw the Communist dominated E.A.M. (National Liberation Front) and the rightists E.D.E.S. movement under the leadership of General Zervas engaged in one of the bloodiest struggles Greece had ever known. The economy was ruined and an army of over 100,000 men absorbed most of the financial help Britain was able to offer. Maintenance of the large army and an almost 50,000 man police force was becoming impossible. The U.N.R.R.A. program was nearing an end, exacerbating a very critical economic situation in early 1947. *(7)* Greece was clearly on the verge of collapse. These were the circumstances under which the Communist guerilla forces launched their final attack in August 1946. Thus, the fall of 1946 was full of bright prospects for the Soviet Union. Until then, Great Britain had been the chief stabilizing element in the eastern Mediterranean and the Middle East. London had financed the Greek army, stationed 16,000 troops around Athens, and supported the Turkish government against Soviet demands. But Britain itself became the victim of enormous economic and social difficulties. Anne O'Hare McCormick dramatically described the implications in the *New York Times*:

> The crisis in Britain and France pointed up a truth the United States knows but shrinks from facing. They are primarily economic crises, signs of the difficulty of treating postwar breakdown by democratic means. They reveal how battered and shaken are the old strongholds of democracy in Europe... Most of all they throw the ball to us, giving notice that if freedom as we understand it is to survive it's up to the United States to save it. *(8)*

On 21 February 1947 the British government informed the Truman administration that it could no longer meet the financial burdens of supporting both Greece and Turkey. It projected a substantial reduction of its commitments after March 31. Suddenly faced with the power vacuum in the eastern Mediterranean as a result of the British withdrawal, the United States had no

6  D. Acheson, *Present at the Creation* (New York, 1969), p. 200.
7  Between 1 April 1945 and 30 June 1947 assistance from U.N.R.R.A. totaled $ 416 million. The bulk of the aid consisted of food, clothes, medicaments, and provisions for industry and agriculture. The criticalness of the situation is demonstrated by the fact that foreign aid constituted fifty-eight percent of Greek governmental income during the fiscal year 1946-1947. *Documentation Française, Notes et Etudes Documentaires*, 2052, p. 6.
8  Quoted in P. Y. Hammond, *The Cold War Years: American Foreign Policy since 1945* (New York, 1969), p. 20.

alternative but to intervene. As Spanier indicates, inaction would have meant the collapse of both Greece and Turkey, and a Soviet breakthrough in the Middle East and the Mediterranean; this would have had a devastating effect on an already demoralized and ruined Western Europe. *(9)*

In less than three weeks the American Congress had approved the military and economic aid program for Greece and Turkey known as the Truman Doctrine. Appearing before both houses of Congress, President Harry S. Truman made it clear that the United States could only survive in a world in which freedom flourished. His message undoubtedly contained a strong ideologocal base. He made no direct reference to either the Soviet Union or international Communism, yet he compared the Communist and American ways of life with dramatic effect:

> One way of life is based upon the will of the majority, and is distinguished by free institutions, representative government, free elections, guarantees of individual liberties, freedom of speech and religion, and freedom from political oppression. The second way of life is based upon the will of a minority forcibly imposed upon the majority. It relies upon terror and oppression, a controlled press and radio, fixed elections and the suppression of personal freedoms. *(10)*

In focusing on Greece and Turkey President Truman stressed the following points:

> It is necessary to glance at a map to realize that the survival and integrity of the Greek nation are of grave importance in a much wider situation. If Greece should fall... the effect upon its neighbor Turkey would be immediate and serious. Confusion and disorder might well spread throughout the entire Middle East.... Should we fail to aid Greece and Turkey in this fateful hour the effect will be farreaching... we must take immediate and resolute action. *(11)*

The Truman Doctrine initiated a dramatic change in American foreign policy. Intervention clearly went beyond aid to Geat Britain; the United States was in fact acting on its own. Its commitments were part of a global policy and must be considered "in the context of global relations with the Soviet Union; they were reflecting a hardening of American policy against Soviet encroachment in Europe, the Far East and elsewhere." *(12)* The rationale behind the American actions seems quite obvious. Had the United States acquiesced in the Soviet aggrandizement in the Mediterranean, the British

9  Spanier, *op. cit.*, pp. 34-35.
10  H. S. Truman, *Memoirs, Vol. II, Years of Trial and Hope* (Garden City, 1955), p. 106.
11  Quoted in M. A. Dendias, *The Truman Doctrine and the Freedom of Greece* (Athens, 1967), pp. 11-12.
12  J. C. Campbell, *Defense of the Middle East* (New York, 1960), p. 33.

position would have been extremely tenous. But at the beginning of the Cold War, the United States obviously could not afford to let its wartime partner forced out of a strategic area. Loy Henderson, director of the Office of Near Eastern and African Affairs at the Department of State, evanuated the United States interests:

> In view of their economic and strategic importance, the Middle East and South East Europe are most tempting to an aggressive and ambitious power. Such a power might well be able, if once in the possession of the strategic facilities and economic resources of this area, to decide the destinies of at least three continents. *(13)*

The net result of Truman's message was a landmark Cold War statement in which the aid to Greece and Turkey was formulated in the framework of universal policy rather than, as George Kennan remarks "in that of a specific decision addressed to a specific set of circumstances." *(14)* For Greece and Turkey the Truman Doctrine was a decisive step toward association with the West, especially the United States. However, the alignment process took a different form in each country.

## GREECE

Since the emergence of Greece as an independent state, it has had to accommodate itself to foreign interference and the protection of outside powers. The geographic location and the strategic importance of this small Mediterranean country has made it the object of international attention from its creation. Greece owed its independence to the support of Russia, France, and Great Britain against the Ottoman empire. The influence of outside powers on Greek internal political life was so great that the existing political parties were characterized by their allegiance to one or another European power. Couloumbis describes this phenomenon as a key variable of Greek political life which facilitated the "infusion of external interventions, intrigues, and subterfuges." *(15)* Moreover, this pattern remained a constant in Greek parties. During the first world war the country was split into two opposing camps. In the power

13 See article by Loy Henderson, *Department of State Bulletin*, 17 (13 November 1947), p. 997.
*14* G. Kennan, *Memoirs* (Boston, 1967), p. 320. Kennan's main criticism focuses on this generalization of the aid to Greece and Turkey. "It implied that what we had decided to do in the case of Greece was something we would be prepared to do in the case of any other country, provided only that it was faced with the threat of subjugation by armed minorities or by outside pressures". See *ibid.*, p. 320.
*15* T. A. Couloumbis, *Greek Political Reaction to American and Nato Influences* (New Haven, 1966), p. 11.

struggle between King Constantine I and republican leader E. Venizelos, foreign policy was an important element; the former was sympathetic to the central powers, and the latter favored Greece's participation in the war on the side of Britain and France. An intense struggle between royalists and republicans characterized the interwar period. Growing political instability and several military coups eventually resulted in the Metaxas dictatorship in 1936. The general's political philosophies as well as his personal affinities for Nazi Germany were directly responsible for the gradual fascization of Greece. On the eve of Germany's attack he articulated the fascist ideology of his regime:

> Since August 4th Greece has become an anti-communist, anti-parliamentary, totalitarian state. Its agrarian and labor foundations make it anti-plutocratic. Thus if Hitler and Mussolini were really fighting for the ideology they preach, they would be supporting Greece with all their forces. (16)

The heavy economic dependence on Great Britain and the personal intervention of King George II created a very difficult situation for Metaxas. His attempts to pursue a neutral policy were futile. When the king, who firmly controlled the Greek armed forces, began purging them of pro-Metaxas military commanders, the government had no alternative but to sign an agreement with Great Britain which, as Tsoucalas puts it, brought "fascist Greece by necessity to the side of the democracies." (17)

Invasions by Italy and Germany brought the country to total collapse and in May 1941 all of Greece came under firm Axis control. The king and the government had fled to London, where a Greek government-in-exile was formed under Premier Tsouderos. In the wake of a disrupted economy and widespread famine, the situation in occupied Greece quickly became desperate. These were the circumstances that convinced the Greek people that their physical survival necessitated armed resistance against the enemy.

The Greek government in London was totally cut off from the country. It was simply unable to provide the inspiration and the leadership in the struggle that was to come, and with only nominal authority it was bound to become merely the symbol of the legal continuation of the Greek state. In this environment the outlawed Communist party emerged as the initiator and organizer of the resistance movement. (18) In collaboration with several smaller parties

---

16  C. Tsoucalas, *The Greek Tragedy* (Hermondsworth, 1969), p. 55.
17  *Ibid.*, p. 56.
18  The K.K.E. (Communist Party of Greece) was outlawed after the Metaxas coup d état in 1936, which led to the suspension of parliamentary democracy in Greece.

the Communists created the National Liberation Force (E.A.M.) with its People's Army of Liberation (E.L.A.S.); a smaller rightist movement led by General Zervas (E.D.E.S.) soon followed its example. The two guerilla groups cooperated for a time in their struggle against the enemy, and the E.A.M. forces were so effective that they soon enjoyed the moral and material support of the British government. *(19)* But by 1943 the first signs of a split emerged. Throughout the war E.A.M. undoubtedly had achieved political supremacy in most parts of Greece, and General Zervas saw that unless he could secure British support away from the Communists in his own favor, the odds would be against him. And he succeeded in doing exactly that. The only other contender for power in postwar Greece was the royalist government-in-exile. British Prime Minister Winston Churchill felt a strong obligation to the king; Greece was a faithful ally and the king was its head and symbol. Churchill's attitude was perhaps more crucial than any other in determining the postwar developments in Greece:

> Our relations are definitely established with the lawfully constituted Greek government headed by the King... Neither can Greece find constitutional expression in particular sets of guerillas, in many cases indistinguishable from banditti, who are masquerading as the saviours of their country while living on the local villagers... Our only desire and interest is to see Greece a glorious, free nation. *(20)*

In its turn, the Greek government in London soon realized that only the British could prevent an eventual seizure of political control by the Communists. Prime Minister Tsouderos reiterated on various occasions that Great Britain would continue to play a decisive role in postwar Greece. In fact, the fear of abandonment by their protectors caused many a nightmare to the London Greeks, and Tsouderos at least saw a formal alliance with Britain as the only bulwark against this threat to Greece's territorial integrity. *(21)* In a letter to Anthony Eden written in March 1943, Tsouderos described in detail the strategic importance of his country for any power interested in the control of the Mediterranean. In addition, the prime minister played perhaps his strongest card. He offered London the use of Greek bases and access routes. *(22)* At the time, the British position had not yet been clearly defined. London was evidently

---

*19* L. S. Stavrianos, *Greece: American Dilemma and Opportunity* (Chicago, 1952), pp. 64-90.
*20* Quoted in Jones, *op. cit.*, pp. 69-70.
*21* For obvious reasons the Greeks feared certain territorial aspirations of their northern neighbours in Bulgaria and Albania, while a rupture in British-Greek relations would only benefit the E.A.M. forces.
*22* Quoted in S. G. Xydis, *Greece and the Great Powers: 1944-1947* (Thessaloniki, 1963), pp. 26-27

unwilling to give up its hold on Greece. The country was strategically located in an area traditionally within Britain's sphere of influence. Yet the outcome of the war was still uncertain, and it was equally important not to neglect the effort of the Greek resistance movements. A direct confrontation with E.A.M. was certainly not opportune, and in fact, at least for a certain period, London made no discrimination in its provision of weapons, money, and supplies. *(23)* Gradually, however, the E.A.M. leadership found itself driven into a corner, given the triangular relationship among the Zervas movement (E.D.E.S.), the king, and the British government. At this stage a propaganda campaign to prevent the king's return and undermine the political authority of the government-in-exile was initiated. The E.A.M. leadership also established the Political Committee of National Liberation (P.E.E.A.) probably intended as the embryo of a postwar Communist government, and a successful revolt of Greek republican officers in April 1944 led to a broadening of the government-in-exile, which now included six members of P.E.E.A.. *(24)* The signing of the important Caserta agreement in September 1944 placed all guerilla forces under the government of national unity, which in turn was under the military command of the British. *(25)* Neither the Caserta agreement nor the coalition government lasted much longer than a month, as serious disagreements arose. *(26)* A concerted attack on Athens followed a Communist coup d'état in December 1944, but the arrival of additional British troops forced the E.A.M. leaders to accept a peace treaty. The agreement signed at Varkiza in February 1945 provided for the disarmament of the E.L.A.S. forces, a referendum on the king, and the holding of general elections under allied supervision. As Tsoucalas remarks, allegiance was by now switching gradually from left to right, mainly because the Communist began holding civilian hostages by the thousands. *(27)* I want to stress, however, that terrorism and atrocities were not confined to one side. *(28)*

23   According to recently published documents, Great Britain's sole objective was to restore the rule of King George II. From November 1943 on, the British government decided to take measures to liquidate the E.L.A.S. forces against the advice of the British chief of staff. See *Le Monde*, 2 November 1972.

24   Couloumbis, *op. cit.*, p. 16.

25   *Ibid.*, p. 17.

26   After the German evacuation British troops entered Greece following a formal request by the Greek coalition government, which included the Communists.

27   Tsoucalas, *op. cit.*, p. 92.

28   Right-wing extremists and General Grivas's "X" organization were notorious for the so-called white terror. See *ibid.*, pp. 92-95.

The general elections of March 1946, supervised by American, French, British, and South African officials, gave the right-wing parties a large majority. The king was recalled by referendum a few months later. *(29)* At the end of 1946 the Communist party launched a new armed attack in a final effort to gain control over Greece. Communist guerilla forces operated from Albania, Yugoslavia, and Bulgaria, but the exact role of the Soviet Union in those crucial days is still a matter of speculation. The entire operation undoubtedly had been launched with Moscow's blessings, although Djilas reveals that Stalin had no intention of risking a war with the West over Greece:

> If, if! No, they [the Greek Communists] have no prospect of success at all. What do you think that Great Britain and the United States -- the United States, the most powerful state in the world -- will permit you to break their line of communication in the Mediterranean Sea! Nonsense. And we have no navy. The uprising in Greece must be stopped, and as quickly as possible. *(30)*

While full-scale warfare was raging, Great Britain began to show signs of economic difficulties dramatically affecting its military and financial efforts in Greece. On 3 February 1947, the British government decided to withdraw 8,000 of its troops stationed in the country. Three weeks later the British ambassador in Washington notified the U.S. government that Greece would collapse in a matter of weeks if substantial military and financial assistance was not forthcoming. Moreover, various demands from the Greek government had preceded the British appeal, and, in fact, in 1946 the Truman administration had granted credit of $ 25 million, about all that was possible under the existing appropriations. Whenever possible, Greek Prime Minister Tsaldaris argued his case. He approached Secretary of State Byrnes for more financial and military assistance but his demands were denied; he could give no reasonable assurance of repayment. *(31)* According to Acheson, Tsaldaris was more obsessed with Greek territorial claims than anything else. *(32)* Many State Department officials were convinced that the Greek economic, financial and administrative system was in complete chaos and "that the Greeks had no

---

29 Both the Communists and a large number of the republicans had decided to abstain from the electoral process. Almost fifty percent of the eligible voters abstained. For a more detailed discussion, see *ibid.*, pp. 96-97.

30 Quoted in M. Djilas, *Conversations with Stalin* (New York, 1962), p. 182.

31 Jones, *op. cit.*, p. 75.

32 Acheson, *op. cit.*, p. 199. Solidifying certain territorial claims was a basic objective of the postwar Greek governments. The most important of these were Albania's cession of northern Epirus conflicts over land held by Bulgaria and the Dodecanese Islands held by Italy. These islands were Greece's only success. See Couloumbis, *op. cit.*, p. 19.

documented case for loans but just wanted money and arms on a large scale, and that if granted they would probably be wasted." *(33)*

American hesitation can be explained on two counts. Greece in 1946 was still considered a British concern; convincing Congress to appropriate huge amounts of money was difficult. Besides, American public opinion had never favored British intervention in Greece. As Jones points out, there was "considerable public concern in the United States over aiding a corrupt, monarchial, "fascist regime in Greece, and "pulling British chestnuts out of the fire." *(34)* The alarming reports of the American ambassador in Athens were so convincing that Byrnes, Acheson, and Forrestal sent an American economic mission, headed by Paul Porter, to thoroughly survey the situation. By mid-February 1947 the Porter mission concluded:

> Unless Greece received immediate assurance of large-scale military and financial aid, the last vestiges of the authority of the Greek government would disapear within a matter of weeks.... Aid in the old pattern, no matter how extensive would not save the situation. Large-scale economic aid was necessary over a period of years, but it was equally important that this should be administered on the spot by an American mission.... exercising sufficiently direct participation in and sanctions over the Greek Government to bring about a thorough reorganization of the Greek economy and administrative system. *(35)*

In other words, American intervention in the internal affairs of Greece was considered necessary for an effective management of American aid. The Greek government, its back against the wall, undoubtedly had no moral inhibitions against this rather unpleasant prospect. As a matter of fact, Greek politicians were eager to secure an American presence at any price, even if it meant a substantial American influence in Greek internal affairs. In Washington there was never any doubt that American aid was conditional. On 3 March 1947, the Greek government sent another urgent appeal. Premier Maximos also asked for American experts to assure the effective utilization of financial and other assistance. Strangely, this message was drafted in Washington and suggested to the Greek government. *(36)* About a week later the president appeared before both houses of Congress and delivered his famous speech instituting the Truman Doctrine. A grant of $ 300 million was made available through the American Mission for Aid to Greece (A.M.A.G.). The dramatic military situation in 1947 necessitated an increase in the military effort, and the percentage of American aid used for national defense purposes jumped to fifty-eight

33   Jones, *op. cit.*, p. 75.
34   *Ibid.*, p. 73.
35   Quoted in *Ibid.*, p. 76.
36   *Ibid.*, pp. 76-77.

percent. *(37)* The massive quantity of American military and economic aid was, undoubtedly, a decisive factor in the final victory over the Greek Communists in August 1949. *(38)* The aid bill to Greece, however, resulted in two more important consequences. It was the first formal expression of the growing Greek association with the United States. In addition, it brought the United States into the important eastern Mediterranean area and the American navy assumed an expended strategic role. Most of all, as Tsoucalas remarks, the Truman Doctrine provided "a permanent and highly efficient mechanism of intervention in Greek affairs." *(39)* Officials realized that American intervention would limit their sovereign rights to a certain degree. The minister counselor of the Greek embassy in Washington, Economou-Gouras, reported to the Greek government that:

> Although the United States Government had no desire to intervene in Greek internal affairs, it recognized, nevertheless, that the full implementation of the proposed plan could not but involve some kind of interference in these affairs. The United States plan would be accompanied by a limitation, in some measure, of the sovereign rights of Greece. *(40)*

Under the aegis of the Truman Doctrine and the Marshall Plan, Greece entered the Cold War era linked firmly with the Western powers, in particular the United States. The most important objective of the postwar government was securing a peacetime alliance with Great Britain and the United States which would guarantee Greece's territorial integrity. Some Greek politicians regarded such a partnership as the most effective device for checking the aggressive designs of Greece's northern neighbors, and that the prohibitive cost of modern weaponry made a small power's dependence on large nations for security and defense absolute. Hence, as in the past, Greece should remain on the side of the major seapowers, which "also represented the liberal, democratic ideals of the Western World." *(41)* When the North Atlantic Treaty Organization was formally established in 1949, neither Greece nor Turkey was

---

37 Between May and December 1947 A.M.A.G. distributed $ 73 million (fifty-eight percent went for defense, twenty-four percent for food, and only sixteen percent for economic reconstruction). See *Notes et Etudes Documentaires*, 2.052, p. 6.

38 From May 1947 to July 1951, American military and economic aid amounted to $ 1,672.6 million, the highest per capita aid received by any underdeveloped country in that period.

39 Tsoucalas, *op. cit.*, p. 106. For examples of American intervention in internal Greek affairs, see *ibid.*, pp. 106-107.

40 Quoted in Xydis, *op. cit.*, pp. 479-480.

41 Couloumbis, *op. cit.*, pp. 18-19, passim.

among the founding members, despite their various diplomatic efforts. *(42)* The stubborn opposition of Great Britain, combined with the reluctance of the Scandinavian and Benelux countries, determined this exclusion. In line with Britain's still predominant position in the Middle East, the British Labour government insisted that Greece and Turkey were to be key states in the envisaged Middle East defense organization. The Scandinavian and Benelux countries feared that obligations under the NATO treaty might force them to intervene in the Greek civil war. However, from 1949 on, both countries, especially Turkey, engaged in an endless diplomatic campaign to gain United States support. The Turks very cleverly refused to cooperate in the proposed Middle East Command unless they were invited to join the Atlantic alliance. *(43)* Political turmoil in the Middle East, the Korean War, and the first successful nuclear explosion in the Soviet Union were determining factors in softening the previous opposition. At the NATO council meeting in Ottawa from September 15 to 20, 1951, Secretary of State Acheson admitted that the dramatic change in the international environment left no feasible alternative but to accept both countries as fullfledged NATO members. *(44)* American sponsorship guaranteed a positive response and the NATO council voted unanimously to extend the invitations. On 18 February 1952 both countries were formally admitted as members of the Atlantic alliance.

In assessing the advantages and disadvantages to Greece of its NATO membership the motives of the Plasteras government offer perhaps the best indication of the two major political parties' perceptions of the question. *(45)* Both parties regarded NATO participation as an invaluable asset and as the cornerstone of Greek foreign policy. The alternative, neutralism, was actively discussed in newspapers and among politicians but was rejected as not feasible and in contradiction with the country's national interests. The memory of the civil war and the continuing threat of the northern Communist neighbors on

---

42 The NATO council, recognizing the strategic importance of the eastern Mediterranean, had tried to associate both countries through a defense planning agency. The proposals failed because both countries, especially Turkey, insisted on full membership.
43 The Middle East Defense Command was proposed in October 1951 by the United States, Great Britain, France, and Turkey as a regional defense organization; Egypt's acceptance was essential to the rallying of the other Arab countries. The proposal died with Egypt's rejection.
44 *Ibid.*, pp. 569-570.
45 The Plasteras government was formed out of a coalition of the two major center parties (the Liberal party and the National Progressive Union).

the one hand, and Greece's geographic and strategic location on the other, did not permit the consideration of nonalignment or a neutral policy. *(46)* With the economy heavily dependent on its merchant fleet, Greece had no alternative but to secure the cooperation of those countries controlling the Mediterranean. In assessing the advantages, the center parties emphasized the security factor as the most crucial. NATO membership would guarantee the territorial integrity of the country, while the NATO shield would solve the perennial security problem. Greek politicians also saw NATO as advantageous to the country's internal security. In fact, the Greek Communists, who had sworn to fight a final round in their attempt at supremacy, would find it very difficult to overcome a Greek governmental force newly equiped with modern sophisticated weapons. The Truman Doctrine and the Marshall Plan poured huge amounts of economic and military aid into the war-ravaged country. *(47)* And NATO membership promised additional benefits. Because of its strategic location as a communication bridge, Greece had to be provided with the roads and airfields necessary to its role. This would at least temporarily alleviate the tremendous unemployment problem. As Couloumbis remarks, material benefits, military and economic aid, were powerful incentives to join NATO. *(48)* In short, alliance was an almost miraculous solution to the most pressing national problems. And as parliamentary debates show, the eagerness to join was so great that membership was ratified in a matter of minutes, without even an exact knowledge of the obligations involved. It was "considered such a good thing that even prolonged debate on the subject was discouraged for fear of

---

46 Couloumbis, *op. cit.*, p. 35.

47 *U.S. Foreign Aid to Greece* (In Millions of Dollars)

| Year | Total Assistance (Economic and Military) | Military | Military Aid as Percentage of Total |
|------|------|------|------|
| 1946-1948 | 723.6 | 198.4 | 27.4 |
| 1949 | 362.0 | 158.7 | 43.8 |
| 1950 | 215.8 | 22.5 | 10.4 |
| 1951 | 240.0 | 83.0 | 34.6 |
| Total | 1,541.4 | 462.6 | |

*Source:* U.S. Embassy, Athens: AID, *Statistics and Reports, U.S. Foreign Assistance and Assistance from International Organizations*, July 1945-30 June 1961.

48 Couloumbis, *op. cit.*, p. 35.

insulting the allies." *(49)* Parliamentary records also illustrate the willingness of center and rightist politicians to accept reasonable limitations in sovereignty and independence as the price for the greater security. *(50)* The only opposition at the time came from the Unified Democratic Left (E.D.A.), which was established in 1951 under the leadership of J. Passalides. E.D.A. protested any move that allied Greece with the Western world and instead advocated a neutral policy. They saw participation in NATO as detrimental to Greece's national interests, as it prevented closer cooperation with Eastern European countries.

Greece was finally admitted to NATO in 1952, but the country had come a long way since 1947. Although the most decisive factor in the alignment process with the West appears to have been security, the threat from Bulgaria and Albania may have been exaggerated to some extent, since Greece had enjoyed a high margin of de facto security since the proclamation of the Truman Doctrine. In 1952 Greece was protected by the American Sixth Fleet, the air force, and the American nuclear arsenal despite the absence of any formal defense treaty. NATO membership was only a formal confirmation of a situation in existence since 1947. Greece enjoyed American protection between 1947 and 1952 simply because the U.S. and other Western nations had too much at stake in this vital area not to protect it. From this point of view, it seems highly probable that other considerations were as important as the security factor. For one thing, the formal framework of an international organization seems to offer more prestige and equality to a smaller state than an unequal relationship with a far stronger partner. As a member of the Atlantic alliance, the small Balkan country enjoyed the same rights and privileges as the other members. In a sense, NATO institutionalized Greece's longstanding dream of a final association with the West in the political, military, economic, and cultural fields.

## TURKEY

Since the 1920s, Kemalist Turkey had pursued neutrality based on Atatürk's basic foreign policy directive, "peace at home, peace abroad". The Kemalist doctrine on foreign affairs included national independence and territorial integrity, and implied that Turkey had no territorial claims, being only interested in the preservation of the status quo. The policy of neutralism and good

---

49  *Ibid.*, p. 47.
50  For a detailed analysis of the parliamentary debates, see *ibid.*, pp. 34-40.

neighborship resulted in cordial relations with Greece, Great Britain, France and especially with the nation's traditional archenemy, Soviet Russia. *(51)* In 1925 Turkey and the Soviet Union signed the treaty of Friendship and Neutrality which constituted the basis of Turkish-Soviet relations until the end of World War II. The cordial Soviet-Turkish relations were certainly not based on common ideological grounds, rather they were an expression of a mutual interest in safeguarding peace and security in the Black Sea area. Atatürk envisioned transforming Turkey into a Westernized country because he believed in one type of civilization, the Western one. *(52)* Although urged by some of his advisers to apply his internal policies to the foreign sphere Atatürk constantly refused to ally his country with one of the Western powers.

When Atatürk died, war on the European continent was imminent. The growing Italian menace in the Mediterranean and the now unavoidable clash between the Western democracies and the Axis powers forced the Turkish government to reconsider its traditional foreign-policy attitudes. Consequently, Ankara decided to abandon neutrality and begin negotiations with Great Britain and France to form an alliance with the West. In accordance with its policy of friendship with the Soviet Union, the Turkish government informed the Soviet leaders of these negotiations, expressing the hope that a similar mutual assistance pact with Moscow might be forthcoming. Moreover, the Soviet Union was also negotiating with the West, and Turkish leaders no doubt acted on the assumption that Moscow would join the Western powers against Germany. The news of the Hitler-Stalin nonaggression pact in August 1939 came as a sudden shock to the Turkish government, and almost immediately relations between Moscow and Ankara deteriorated. Nevertheless, the Turkish government hoped to reach a workable solution with the Kremlin before signing the treaty with France and Great Britain. But after several weeks of negotiations, the Turkish foreign minister categorically refused to accept the Soviet conditions, and on 19 October 1939 Turkey entered into an alliance with Britain and France. *(53)* The two West European allies agreed to cooperate effectively with Turkey and to provide aid and assistance in case Turkey was

---

51  Greece, Great Britain and France were Turkey's principal enemies during the war of independence. The anti-Russian sentiment in Turkish society is an historic factor, partly explained by the thirteen wars fought between those countries since 1677.

52  F.A. Váli, *Bridge across the Bosporus. The Foreign Policy of Turkey* (Baltimore, 1970), p. 22.

53  Soviet Foreign Minister Molotov wanted Turkey to remain absolutely neutral. He also wanted Ankara to violate certain provisions of the Montreux Convention by closing the straits to the fleets of non-Black Sea countries.

attacked by a European power. Turkey, on the other hand, pledged to support Great Britain and France if those countries became involved in a Mediterranean war as a result of open aggression by a European power. Significantly, Turkish diplomats secured the insertion of an exemption clause which absolved Turkey of all obligation in the event of an armed conflict between its allies and the Soviet Union. *(54)* In these ways, Turkey positioned itself on the side of the Western democracies. It managed to stay out of the armed conflict by arguing that its armed forces were unprepared to confront the far superior German army. In short, the core of the Turkish argument held that a neutral but pro-Western Turkey would far better serve allied interests than what was seen as the other eventuality, a completely occupied country. Soviet reaction to Ankara's alignment policies contained a stern warning. It was almost prophetic. In a speech before the Supreme Council of the U.S.S.R. Molotov declared:

> By concluding this pact with England and France, Turkey had linked her fate to that of the Western Powers and had thus taken a hazardous line which she would regret. *(55)*

Once the nonaggression treaty was in effect, Soviet foreign policy made every attempt to secure absolute Turkish neutrality. With German backing Moscow hoped to aquire its own sphere of influence in the Balkans and a revision of the Montreux Convention. The defeat of Greece and Yugoslavia and German penetrations into Bulgaria and successes in northern Africa almost completely isolated Turkey. Fully aware of its extremely dangerous situation, the Turkish government informed the Western allies of its intention to seek some kind of an accord with Germany to safeguard the country from German aggression, even occupation. With Western approval, a German-Turkish treaty of friendship and territorial integrity was signed; four days later, on 22 June 1941, Hitler launched Operation Barbarossa, much to the relief of the Turkish government. The Turkish foreign minister could not hide his feelings when he remarked that this was not a war but a crusade. *(56)*

Once the Soviet Union had joined the Western allies, the Kremlin immediately changed its attitude toward Ankara. At times the Soviets had praised Turkish neutrality; now the Soviet Union wanted Turkey to declare war on Germany. However, the Turkish government still refused, despite Western pressures, to abandon its armed neutrality, mainly because the Axis powers

---

54  J. Daniel, "Turkey's Position in the Post-War World", *The Yearbook of World Affairs 1951* (London, 1951), p. 209, and J.C. Hurewitz, *Diplomacy in the Near and Middle East: A Documentary Record* (Princeton, 1956), II, pp. 226-228.
55  Quoted in N. Sadak, "Turkey Faces the Soviets", *Foreign Affairs* (April, 1949), p. 454.
56  See M.P. Cabiaux, "Les Relations Turco-Soviétiques", *Chronique de Politique Etrangère* (November, 1966), p. 643.

were still very strong in the Mediterranean and Turkey had no desire to be occupied by Germany only to be liberated by the Soviets. *(57)* Turkish fears about ultimate Soviet intentions were certainly not imaginary; Nazi Germany had informed Ankara of Soviet designs in the Balkans and the straits. *(58)* In response, the Soviet government tried to convince the Turkish leaders that these allegations were sheer Nazi propaganda. The Soviet government reaffirmed its fidelity to the Montreux Convention and assured Turkish leaders that it had no aggressive intentions toward the straits. In spite of these assurances, Turkey remained neutral, although complete neutrality was gradually abandoned with the growing successes of the Western allies.

Western pressures finally persuaded Turkey to declare war on Germany in March 1944 although by then the Soviet Union had ceased to call for Turkish participation in the common war effort. *(59)* The German threat in the eastern Mediterranean had disappeared by that time, and even if skillful Turkish diplomacy had managed not to arouse the belligerents, once the Soviet Union considered it time to turn against Turkey there was little Turkey could do. Turkish leaders no doubt hoped to continue Atatürk's nonalignment policy as soon as the European war operations were over; after all, it had saved Turkey from the calamities of war. But the brutal Soviet diplomatic campaign against Ankara at the close of the war inevitably undermined Atatürk's "peace at home, peace abroad" concept. Especially in view of the developments in Eastern Europe, the Soviet threat became a matter of life and death. Stalin's objectives were pretty well known in Ankara, and since 1939 Turkish leaders had bluntly refused to comply with Soviet demands aimed at disrupting the existing status of the straits.

On 19 March 1945, the Soviet government denounced the Turkish-Soviet Treaty of Neutrality and Non-Aggression, arguing that it needed adapting to the new circumstances. The Turkish government, still hoping to reestablish

---

57  Váli, *op. cit.*, p. 32.

58  During the Berlin conversations in November 1940, Molotov had stated that the security of the Soviet Union required the establishment of a base of Russian land and naval forces within the range of the Bosphorus and the Dardanelles. This was to be done through a long-term lease. Moreover, the area south of Batum and Baku in the direction of the Persian Gulf should also be recognized as the center of Soviet aspirations, See P. McGhee, "Turkey Joins the West", *Foreign Affairs* (July, 1954), p. 620.

59  This, according to Váli, was done in order to exploit Turkish aloofness after the war. Interestingly, the Turkish wartime policy had also created some animosity among the Western allies, and the Turkish government considered it of utmost importance not to be castigated as fascist. It wanted to join the democratic club, especially as a founding member of the United Nations Organization. See Váli, *op. cit.*, pp. 33, 64.

good-neighbor relations, was offered a new treaty on two very important conditions. First, the Turkish-Soviet frontier needed rectification, which meant the
return of the Kars-Ardahan districts to the Soviet Union. Second, the Soviets
demanded a revision of the 1936 Montreux Convention and the establishment
of Soviet bases in the straits. *(60)* In other words, the Soviet Union claimed the
joint defense of the straits by arguing that Turkey was too weak to defend them
alone. After an exchange of diplomatic notes the Turkish government flatly
rejected Moscow's proposals on the grounds that they violated Turkey's
national independence and territorial integrity.

Throughout 1945, Turkey remained firm in its resistance to Soviet ambitions.
This was especially difficult because both Great Britain and the United States
had agreed in principle to a revision of the Montreux Convention at the Potsdam Conference in February, 1945. For more than a year Turkey stood alone
in the nerve war against the Soviets, while the Red Army concentrated steadily
along the Turkish-Russian border. But the prospects for Turkey's holding out
diminished with growing Soviet expansion in the adjacent areas. In the north,
Bulgaria and Rumania were under Soviet control; in Greece, Communist
guerilla forces were swiftly gaining control over the country, while a Soviet
puppet regime was established at Turkey's eastern border. *(61)* And external
dangers were certainly not the only ones pressing. Turkey faced tremendous
economic problems, essentially due to excessive military expenditures. Since
1939 the Ankara government had maintained an army of a half million men
and spent almost half the national revenue on defense. *(62)* This extremely
high defense budget coupled with other factors caused an inflationary process
which the Turkish government was apparently not able to curtail. Consequently, the note circulation had risen from 190 million Turkish pounds in
1939 to 1000 million in 1949. The prices of food and other essential commodi-
ties had multiplied sixfold in ten years and continued to rise.

From 1946 on, the Truman administration had realized that Stalin's grand
design not only threatened vital Western interests in the Mediterranean but
also that the strategically important Middle East area might be the next target
of Soviet encroachment. *(63)* The American willingness to contain Soviet

---

60  *Ibid.*, p. 172, passim.
61  The Azerbaijan regime in Iran.
62  The defense expenditures as a percentage of the budget was 36.4 in 1939-1940; 31.3 in
1940-1941; 27.8 in 1941-1942; 30.4 in 1942-1943; 32 in 1943-1944; 58.5 in 1944-1945; 31.7 in
1946, and 44 in 1947. See Daniel, *loc. cit.*, 198.
63  Official American concern over the Middle East was the strongest in the Defense Department headed by James Forrestal. Middle East oil was perhaps the most determining factor

expansion was amply demonstrated when Secretary of Defense Forrestal declared that the American fleet would remain in the Mediterranean as a token
of U.S. interests in that part of the world. Washington illustrated its point
further by sending a unit of the Sixth Fleet to Istanbul, where American
servicemen received an unprecedented welcome. On 18 October 1946 the
Turkish government, now diplomatically supported by the Western powers,
sent its last note to Moscow. Soviet proposals were once again denounced as
being completely incompatible with the country's territorial integrity. Two
years of extremely powerful Soviet pressure had resulted in the complete renunciation of neutrality. More than anything else the Soviet threat was the
overriding factor compelling the Inönü government to ally itself with the
West, especially the United States. From then on the ideological orientation
of Ankara's foreign and military policy would be exclusively oriented toward
the West. *(64)*

The Truman Doctrine of March 1947 was just the start of the special relationship that was to evolve between Ankara and Washington. Beyond a doubt,
the security factor was paramount in the Turkish decision to seek military and
political ties with the West. The Soviets quite simply threatened the survival of
Turkey as an independent nation. In addition, many Turkish leaders were
aware of the deplorable state of the Turkish army, especially its equipment.
There was also the ideological factor; Turkey wanted to be a Western European country, and this desire, as Váli remarks, provided an additional impulse
to ally with the West. *(65)* The newly established ties with the United States
also had a profound impact on national affairs; it accelerated the democratization of Turkish political life. Turkey took belonging to the democratic club very
seriously. The Inönü government decided to create the embryo of a real democracy by ending the one-party system. *(66)* The Democratic party was formed and the first general elections were held in 1946. According to Váli, this
was a voluntary process which Turkey initiated to impress the West with its
allegiance to Western democracy and civilization. *(67)* For postwar Turkey,
identification with the West, and especially the United States, meant military
security, economic development, and a share in Western civilization.

in shaping the department's attitude in view of rumors of dwindling American oil resources.
See W. Millis (ed.), *The Forrestal Diaries* (New York, 1951), pp. 356-358.
64 Váli, *op. cit.*, p. 36.
65 *Ibid.*, p. 155.
66 Since the creation of the Turkish republic, the country had been ruled by the Republican
People's party (hereafter R.P.P.), the only political party until 1946.
67 *Ibid.*, p. 37.

In accordance with the Truman Doctrine, Turkey and the United States signed a military assistance agreement in July 1947. *(68)* Almost $ 100 million poured into Turkey in one year. Nearly all of it was spent on a large-scale modernization of the Turkish army. Washington supplied modern equipment and weapons, while American instructors provided an on-the-spot training program. American military aid also positively affected the general economic situation. As in Greece, many jobless Turks engaged in the construction of roads, transportation facilities, and military installations. American military aid at least temporarily offered a healthy solution to chronic unemployment. The rapid modernization of the army also made it possible for the Turkish government to announce a program of progressive demobilization. *(69)*

From 1948 on, American aid to Turkey became part of the overall European scheme called the Marshall Plan. The inclusion of Turkey in a global European recovery program in turn meant fundamental repercussions on the Turkish economic system. Specifically, aid to Turkey under the Marshall Plan was coupled with far-reaching American control of the country's economy. Some scholars refer to a much wider range of American influence; apparently it was not limited to the economic sector but also included internal and external policies. In the economic field, Turkey had followed Atatürk's principle of statism, which implied strong governmental control over the economic sector, since the 1920s. Statism was given an indigenous Turkish flavor; certainly it did not follow the usual Communist pattern. Private initiative prevailed, and the state took over only when capital or private initiative were insufficient or nonexistent. By the late 1940s American advisers were urging the Turkish government to develop economic concepts and institutions that corresponded to those in the West. This meant a radical liberalization of the economy, including quite substantial contractual guarantees to attract foreign enterprise. Some Turkish newspapers did criticize the American intervention in Turkish economic affairs and even hinted at a revival of the old system of capitulations. *(70)* However, as long as the Inönü government remained in power little was done to liberalize the economy. The R.P.P. was much too identified with

68 World Peace Foundation, *Documents on American Foreign welations, 1947*, IX (Princeton, 1949), pp. 730-732.
69 In 1945-1946 the Turkish army consisted of 1,000,000 men and was gradually reduced to ± 600,000.
70 Cabiaux, *loc. cit.*, 667. The capitulatory regime consisted of a number of treaties signed between the Ottoman empire and various European states. For example, France signed a capitulation traty in 1535. It provided extraterritorial rights for French citizens, including criminal and civil jurisdiction. In general, under these agreements foreign residents enjoyed a number of privileges in financial and legal affairs.

120

Atatürk's policies to take such a fundamental and far-reaching decision. However, the leaders of the emerging Democratic party had made it publicly known that they were convinced of the limitations inherent in state enterprise. Supported by a growing capitalistic business group, the Democrats committed themselves to private entreprise and the encouragement of foreign investments. Once in power, the Democratic government under Premier Menderes took important steps to gradually transform the Turkish economic system along the lines the Americans had suggested. American influence had certainly been decisive, although changes in the internal political life of the country had been initiated by Inönü, who gave Turkey the substance as well as the form of democracy by granting full rights to opposition parties. When the R.P.P. was defeated in May 1950 Inönü again acquiesced to the popular will and the peaceful transfer of power proved that Turkey had in fact become a Western-type democracy.

The attitude of the Menderes government toward private enterprise certainly found favor in Washington, although the available evidence indicates that American pressure was less intense in Turkey than in Greece. *(71)* Alignment with the United States meant enormous advantages for Turkey in the economic and military spheres. *(72)* The most spectacular achievement was the complete reorganization and modernization of the Turkish army.

The Inönü government began in 1948 to indicate its willingness to enter a formal alliance with the United States. By then Turkish leaders had concluded that the United Nations would be unable to guarantee their national security in case of a Turco-Soviet confrontation. The collapse of the collective security system as envisaged in the U.N. Charter was all too obvious to Ankara. The Western unwillingness to invite Turkey to be a founding member of the North Atlantic Treaty Organization created bitterness and frustration. Angrily, the

---

71 Lewis reveals that the American Information Service in Ankara attempted to influence the 1950 elections. In a booklet printed in Turkish the A.I.S. expressed in a veiled way its preference for a new Democratic government. See Lewis, *La Turquie* (Verviers, 1968), p. 150.

72 *American aid to Turkey* (In Millions of Dollars).

| Year | Economic | Military | Percentage of total |
|------|----------|----------|---------------------|
| 1946-1948 | 44.5 | 68.8 | 61 |
| 1949-1952 | 225.1 | 235.9 | 51 |
| Total | 269.6 | 304.7 | |

*Source:* A.I.D., *U.S. Overseas Loans and Grants*, 1 July 1945-30 June 1967.

Turks refused the cession of several bases which the American government apparently was seeking. These bases were eventually put at the disposal of the Strategic Air Command in 1951, but by that time Washington had already decided to sponsor the accession of Greece and Turkey to NATO. The heroic conduct of the Turkish contingent in the Korean War had not gone unnoticed in American official circles. *(73)*

When Turkey was finally admitted, the Turkish Parliament cast no negative votes almost as a point of honor. Of interest, the vote was 404 to 0, with only one abstention. *(74)* Turkish public opinion as recorded in the Turkish press wholeheartedly supported the direction of their government's foreign policy. A leading Turkish newspaper editorialized:

> Our entry into the Atlantic Alliance... is a great victory for our foreign policy. Turkey will no longer face the Russian danger alone. *(75)*

An article in the newspaper "Ulus" read:

> The invitation to Turkey and her subsequent admission in the Alliance cannot be considered as a mere gesture or present from the NATO members... They have invited Turkey because they realized that the protection of Turkey would better serve their interests. *(76)*

In sum, among Turkish motives for joining the Atlantic alliance fear was definitely the most important. The Soviet Union and the adjacent Communist states were regarded as a permanent threat to Turkish security despite the fact that the Soviet Union had stopped its intimidation campaign in 1946, and although Turkey was a de facto ally of the United States it still lacked a definite formal commitment to its defense. *(77)* In one sense this argument was academic, since the U.S. was already committed to the survival of Turkey. To pour millions of dollars into a country and then allow it to be isolated or overrun by

---

73 Turkey was the first country after the U.S. to respond to the U.N. appeal. The Turkish contingent (4,500 men) distinguished itself in combat and sacrificed many soldiers to permit a safe retreat for American troops. Turkey's prestige in the United States was undoubtedly a factor in persuading Washington to give up its previous opposition to Turkish membership in the Atlantic Alliance. See McGhee, *loc. cit.*, 623, and Cabiaux, *loc. cit.*, 673.

74 McGhee, *loc. cit.*, 617.

75 Quoted in Cabiaux, *loc. cit.*, 674.

76 Quoted in *ibid*.

77 However, Great Britain and France had reaffirmed the validity of the 1939 alliance. London and Paris even suggested that they would guarantee Turkey's territorial integrity against any outside attack or aggression. Daniel, *loc. cit.*, 218.

the enemy would be senseless. The prestige factor, closely linked with ideology, had been part of the argument since the renunciation of neutrality. Besides, Turkey wanted to be a European state, an integral part of the West. NATO provided an institutional arrangement in which the Turkish voice would be heard as a European voice. Moreover, a multilateral organization offered a better guarantee of equality than a bilateral relationship with the American giant. For historical reasons, the Turks are very sensitive about a relationship that creates patterns of dependency. In addition to the security factor, economic considerations were a major incentive in the alignment process; Turkey had been struggling with an unbalanced economy for years. The agricultural and industrial output was insufficient and the very high defense budget only complicated matters. The formal political and military association with the West promised new and favorable opportunities.

In gauging the advantages and disadvantages of Turkey's participation in NATO one must keep in mind that the geopolitical situations of both Greece and Turkey were among the most crucial considerations leading to their admission. Militarily, Turkey's importance for NATO's southern flank lies in its location and in the strength of its armed forces. Even more important in terms of defense is the Anatolian area, which has natural boundaries and a fortress-like interior. (78) In an armed conflict Asian Turkey would be the real battle area, since the European section as well as the straits are difficult to defend and vulnerable to large-scale bombing. Turkey's strategic importance was amply demonstrated by the continuous American insistence on locating several bases on Turkish territory. Eventually the Menderes government offered three, which were put at the disposal of S.A.C.

Not only did the geopolitical situation make Turkey a key factor in containing the Soviet Union, the contribution of the Turkish armed forces to the alliance was also regarded as a gain. Turkey has the third largest military force in the alliance and the skill and bravery of the Turkish soldier are famous. (79) The economic, military, and political advantages of NATO membership, plus the psychological satisfaction of belonging to the Western world, certainly outweighed any disadvantages in the eyes of the average Turk. On the other hand, such an alliance involved several risks. In case of conflict with the Soviet Union, Turkey would be among the first targets. For obvious reasons, a Soviet military operation would try to control the straits as a first move toward the eastern Mediterranean, and a foothold in the areas adjacent to the Middle

78 Váli, *op. cit.*, p. 46.
79 The number of the total armed forces has remained around 500,000. In times of emergency it can be tripled by calling in reserves.

123

East would cut off the oil supply vital for Western Europe's defense. Another adverse effect of NATO membership was its deteriorating influence on Arab-Turkish relations since Ankara was joining the camps of Western imperialists. Finally, despite massive Western assistance, the enormous economic costs of keeping up the third-largest army in the alliance would become, as in Greece, a highly debated issue. *(80)* To the average Turk in the 1950s these disadvantages were only marginal when compared with the military, economic, political, and cultural advantages of Turkey's inclusion in the Atlantic community.

80   The Turkish defense expenditures as a percentage of gross national product are among the highest in NATO. See *Nato, Facts and Figures* (Brussels, 1969), pp. 226-227.

*Turkish Defense Expenditures as a Percentage of G.N.P.*

| 1949 | 1950 | 1951 | 1952 | 1953 | 1954 | 1955 | 1956 | 1957 | 1958 | 1959 |
|------|------|------|------|------|------|------|------|------|------|------|
| 6.7  | 6.4  | 5.8  | 5.6  | 5.4  | 6    | 5.6  | 5.2  | 4.5  | 4.5  | 5.3  |

| 1960 | 1961 | 1962 | 1963 | 1964 | 1965 | 1966 | 1967 | 1968 | 1969 | 1970 |
|------|------|------|------|------|------|------|------|------|------|------|
| 5.5  | 6.1  | 5.9  | 5.5  | 5.6  | 5.8  | 5.2  | 5.4  | 5.5  | 5.2  | 4.9  |

# Chapter II

# GREECE, TURKEY AND NATO

## AMERICAN INTRUSION IN GREEK POLITICS. THE ISSUE OF GOVERNMENTAL STABILITY

For decades, political and economic instability had been a constant element in Greek politics, and there was no reason to expect improvement with the rise and fall of the postwar governments. Americans had often advised economic and political stability as a prerequisite for the successful reconstruction of the devastated country. Consequently, some Greek politicians have argued that the United States did influence the internal political developments in Greece and that Greek participation in the Atlantic alliance was a "by-product of extremely close Greek American relations." *(1)* Yet perpetual governmental instability was again accelerated when the liberal forces eventually split in numerous hostile factions. The liberal Plasteras-Venizelos coalition government, formed after the elections in March 1950, lasted for only eight months, and it became clear that the liberals were more involved in fighting each other than in providing a firm and sweeping reform program. In these circumstances Field Marshall Papagos emerged as a new political figure. Aroused by the economic and political chaos, Papagos proposed to unite the Greeks in much the same way as General de Gaulle had roused France with the Rassemblement Français. The Greek Rally (Ellinikos Synaghermos), as his party came to be known, was superior to the other parties, according to Papagos, since both had supported "a regime of the parties which had failed to give Greece much-needed political and economic stability." *(2)*

The elections of September 1951 were very significant for the progress of Synaghermos; Papagos's refusal to enter a coalition with the Liberals and

---

1 Couloumbis, *op. cit.*, p. 50.
2 J.P.C. Carey and A.G. Carey, *The Web of Modern Greek Politics* (New York, 1968), p. 150.

Populists eventually led to the last liberal government. *(3)* At this stage, American intervention in Greek politics was decisive. It was no secret that the rightist Papagos movement had favorably impressed American policy makers, who felt that it contained the seeds of a stable and uncompromising anti-Communist government. A controversy over the electoral system in the spring of 1952 triggered American interference. *(4)* Greece was receiving more American aid than at any previous time when J. Peurifoy, U.S. ambassador to Greece, issued the following declaration:

> Because the American government believes that the reestablishment of the "simple proportional" election method, with its unavoidable consequences of the continuation of governmental unstability, would have destructive results upon the effective utilization of American aid to Greece, the American Embassy feels itself obliged to make its support publicly known for the patriotic position of the Prime Minister Plasteras with regard to this subject. *(5)*

Tsoucalas accuses Peurifoy of threatening secretly to suspend U.S. assistance if the majority system was not accepted. *(6)*

The center parties and E.D.A. reacted very strongly against outright American support for General Papagos. Anti-American feelings appeared in the Greek press, and the editor of *Eleftheria* even mentioned NATO in a rethorical question:

> In the name of what logic can a military alliance, which aspires to the fortification of the independence of nations, remove from its members even their political rights? *(7)*

The United Democratic Left was even more outspoken in its criticism. The party's paper regarded Peurifoy's announcement as just one step in a series of actions to oust the center coalition government and "replace it with Synaghermos, the American-supported Conservative party, whose policies would best suit the interests of the United States." *(8)* The paper also quoted Minister

3 The Rally received thirty-six percent of the votes, while the United Democratic Left (herafter E.D.A.) secured about nine percent.
4 The issue at stake was whether the majority system or the simple proportional system would rule in the forthcoming elections. Papagos and Plasteras were both in favor of the majority system, while Venizelos and most of the other center politicians advocated proportionality. This implies that smaller parties were better off under the former system, while the steadily growing Rally expected more seats from the majority system.
5 Quoted in Couloumbis, *op. cit.*, p. 54. In the 1949-1952 period Greece received $ 733.4 million in economic aid, while Turkey, with three times the population, received only $ 225.1 million.
6 Tsoucalas, *op. cit.*, p. 125.
7 Quoted in Couloumbis, *op. cit.*, p. 55.
8 *Ibid.*, p. 57.

T. Havinis, who resigned in March 1952:

> Instead of recognition they [United States] have driven us to a condition where the Minister, and I say this with bitter complaint, not being able himself, nor the appropriate agency he heads, to have an opinion and to make responsible decisions without the prior approval of other persons.... I protest, as a Greek and as a representative of the Greek people, for the unjust humiliation which occurs to our motherland and which I consider unacceptable. *(9)*

Despite the long-standing tradition of foreign intervention in Greek politics, Peurifoy's only support came from the right-wing forces, who contended that the United States had the right to be concerned about the disposition of its own money. The American orientation of Synaghermos became all too clear when Papagos said:

> I like to state the unadulterated truth. When we exist not only thanks to our decision, but because the Americans exist, and they report to their citizens, under what type of logic can we deny them the right to have their own opinion. American aid is given for a specific purpose. It does not constitute charity, and neither would we as proud Greeks accept it as such. As a consequence, when its purpose is misunderstood we cannot claim its continuation. *(10)*

The government decision to apply the majority system to the up-coming elections proves without doubt the effectiveness of American influence in Greek internal affairs. American officials and diplomats openly admitted that Washington wanted a strong, stable, anti-Communist government that could implement firm economic policies and effectively utilize the huge amounts of American aid.

In order to prod the Greek economy, the center government applied to NATO for $ 28 million to make up the deficit in the national budget. When this request was turned down, Venizelos decided to curb the military budget by almost $ 35 million. *(11)* Among the measures contemplated were a reduction of the army's size form 140,000 to 120,000 men and two years' service instead of

---

9 Quoted in *ibid.*, pp. 57-58.
10 "Interview with General Papagos", *Vema*, 27 April 1952; quoted in Couloumbis, *op. cit.*, p. 59.
11 Tsoucalas points out that the center government was actually forced to cut the military budget because of a continued embargo of American aid The sharp reduction of U.S. aid began in January 1952 reflecting the growing distrust of the U.S. toward the center government. See Tsoucalas, *op. cit.*, pp. 124-125.
As a matter of fact, American military aid was sharply reduced in 1952. Once the Greek Rally was in power, the American military aid bill increased by more than 100 percent.

three. *(12)* Washington immediately responded to these proposals negatively, as did its close Greek ally, Synaghermos. Among other things the government was accused of seriously endangering the country's military capabilities and of weakening NATO's entire southern flank. It should be stressed, however, that the Greek leaders decided to lower the military budget only after comparing Greek defense expenditures with those of its allies. *(13)* Its research showed unmistakenly that Western Europe was spending proportionally less on defense, while its economic development was moving at a much higher rate than Greece's. The resentment provoked by this dichotomy would become a major issue in the forthcoming elections. The center parties argued that military expenditures had to vary directly with the amount of U.S. aid; the Greek Rally supported a rigid defense posture independent of fluctuations in American contributions.

The defection of two E.D.A. deputies to the Plasteras party and the resultant slim government majority hastened Ambassador Peurifoy's second intervention in Greek internal politics. In statements to the Greek press the American ambassador tactlessly asserted that Greece needed new elections under a single-member district, and that only a strong, anti-Communist regime would make effective use of American aid. No other kind of government, according to Peurifoy, would be able to implement controversial but important anti-inflationary measures needed to spur an economic revival. *(14)* Such basic disagree-

| | *U.S. Foreign Aid to Greece* (in Million of Dollars) | | |
|---|---|---|---|
| *Year* | *Total Assistance* *(Economic & Military)* | *Military* | *Military aid as a* *Percentage of Total* |
| 1946-1948 | 723.6 | 198.4 | 27.4 |
| 1949 | 362.0 | 158.7 | 43.8 |
| 1950 | 215.8 | 22.5 | 10.4 |
| 1951 | 240.0 | 83.0 | 34.6 |
| 1952 | 239.1 | 59.3 | 24.8 |
| 1953 | 202.5 | 121.3 | 59.9 |

*Source:* U.S. Embassy, Athens; AID, *Statistics and Reports, U.S. Foreign Assistance and Assistance from International Organizations*, July 1945-30 June 1961.

12 Couloumbis, *op. cit.*, p. 61.
13 Between 1948 and 1951 military expenditures accounted for almost thirty-three percent of the national budget, reaching 43,5 percent in 1950-1951. Defense expenditures as a percentage of G.N.P. were 6,4 in 1949, 6,9 in 1950, 7.4 in 1951. See *NATO: Facts and Figures op. cit.*, p. 226,
14 Couloumbis, *op. cit.*, p. 62.

ments between the center government and the U.S. precipitated direct American involvement in Greek politics, eventually causing the fall of the liberal government in the autumn of 1952. The elections in November brought the Greek Rally into power. The party polled just less than fifty percent of the votes, but gained more than three-quarters of all the seats. *(15)* Considering America's long-standing objective to stabilize and strengthen the Greek government, it seems fair to conclude that the American maneuvers favored the rise and consolidation of the rightists. *(16)*

If Peurifoy intended to gradually undermine the position of the center government, his intervention was very successful. However, the episode was most significant as an indication of the leverage the United States had over the small Balkan country. It illustrates as well the effectiveness of American aid as a weapon to pressure the liberal government, and as a means of imposing U.S. objectives. *(17)* American manipulations undoubtedly facilitated the rise of the Greek Rally, but it also generated an era of conservatism which, as Tsoucalas remarks, was "alas, a deadly one." *(18)*

## GREEK FOREIGN AND NATO POLICIES UNDER THE PAPAGOS GOVERNMENT

The basic foreign-policy objectives of the newly established government were formulated by General Papagos in his first address to the Greek Parliament. As could be expected, he described NATO as the cornerstone of Greek foreign policy, and he especially emphasized a thorough understanding of the obligations membership imposed. Papagos proposed a policy of improved relations with Yugoslavia, nonaggression policy toward Albania, and, importantly, a very close cooperation in all fields with Turkey. Focusing on the Greek armed forces, Papagos substantially modified his campaign stand that the strength of the armed forces had to be maintained at its present level despite cuts in American economic and military aid. Once in power Papagos declared that defense

---

15 Through the majority system of voting, the Rally obtained 247 out of 300 seats in Parliament. E.D.A. won no representation at all, while the two center parties elected fifty-one deputies.

16 The minister of coordination, George Kartalis, admitted disagreeing with the United States "because the latter had reduced Greek economic development to a position of secondary importance, judging from its insistence on strictly anti-inflationary policies coupled with decreases in aid and continuation of the staggering defense costs". Quoted in *ibid.*, pp. 64-65.

17 Prime Minister Venizelos remarked in this connection that the handling of the aid issue would determine the future of Greece and the survival of the Greek people. See *ibid.*, p. 67.

18 Tsoucalas, *op. cit.*, p. 126.

expenditures were automatically linked with increases or decreases in foreign aid. *(19)* Ideologically the Papagos government adopted a firm pro-Western and vigilant anti-Communist position. This made close cooperation with the U.S. and NATO imperative. Greek forces had to be highly trained and well equipped to deter possible aggression from Bulgaria and Albania. Culturally and ideologically, Greece belonged to the Western world, and Greek membership in NATO "was not interpreted merely as a policy of cold national interest but also as one of moral and ideological compulsion." *(20)* Papagos's understanding that unlimited sovereignty was a thing of the past paralleled his willingness to accept curtailment in Greek national independence. This attitude was also reflected in the signing of a Greek-American military agreement in October 1953. Acting in a typical "let's get it over with" move when Parliament was not in session and the king was absent, the government had not even informed the major opposition leaders of the entire plan. The agreement stipulated that the United States could use Greek roads, railways, and territories and construct the military facilities necessary for the implementation of NATO plans; U.S. personnel could enter, leave, and circulate freely. Most important, perhaps, was the right of extraterritoriality extended to involved Americans military and civilian. All imports of machinery, parts, and supplies were free of taxation and inspection and could be removed at will. Greece, on the other hand, would compensate the U.S. for facilities and equipment left behind. Assessing the overall value of the agreement, Papagos pointed out that the close cooperation with the U.S. enhanced Greek security more than ever. *(21)* Besides, Greek personnel would construct the military infrastructure, thereby benefitting the whole Greek economy. He referred to similar treaties between the U.S. and other allies, and described the Greek-American treaty as based on the same terms. *(22)*

The Greek military establishment emphasized the strategic value of the treaty, saying it enhanced the security of Greece's vulnerable northern frontiers. The geographic position of northern Macedonia makes it almost defenseless

---

19 Papagos declared in Parliament that "Greece's capabilities to continue contributing substantially in the future to the defensive effort are related by fate to the level of aid provided." Quoted in Couloumbis, *op. cit.*, pp. 72-73, passim.

20 *Ibid.*, p. 75.

21 *Ibid.*, p. 78.

22 Here the Greek government was either uniformed or deliberately misleading the opposition parties, since American forces in Britain and France did not enjoy the right of extraterritoriality. See *ibid.*, p. 79.

against a Soviet-Bulgarian attack; the narrowness of the area offers no possibility of retreat. An alliance with the U.S. guaranteed an air force to support the Greek forces on the Greek-Bulgarian frontier. *(23)* Greece's military and strategic importance must be considered in conjunction with Turkey's, since the two comprise the defense of NATO's southern wing. Turkey seems far more important in terms of conventional warfare. Turkish control of the straits still constitutes a serious handicap for the Soviet Black Sea fleet. On the other hand, Anatolia is the actual defense line of NATO's southern wing, and there the real battle would be fought. The rugged mountainous terrain makes this area a natural barrier against an attack from the north. By contrast, Greece does not possess such a natural northern defense line; its defense perimeter runs somwhere through southern Macedonia or northern Thessalia. Greece's most important function would be as a bridgehead to protect and support NATO air bases in Greece and Crete. Moreover, Greece would defend the vital communication lines enabling the numerous Greek islands to provide protection and other facilities to NATO'S Mediterranean fleet. *(24)* In an actual conflict, the real battlefield would be in Asia Minor, because the geographic composition of Greece makes the country very difficult to defend. On the other hand, the roles of Greece and Turkey are complementary, and therein lies the southern flank's vulnerability: a quick neutralization of one of the two countries would mean the almost immediate disintegration of the southern flank. Interestingly, General Papagos considered a new defense concept for Greece. He envisaged an offensive role for the Greek military forces in case of a worldwide conflict. The core of his plan was the immediate invasion of Bulgaria and the establishment of NATO's defense line along the Danube River. The plan was never accepted. *(25)*

The major opposition parties protested the government's action as unconstitutional. The Center focused on the terms of the agreement, and only a few center politicians attacked the Greek-American treaty itself. They argued that harder bargaining would have resulted in better terms. They were also afraid that the new treaty would mean increased military obligations for Greece, already overburdened under the NATO treaty. *(26)* Many center politicians

---

24  *Ibid.*

23  Luc Crollen. "Les Flancs de l'Alliance sont-ils Menacés", *Revue Générale Belge* (September, 1969), 99-100.

25  Information obtained by Mr. Luc Crollen from Mr. Averoff, Greek foreign minister under the Karamanlis government.

26  A spokesman for the Liberal party pointed out that the Greek concessions were not in

noted Denmark's and Norway's refusal to cede bases to the U.S. Even if the treaty were necessary, Greece still had made many more concessions than other European allies. Finally, some questioned the need for enhanced security as a result of this treaty; they felt that economic aid was much more crucial. *(27)* On the whole, however, criticism from the center concentrated on the provisions of the treaty, not on the issue of close Greek-American cooperation.

The government's counterarguments focused primarily on enhanced Greek security. Defense Minister Kannellopoulos responded that Greece would now be protected against outside aggression. The new treaty dispelled the pressing fear that Greece would stand alone in case of an attack. By itself this consideration outweighed any disadvantages arising from the agreement. Kanellopoulos even claimed that the pact was "a reward for Greece's faithful fulfillment of its obligations within NATO." *(28)* In Parliament Foreign Minister Stephanopoulos argued that the Greek-American pact was part of Greece's membership in NATO; if one opposed the former one also opposed the latter. He announced bluntly that if the treaty was not ratified that Greece would be expelled from NATO. *(29)* The Papagos government responded to every criticism with a counterargument. However, some were neither accurate nor valid. *(30)* In one sense, the conservative argument that the new treaty reinforced Greek security was correct, since in case of aggression the mere presence of American military personnel would insure almost immediate American involvement. On the whole, however, the Greek-American agreement illustrates again the great leverage the United States had on the conservative government. In fact, Washington extracted far more substantial concessions from Greece than from either France or England, and the Papagos government apparently yielded willingly. The only clear-cut condemnation of the agreement came, as could be expected, from left-wing politicians. From its inception, E.D.A. had opposed Greek membership in NATO and close ties with the United States in particular. The Greek-American agreement was described as a Trojan horse sent to destroy

accordance with Greek national dignity Moreover, Greece was offering as many divisions to NATO as all the Western European allies combined. See Couloumbis, *op. cit.*, p. 82.

27  *Ibid*, pp. 79-84, passim. American economic aid was sharply reduced after the boom during the Marshall Plan period. Between 1949 and 1952 total economic aid reached a peak of $ 733.4 million. In the 1953 to 1957 period American aid totaled $ 273.6 million.

28  Quoted in *ibid.*, p. 84.

29  *Ibid.*, p. 85.

30  For instance, Article VIII of the NATO treaty requires only that the parties will not enter into any commitments which may conflict with the treaty. In other words, if Greece had refused to sign or ratify the agreement, NATO would have had no legal grounds to expel Greece.

Greek national independence. Moreover, the bases conceded to the U.S. could be used for the kinds of strategic operations that would make Greece an immediate target of enemy retaliation. In short, Greece was becoming a virtual American colony and war base; according to E.D.A. both the right and center parties were guilty of subservience to alien interests. *(31)*

The issue of American bases in Greece in many ways resembles the issue of the country's adhesion to the Atlantic alliance. In 1952 and 1953 Greece still relied heavily on American military and economic aid, and both center and right-wing politicians accepted a certain loss of national independence as the inevitable price for their country's inclusion in the Western camp. Fear of Communism and memories of the civil war were still omnipresent, and the only safeguard against internal subversion and external threats was accepting an American military presence, even at the expense of national dignity. Refusing the Americans bases contained too many risks, the most important of which was the loss of foreign aid. Except for a small minority, the Greeks endorsed the pro-Western course of the Papagos government. Both the center parties and the Greek Rally concluded that any other alternative would eventually benefit Greece's archenemies, Albania and Bulgaria. Even if Greece's adherence to NATO meant conceding a certain amount of sovereignty, the alternative, a Communist-dominated Greece, would soon lead to total control by the Soviet Union, "which in no way would be commensurate to the minor losses within NATO." *(32)* Most Greek politicians were realistic enough to accept the postwar realities: a nineteenth-century concept of unlimited independence had become an anachronism in the twentieth-century. George Papandreou, one of the opposition leaders, declared:

> Since... the period of independence has passed, those who think that we can live in the current face of the world with the old understanding of sovereignty are wrong. But as it is certain that the period of independence has passed, it is equally certain that the period of subjugation applies only to the Iron Curtain and not the free peoples. *(33)*

The major parties generally accepted ceding bases to the United States because it enhanced Greek security against possible external threats. This and the economic factor were no doubt the chief determinants in the Greek decision to install American bases.

In the 1952 to 1955 period, the Greek government initiated the first steps of

31  *Ibid.*, p. 86, passim.
32  Quoted in *ibid.*, p. 87.
33  *Ibid.*, p. 88.

a new regional policy. Signing the well-known Balkan pact with Turkey and Yugoslavia was the first achievement, one which served at least indirectly to tie Yugoslavia with NATO. Cooperation among the Balkan countries resulted in friendly and beneficial relations with Belgrade as well as several trade agreements with East European countries. Again, both the conservative and center politicians generally endorsed the Papagos initiative and agreed on the amjor foreign-policy options and decisions.

By the end of 1954, however, out of nowhere the Cyprus issue had arisen to threaten NATO's southern flank, making the Balkan pact meaningless and bringing two NATO allies on the verge of war. More than any other factor, Cyprus would prove so disruptive an issue that Greece and Turkey would question their membership in the Atlantic alliance. Relations, especially with the United States, would deteriorate as Washington appeared to be unwilling to take sides in the conflict. American neutrality in that conflict created bitterness and frustrations in both Athens and Ankara, where anti-Americanism and anti-NATO feelings would soon become equally strong.

## THE 1956 CYPRUS CRISIS.
## EFFECTS ON NATO'S SOUTHERN FLANK

Cyprus, once part of the Ottomon Empire, was ceded to Great Britain under the Treaty of Berlin in 1878 and became a crown colony after the first world war. Its population is a mixture of Greeks and Turks, although the former formed a majority. (34) Greek Cypriotes for a long time had hoped for the unification (enosis) of the island with Greece but London had steadily refused to grand self-determination. As long as Great Britain predominated in Greek affairs, the Athens government refused to encourage the aspirations of the island's Greek majority. However, it is very important to note that the two communities had existed harmoniously until the mid-1950s, when peace was shattered by Britain's divide-and-rule policy. (35)

The fierce nationalistic movement no doubt created some ill-feeling among the Turkish minority, but curiously it was the British who "seemed to argue the Turkish case before the Turks ever thought of it." (36) Whatever its source, the controversy heightened and the Turkish government entered the

---

34 In 1881 Cyprus was inhabited by 137,631 Greeks and 45,458 Turks. See Tsoucalas, op. cit., p. 156.
35 T.W. Adams and A.J. Cottrell, Cyprus between East and West (Baltimore, 1968), p. 8.
36 Tsoucalas, op. cit., p. 158.

picture in full support of the Turkish minority, which became in turn more Turkish than it had ever been before. Once Britain began to decline in the Mediterranean the Papagos government moved to effect unification, no doubt on the assumption that American support was assured. The premier brought the issue before the United Nations and asked for a permanent solution. However, Great Britain insisted that the problem was internal and domestic, and consequently the issue was not even listed on the agenda of the General Assembly. In September 1955 rioters in Istanbul and Izmir demonstrated against the Greek minorities there, causing great personal and property damage. *(37)* The incidents effected public opinion in both countries tremendously, and Turkish-Greek relations gradually deteriorated. At this point, hoping to avoid a complete break among three NATO allies, the United States intervened. The Greek and Turkish governments received an identical telegram from Secretary of State John Foster Dulles, who urged them to settle their differences peacefully. The telegram described both countries as equally responsible for the events, although, as Couloumbis points out, "the provocation had been clearly on the part of Turkey." *(38)* Dulles's undiplomatic communication provoked public outrage in Greece. The supposedly neutral attitude of the U.S. and the other Western allies was condemned by a great number of Greek politicians of all party affiliations. Conservatives and liberals openly questioned further association with alliance members, especially the U.S. They felt that Greece had been betrayed by the NATO countries, while the Soviet bloc had voted for the inclusion of the Cyprus problem on the agenda of the General Assembly in the fall of 1955. *(39)* Greece no longer had friends, one conservative pro-Western newspaper wrote, referring to the positive attitude of those considered enemies. Greek foreign policy had always paralleled that of NATO and the U.S.; now the editor appealed for independence, even if it meant clashes with allies. He concluded dramatically: "We do not know what the government wants, but the people want withdrawal from NATO." *(40)* In-

---

37 The mobs were apparently organized by the Menderes government; the Turkish police received orders not to intervene. See W.F. Weiker, *The Turkish Revolution, 1960-1961* (Washington D.C., 1963), pp. 33-35. Tsoucalas reveals that in order to arouse Turkish religious and nationalistic feelings Menderes organized the bombing of a mosque in Salonica. This happened a few days before the planned retaliation against the Greek minority in Turkey. See Tsoucalas, *op. cit.*, p. 159.

38 Couloumbis, *op. cit.*, p. 96.

39 The United States, Britain, France, Norway, and Luxembourg cast negative votes while Poland, the Soviet Union, and Egypt supported the Greek viewpoint.

40 *Ibid.*, pp. 96-97, passim. A review of the headlines in various Greek newspapers speaks for itself: "Shame", *Kathimerini*, 22 September 1955; "U.S. Pressures on Greece", *Vema*,

dicatively, but not at all suprisingly, the editorial expressed anti-American and anti-NATO feelings interchangeably. The identification of the U.S. with the Atlantic alliance is a phenomen characteristic of both Greece and Turkey.

Prime Minister Papagos's death in October 1955 diverted the attention from the highly emotional Cyprus issue, at least for a while. In a surprise move, King Paul appointed Constantin Karamanlis prime minister and instructed him to form an interim government. (41) Karamanlis immediately established a new party (E.R.E.), but apart from its name it was merely a continuation of the Greek Rally in both membership and platform. Elections were scheduled for February 1956, and Prime Minister Karamanlis started his campaign with a particular emphasis on foreign policy. The E.R.E. leader dismissed the possibility of equal friendship with West and East. Such a policy presupposed giving up NATO association, a step he considered detrimental to Greece's national interests. He suggested that the country could better pursue its objectives toward Cyprus by staying where it was. Greece had joined the alliance to safeguard its survival; on the other hand, the partnership "could not be assumed to be beyond review or revision, should this be required by factors of national security, national dignity, and the interests of the Greek people." (42) He pledged his party to a more independent foreign policy based on Greek national interests. This radical language certainly had no precedents in conservative election programs, and was a clear indication of the leftward turn in the party's ideology. On the other hand, Karamanlis's position cannot stand at face value; he definitely proclaimed the country's unquestioned allegiance to NATO. However, the prime minister did shift unmistakebly toward a conciliatory position toward Turkey stressing the need to revive the old friendship. (43)

The center parties' position on the most pressing foreign policy issues was characterized by vague generalizations. (44) In sharp contrast to former preelection programs, it made no mention of what had been the cornerstone of

22 September 1955; "Friends not Vassals", *Vema*, 16 October 1955; "No Mr. Dulles", *Eleftheria*, September 1955; "Greece for Greece", *Auge*, 20 September 1955.

41 Traditionally, the deputy prime minister, in this case Panayotis Kanellopoulos, took over temporarily. According to Tsoucalas, the king's choice was the result of strong American pressure to end the explosive situation caused by the Cyprus problem. See Tsoucalas, *op. cit.*, p. 160.

42 Quoted in Couloumbis, *op. cit.*, p. 98.

43 Tsoucalas, *op. cit.*, p. 160.

44 It is very important to note the preelection cooperation between the center parties and E.D.A. under the name Democratic Union. Again this trend illustrates the leftward turn of the center parties, probably as a result of frustration over Cyprus.

Greek foreign policy, NATO. Rather it emphasized the formulation of a realistic Greek foreign policy based on national interest. Those interests were not defined nor was any clearcut alternative to the proposals of the conservative party presented. *(45)* On the other hand, although more moderate in its attitude on the U.S., E.D.A. described the preelection cooperation with the center parties as "the beginning of the battle to open the way for the adoption of a really realistic foreign policy." *(46)*

In the elections of 1956 E.R.E. received less votes than the center-left coalition, but secured more than half of the seats through the majority electoral system. The Karamanlis government reaffirmed its faith in the Atlantic alliance, blaming the current NATO crisis on Turkey and Great Britain. E.R.E. representatives also felt that NATO should remain the key factor in the country's foreign policy. Greece had joined the alliance to safeguard its independence and security, and this consideration was as valid in 1956 as it was in 1952. Moreover, by joining NATO Greece had enhanced its status; a policy of neutrality would isolate the country, lower international prestige, and diminish chances for a solution on Cyprus. Leaving NATO for the sake of the island would be irrational and unwise. The most prominent center politicians, although more critical of the NATO allies, arrived at the same conclusion. The only strong advocates for neutrality were the E.D.A. representatives. E.D.A. Chairman Passalides argued that instead of enhancing its defense capabilities Greece was becoming a target of Soviet retaliation, paying too high a price for military expenditures and receiving minimal economic aid in return. *(47)*

For the first time since 1952 the center and conservative parties adopted a foreign-policy line that was highly critical of U.S. and NATO policies. Membership in NATO, once the best possible solution to pressing problems, was now openly questioned. Disengagement, neutrality, and disassociation from the West became familiar themes in the Greek press. However, the Karamanlis government concluded realistically that disengagement would jeopardize everything Greece had fought for since 1947. Strategic, geopolitical, and security considerations left no alternative but faithfulness to NATO. As Couloumbis remarks, Greece sacrificed its pride "to what was considered a greater interest -- the shield of NATO association and the security this afforded." *(48)*

---

45  Couloumbis, *op. cit.*, pp. 99-100, passim.
46  *Ibid*, p. 101.
47  *Ibid.*, p. 101-107, passim.
48  *Ibid.*, p. 109.

## TURKEY: A MORE THAN FAITHFUL ALLY?

The foreign-policy objectives of the Menderes government sought to link Turkey with the West in every possible way. One of its first achievements was the signing of a defense alliance with Greece and Yugoslavia, an accord initiated as a result of the American aid program under the Truman Doctrine. In 1952 the American and British governments advised both Ankara and Athens to consider alliance with Yugoslavia to counter a possible Soviet or Bulgarian offensive in the Balkans. Military aggression against the Thracian border of either Greece or Turkey had been a matter of great concern in both capitals. Moreover, the defense of the sensitive Macedonian border necessitated closer Greek-Yugoslav military cooperation. The subsequent Balkan pact of February 1953 was not only a great diplomatic victory, it demonstrated that once distrustful countries could collaborate easily once they were persuaded that it was in their mutual interests.

The Menderes government had secured Turkish membership in NATO, now it indicated that Turkey was ready to participate in a regional Middle East security organization. This organization was a plan sponsored by the West, the objective of which was including the Middle East in a collective defense effort. Egypt's refusal to join resulted in its failure. The Arab states clearly refused to take part in a Western military arrangement, and American, Turkish, and British diplomats spared no effort to find an alternative solution in which Turkey would play the key role. *(49)* At this point, Secretary of State John Foster Dulles put forward his so-called northern tier concept; and the defense of the Middle East eventually evolved from his suggestion. *(50)*

The first step in the creation of the northern tier was the Pakistan-Turkish Treaty of Friendly Cooperation, signed in 1954; it was followed the next year by the Turco-Iraqi pact which came to be known as the Baghdad Pact. *(51)* The successful conclusion of these treaties made the containment of the Soviet bloc almost perfect. Actually, the continuity of the containment concept was

---

49 Campbell, *op. cit.*, pp. 39-48.

50 Dulles proposed to create a chain of allied powers along the Soviet Union's southern border. Major diplomats agreed at the time that Turkey would play the key role in the defense system.

51 In the same year Pakistan, Iran, and Great Britain also decided to join the Baghdad Pact. After the 1958 revolution in Iraq the Baghdad government refused any further copperation in the Western defense arrangement and in the end the Central Treaty Organization (CENTO) was composed of Iran. Pakistan and Great Britain. Although not a member of CENTO, the United States has a permanent representative in the CENTO headquarters in Ankara.

accomplished by both Turkey and Pakistan. Turkey links NATO and CENTO (the Central Treaty Organization), while Pakistan forms the link between CENTO and SEATO (the Southeast Asian Treaty Organization). As the land connection between Iran an Pakistan, Turkey is the key to the success of the both NATO and CENTO. *(52)* In the Balkans Turkey and Greece stand against Bulgaria, while Turkey faces the Soviet Union along its Black Sea coast and the land bordering the Transcaucasian Soviet provinces. In addition, it defends the straits against air and amphibious attack. *(53)* The rugged Taurus-Zagros mountain range is the principal natural protection in the area; in fact, as Rustow points out, it is the first and last defense line of the whole Mediterranean. *(54)*

During the Menderes era, Washington and Ankara apparently lived amicably. Ankara not only followed American advice on every occasion; being America's best and most reliable ally became almost a question of honor. Unlike Greece, the Menderes government made no major objections to the installation of intermediate-range ballistic missiles on Turkish territory.

When the Soviet Union successfully launched its first intercontinental ballistic missile in August 1957, the American government spared no effort in persuading its allies to accept middle-range nuclear missiles to counter the alleged Soviet superiority. The NATO council meeting in Paris in 1957 endorsed the American proposals. Turkey subsequently accepted the installation of fifteen Jupiter missiles, at the same time expressing an interest in tactical nuclear weapons. The U.S. immediately supplied these as well. *(55)* Turkish willingness to comply with U.S. and NATO demands inevitably led to the

---

52  Campbell, *op. cit.*, p. 50.

53  Vàli, *op. cit.*, p. 123.

54  Dankwart A. Rustow, "Defense of the Near East", *Foreign Affairs*, 34, 2, (January, 1956), 274. As a consequence of these expanded commitments Turkey maintains the third largest military force in the Atlantic alliance (following the U.S. and France). In peacetime the Turkish army is divided into three components. The First Army is located in European Turkey (Thracia) where it is expected to cooperate with the First Greek Army against Bulgaria; the Second Turkish Army is stationed in the Southeast along the Syrian and Iraqi borders; the Third Army operates along the frontier with the Soviet Union. The land forces are divided into seventeen divisions while the air force has twenty-seven squadrons. Finally, the Turkish navy consists of a small number of destroyers and submarines. As a rule NATO would only have operational authority in time of war. Turkey officially has assigned fifteen divisions to NATO, but these forces remain under the exclusive control of the Turkish military authorities. See Vàli, *op. cit.*, pp. 119-123, passim.

55  These weapons were controlled by the so-called double key veto system. Both Washington and Ankara had to agree on their use. The weapons were in the custody of United States forces, but would be launched by Turkish servicemen in case of war. See Vàli, *op. cit.*, p. 120.

establishment of a vast American colony in the country. As in Greece American military forces enjoyed substantial privileges in customs control and jurisdiction. Washington and Ankara signed more than fifty agreements but with few exceptions they were neither made public nor ratified by the Turkish Parliament. Although public resentment was hardly noticeable during the Menderes administration, the American military presence would become a highly sensitive issue in the 1960s, with dramatic repercussions on U.S.-Turkish relations. *(56)*

After Stalin's death, Moscow made several overtures of friendship, but was unable to change Turkey's Western orientation. *(57)* The traditional hostility toward Russia was now combined with a stern and vigilant anti-Communism. The Kremlin's "keep smiling" diplomacy met with little success, and for another ten years Turkish-Soviet relations were frozen. On occasion, the Soviet Union adopted a threatening posture toward Turkey; this merely served to entrench the country even more firmly in the Western camp. *(58)* Throughout the Menderes era, Turkish foreign policy paralleled almost perfectly whatever NATO, and especially the United States, considered to be in the interest of the West. For most Americans Turkey had become the unconditional ally, faithful in the worst of circumstances. *(59)* However, by the mid-fifties political evolution inside Turkey began to strain Turkish-American relations. From 1953 on, Prime Minister Menderes gradually enacted oppressive laws designed not only to cripple the opposition parties but to bring the administrative and judicial branches of the government under his party's control. *(60)* Moreover, after a boom in the early 1950s, the economic situation stadily deteriorated.

---

56 American military and civilian personnel figured at about 30,000 in the 1950s. Americans lived almost exclusively on and around the military bases. The lack of communication on the one hand and the high standard of living on the other gradually gave rise to nationalistic even xenophobic, attitudes among various segments of the Turkish public opinion.

57 In May 1953, the Soviet Union renounced every territorial claim on Turkish territory. Moscow also reconsidered its former opinion regarding control of the straits.

58 Turkey was threatened by the Soviet Union when Menderes decided to install middle-range nuclear missiles. Since these offensive weapons were directed against the Soviet Union Moscow made it clear that Turkey would be among the first targets in the event of a military confrontation.

59 According to U.S. General W.H. Arnold, Turkey had become one of the cornerstones of the Atlantic alliance. He pointed out: "For your dollar investment you are getting more for your dollars than in any other place. The Turks are fighters". Quoted in J.C. Satterthwaite, "The Truman Doctrine: Turkey" *The Annals*, (May, 1972), 81.

60 J.C. Hurewitz, *Middle East Politics, The Military Dimension* (New York, 1968), p. 212.

*(61)* New industrial plants were often constructed for political reasons rather than strictly economic ones. Menderes was almost obsessed with forcing the pace of the economy. He wanted to transform the predominantly agricultural country into an industrial state in a minimum of time regardless of methods and effects. The result was widespread inflation and an enormous foreign debt. *(62)*

*61* Between 1950 and 1953 the Turkish economy experienced a real growth in terms of the gross national product. In 1954 an extremely bad harvest resulted in a sharp decline. The expansion of the economy continued after 1955 but the growth rate steadily declined except in 1958. The actual growth of the Turkish economy cannot be properly evaluated without comparing it with the evolution of net per capita income. Per capita income increased 39.2 percent during the Menderes administration, but the biggest increase occured during the period between 1950 and 1953. Moreover, population increased at an average of 2.9 percent per annum, and per capita income at 3.3 percent. See Leo Tansky, *U.S. and USSR Aid to Developing Countries. A Comparative Study of India, Turkey and the U.A.R.* (New York, 1968), pp 40-42, passim.

The following tables illustrate the growth of Turkish G.N.P, as well as the evolution in per capita income.

| Growth of G.N.P. (at 1948 prices) (in Billions of Lire) | | | Growth of Population and Trend of Per Capita National Income | | |
|---|---|---|---|---|---|
| | G.N.P. | Annual Percentage Increase | | Population (Thousands) | Per Capita Income (at 1948 Prices) |
| 1950 | 10.4 | | 1950 | 20,947 | 434 |
| 1952 | 13 | | 1953 | 22,818 | 634 |
| 1953 | 14.5 | 11.1 | 1955 | 24,065 | 555 |
| 1954 | 13.1 | –9.2 | 1956 | 24,771 | 539 |
| 1955 | 14.2 | 7.6 | 1957 | 25,498 | 549 |
| 1956 | 15.1 | 6.8 | 1958 | 26,247 | 597 |
| 1957 | 16.1 | 6.3 | 1959 | 27,017 | 604 |
| 1958 | 17.9 | 11.8 | 1960 | 27,810 | 604 |
| 1959 | 18.7 | 4.3 | | | |
| 1960 | 19.3 | 3.2 | | | |

Source: A.I.D., *Turkish Economic Statistics* (Ankara, 1962), p. 8.

*62* The agricultural production was insufficient to meet the Turkish domestic and export requirements. Consequently, it adversely affected the balance of payments and depleted the foreign-exchange reserves. Between 1953 and 1958 the cost of living rose almost 65 percent, which was especially detrimental to fixed-income groups. This was particularly the case for the Turkish officers corps, whose economic and social status declined. See Tansky, *op. cit.*, p. 40 and Hurewitz, *Middle East Politics, The Military Dimension*, p. 214.

As early as 1955, the Eisenhower administration warned Turkey that it would reconsider its economic aid program if the irresponsible spending and unsound economic policies continued. Nevertheless, U.S. assistance increased in the following years, probably because the successful launching of a Soviet I.C.B.M. magnified Turkey's importance. Washington's contradictory policy indicates clearly that aid to Turkey was a function of the Soviet threat to vital American interests. *(63)* Giritli concludes that the United States needed Turkey as much as the Turks needed the United States. *(64)*

Ankara was realistic enough to realize that American assistance was not altruistic. A Turkish newspaper described the aid program as a "mathematical necessity", since maintaining one American soldier in Turkey cost $ 6,500 while a Turkish soldier could do the same job for just $ 235. *(65)* It should be stressed, however, that Washington's displeasure over Menderes's economic policies remained a strictly intergovernmental issue. Turkish public opinion was not involved. *(66)* By the end of the 1950s, on the other hand, the special Turkish-American relationship became a matter of concern to the urban intellectual community as well as the Republican People's party. Before time, foreign policy had seldom been criticized simply because it was considered an unpatriotic act to discuss such delicate issues. *(67)* On two specific occasions the Democratic government was heavily attacked for pursuing policies that served American aims rather than Turkey's. During the 1958 Middle East crisis the Turkish government allowed the dispatch of American paratroopers from the Andana air base as part of American intervention in Lebanon. *(68)* During a general parliamentary debate, General Inönü objected sharply to the government's aggressive actions which he said were only damaging the already low Turkish image in the Arab world. Inönü advocated more caution in general,

---

63 The average in U.S. economic aid to Turkey in the 1953-to-1957 period was $ 125.6 million. There was a slight increase in 1958 ($ 130.8 million) and a sharp upward trend in 1959 ($ 216.4 million). The same pattern appeared in the military aid program, where there was a substantial increase in 1958. Again the average in the 1953-to-1957 period amounted to $ 183.3 million, whereas 1958 brought in a total of $ 249.4 million.

64 I. Giritli, *Fifty Years of Turkish Political Development, 1919-1969* (Istanbul, 1969), p. 93.

65 *Ibid.*

66 A.H. Ulman and R.H. Dekmejian, "Changing Patterns in Turkish Foreign Policy, 1959-1967", *Orbis*, XI, 3 (Fall, 1967), 773.

67 Váli, *op. cit.*, p. 78.

68 The Turkish army was placed on a state of alert during those critical days. Arab-Turkish relations were very strained following Turkey's decision to back the Eisenhower Doctrine. The state of alert was also a response to Soviet troops movements along the Caucasian border. See *ibid.*, pp. 126-127.

and noninvolvement in the Middle East. *(69)* The next year, on 5 March 1959, Turkey and the United States signed a bilateral defense pact. The Turkish government had been insisting on such an agreement for almost a decade. The pact provided that in case of aggression the United States would take any appropriate action, including the use of armed force, as mutually determined by the two countries. A storm of criticism arose in the Turkish press and in the Republican party. The new pact was seen not only as an extension of the Eisenhower Doctrine to a country already covered by the Atlantic alliance, but an American pledge to help the dictatorial Menderes regime even against internal revolution. The opposition parties feared that the U.S. would support Menderes even if he were defeated in a legal election. *(70)* Interestingly, the identification of the Menderes government with America's stake in Turkey caused even General Inönü to declare publicly that Turkey's pro-Western and pro-American policy would remain unchanged if the R.P.P. assumed power. *(71)* The bloodless military coup of 27 May 1960 overthrew the oppressive and authoritarian Menderes government. *(72)* Although U.S. officials had criticized the prime minister's economic policies, overt American support of a government violating basic democratic principles had unquestionably begun to alienate the Turkish intellectual community. The fall of the Menderes government marked the end of the honeymoon in U.S.-Turkish relations.

*69*  Giritli, *op. cit.*, p. 92.
*70*  Ulman and Dekmejian, *loc. cit.*, 773.
*71*  *Ibid.*, 774.
*72*  An analysis of internal political developments in Turkey goes beyond the scope of this study. Suffice it to note Menderes's repressive measures against the opposition parties and the press. Menderes was undermining the basic principles on which the Turkish republic had been founded. As the real protector of the Kemalist revolution, the army was left very little choice but to intervene in order to prevent a real civil war.

# CHAPTER III

# THE SEEDS OF NEUTRALISM
# IN GREECE AND TURKEY

## A. GREECE

### THE GRADUAL DECLINE OF THE CONSERVATIVE GOVERNMENT

Once in power, the Karamanlis government was immediately confronted with the tenuous Cyprus problem. For obvious political and electoral reasons, the new premier dared not dissociate his government from the uncompromising *enosis* position. Throughout 1956 the E.O.K.A. guerilla organization intensified its struggle against British forces. *(1)* As a countermeasure, London arrested and deported Archbishop Makarios, but even this could not break Cypriote resistance. Greek-British relations became so strained that Greece recalled its ambassador in London. Again a flow of articles in the Greek press discussed the pros and cons of a neutralist policy. Some even made concrete proposals for a Belgrade-Athens-Cairo axis. *(2)* When Great Britain proposed

---

*1* E.O.K.A. (National Organization of Cypriot Fighters) was a secret terrorist organization formed by General Grivas in 1953. It intended to clear the island of British rule. E.O.K.A. rapidly dominated the island, but bloody conflict continued until 1959, when Cyprus was promised independence. The British failed to completely subdue the resistance movement. As a matter of fact, many E.O.K.A. survivors now hold important posts in the Cypriote government. General Grivas had been the commander of the Greek Cypriot National Guard, which was composed partly of supposed volunteers from the regular Greek army. During the 1967 Cyprus crisis when Greece and Turkey were once again on the verge of war, Ankara threatened to invade the island if the Greek junta government refused to meet four specific Turkish demands. The most important were the disbanding of the 20,000 men Greek National Guard and the removal of General Grivas and his 12,000 illegal volunteers. This time the U.S. government, mindful of the damage done by the Johnson letter in 1964, apparently decided not to worsen relations with the Demirel government. Consequently, the Greek government was left no other alternative short of war but to accept the Turkish demands. General Grivas was removed from the island. Between 1967 and 1972 General Grivas's liberty was restricted but quite surprisingly he managed to reappear in Cyprus in April 1972. See Adams and Cottrell, *op. cit.*, pp. 70-72, 88.
*2* Couloumbis, *op. cit.*, p. 110.

the Radcliffe Plan, which granted full autonomy to Cyprus except in defense and foreign affairs, the Greek government refused to discuss the matter. London followed that with an alternative solution: the partition of Cyprus. Tsoucalas describes the British move as pure blackmail, an impossible measure the purpose of which was to soften Greek opposition to the Radcliffe Plan. *(3)* Ankara hailed the partition proposal; Athens unequivocally rejected it. As Tsoucalas remarks, from then on whenever Greek pressure mounted, the Turkish government threatened to take its own slice, by force if necessary. *(4)* The question was no longer one of preserving and maintaining British bases on the island. NATO's southern flank was in danger of collapse. In February 1958 the situation in Cyprus was deteriorating at a very fast pace, and at the same time serious disagreements within his party over the election system forced Karamanlis's resignation. A few months earlier, in December 1957, the NATO conference in Paris had discussed the possibility of installing intermediate-range ballistic missiles in various NATO countries. Greek military leaders had on various occasions stressed the advantages of locating nuclear weapons on Greek soil. *(5)* Any future war would escalate into all-out nuclear conflict, they argued, and Greek security and effectiveness required such equipment. Moreover, refusing it would look like the Athens government had succumbed to Soviet propaganda then circulating which attempted to discourage the possession of nuclear missiles by NATO countries. The prestige factor was also important. Another argument emphasized the increased ability to contain Bulgaria in case that country attacked Thrace or Macedonia. *(6)* The Karamanlis government had until then taken a "temporizing" position, in response to the anti-American and anti-NATO sentiments among the Greek people. As might be expected, the 1958 election campaign focused primarily on the installation of nuclear bases and the perennial Cyprus problem.

The preelection program of the liberal party, headed by S. Venizelos and G. Papandreou, primarily concerned the necessity of formulating and implementing a truly Greek foreign policy, based only on Greek national interests. From the liberal point of view, both the right and the left were representing the interests of foreign powers. In contrast, the center promised a foreign policy formulated in Athens, not in Washington or Moscow. The E.R.E. government was accused of subservience and a fatalistic attachment to a Western orienta-

---

3 Tsoucalas, *op. cit.*, p. 161.
4 *Ibid.*
5 The military specialists apparently based their evaluation on the fact that Greece would control and dispose of the missiles on Greek territory. See Couloumbis, *op. cit.*, p. 111, note.
6 For a detailed analysis of the military viewpoint on the installation of nuclear bases, see *ibid.*, pp. 111-112.

tion. *(7)* Furthermore, Papandreou made it clear that a center government would refuse the installation of nuclear weapons on Greek territory. Such a measure was not one of Greece's responsibilities within the Atlantic alliance. He went on to stress that the liberal party would remain uncommitted to any geographical region, although the interests of Greece required that it remain a member of NATO. *(8)* Venizelos, on the other hand, described E.R.E. policies as "masochistic subservience". He accused the Karamanlis government of indifference to the sharp cuts in American aid to Greece occuring while the Turkish aid program basically remained unchanged. *(9)* Interestingly, over a few years the liberal party had switched from a staunch pro-Western position to one with definite overtones of neutrality. Speaking for the conservative E.R.E. party, Karamanlis described NATO as necessary to Greek security. His party would support continued membership no matter how the Cyprus situation evolved. On the matter of the bases Karamanlis was cautious. He said that as those weapons had not been offered to Greece there was no need to decide whether to accept them or not. In any case he promised that the Greek Parliament would play its constitutional role if an E.R.E. government decided to act on the NATO recommendation. *(10)* The United Democratic Left reiterated its usual argument that Greece should leave NATO recommending good relations with all nations regardless of their political and social systems. *(11)* In the May 1958 elections the E.R.E. party captured a winning 41.16 percent of the vote and 171 seats out of a total of 300. *(12)* The big surprise was the crushing defeat of the center and the huge success of the left, which succeeded as major opposition party. The complex electoral system was one of the reasons for the large increase of the leftist forces in Parliament. Another obvious reason was the conservatives' handling of the Cyprus problem, which frustrated and alienated large segments of the Greek population. But

7    *Ibid.*, p. 121.
8    *Ibid.*
9    Mr. Venizelos's statement implies a preferential treatment of Turkey by the U.S. government. This was certainly not the case in 1958. The per capita American aid to Greece was $ 17.5 in military aid and $ 7.5 in economic aid. For Turkey, it was $ 9.5 and $ 4 respectively.
10    *Ibid.*, pp. 122-123, passim.
11    *Ibid.*, p. 124.

12    Results of the 1958 election:

|  | Valid | 3,847,785 |
| --- | --- | --- |
| E.R.E. (conservative) | 1,583,885 -- 41.16% -- | 171 seats |
| E.D.A. (left) | 939,902 -- 24.42% -- | 79 seats |
| Liberal (center) | 795,445 -- 20.76% -- | 36 seats |

primarly, many liberal supporters "were sick and tired of the endless disputes between the Centrist leaders." *(13)*

The new Karamanlis government reaffirmed its faith in the Atlantic alliance as the only institution protecting national and territorial integrity. However, Karamanlis openly promised that Greece would also cultivate friendly relations with Eastern Europe and the Arab world, a course apparently motivated, as Couloumbis remarks, by "the desire to start paving the way for possible alternatives to membership and association with NATO and the West." *(14)* Throughout 1958 the Cyprus problem remained explosive. Greece and Turkey were on the verge of war in July, and for the first time Greek Foreign Minister Averoff stated that "Greece could not sacrifice the interests of the Cypriotes for the sake of allied solidarity." *(15)* This, of course, was a surprising modification from the earlier conservative position, which regarded continued Greek participation in NATO as essential regardless of what happened in Cyprus. War seemed imminent, especially after the Greek government withdrew the Greek officers from the NATO headquarters in Izmir. The move touched off an atmosphere of hysteria in Athens. War would undoubtedly have destroyed NATO's southern flank completely; the Soviet Union would have emerged the real victor. Under the leadership of its secretary general, P.H. Spaak, NATO took immediate steps to bring the leaders of both countries to the conference table. *(16)* Although without solution, the meetings lessened tensions and prepared the way for further negotiations. At this stage, according to Tsoucalas, the United States and NATO coerced the Greek government into accepting independence for Cyprus. Eventually Karamanlis acquiesced, and in February 1959 Greece and Turkey signed the Zurich agreements granting Cypriote self-determination. *(17)* A week later the British government ratified the document. *(18)* Western unity had been preserved for the time being at the cost of Greek pride. All the Greek opposition parties voted against the London-

13　Tsoucalas, *op. cit.*, p. 169.

14　Couloumhis, *op. cit.*, p. 126.

15　Quoted in *ibid.*, p. 128.

16　For a detailed analysis of Mr. Spaak's role, see P.H. Spaak, *Combats Inachevés. De l'espoir aux déceptions*, II (Paris, 1969), pp. 136-163.

17　Several factors explain Mr. Karamanlis's decision to accept a non-*enosis* solution. For one thing, Karamanlis had just won the 1958 elections and apparently risked internal discontent and opposition to his stand. Moreover, certain signs seemed to indicate that the Cyprus issue had lost its appeal; the possibility of war with Turkey was causing second thoughts even among the most intransigent *enosis* supporters. See Tsoucalas, *op. cit.*, pp. 161-162.

18　Britain ratified the agreement only after securing its military interests. Consequently, the British bases on the island remained under the exclusive control of London.

Zurich agreements, which they described as a betrayal of Greek national interests. *(19)* However, the complex Zurich settlement would soon prove to be only a short-run solution; Cyprus was to remain a disintegrative factor in NATO's southern flank.

## CHANGING PATTERNS IN DOMESTIC POLITICS:
## THE RISE OF THE PROGRESSIVE FORCES.

The remarkable success of the E.D.A. party in the 1958 elections was perhaps a symptom of the growing frustration of a large segment of the Greek population, although it effected the political convictions of the average Greek only slightly. However, as Tsoucalas points out, the emergence of the left had a substantial impact on Greek internal politics. With one-third of the parliamentary seats, E.D.A.'s voice could no longer be neglected. Another important event was the radical reorganization of the center parties after the debacle in early 1958. They used their dramatic defeat as an incentive to settle their differences, and in the fall of 1961 the Center Union emerged as a coalition among almost all forces on the scale between the conservative E.R.E. and the leftist E.D.A. Between 1958 and 1961 the major foreign policy issue was Greece's association with the European Economic Community (E.E.C.). The association agreement was signed in July 1961, and many regarded it as a step toward a growing Atlantic community. *(21)*

The elections of October 1961 returned the conservatives to power. The Center Union succeeded in polling 34.3 percent of the votes, while the left suffered a disastrous defeat. The 1961 elections were important in that the Center Union offered a new alternative to the predominance of the right. *(22)* They saw the emergence of three political blocks, right, center, left, which would undermine the strongholds of the conservative party. *(23)* The 1961 elections also affected Greek-American relations. The rise of the leftist forces after 1958 had worried many American officials. Although they still supported Karamanlis, they felt that a strong center movement was needed. They urged

*19* Couloumbis, *op. cit.*, p. 130.
*20* *Ibid.*, p. 135.

*21* The election results were as follows:

| | | | |
|---|---|---|---|
| Conservatives (E.R.E.) | 2,181,607 votes | 49.6% | 174 seats |
| Center Union | 1,515,284 | 34.3% | 103 seats |
| Left | 670,373 | 15.1% | 23 seats |

*22* Tsoucalas, *op. cit.*, p. 171.
*23* *Ibid.*

the reorganization and unification of the center parties and even implied that they "would eventually welcome a center government" (24) to check the rise of the left and reduce the political spectrum to two large parties. (25)

The Center Union's foreign policy was spelled out by George Papandreou during his campaign. He said that Greece was a member of the Western world because of its history, geographic position, and its belief in Western civilization and values. As part of the West Greece had assumed its share of the military responsibilities, but because of subservient E.R.E. policies had been denied the rights it should enjoy as an equal member of the Atlantic alliance. He continued with his now-famous declaration "We are allies with the West and we want to be friends with the East", clearly an indication that a center government would attempt a far more independent foreign policy. (26) Greece would also remain in NATO not as a "passive receiver of directives, but [as] an active, creative member." (27) In addition, Papandreou was very critical of Greek military expenditures, which were proportionally much higher than in other NATO countries.

The foreign-policy program of the new Karamanlis government focused on familiar themes. Greece would remain a faithful NATO ally because geopilitical considerations left the country no other alternative. On the touchy issue of military expenditures Karamanlis argued: "The need for increased investments toward Greek economic development, in connection with the economic burden resulting from... defensive organization, renders inevitable the dependence of the Greek economy on sufficient economic reinforcement from foreign nations." (28) The real dilemma for the Karamanlis government was one of priorities. Either security or economic development had to be emphasized, or enough Western military and economic aid procured to maintain the present level of defense expenditures. (29) Karamanlis cited the strong, rich Western

24  Ibid., p. 171.
25  The American ambassador in Athens was quite satisfied with the outcome of the elections. He said that "the elections have given concrete proof of the Greek people's faith in the ideal of individual freedom and human dignity". See Le Monde, 29 December 1961.
26  Quoted in Couloumbis, op. cit., p. 138.
27  Quoted in ibid., p. 139.
28  Quoted in ibid., p. 140.
29  Greek defense expenditures as a percentage of the budget and G.N.P. at factor cost:

|  | 1957 | 1958 | 1959 | 1960 | 1961 | 1962 | 1963 | 1964 | 1965 | 1966 | 1967 |
|---|---|---|---|---|---|---|---|---|---|---|---|
| Budgetary Expenditures | 29.0 | 28.2 | 27.0 | 26.8 | 23.1 | 26.1 | 24.7 | 21.3 | 20.6 | 20.8 | 22.4 |
| G.N.P. | 5.5 | 5.3 | 5.4 | 5.4 | 4.7 | 4.5 | 4.3 | 4.1 | 4.0 | 4.2 | 5.1 |

Source: American Embassy, Athens.

European allies who might eventually relieve the United States of some of its commitments. At the Nato council meeting in Athens in May 1962, the Greek government insisted on permanent military and economic aid from NATO and asked for $ 100,000,000 yearly. Eventually NATO established a consortium to assess the need for aid. They planned a global analysis of the Greek economy. *(30)* The Center Union, headed by G. Papandreou, attacked the idea as a device for foreign control in the economic affairs of Greece. Papandreou wanted the government to make an assessement of its own, and inform NATO that Greek defense expenditures had to be lowered if it showed that the Greek economy could no longer absorb the high military expenses. Holland, Denmark, and Britain had all successfully followed this procedure. *(31)*

By the end of 1962 despite its dissatisfaction, Greece remained as faithful an ally as ever. The year marked the termination of direct American aid, although only outright grants were affected. Other types of aid and assistance were normally continued, as table I illustrates.

In the end internal politics rather than international issues brought about the fall of the Karamanlis government. George Papandreou, leader of the newly-established Center Union, perhaps more than anyone else was responsible for this outcome. He relentlessly attacked every aspect of the state structure the conservatives had developed. *(32)* The Center Union's appeal to the workers and peasants was more effective than the E.R.E. claims of their own achievements, a remarkable phenomenon considering that the center's economic and social program was as general as Karamanlis's. In fact, Papandreou's articulateness rallied the broad masses of the working people who hoped for some kind of social justice. *(33)* Items such as income redistribution, pension, and free medical treatment were for the rural classes "what no cool-headed political programme could ever become." *(34)* Papandreou also criticized army involvement in politics, and he bluntly asked King Paul to dismiss Karamanlis and call for new elections. When the king refused, Papandreou questioned the system of constitutional monarchy. *(35)* Social unrest intensified and the

---

30  Couloumbis, *op. cit.*, p. 144. The NATO consortium would also assess Turkish needs. The Greek concerns in the field of foreign aid were based on the projected termination of direct American aid to Greece in 1962.

31  *Ibid.*, p. 145.

32  The state structure or apparatus refers to the armed forces, police, gendarmerie, the court, educational system, radio, television, and the like.

33  Tsoucalas, *op. cit.*, p. 174.

34  *Ibid.*, p. 175.

35  Tsoucalas remarks that although the monarchy as such was not really questioned, the activities of some royal advisers were. The king was asked to return to his proper constitutional role. *Ibid.*, p. 176.

## TABLE I

### Greece

(U.S. Fiscal Years -- Millions of Dollars)

| Program | Post-War Relief Period | Marshall Plan Period | Mutual Security Act Period | | | | Foreign Assistance Act Period | | | | |
|---|---|---|---|---|---|---|---|---|---|---|---|
| | 1946-1948 | 1949-1952 | 1953-57 | 1958 | 1959 | 1960 | 1961 | 1962 | 1963 | 1964 | 1965 |
| *AID and Predecessor Agencies* | – | 706.7 | 188.0 | 27.7 | 20.7 | 56.6 | 20.4 | 30.3 | 31.5 | 7.8 | -9.9 |
| -- Loans | – | – | 35.0 | 12.0 | – | 31.0 | – | 10.0 | 31.6 | 7.7 | -9.9 |
| -- Grants | – | 706.7 | 153.0 | 15.7 | 20.7 | 25.6 | 20.4 | 20.3 | -0.1 | 0.1 | ss |
| *Food For Peace -- Total* | – | 0.5 | 85.6 | 33.4 | 11.6 | 10.8 | 20.8 | 15.1 | 14.6 | 18.0 | 25.1 |
| *Export -- Import Bank Long-Term Loans* | 14.6 | – | – | – | – | – | 1.2 | 2.0 | 3.0 | – | 17.5 |
| *Other U.S. Economic Programs* | 510.5 | 26.2 | | | | | | | | | |
| *Total Economic* | 525.2 | 733.4 | 273.6 | 61.1 | 32.3 | 67.4 | 42.4 | 47.4 | 49.1 | 25.8 | 32.7 |
| -- Loans | 111.3 | – | 61.6 | 24.8 | – | 34.6 | 10.9 | 18.2 | 36.1 | 12.0 | 29.4 |
| -- Grants | 413.9 | 733.4 | 212.0 | 36.3 | 32.3 | 32.8 | 31.5 | 29.2 | 13.0 | 13.8 | 3.3 |

ss Less than $ 50,000

Source: AID, *U.S. Overseas Loans and Grants.*

152

situation became more and more explosive. Strikes, rallies, and demonstrations were daily events to which the police responded sternly. Events climaxed in May 1963 when Gregory Lambrakis, an E.D.A. parlementarian, was murdered after a party meeting in Salonica. First the police, then the army, the government, and finally the palace were implicated in the affair. *(36)* The accusations shattered the Karamanlis government.

A month after the dramatic events Karamanlis resigned, ostensibly over a disagreement with King Paul on a scheduled royal visit to England. This issue was probably a pretext to resign; rumors circulating spoke of more basic disagreements between the king and his prime minister. *(37)* Against Karamanlis's advice, the king instructed Panayotis Pipinellis to form a transitional government. When Venizelos moved to support Pipinellis, Papandreou expelled his partner from the party and emerged as leader of the Center Union. *(38)* Under renewed pressures from the center, the king finally scheduled new elections for November 1963.

The Center Union won the election but was unable to secure a parliamentary majority. *(39)* This meant that Papandreou needed either E.D.A. support or a coalition arrangement with the conservatives. When King Paul asked him to form a government Papandreou constructed one composed entirely of his own supporters, and secured a parliamentary vote of confidence with only the help of E.D.A. deputies. However, unwilling to depend on the left, Papandreou resigned, apparently hoping that new elections would give the Center Union an absolute majority. The elections of February 1964 finally brought the center to

36  These connections were never disclosed but the role of the police as immediate instigators of the murder was common knowledge. See *ibid.*, pp. 176-177.
37  The true nature of this disagreement is unknown, although the enmity between the premier and Queen Frederika was an open secret. See *ibid.*, p. 166.
38  Venizelos, who had reluctantly continued Papandreou's "intransigent struggle", was supported by a large number of center deputies. By undermining Papandreou he only accelerated his colleague's charismatic rise, and Papandreou became the most important national leader at the age of eighty.

39  Results of the elections held in November 1963:

|  | Votes | Percentage of Total Votes | Parliamentary Seats |
|---|---|---|---|
| Conservatives | 1,786,008 | 39.01 | 132 |
| Center Union | 1,931,289 | 42.18 | 138 |
| Left | 666,233 | 14.54 | 28 |

power with 173 deputies and fifty-three percent of the votes. *(40)* After three years of "relentless struggle", the supremacy of the right was over.

The center's foreign policy and its attitude toward NATO was almost identical to its pre-election platforms of 1958 and 1961. Historical and geographical factors forced Greece to ally with the West. The reasoning behind Greek participation in the organization remained basically unchanged, although Papandreou qualified his pro-NATO stand by proposing that Greece cultivate friendly relations with Communist countries. Rather than question the alliance itself, Papandreou deplored the fact that although Greece had always fulfilled its NATO obligations it had not enjoyed the same rights as most other members. *(41)* The familiar complaint centered on the dichotomy between high defense eexpenditures and the general state of the Greek economy. Henceforth, he favored reducing military expenditures, especially since the NATO treaty itself stipulated that "defense efforts of NATO members should be founded on healthy social and economic conditions." *(42)* Papandreou charged that his country's expenditures were proportionally the highest in the Atlantic alliance. This was certainly not the case in 1964 and 1965. The Greek government spent less on defense than Turkey, while American military aid to Greece was three to four times higher. Moreover, while Greek politicians occasionally alleged that Turkey received preferential treatment from the Americans, this is certainly exaggerated. As a matter of fact, the record of American aid to both countries demonstrates preferential treatment of Greece. The average of American assistance per capita over the entire period indicates almost a three to one ratio in economic and a two to one ratio in military aid in favor of Greece. Of course Greece was almost completely destroyed during the second world war and the civil war. This certainly explains the sharp disproportion in

40 Elections of February 1964:

| Conservatives | 1,576,550 | 35.0 | 105 |
|---|---|---|---|
| Center | 2,377,647 | 52.78 | 173 |
| Left | 540,687 | 12.0 | 22 |

*41* The Center Union's policy on foreign issues and NATO was heavily influenced by Sophocles Venizelos, who probably would have been foreign minister in a center cabinet had he not been expelled from the party. Venizelos emphasized the necessity for Greek participation in NATO as well as a common Western military strategy. He saw Greek neutrality as unfeasible, although he was aware of the negative repercussions of the alternative on the Greek development effort. Venizelos advocated an active détente with the Communists, even suggesting negotiations on the Soviet proposal to make the Balkans an atomic-free zone. He specified, however, that in such discussions Greece should act within the framework of its NATO obligations. See Couloumbis, *op. cit.*, pp. 153-156, passim.

*42* *Ibid.*, p. 173.

American aid until the mid-fifties. However, the 1960 to 1965 periode shows the same pattern in American spending, while the Turkish defense effort was higher. Whether Turkey was a more faithful ally remains an open question; the fact remains that Turkey was consuming more national resources for its defense than Greece. The year 1962 is the only one in which Turkey received more American military aid. Greece received the larger amount of economic aid until 1960, also understandable given the dramatic situation after the war. The 1961-to-1965 period shows Turkey's holding a slight advantage, but this cannot be considered proof of preferential treatment.

The general trend of the center's program clearly defined the priorities of the Papandreou government. Social and economic projects were imperative and their implementation required reducing the defense budget. (43) Papandreou

TABLE II
Per Capita American Foreign Aid
(in dollars)

| Greece | Military Aid | Economic Aid | Total |
|---|---|---|---|
| 1949-1952 | 42.5 (average) | 96.5 (average) | 139 |
| 1953-1957 | 54.4 (average) | 34.3 (average) | 88.7 |
| 1958 | 17.5 | 7.5 | 25 |
| 1959 | 10.8 | 3.9 | 14.7 |
| 1960 | 14 | 8 | 22 |
| 1961 | 5 | 5 | 10 |
| 1962 | 4.1 | 5.6 | 9.7 |
| 1963 | 10.1 | 5.7 | 15.8 |
| 1964 | 9.7 | 3 | 12.7 |
| 1965 | 12.1 | 3.8 | 15.9 |

| Turkey | Military Aid | Economic Aid | Total |
|---|---|---|---|
| 1949-1952 | 11 (average) | 10.5 (average) | 21.5 |
| 1953-1957 | 38 (average) | 18.9 (average) | 56.9 |
| 1958 | 9.5 | 4 | 13.5 |
| 1959 | 7.4 | 7.5 | 14.9 |
| 1960 | 3.6 | 4.2 | 7.9 |
| 1961 | 3 | 7.7 | 10.7 |
| 1962 | 5.3 | 6.3 | 11.6 |
| 1963 | 5.3 | 6 | 11.3 |
| 1964 | 3.3 | 5.8 | 9.1 |
| 1965 | 3.7 | 6.4 | 10.1 |

Source: AID, *U.S. Overseas Loans and Grants, 1966.*

43 Various NATO members had indicated their willingness to offer Greece the necessary financial contribution in order to keep the Greek defense expenditures at an adequate level. In 1963, NATO contributed $ 23.5 million, which was almost twenty percent of the total Greek defense budget. See Couloumbis, *op. cit.*, p. 175.

155

## TABLE III

Average par Capita of American Foreign Aid
(in dollars)

| Greece | Military Aid | Economic Aid |
|---|---|---|
| 1949-1960 | 11.5 | 12.5 |
| 1961-1965 | 8.2 | 4.6 |
| Turkey | | |
| 1949-1960 | 5.8 | 3.7 |
| 1961-1965 | 4.1 | 5.3 |

Source: AID, *U.S. Overseas Loans and Grants, 1966.*

## TABLE IV

Average Per Capita of American Foreign Aid
(in dollars)

| Greece | Military Aid | Economic Aid |
|---|---|---|
| 1946-1965 | 220 | 233 |
| Turkey | | |
| 1946-1965 | 102 | 82 |

Sources: AID, *U.S. Overseas Loans and Grants, 1966.*
         *NATO, Facts and Figures, op. cit.,* pp. 222-223.

## TABLE V

Average Defense Expenditures as a Percentage of GNP

| Greece | |
|---|---|
| 1949-1965 | 5.5 |
| Turkey | |
| 1949-1965 | 5.6 |

Source: *NATO, Facts and Figures, op. cit.,* pp. 224-225.

156

## TABLE VI

Defense Expenditures as a Percentage of GNP

|        | 1961 | 1962 | 1963 | 1964 | 1965 |
|--------|------|------|------|------|------|
| Greece | 4.7  | 4.5  | 4.3  | 4.1  | 4.0  |
| Turkey | 6.1  | 6.3  | 5.5  | 5.6  | 5.8  |

Source: *NATO, Facts and Figures, op. cit.*, p. 225.

also emphasized the need for friendly relations with Greece's northern neighbors. He made no reference to the Cyprus problem, but very soon the situation became explosive. Archbishop Makarios had proposed revising the Cypriote constitution, and in response Turkey threatened to invade the island. Mainly as a result of U.S. pressure war was avoided. The United States had painstakingly refused to take sides, since its doing so would have meant the complete breakdown of NATO's southern wing. Rather than pushing the issue, Washington had until now relied on quiet diplomacy, although President Johnson's threatening letter to Turkish President Inönü constituted an ultimatum. *(44)* Ambassador Stevenson's remarks in the U.N. also reflected U.S. neutrality.

> The United States had no position as to the form or the shape of a final settlement of the Cyprus problem... [thus] it is not for my government to say what the solution would be. *(45)*

As in 1956, the Cyprus problem became the most important foreign policy issue in Greece. In strong language Premier Papandreou warned the Turkish government that Greek forces would retaliate in case of Turkish intervention. Nevertheless, he hoped that the Inönü government would show the necessary restraint. *(46)* Papandreou's position was moderate compared to other center leaders, who expressed opinions similar to the E.D.A. viewpoint. These politicians argued that Greece could not challenge the Turkish position within the framework of NATO because Turkey was strategically far more important than Greece. The spokesman for the left wing of the Center Union, Loukis Akritas, even implied that Greece might gain more by adopting a neutral course. *(47)* He cited Egypt and Yugoslavia as small countries that played an important role in world affairs independent of foreign powers. Turkey's prime

44  For more details on the 1964 Cyprus crisis and the Johnson letter, see pp. 170-171.
45  Quoted in Adams and Cottrell, *op. cit.*, p. 57.
46  Couloumbis, *op. cit.*, pp. 179-180.
47  *Ibid.*, pp. 181-182.

position in NATO's southern flank convinced many Greek politicians that a NATO-imposed solution on Cyprus would be advantageous to Turkey. Premier Papandreou insisted that the United Nations should solve the Cyprus problem. *(48)*

As in Turkey, the allied handling of the 1964 Cyprus crisis created only frustration and disillusion. Again anti-American and anti-NATO sentiment in Greek public opinion became apparent. The Papandreou government responded in a way quite similar to Turkey's after the famous Johnson letter. Exhibiting his growing independence in foreign affairs, Papandreou ordered the Greek army not to participate in regular NATO maneuvers. Another measure, apparently irritating to Washington, made the Greek intelligence service less dependent on the C.I.A. Tsoucalas also says that Papandreou did nothing to prevent Makarios from buying Soviet weapons. Finally, Papandreou planned to cut Greek military expenditures, despite strong NATO pressures. *(49)* The planned cuts alarmed some of the military leaders. The former chief of staff, General Frontistis, openly declared in parliament:

> Is the government prepared to reach that point [i.e., reduce the military forces further]? Will she find a military leadership that will accept it? You see I am avoiding to speak about the reaction of the allies, because the allies might perhaps prefer the change of the missions, rather than any further weakening of the force backing the present mission. *(50)*

While Frontistis may not have spoken for the entire military establishment, his statement does give some indications of the position of the army leaders. *(51)* The general felt that further cuts in military expenditures or present troop levels would not only weaken Greece's military position vis-à-vis Bul-

---

48 This might be interpreted as an implicit rejection of the solution proposed by the NATO council. According to this plan, NATO troops would land on the island to prevent further intercommunity fighting. Both belligerents agreed at the time, although Greece was then under an interim government appointed to supervise the elections of February 1964. Greek acceptance of the plan had been reached only after broad consultations among party leaders, including Papandreou. Elias Eliou, spokesman for E.D.A., detailed the way NATO would operate. He claimed that the plan had the Turks invading the island, followed by a Greek countermove in another part of Cyprus. NATO forces would be brought in as a result and would probably be stationed permanently. According to Eliou's information General Lemnitzer even sent telegrams to Ankara and Athens to begin the implementation of the program. However, Papandreou denied the existence of such a telegram. See *ibid.*, pp. 183-184, passim.
49 Tsoucalas, *op. cit.*, p. 187.
50 Couloumbis, *op. cit.*, p. 187; see also Tsoucalas, *op. cit.*, p. 187.
51 Referring to Frontistis's "astonishing statement", Tsoucalas implies that this was a consensus and predicts an eventual military takeover. Frontistis himself denied such an interpretation, and explained that he only referred to the right of military leaders to resign. See Tsoucalas, *op. cit.*, p. 187, and Couloumbis, *op. cit.*, p. 188.

garia, which he still considered Greece's main enemy, but might lead to NATO's revision of the country's military and defensive mission. *(52)* His exact meaning is unclear, but some of Frontistis's earlier writings hint at his fears. His analysis of NATO's southern flank concluded that in the event of a conventional confrontation Greece and Turkey would be unable to withstand the superior Bulgarian forces unless NATO provided massive support. Moreover, Frontistis insisted that NATO apply the forward strategy in both Greece and Turkey, delineating the defense perimeter at the nothern borders of the two countries. *(53)* This implies that he speculated that a reduction in manpower and military expenditure would lead to the reappraisal of the forward strategy in Greece. In short, the defense line would move south at the expense of Greek territory. *(54)*

The independence of the Papandreou government from NATO and the U.S. no doubt accelerated strong anti-American feelings in Greece and, as in 1956, neutralist tendencies again gained popularity. On the domestic front, Papandreou was gradually confronted with an unprecedented radicalism among students, workers, and peasants. Social pressures began mounting, to the discomfort of the Central Union, as the results of Papandreou's political liberali-

---

*52* General Frontisis provided statistical data which showed that despite strong NATO pressures the Karamanlis government had initiated a gradual reduction of military expenditures

Proportion of Budget Spent on Defense

| Year | Percentage | As a Percentage of G.N.P. |
|------|------------|---------------------------|
| 1936-1940 | 30.0 | 5.5 |
| 1957 | 23.9 | 5.5 |
| 1958 | 20.5 | 5.3 |
| 1959 | 18.0 | 5.4 |
| 1960 | 19.2 | 5.4 |
| 1961 | 17.4 | 4.7 |
| 1962 | 15.0 | 4.5 |
| 1963 | 14.3 | 4.3 |

Couloumbis, *op. cit.*, p. 187, note.

*53* A. Frontisis, "The Defensive Problem in the Greek Area", *International Relations* (Athens, 1962), p. 33-34.

*54* Frontisis could foresee additional reductions only if Bulgaria reduced its forces and the problems with Turkey were solved. In the absence of such improvements, Greece should maintain the current force levels. See Couloumbis, *op. cit.*, p. 188.

zation seemed to move beyond control. In order to prevent a massive growth of E.D.A. the Center Union, was forced to develop policies clearly designed to undercut the rival party's appeal. *(55)*

From these circumstances Papandreou's son Andreas emerged as indisputable leader of the Center Union's left wing. Ambitious as he was, Andreas Papandreou probably sensed that time was in his favor and he developed a program of radical economic and social reforms. Conflicts with the elder Papandreou, a moderate and an anti-Communist, were unavoidable. Andreas Papandreou soon united those who had attacked U.S. interference in Greek affairs behind a foreign policy with definite anti-American overtones. As Andreas's popularity grew, George Papandreou gradually lost control of the Center Union, and the appearance of factionalism led to the downfall of the government. Another important factor contributing to Papandreou's fall was his inability to handle the army structure. Although he had continued to attack the army throughout his premiership, he finally decided to effect a purge. *(56)* The move was fatal to his political career. *(57)*

The alleged American role in undermining the Papandreou government cannot be proven, although C.I.A. agents were said to have attempted to bribe several politicians who were prepared to disavow the Papandreous and to accept parliamentary support from E.R.E.. *(58)* Whether U.S. intelligence was involved or not Papandreou's independent policies were almost certainly creating second thoughts among American officials. The Aspida Affair as well as George Papandreou's attempt to name himself minister of defense, precipitated a collision with young King Constantine. *(59)* King Constantine refused to allow the premier the second title, apparently because he saw it as a tactic to save Andreas Papandreou, who was involved in the Aspida Affair.

---

55 Again there is a striking parallel with political developments in Turkey, where one faction of the Republican Peoples' Party, headed by Bülent Ecevit, introduced the left-of-center policy. Although Inönü initially supported the group, a fundamental disagreement over party policies led to Inönü's resignation as party leader in May 1972.

56 Tsoucalas, *op. cit.*, pp. 186-187, passim. According to Tsoucalas, Papandreou hesitated to liberalize the army because he feared a reaction from the palace.

57 Papandreou exposed a series of documents he had discovered that described army interference in the 1961 elections.

58 *Ibid.*, p. 190.

59 Aspida, a small left-wing army organization, was accused of planning to overthrow the constitution. Some thirty officers were involved in this case, and given their republican leanings their accusers assumed that the attack was directed primarily against the king, although evidence on this charge is still lacking. Premier Papandreou requested the removal of his defense minister, and when the king refused to appoint a new one Papandreou proposed taking that post as well.

160

When the premier threatened to resign, the king immediately accepted his offer and a new government was formed within two hours. *(60)* The ouster of George Papandreou on 15 July 1965 was the beginning of the end for the Center Union. Greece was within two years of a military dictatorship.

## THE FAILURE OF LIBERALISM AND THE COLONELS' COUP

King Constantine dealt one of the first fatal blows to democracy in Greece. The constitutionality of his action is not a matter to be discussed here; more important for our analysis is that in effecting his own political decisions the king neglected the mandate George Papandreou had received from the Greek electorate. The Greeks were used to the crown meddling in politics. On the other hand, Constantine had clearly violated the principles of parliamentary democracy. Public indignation led to unprecedented mass meetings in which the king and his policies were severely attacked. *(61)* Tsoucalas describes these meetings as a new development in Greek politics: "an authentic feedback process emerged between political activity in the broad sense and popular pressure." *(62)*

Royal intervention made Papandreou's popular base even stronger than before, and no one doubted the outcome of the May 1967 elections. From 1966 constant rumors circulated that the army planned a takeover to end political and social unrest. As a matter of fact, the right had emphasized the danger of a Communist menace ever since the liberals had come to power. One E.R.E. politician even described Georpe Papandreou as the Kremlin's agent in Greece. *(63)*

Apparently the failure to do away with the center brought the military into the political picture. Remarking that it seems impossible to keep the army out of politics, Sulzberger reveals that I.D.E.A. generals on the Supreme Military Council had decided to "interfere in the political situation" without fixing a

60 According to Sulzberger, King Constantine had been advised to intervene in the political arena. See G.L. Sulzberger, "Greece under the Colonels", *Foreign Affairs*, 48, (January, 1970), 302. The swiftness of the operation leads Tsoucalas to conclude that it had been carefully planned in advance.

61 Leftist youth organizations were very active in the demonstrations, but Tsoucalas suggests that they were only a part of a much more general and varied mass movement. What the people wanted was not a change of regime but the reestablishment and consolidation of popular sovereignty. See Tsoucalas, *op. cit.*, p. 194.

62 *Ibid.*, p. 194.

63 *Le Monde*, 11 September 1965. George Rallis referred to Papandreou this way not because he thought him to be a Communist but because Papandreou's program threatened to disrupt the conservative state system.

specific day. *(64)* The available information implies that the king was still
hesitating over methods to solve the political crisis. He did not rule out a
military solution, but the evidence suggests he would only have resorted to that
if nonmilitary solutions had failed. When the generals made their decision,
however, the word was passed to a junta of colonels who had been planning a
coup of their own for at least a decade. *(65)* General Zoetakis informed them
of the king's plan and the colonels struck. The entire operation, based on a
NATO contingency plan, was a complete success. *(66)* The exact role of the
United States in the affair is far from clear, although the colonels referred to
U.S. support in their first meeting with an astonished King Constantine. In
fact, some sources refer to the active participation of the C.I.A., but the evidence is inconclusive. Of course, given the strong anti-Communist feeling
among the military leadership and their unquestioned allegiance to NATO,
U.S. interests in Greece were better served by a government that would reestablish political and social stability even by infringing on democratic institutions. The record of U.S. policy suggests that the Americans favored conservative and center-right governments, which were far more manageable than
their liberal counterparts.

The principal justification for the military action appeared in a statement by
Prime Minister Kollias. He argued that Greece had been gradually leaving the
Western camp. "We were heading towards chaos. If the army had not acted
Greece would have to withdraw from NATO and would become a communist
state." *(67)* In other words, the "raison d'être" of the military intervention
was the alleged threat of a Communist take-over. Consequently, one of the
new government's first moves was the dissolution of E.D.A., which had hoped
to bring Greece more closely into the Soviet orbit. *(68)* On the domestic
scene, the new leaders organized a large-scale campaign to "purify" the country. Thousands of leftists were arrested and brutally treated by the military

---

64   Sulzberger, *loc. cit.*, 303. I.D.E.A. was a Greek officers' organization which was definitely
anti-Commuhist, pro-E.R.E., and royalist.

65   *Ibid.*, p. 304. The generals decided to intervene after a mass meeting in Saloniki was
announced in which Andreas Papandreou would be the leading figure. They were afraid that
things would get out of control. Again no exact date was scheduled. According to Tsoucalas,
only on 21 April 1967 were the generals and the king to meet to decide on the intervention
and its timing. See Tsoucalas, *op. cit.*, p. 203.

66   As early as 1958, General Nicolopoulos, head of the Supreme Military Council, had
brought the colonels' plot to the attention of the other generals. Among the plotters were
G. Papadopoulos, N. Makarezos, and John Ladas. Sulzberger, *loc. cit.*, 304.

67   "The Government Position on NATO and Foreign Policy in General", *International
Relations* (Athens, 1967), 7.

68   *Ibid.*

police, whose coercive activities almost became administrative practice officially tolerated by the Greek government. *(69)* At least this was the conclusion reached by the Special Committee of the Council of Europe's Human Rights Commission.

The unsuccessful royal countercoup in December 1967 and subsequent exile of the royal family eliminated the last power element that could have been a problem for the junta. With the king out of the picture, Papadopoulos could tackle the army and purge the royalist establishment. Slowly but effectively he consolidated his position, and does not seem anxious to restore democracy, although the government nominally guarantees that democracy will be restored when Greeks show the necessary maturity. *(70)*

The events in Greece confronted the United States government with a real dilemma. Should it continue supporting an oppressive, authoritarian regime that made a mockery of democracy, or oppose the Athens junta with certain specific measures. From the beginning the Johnson administration expressed its displeasure with the new regime by imposing an embargo on all heavy weapons. This measure was intended to have a profound impact on the Greek army officers, who might be persuaded to overthrow the government.

With the Nixon administration, a slight change in attitude became discernible. Some policy makers were apparently urging the government to distinguish between the military and political aspects of U.S. policy toward Greece. The Pentagon and officials in the Defense Department argued that Greece's strategic importance to NATO was far more important than ideological and moral considerations, and that Greek heavy military equipment was becoming obsolete at a time when the Soviet Union was not only increasing its naval presence in the Mediterranean but was delivering up-to-date materiel to Bulgaria. *(71)*

The invasion of Czechoslovakia, the growing Soviet presence in the Mediterranean, and the lingering Middle East conflict compelled the Nixon administration to yield to Greek and Pentagon pressures. The embargo was

---

69  *Time*, 12 December 1969. Martial law was imposed on the entire country and had been only partially lifted by December 1971. It still covers the major cities.

70  Papadopoulos stated in December 1970 that he would not permit a return to normal political life until he decided the time was right. See *Le Monde*, 22 April 1972.

71  The Soviet Union shipped several hundered of their latest tanks to Bulgaria. The American-made M-47s and M-48s in the Greek arsenal were at least fifteen to twenty years old. However, 200 American tanks were blocked in the Italian port of Livorno following the Johnson administration's embargo. Those tanks cost $ 1,000,000 a year for storage, and had been sitting there since 1967. See *Time*, 21 September 1970.

limited and eventually lifted in September 1970. *(72)* The differentiation between military and political policies toward Greece became apparent when
Washington tried in vain to prevent its ally's suspension from the powerless but
prestigeous Council of Europe. The 1,200-page report of the European Commission of Human Rights clearly recorded the majority's disappointment at
the failure of the Greek junta to allow an early return to democratic rule. In a
final effort to change the Commission's decision, the Greek government
threatened an "agonizing reappraisal" of Greek defense expenditures within
NATO. Bluff or not, it did alarm Secretary of State William Rogers, who
warned the European NATO allies of the negative side effects of disciplinary
action against Greece. *(73)* Despite attempts to balance American national
interests with moral principles, the Nixon administration clearly demonstrated
the priority of strategic and balance-of-power considerations. Members of
Congress had criticized U.S. support of the Greek junta, but government
officials continued to argue that U.S. arms and military aid were not crucial
to the success of the present Greek government, since Papadopoulos could
always purchase the arms elsewhere. *(74)* Moreover, the Soviet naval expansion in the Mediterranean and Moscow's acquisition of bases in Egypt and
Syria had increased the strategic importance of Greece, which Washington
now regards as the key bastion of NATO's southern flank. *(75)*

Critics of Nixon's policies have argued that the U.S. government had the
power to force the restoration of democratic institutions in Greece. *(76)*
Senators Moose and Lowenstein determined that exchanges between Greece
and America had hardly been on an equal basis. Whatever the Greek govern-

72  The embargo on heavy equipment was apparently not paying off. As a means to pressure
the colonels into restoring democracy it obviously failed. Moreover, constant rumors in the
summer of 1970 said that Athens would purchase tanks, minesweepers, artillery, and other
military equipment in France on very favorable conditions. The delivery of small arms,
trucks, and helicopters had not been suspended. After the invasion of Czechoslovakia American military aid was stepped up, and included jet fighters (F 102, F 104, and F 5), minesweepers, and large quantities of ammunition, exactly what the colonels needed to keep the
country under firm control. See *Keesings Historisch Archief*, 12 February 1971, p. 105.
73  *Newsweek*, 22 December 1969.
74  *International Herald Tribune*, 17 April 1972.
75  The Greek-American agreement of 7 February 1972 on homeport facilities for the
Sixth Fleet in Pireus and the delivery of thirty-six Phantom jets were described by Pentagon
sources as a vital counterweight to the Soviet military presence. See *International Herald
Tribune*, 17 April 1972.
76  Senators James Lowenstein and Richard Moose investigated the Greek political situation on the request of Senator W. Fulbright, chairman of the Senate Foreign Relations Committee. See *Newsweek*, 3 May 1971.

ment obtained, it gave nothing in return. For example the U.S. ambassador in Athens, Tasca, informed Washington in the summer of 1970 that the Greek government was prepared to lift martial law if heavy arms shipments to Greece were resumed. The Nixon administration agreed and made $ 56 million in planes, tanks, and helicopters available over a two-year period. The deliveries were described as necessary for the Greek defense effort in the Atlantic alliance. *(77)* To the present day martial law remains in effect in major Greek cities. Any promises made have been broken. The United States has suffered a loss of prestige as the tacit supporter of the Greek military government. Moose and Lowenstein concluded that Athens has been able to pressure Washington more than that Washington has been able to pressure Athens. They labeled Nixon's policies a complete failure since they were contributing to the final consolidation of the military regime. *(78)* Congressional opposition reached a climax when the House voted to suspend the military aid to Greece for fiscal year 1971-1972. *(79)* This was the sternest warning to Athens and the president since the 1967 coup although its immediate impact was lessened by a special clause allowing the president a maximum of $ 70 million if aid to Athens proved vital to U.S. national security. *(80)* Congressional action at least showed that most politicians were concerned with the American image, already damaged in the Vietnam tragedy. As one *Newsweek* reporter observed, to many Americans "there is a vague but nonetheless disturbing parallel between Washington's acquiescence to the Greek junta and its earlier support for undemocratic governments in places like Saigon" *(81)*. The continuation of American aid to Greece may pay off in terms of defense, but in the long run it will damage the reputation of both the United States and NATO and completely erode the spirit of the preamble of the North Atlantic Treaty. But, as

77  *Ibid.*
78  *De Standaard*, 10 March 1971.
79  The House denied Greece the $ 118 million in military aid by a margin of 122 to 57 votes. See *Newsweek*, 16 August 1971. In october 1971 the Senate Foreign Relations Committee seconded the House resolution. See *Keesing Historisch Archief*, 5 November 1971, p. 712.
80  *Newsweek*, 16 August 1971. As a matter of fact, President Nixon used the national security clause in March 1972, when $ 72 million was made available for the Athens regime. In February 1973 the Greek government announced that it would no longer accept free American military aid. According to the minister of economic affairs, Koulis, Greece would pay for American military equipment. Diplomatic sources described this measure as primarily intended to counter congressional opposition in the U.S. Moreover, international prestige consideration certainly played a role, since Greece is the first country in the alliance to refuse American aid. See *De Standaard*, 17 January, 1973.
81  Quoted in *Newsweek*, 19 January 1970.

Sulzberger remarks, "policy making is a cold and calculated business where the national interest is the final criterion for the shaping of foreign policy." *(82)*


## B. TURKEY

## THE 1960 REVOLUTION AND ITS AFTERMATH

The members of the Atlantic alliance generally received the military coup in Turkey with mixed feelings. The leaders of the coup, especially the R.P.P., clearly promised a return to the Kemalist reforms as the first task of the new government. Some Western observers even speculated on a reversion to Atatürk's foreign policy directives and an eventual reconsideration of Turkey's participation in the Atlantic alliance. Another major concern for Turkey's allies was the prospect of permanent rule by a military dictatorship and the possible abrogation of democratic practice and institutions. As things turned out, however, the usual patterns of military rule were absent, and on the very day of the coup its leaders promised the restoration of democratic rule through free elections and civilian government. General Gürsel, chairman of the National Unity Committee as the junta was called dispelled rumors of disengagement and neutrality by declaring that Turkey would remain faithful to its commitments within NATO and CENTO. The core of his message read:

> We are loyal to all our alliances and undertakings. We believe in NATO and CENTO and we are faithful to them. We repeat: our ideal is peace at home, peace in the world. *(83)*

A copy of this message was immediately delivered to the American embassy in Ankara. Old suspicions of American intentions in Turkey were still very much alive among R.P.P. leaders, who now feared that the United States might prefer the permanent rule of the loyal military establishment rather than risk government instability under civilian rule. In an unusual public gesture General Inönü again assured Washington that "the foreign policy of Turkey had remained almost unchanged for many years; it is a national, bipartisan policy and the R.P.P. would observe its continuity. Therefore, there is nothing to worry about." *(84)* Within seventeen months the junta managed to fulfill its

---

*82* Sulzberger, *loc. cit.*, 311.
*83* Quoted in Weiker, *op. cit.*, p. 21.
*84* *Ulus*, 20 July 1961. Quoted in Ulman and Dekmeijian, *loc. cit.*, 775.

promises, and on 15 October 1961 elections leading to the first postwar coalition government were held. *(85)*

The junta's record on foreign policy shows no dramatic changes. In fact, international issues became secondary to the stabilization of the internal political situation. Hence, most scholars argue that the real change in the country's foreign policy became discernible only in the mid-sixties. Clearly, however, the profound change in the domestic political scene had a fundamental impact on the foreign policy-making process. The reconstruction of constitutional government and the free atmosphere after the coup completely altered the handling of foreign affairs. Since Atatürk's time foreign policy had been formulated by a small group of experts; the authoritarian Menderes regime allowed no public criticism of the government's policies. With the free atmosphere characterizing Turkish politics after 1960, foreign policy-making now entered interparty discussions, and for the first time in Turkish history a progressive, left-wing movement emerged which openly questioned Turkey's exclusive Western orientation.

The emergency of the Turkish left was a direct result of the internal political liberalization which permitted freedom of discussion and the expression of opinions highly critical of governmental policies. The parallel between the Greek E.D.A. party and the Turkish Labor party (T.L.P.) is remarkable, especially in the field of foreign affairs. *(86)* Since 1962 the party has openly advocated disengagement and a return to neutralism. They describe Turkey as a colony of the American imperialists saying that a one-sided foreign policy had led to the country's complete isolation.

Students and journalists often reiterated that the American aid program was merely a device to bring Turkey within an American hegemony, and in addition that American aid contained several conditions incompatible with national sovereignty. Turkey was the only member within the Atlantic alliance

---

85 The military leaders almost forced the R.P.P. and the newly-created Justice party into a coalition. They left no doubt about their preferences: a coalition government in which the R.P.P. would play a major role. Consequently, General Inönü became prime minister, while General Gürsel assumed the presidency after retiring from the army. See Hurewitz, *op. cit.*, p. 221.

86 Of course the parties, although similar in outlook, were not so in terms of time. Greece had had an extreme left since World War II. Turkey, on the other hand, had never experienced such a movement, although it had fostered a clandestine Communist party. The T.L.P. was founded in 1962, ten years after the Greek E.D.A. party, and consisted almost exclusively of young, leftist intellectuals. Only a small minority of trade union leaders joined the party's rank and file. Formal collaboration with the trade unions was almost nonexistent.

that had yet to seek a rapprochement with the Soviet Union and the Eastern bloc countries. Moreover, the country was lagging behind in the détente process because of its outspoken subservience to Washington. The leftists also criticized their government's identification of Turkish national interests with the global interests of Washington. The installation of American bases and nuclear missiles on Turkish soil was not only a flagrant violation of Turkish national sovereignty but, even worse, it made Turkey a first target in an East-West confrontation. In fact, the leftist argument made a great deal of sense, as the Cuban missile crisis amply demonstrated. When the Soviet Union linked the withdrawal of its I.R.B.M.s on Cuba with the removal of the American missiles in Turkey, many Turks realized that a decision made in Washington might jeopardize their country's safety or even existence. (87) This dramatic episode only gave more weight to the leftist argument, and a wave of public indignation and criticism spread over the country.

The new leadership gradually took account of the changes in the international environment and a more flexible and pluralistic approach to foreign policy slowly began replacing the exclusive, one-sided Western orientation. Differences at first were only slight, but the new emphasis on Turkish independence left no doubt about the country's changing foreign policy patterns. The military regime modified the traditional foreign policy by supporting the liberation movements in Africa and Asia. Its leaders indicated their interest in bettering relations with their traditional enemy, Russia, even to the extent of accepting Soviet economic aid offers. (88)

Difficulties with the United States also came to a head when the Kennedy administration introduced the flexible response instead of the massive retaliation concept into its defense strategy. In purely military terms, the two countries that make up NATO's southern flank could hardly be less defensible as an entity. Both Greece and Turkey can be attacked separately; except in Greek-Turkish Thrace the possibility of mutual support is rather marginal. Moreover, each country has specific geographic features which complicate its defense capabilities. As Mediterranean countries, they can be supported by available alliance seapower and tactical air support, but territorial operations, the most

---

87 Váli, *op. cit.*, p. 129.

88 Ulman and Dekmeijan, *loc. cit.*, 774. Interestingly even Menderes had considered the possibility of Soviet economic aid to overcome growing economic difficulties. In fact, he decided to visit Moscow but the 1960 coup changed his plans. The military government also took the unprecedented step of voting with the Afro-Asian bloc in the United Nations on the issue of Algeria's independence.

important in the forward strategy, remain an individual country effort. Further, Turkey's main defense line lies in the south where it faces Iraq and Syria, nations hostile toward Turkey since the Ottoman Empire. *(89)* Many intellectuals and party politicians pointed out that the adoption of the flexible response concept would not fit Turkey's strategic needs. They especially feared that Turkish territory might be traded for time in the case of a Soviet attack. *(90)* In other words, Anatolia might not be defended at all. If the NATO defense perimeter ran along the Zagros-Taurus mountain range, almost the entire country would be sacrificed at the very beginning of a conflict. This special strategic problem was emphasized by Retired Admiral Orkunt during our discussions in Ankara. He felt that NATO would apply the forward strategy only in Central Europe, while its wings would be considered expendable. If its northern and southeastern flanks were attacked, NATO would do nothing or very little. Its response would be limited to various diplomatic efforts or perhaps the sending of a token force. *(91)*

For the most part, difficulties between Turkey, the U.S., and NATO had involved only the attentive foreign policy elite. Now anti-American or anti-NATO sentiments began to appear in the Turkish press and in the speeches of leftist politicians, still without affecting the larger public. As a matter of fact,

---

*89* James V. Galloway, *"Nato's Southern Flank"* (unpublished paper, Harvard University, 1967), pp. 12,13, passim.

*90* Váli, *op. cit.*, p. 120.

*91* Some measures were suggested to overcome these difficulties. At first the allies thought that the American M.L.F. (multilateral force) proposals would calm the anxious Turks. After initially supporting the plan, the Turks suddenly withdrew their support. Another proposed a chain of atomic mines (atomic demolition munitions) along the Turkish-Soviet and Turkish-Bulgarian borders. The plan raised some interest, especially since the detonations would take place underground with almost no danger of fallout. The mines would remain under American control and the double-key veto system would guard against accidental use. The plan was eventually dropped since it required the evacuation of more than three million people and their livestock. Among the other reasons was that detonation had to be swift in order to be effective, but the decision to detonate could not be reached in the required time because U.S. law made a permanent delegation of authority to Turkish commanders impossible. Even if these weapons were purely defensive, their detonation might result in an all-out nuclear escalation. With the expansion of Soviet naval activity in the Mediterranean, the NATO council suggested creating a new integrated command with vessels from the U.S., Great Britain, and France. Greece and Turkey were also asked to assign some of their naval units periodically. This force would include about five aircraft carriers, five or six cruisers, and thirty to forty destroyers. It was expected that Greece and Turkey could not cooperate on a larger scale unless more financial assistance was forthcoming. For a time the Turkish government remained skeptical, then expressed its readiness to participate. See *ibid.*, pp. 121-122, passim.

the post-revolutionary governments pledged unequivocal allegiance to the Atlantic alliance. In 1963 Foreign Minister Cemal Erkin declared:

> Turkey was not and has never been the outpost of the East. Turkey has always been, and even more so today, the bastion of the West and the advanced guard of Europe against any danger threatening from the East. Mankind has reached the stage where it is impossible to adopt a neutral policy when faced with war and peace. Fear and the attempts to escape danger no longer help either to avoid the danger nor to maintain peace. *(92)*

Between 1960 and 1963, governmental foreign policy remained basically unchanged. Although friction existed between Turkey and NATO, the Turkish commitment to the West remained a total one. The appeal of neutralism, which was steadily growing in developing countries, apparently had no effect on the Turkish decision makers. The Turkish determination to remain a military partner of the West can only be explained by the threatening Soviet attitude after World War II. The long-standing, profound hostility between the two countries adds a more subjective factor perhaps as important as the Cold War experience. The traditional fear and aversion for Russia, whether Communist or czarist, is a permanent feature of the Turkish psychology and helps to explain Turkey's unconditional loyalty to the Atlantic alliance.

## THE CYPRUS PROBLEM
## AND ITS EFFECT ON NATO'S SOUTHERN FLANK

Until 1963 anti-American and anti-NATO feelings had been confined to a small but active left-wing minority represented in politics by the Turkish Labor party. The 1964 Cyprus crisis became the turning point in Turkish-American relations. Previous anti-American trends expanded suddenly, and the catalyst was President Johnson's undiplomatic letter to Prime Minister Inönü. Again the situation curiously parallels the 1956 developments in Greece. On both occasions an American diplomatic intervention triggered an anti-NATO and anti-American process until the public questioned further participation in the Western alliance.

In December 1963 Archbishop Makarios made a unilateral attempt to change the Cypriote constitution, and fighting erupted between the Greek and Turkish communities on the island. *(93)* In January 1964 Makarios announced

---

92  Quoted in Cabiaux, *loc. cit.*, 684.
93  Makarios had informed the Greek, Turkish, and British governments of certain desirable constitutional amendments. These provisions would have abrogated specific rights of the

the unconditional abrogation of the Zurich-London agreements, which was swiftly followed by the Turkish threat to invade the island. *(94)* The United States then proposed to send a NATO force to Cyprus, but in accordance with his policy of nonalignment Makarios categorically refused. The archbishop brought the case before the United Nations, indicating that he would accept a U.N. peace force on the island. The dispatch of 5,000 U.N. troops reduced the intensity of the fighting somewhat, but could not promote a solution to the problem. *(95)* Moreover, despite the U.N. presence, Greece and Turkey continued to supply their communities with arms. *(96)*

The Turkish government retaliated by expelling Greek citizens from Istanbul, and in August 1964 Turkish aircraft bombed Greek positions on Cyprus. Premier Inönü finally decided to intervene, and informed the NATO allies of his intentions. President Johnson sent him a letter very much in the nature of an ultimatum. The president's message reminded Turkey of its NATO obligations, which prohibited members from waging war on each other. Johnson also reiterated that Turkey needed Washington's consent to use arms for purposes other than those for which they were given. Johnson referred to the possibility of direct Soviet involvement, stating:

> I hope you will understand that your NATO allies have not had a chance to consider whether they have an obligation to protect Turkey against the Soviet Union if Turkey takes a step which results in Soviet intervention without the full consent and understanding of its NATO allies. *(97)*

In other words, Turkey's most trusted ally refused to intervene in a Soviet-Turkish confrontation which might follow a Turkish invasion of Cyprus.

American intervention resulted in the cancellation of the planned invasion, but the repercussions on Turco-American relations damaged them almost beyond repair. The Turks were disillusioned with their allies' neutrality; the American ultimatum wounded their pride. In a sense these factors "institutionalized for the first time a deep-seated anti-Americanism in Turkey." *(98)*

---

Turkish minority, and were consequently rejected by the Turkish government on the grounds that they constituted a violation of the 1959 Zurich-London agreements.

94   Turkey relied on Article IV of the Treaty of Guarantee, which gave the three guarantor powers the right to intervene when a violation of the agreements occured. See Váli, *op. cit.*, pp. 245-246.

95   *Ibid.*, p. 254.

96   At the same time a number of regular Greek forces infiltrated the island. General Grivas took over their command. Finally, Makarios ordered an economic blockade against the Turks. See *ibid.*, p. 255.

97   Quoted in *ibid.*, p. 130. Although the Johnson letter was not made public until 1966, most of it had already been leaked to the press.

98   Ulman and Dekmejian, *loc. cit.*, 778-779.

For the first time also Turkish public opinion, the press, and politicians expressed serious doubts about the value of the North Atlantic alliance. As in Greece a decade earlier, the feeling was that Turkey had been betrayed by its friends, and the issue of neutralism suddenly reached the realm of public discussion. Premier Inönü supposedly declared, "Our friends and our enemies have joined hands against us." *(99)* The Turkish press complained that Turkey had been among the first to join the U.S. in Korea; now they were the first to be abandoned. *(100)* The parallel between Greek and Turkish reactions is striking.

As discussed earlier, the Greeks resented a U.S. policy which purportedly favored Turkey because of its greater strategic importance. Turkey, on the other hand, resented the Americans' so-called neutral attitude, which in Turkish public opinion amounted to overt support of *enosis*. Moreover, Washington and NATO had done nothing to prevent the infiltration of thousands of Greek regular forces on Cyprus. *(101)* Ankara saw the United States as opposed to an independent Cyprus whose allegiance would be to Moscow rather than the West, while the Cypriote and Greek governments objected to the Turkish *taksim* or partition proposals. During the 1964 crisis the Turks had expected full support from Washington, assuming that Turkey was far more important to NATO than was Greece. After all, while Greece had refused to install nuclear missiles on its soil, Turkey had complied unconditionally with its allies' demands. They failed to realize, however, that their strategic importance had sharply declined once the U.S. had made its I.C.B.M.s operational. In fact, Turkey's obsolete Jupiter I.R.M.B.' had been withdrawn in 1962. In other words, Turkish bases were no longer necessary for the maintenance of the nuclear balance of power. *(102)* Ulman and Dekmeijan also indicate that the American economic leverage on Athens used at the time of the London-Zurich agreements, had substantially diminished once Greece became an associated member of the Common Market. This experience plus profound disillusion over U.S. and NATO policies led to a reconsideration of Turkey's relations with both the United States and NATO. In 1964-1965 the United States lost "that extra quality of unconditional loyalty from one of the few nations still disposed to offer it." *(103)*

---

99  *The Times*, 27 August 1964.
100  N. Eren, "Die Internationalen Positionen der Turkei", *Aussenpolitik* (October, 1965), 705.
101  The official access routes to the island are under Greek control. The number of Greek forces has been estimated between 2,000 and 5,000. See Váli, *op. cit.*, p. 255.
102  Ulman and Dekmeijan, *loc. cit.*, 777.
103  Claire Sterling, "Ankara: Inönü Looks Left", *The Reporter*, 9 September 1965, p. 18.

The most significant foreign policy reorientation was Ankara's rapproachement with the Soviet Union and the establishment of cordial relations with the Arab world. The government envisioned a many-sided, independent foreign-policy determined only by Turkish national interest. In practical terms, the new approach would result in four major foreign policy changes: (a) political rapprochement with the Communist world especially the Soviet Union; (b) better relations with the Arab Middle East; (c) closer relations with neutral countries; (d) more independence from NATO and the U.S. *(104)*

The détente in Soviet-Turkish relations was initiated by Turkish Foreign Minister Erkin's visit to Moscow in October 1964. *(105)* After almost twenty-five years of strained relations, both countries engaged in an active diplomatic exchange. *(106)* The Turkish overtures of friendship were directly linked with Turkey's frustrations over Cyprus. Moreover, the Turks rightly indicated that all the other NATO allies had responded to Moscow's peaceful coexistence policies, while Turkey had isolated itself as the Cold War warrior. Ankara also hoped to extract Soviet support in the Cyprus conflict, but most of all the reorientation of Turkish foreign policy was expected to have a profound impact on the West and on the U.S. in particular. *(107)* Finally, the reestablishment of

---

*104* Váli, *op. cit.*, p. 133.

105 This was the first Turkish official visit since 1939.

*106* After Foreign Minister Erkin's official visit to Moscow, the Soviet Union reciprocated by sending a delegation headed by President Podgorny. In May 1965 Soviet Foreign Minister A. Gromyko visited Ankara, where he held high-level talks with the new Turkish prime minister, Urgüplü, and President Gürsel. This was followed by Premier Urgüplü's visit to Moscow in August 1965, where he discussed policy matters with Premier Kosygin and Party Secretary Bresjnev. Finally, Soviet Premier Kosygin visited Turkey in January 1967.

*107* Soviet policies toward Cyprus have been ambivalent, even contradictory. However, there seems to be no doubt about the ultimate Soviet aims:

a) To exploit tensions on the island so as to exacerbate divisions within the Atlantic alliance. With Greece and Turkey on the verge of war, NATO's southern flank would slowly disintegrate.

b) To remove all Western influence on the island, especially the British military facilities.

c) To keep the conflict over the island alive in order to divert the attention of the NATO allies from other pressing problems.

Soviet policy toward Cyprus has included several tactical phases. As the Greek favored *enosis* solution gained favor in the United Nations and even in NATO circles, the Soviet leaders apparently reconsidered their position. Union with Greece had little value for the Kremlin. For one thing, it would have meant political suicide for the Cypriot Communist party (Akel). With the ouster of the liberal Papandreou government in Greece, the Soviet leaders apparently recognized that Turkish cooperation outweighed any advantages to be gained from an independent Cyprus and adopted a pro-Turkish attitude. See Adams and Cottrell, *op. cit.*, pp. 29-30, passim, and Sterling, *loc. cit.*, 19.

Soviet-Turkish relations ended an almost exclusive Western monopoly in the economic and cultural fields. In October 1964 the two countries signed an agreement in which the Soviet Union promised to increase its agricultural imports from Turkey, while Ankara would bring in more Soviet technical equipment. The document established a barter system whereby Turkish agricultural exports were traded for Soviet technical equipment. *(108)*

The most important point of the agreement, at least for Turkey, was the Soviet condemnation of *enosis*. According to the agreement, the Soviet Union supported the independence and territorial integrity of Cyprus. The Kremlin furthermore accepted the two-community proposal and stressed the importance of laws guaranteeing the legitimate rights of each community. Along with increased trade with the Soviet Union, the Turkish government had indicated on various occasions that it would seriously consider the possibility of Soviet economic aid. They were motivated not only by the more independent character of Turkish foreign policy but also by another factor. Since the early sixties American assistance programs to Turkey had decreased steadily; the Turkish government had no alternative but to look for additional sources to finance its development plans. *(109)* On the other hand, the Soviet Union seemed far less enthusiastic about offering economic help. In general, the Soviet Union provides loans over a period of twelve years with a 2.5 percent interest rate. By 1965 the Kremlin had given $ 1.4 million to various Middle Eastern states,

---

*108*  The exports and imports under this agreement have varied between $ 10 and $ 12 million annually. In terms of the total Turkish foreign trade figures, Turkish-Soviet trade represented 1 to 1.2 percent. See Eren, *loc. cit.*, 707. In 1968 the Soviet Union ranked fifth among Turkey's trading partners. First was West Germany with 20.4 percent of Turkey's imports and 17.4 of its exports. The United States was second with 15.8 percent of Turkey's exports and 14.6 of its imports. Great Britain was third and Italy fourth. See Váli, *op. cit.*, p. 332.

*109*  The following table suggests the sharp reduction in American economic aid:

| U.S. Fiscal Year | Total U.S. Economic Aid (in Millions of Dollars) |
|---|---|
| 1963 | 237.2 |
| 1964 | 148.8 |
| 1965 | 152.9 |
| 1966 | 126.6 |
| 1967 | 132.2 |
| 1968 | 135 |
| 1969 | 60. |
| 1970 | 43.5 |

Source: AID, *U.S. Overseas Loans and Grants*, 1 July 1945 - 30 June 1967. See also the *New York Times*, 13 January 1969 and 20 March 1970.

especially Egypt. The amount proved to be an overexpenditure, and various domestic projects had to be suspended. This explains the Soviet hesitation when faced with Turkish foreign aid demands. *(110)* When considering the Turkish viewpoint, one has to take into account the shaky condition of the Turkish economy. From 1962 to 1967 Turkey experienced permanent deficits in the trade balance ranging between $ 310 and $ 108 million. Moreover, Turkey was also obligated to make amortization and interest payments on its debts of over $ 100 million a year. The deficit on the balance of payments was met by loans and grants from the United States and the O.E.C.D. consortium. *(111)* In March 1967 the Soviet Union loaned their neighbor $ 200 million in the form of equipment, technical assistance, and material help for the construction of several industrial plants. The repayment consists of Turkish export deliveries and include tobacco, nuts, raisins, olive oil, and manufactured goods. *(112)*

The record of Turco-Soviet trade and Moscow's aid program is certainly not spectacular. Nevertheless, as Váli remarks, the new independent line in the economic field attracted much attention in Turkey and abroad and was a logical result of Ankara's new independent foreign policy. Turkish overtures to Moscow and the increased trade and aid should certainly not be exaggerated into evidence that Turkey is slowly slipping out of the Western camp. On the contrary, Soviet assistance represented less than four percent of the total Western economic and military assistance provided Turkey since 1950. *(113)* The country has no intention of loosening its economic contacts with the West. The best indication of this is Turkey's association with the European Economic Community (E.E.C.) and its expected full membership within a few decades.

The accord with Moscow turned out to be most fruitful as far as Cyprus was concerned. On several occasions Soviet leaders indicated that the two-

---

*110* Eren, *loc. cit.*, 708.

*111* Väli, *op. cit.*, p. 325. The balance of payments deficit was also partially met by the remittances of Turkish workers in Western Europe and tourist receipts.

*112* *Ibid.*, p. 333. Repayment must take place within fifteen years at an annual interest of 2.5 percent.

*113* A comparison of U.S. and U.S.S.R. aid to Turkey illustrates the insignificance of Soviet assistance (In Millions of Dollars).

| U.S. Economic Aid | | U.S.S.R. Economic Aid | |
|---|---|---|---|
| July 1945 - June 1965 | Percent of Total | 1954-1965 | Percent of Total |
| 2,279 | 5.1 | 210 | 4.2 |

Source: *New York Times*, 25 February 1965, and 13 November 1965.

community proposal was the consensus of both the Soviet Union and Turkey and that the Cyprus problem might best be solved through a federal arrangement allowing a high degree of autonomy to the Greek and Turkish communities. *(114)* Support for Turkish interests resulted in the abstention of the Communist bloc in the General Assembly in December 1965. *(115)* For the first time, centuries-old enemies had become allies.

An evaluation of the effects of the normalization of Turco-Soviet relations on Turkish participation in NATO should make a clear distinction between government policy and the measures advocated by a small, active left-wing elite with "considerable influence among the press, universities and students." *(116)* During President Podgorny's visit to Turkey in January 1965, the government publicly announced the withdrawal of support for the American-sponsored M.L.F. plan. Turkish officials described the plan as not of vital importance for Western defense, while its costs were too much for the Turkish economy. *(117)* Some observers have hinted that the Turkish decision was the price for Soviet support on Cyprus, although this was categorically denied in Ankara. *(118)* The Inönü and Urgüplü governments consistently reiterated that Turkey would remain a faithful ally of the West, respecting all obligations under the NATO treaty. Nevertheless, their tone had changed; the pursuance of a course more independent of the West would become a permanent feature of Turkish foreign policy.

Premier Demirel continued in this direction after the Justice party's electoral victory in 1965. Although foreign policy had not been a central issue during the campaign, the Turkish Labor party came out immediately with a strong anti-American and anti-NATO program. Since 1961 the T.L.P. had been the spokesman for a return to neutralism, angrily calling the U.S. "the source of all evils which had fallen on Turkey." *(119)* The political atmosphere certainly suited T.L.P. interests, for anti-American sentiments were exploited almost daily by leftist and extreme rightist groups. *(120)* But despite the favo-

---

114 For a more detailed analysis, see Adams and Cottrell, *op. cit.*, pp. 41-50.

115 The Communist bloc abstained on a pro-Greek Cypriot resolution which called on all members to "respect the sovereignty, unity, independence and territorial integrity of Cyprus and to refrain from any foreign intervention or interference". Adams and Cottrell, *op. cit.*, p. 44.

116 Váli, *op. cit.*, p. 143.

117 Turkey was to bear one percent of the total costs or $ 50,000. Váli, *op. cit.*, p. 121.

118 *New York Times*, 14 and 15 January 1965.

119 I. Giritli, "Turkey since the 1965 Elections", *The Middle East Journal* (Summer, 1969), 354.

120 The extreme right is basically xenophobic. They resent the presence of American

rable circumstances, the T.L.P. polled only three percent of the votes, earning fifteen elected deputies out of 450. There are a number of reasons for their poor showing; the identification of the party with Communism in this traditional anti-Russian country definitely hampered its progress. Most of its supporters belong to the small, urban, and leftist intellectual community, for whom the vast majority of the Turkish peasants produce no following whatsoever. Moreover, the interest of the average Turk in foreign affairs remains only marginal, leading Váli to conclude that "foreign affairs is still a stepchild of public opinion on politics." (121) The only public interested in the realm of foreign affairs seems to be the urban, left-wing minority, but its influence on official foreign policy-making seems to be more vocal than real. The failure to attract the Turkish workers and trade unions on the one hand and the conflicts within the T.L.P. leadership on the other indicates that the party's influence on domestic and foreign policy will continue to be marginal.

Following the Cyprus crisis of 1964 and the rise of anti-American and anti-NATO feelings, the American military presence became the target of public criticism. Most of the bilateral agreements regulating the status of American forces had been secret, and the opposition parties demanded their publication, revision, or abrogation. (122) The privileges enjoyed by the Americans were seen as an outright violation of Turkish sovereignty. (123) More than everything else, nationalism appeared to be the most powerful source of anti-Americanism, and the secret military agreements and exclusive American jurisdiction within the bases gave rise to memories of the old Ottoman Empire, so afflicted by economic and judicial servitudes. The American military presence had come under constant attack. Rumors that the U.S. owned and controlled the bases were widely believed despite constant denials by the Demirel government. Turkish leaders reiterated that the joint defense installations were state pro-

military and civilian personnel on Turkish soil. Although they support membership in NATO, they do so only for reasons of nationalism and anti-Communism. See Váli, op. cit., p. 104. Rumors in Turkey allege that the Soviet Union actually provides funds to the extreme right and left. Although evidence for these accusations is lacking, the growing political turmoil and governmental instability obviously suit Soviet interests.

121   Ibid., p. 100.

122   Ibid., p. 139.

123   Among the various accusations some are worthy of mention; opponents argued that although the U.S. had the right to occupy Turkey for security reasons, Turkey, like Korea and Vietnam, will be turned into a battleground whenever the U.S. decides to do so. The Americans use Turkish soil for espionage missions and reconnaissance flights over Soviet territory. For example, the now-famous U-2 flight of 1960 originated in Turkey. See ibid., p. 135.

perty under Turkish control. The American military could not use them against any foreign country without the consent of the Turkish government. *(124)* But the American presence had become too obvious; the privileges and incomparable high standard of living enjoyed by the American colony was a thorn in the side of the average Turk. In addition, some Turkish military leaders were convinced that Turkish soldiers and officers could perform the tasks now entrusted to foreigners. *(125)* Under constant pressure from the opposition parties and the press, the Demirel government took steps to revise the bilateral agreements. *(126)* Negotiations initiated in March 1966 for this purpose lasted for almost three years, clearly an indication of the difficulties surrounding this highly sensitive and complex issue. In January 1969 a new basic agreement was concluded. Its most specific features designated that:

(a) The joint defense installations were the property of the Turkish state. The establishment of new installations required the approval of the government.

(b) These installations were under the exclusive control of the Turkish government and Turkey has the right to station as many troops there as it considers necessary.

(c) The Turkish government must be informed of any increases, decreases, and replacements in American personnel.

(d) Non-Turkish personnel would continue to be subject to the provisions of the Status of Forces Agreement which was signed by Turkey in 1956. This agreement divided jurisdiction between the territorial authorities and national command authorities of the visiting forces. *(127)*

In July Turkish and American officials signed the new Cooperative Agreement concerning Joint Defense in Turkey. The document revised some bilateral arrangements, but its spirit based the American-Turkish defense effort on a mutual respect for the sovereignty and equal rights of both parties. It provided, for example, that Turkey could restrict the American utilization of bases in case of a national emergency, while American servicemen were also expected to observe and respect Turkish laws. *(128)* The successful conclusion of this

---

124   *Ibid.*, p. 138.

125   The Turkish military did ask for a greater operational control of the joint installations and a larger share in the facilities, such as housing, hangars, and runways. See *New York Times*, 28 March, 1966.

126   Some of the agreements signed during the Menderes era were lost in the confusion that followed the 1960 coup.

127   Váli, *op. cit.*, pp. 139-140. However, a serviceman committing an offense while on duty was no longer automatically removed from Turkish jurisdiction, as had previously been the case.

128   *Ibid.*, p. 141. In February 1970, Premier Demirel pointed out that the joint defense installations are under the joint control of Turkish and NATO authorities, and that the U.S.

important agreement was generally acclaimed by the moderate segment of Turkish public opinion, but it had no effect on the militant leftist elite. *(129)* An interesting corollary to the normalization of U.S.-Turkish relations was the agreement to begin a gradual withdrawal of American servicemen. In spite of Pentagon insistence on the need for a certain level of American troops for Western defense, their number gradually decreased from 10,000 to about 6,000 men in 1970. *(130)*

In 1966 Premier Demirel firmly refused to send a Turkish contingent to Vietnam despite a formal request by U.S. Undersecretary of Defense McNaughton. *(131)* Actually, American policies in Vietnam were an additional factor in increasing anti-Americanism, and the left exploited America's entanglement in Southeast Asia on every occasion. Similarly, the Turkish government refused passage into the Black Sea of American destroyers equipped with weapons that did not fall specifically under the Montreux Convention, although it had previously been quite liberal in its interpretation of the 1936 standards. Again history can help explain present behavior. Turkey's limitations on American vessels are undoubtedly connected with the fact that Turkey's participation in World War I resulted directly from the bombardment of the Russian Black Sea by two German warships. In 1970 the Turkish government allowed the Soviet Union to transport arms and equipment to Syria.

forces could engage in activity only after having informed the Turkish government of its intentions. *Ibid.*, note.

129 On various occasions American soldiers were harassed by left-wing demonstrators, and four servicemen were kidnapped in 1971. In 1969 American sailors were thrown into the sea when a unit of the U.S. Sixth Fleet paid a customary visit to Istanbul. These outbursts of violence were publicly condemned by Prime Minister Demirel, who warned that the government would not allow Turkish foreign policy to be governed in the street. Moreover, both the extreme left and rightist groups have made American actions the target of their criticism. Undoubtedly some accusations were justified but some stories of American behavior have been exaggerated or invented. For instance, some blamed the United States for the failure of Turkish heart transplants because Washington deliberately prevents the development of medicine in the country by drawing away Turkish doctors. American wheat deliveries were described as an attempt to poison the Turkish nation. A Turkish columnist with a sense of humor even remarked that "they [the extremists] would blame the U.S. if a meteor fell here and try to associate it with the American satellites". See Giritli, *loc. cit.*, 354 and Váli, *op. cit.*, pp. 141-143, *passim*.

130 Several American-controlled bases were handed over to the Turkish authorities in 1968, as were radar stations along the Black Sea and the communication base in Gölbaçi, south of Ankara. By 1 July 1970 all U.S. bases and facilities in Turkey, with the exception of the air base at Incirlik near Adana, had been returned. See *Britannica, Book of the Year, 1971* (Chicago, 1971), p. 774.

131 Ulman and Dekmeijan, *loc. cit.*, 780.

Trucks loaded with Soviet weapons and supplies crossed Turkish territory. *(132)*

The essential change in Turkey's foreign policy since 1964 has been one of emphasis. The Menderes government had almost taken it for granted that Turkish, American, and NATO interests were identical. In the sixties NATO was no longer regarded as an end in itself. Whenever NATO arrangements clashed with Turkish interests, Ankara would not hesitate to say so. This was amply demonstrated during the 1967 Arab-Israeli confrontation. The possibility of Arab support on Cyprus prohibited any actions that might arouse Arab hostility, and Turkey adopted a position of nonalignment in the United Nations. *(133)*

The independent foreign policy pursued by the Inönü, Urgüplü, and Demirel governments did not lead, as many intellectuals and leftists perhaps hoped, to disengagement or neutralism. Government foreign policy remained basically pro-Western and pro-NATO and Ankara worked to minimize the importance of anti-American and anti-NATO sentiments, saying that they were only the expression of a small minority. *(134)* The official Turkish-American relations remained cordial and the government left no doubt about Turkey's continued allegiance to NATO. Premier Demirel declared in the National Assembly that:

> The desire to reinforce our security within a collective framework led us to join the NATO Alliance. We consider our alliance with NATO as manifestation of the identity of fate among the countries embracing freedom and democratic ideals... Besides the security aspects of the NATO alliance I should like to stress the additional uses of NATO, the contribution it makes to our defense power and economy. *(135)*

The invasion of Czechoslovakia by the Warsaw Pact forces in 1968 marked a definite turning point in the nationwide debate over Turkey's prolonged participation in NATO. For months the press, politicians, and intellectuals had been analyzing the implications of a possible return to neutrality. *(136)*

---

*132* J.C. Campbell, "The Soviet Union and the United States in the Middle East", *The Annals* (May, 1972), 132.

*133* *Ibid.*, p. 784. The nonaligned option was adopted to avoid alienating either the U.S. or the Soviet Union.

*134* This may be correct, as Sulzberger remarks. On the other hand, forty-two percent of Turkey's population is fifteen years of age or less, and these youngsters are under the constant influence of radical leftist teachers and professors. This may eventually produce a generation far from friendly with the U.S. and the West in general. See Sulzberger, "Too Much of an Ally", *Outlook*, 21 August 1968.

*135* Quoted in Váli, *op. cit.*, p. 125, note.

*136* In 1969 NATO members were scheduled to decide whether they should continue their participation in NATO.

General Inönü's outright support for Demirel's foreign policy plus its growing bipartisan nature decided the issue of Turkey's continued participation in the alliance. Inönü pointed out that Turkey's experiences during and after the second world war made Ataturk's nonalignment policy impossible. He recommended that Turkey remain an official ally of the West without neglecting its new friendship with the Soviet Union. His conclusion was reinforced after the Czeck invasion. "We have examined the NATO agreement and announced our stand. The recent Czeck events have shown how correct this stand was." *(137)* Professor Erim, one of the party's foreign policy experts, evaluated the R.P.P. position on neutralism this way:

> Turkey will follow a western-oriented policy as Atatürk showed. Turkey's legislation and state organization are proof of Western civilization. Turkey is a country which is striving to be Western and taking her place in the front ranks of Western civilization. Today there are countries which appear at first glance to be outside the blocs, but in reality there is no such country as a neutralist one. Here we have Egypt... Today she is under the control of Russian technicians, Russian experts, Russian money. This shows that the Third World countries have to choose one of the blocs in the first serious clash. *(138)*

The Soviet Union's brutal use of force in a country which was a formal ally raised second thoughts among those who had been wavering between Western alignment and neutralism. *(139)* The events of August 1968 were for the vast majority of politicians and journalists proof that Turkey, with its exposed geographical position, still needed NATO protection. One newspaper illustrated its pro-American and pro-government position as follows:

> The propaganda made by the Soviets at the expense of millions of rubles fell to dust in a night. Oh, masquerades of independence who pretend it to be a violation of our honor and dignity when the sailors of the sixth fleet stroll with prostitutes, look well with your

---

*137* Quoted in *ibid.*, p. 83.

*138* *Ibid.*, p. 86. The R.P.P. had undergone a significant change in the late sixties in accepting a left-of-center program. The alteration was almost exclusively related to domestic affairs (economic development and social justice) and was not expected to have serious repercussions on the party's foreign-policy line. Inönü has been extremely cautious in his approval of the leftist orientation. Others disagreed and left to found the Reliance party. Although some R.P.P. leaders have on occasion flirted with neutralism, the official party line seems in accordance with government foreign policy. *Ibid.*, pp. 82-87. In May 1972 basic disagreements between Inönü and Bulent Ecevit, leader of the left-wing faction in the R.P.P., could no longer be suppressed. During an extraordinary party congress, Ecevit was elected as the new party leader. Consequently, Inönü resigned, and various rightist dissidents left the R.P.P. to form the Republican party. See *Keesing Historisch Archief*, 13 October 1972, p. 664.

*139* Aware of the traditional anti-Russian feelings in Turkey, even the T.L.P. considered it necessary to condemn the Soviet invasion. They claimed that Turkish socialism would be liberal and benevolent. See Giritli, *loc. cit.*, 357.

eyes! When the Soviets move in, the place of the prostitutes will be taken by your mothers, wives, and sisters. *(140)*

The bipartisan nature of foreign policy proved that the handling of foreign affairs was no longer the monopoly of the ruling party. General Inönü's pro-NATO stand was probably more decisive in undermining the neutralist appeal than most of the government's arguments. Interestingly, the reaction of the Demirel administration to the invasion was far less outspoken than one might have expected. Official statements by the premier and Foreign Minister Çağlayangil deplored the Czeck events without once mentioning the Soviet Union. On the other hand, even at the risk of jeopardizing recent improvements in Turco-Soviet relations, the Turkish government stressed once again the necessity of the NATO and CENTO alliances. President Sunay referred to Czechoslovakia when he denounced those who labeled Turkey a mere U.S. satellite:

> To consider those commitments incompatible with national sovereignty, national dignity and interests, and to regard them as having caused Turkey to fall into the satellite-ship of other states is a mistaken view. The latest developments have proved once again the necessity for and usefulness of our alliances. *(141)*

In analyzing the debate on a possible withdrawal from NATO, we must distinguish clearly between the objective and balanced inquiries of a number of scholars and politicians and the biased, highly prejudiced literature of the extreme left. As we discussed in the first chapter, a number of compelling factors left Turkey no alternative to an exclusive alliance with the West, and with the U.S. in particular. The international political environment of the late forties had undergone dramatic changes and the bipolar world pattern of the 1950s gradually evolved into a multipolar political system. Polycentrism both in the East and the West made it possible for various smaller states to enjoy a degree of maneuvrability in foreign relations. These objective changes prompted Turkey's active rapprochement with the Soviet Union, although disillusion over the allied handling of the Cyprus problem was certainly the determining factor. Moreover, a look at the factors that forced Turkey into alignment with the West shows that at least some of them were losing their importance. Fear of the Soviet Union had been the overriding alignment factor. But Soviet policies had changed and the reestablishment of cordial relations eventually eroded the importance of the security factor. Alignment with the West also accelerated the democratization of internal Turkish politics, resulting in a high margin of

140  Váli, *op. cit.*, p. 105.
141  Quoted in *ibid.*, p. 136.

governmental stability. However, association with the United States in the contemporary world has become a contributing factor to internal turmoil and unrest, with negative repercussions on internal political stability. Economic and military aid was perhaps as important as security considerations once, but the exclusive economic dependence on the West has also been undermined by the trade and aid agreements with the Soviet Union. Ideologically Atatürk's Turkey had always belonged to the West despite his refusal to align his country militarily. In short, a neutral Turkey would be as much a Western Turkey as a Turkey entrenched in the Atlantic alliance.

In view of the changes in the internal and external environment, various scholars and party politicians embarked on painstaking research to determine whether the alignment factors were still as important as they had been. What would Turkey gain or lose if it broke its military ties with the West? Professor Ülman determined that Turkey would gain by leaving NATO. He argues that the Turkish economic development effort is seriously hampered by the high defense expenditures an oversized army necessitates. *(142)* Ülman's conclusion contains certain valid points. The armed forces expanded after the 1960 coup and military expenditures rose at a more rapid rate. Compared with the government's investment in development, the defense expenditures since 1960 were higher than in the 1956 to 1960 period, and the Turkish armed forces were consuming national resources faster than during the Menderes era. *(143)* Table VII illustrates the jump both in force levels and defense expenditures after the military coup. Ülman describes the Soviet threat as no longer of a military nature. Rather it is political and subversive, and the best defense against this menace lies in a firm program of economic and social reforms instead of an oversized army. As a member of NATO, Turkey would be dragged into a war whether it was the victim of an aggression or not. Moreover, if the Soviet Union attacked, Turkey would receive Western support even without formal military ties. Vital interests in the Eastern Mediterranean and the Middle East would leave the

---

*142* In 1968 Turkey alloted 4.3 percent of its $ 280 per capita national income to the armed forces, which in fact means $ 12 per annum for every citizen. In the same year, military expenditures represented 18.4 percent of the national budget. Half of Turkey's military expenditures were covered by military assistance programs from various NATO countries. The United States military aid to Turkey totaled $ 2,520 million to 1968. Interestingly, West Germany has been steadily increasing its military aid to Turkey, while American aid was reduced to $ 75 million in 1971. German military assistance varied between $ 15 and $ 25 million per annum. See *ibid.*, pp. 123-124, passim.

*143* Hurewitz, *Middle East Politics: The Military Dimension*, pp. 225-226.

## TABLE VII

Turkey: Force Levels, Government Expenditures, and G.N.P., 1956-1966.

*Government Expenditures (Millions of Turkish Lira)*

| | Population (Millions) | Force Levels (Thousands) | Defense (including International Security and Justice) | Development | Total | G.N.P. (in Millions of Lira) | Defense Expenditures (as Percent of G.N.P.) |
|---|---|---|---|---|---|---|---|
| 1956 | 24.8 | 400,000 | 1,074 | 920 | 3,444 | 24,330 | 4.4 |
| 1957 | 25.5 | | 1,273 | 1,240 | 4,144 | 30,530 | 4.2 |
| 1958 | 26.3 | | 1,313 | 1,300 | 4,627 | 38,510 | 3.4 |
| 1959 | 27.0 | | 1,600 | 1,725 | 6,232 | 47,730 | 3.4 |
| 1960 | 27.8 | 400,000 | 1,844 | 2,350 | 7,640 | 50,970 | 3.7 |
| 1961 | 28.5 | | 2,800 | 2,358 | 9,035 | 53,720 | 5.2 |
| 1962 | 29.3 | | 3,288 | 2,247 | 10,468 | 60,300 | 5.5 |
| 1963 | 30.0 | | 3,667 | 2,835 | 12,563 | 68,490 | 5.4 |
| 1964 | 30.7 | | 3,813 | 3,246 | 14,021 | 74,198 | 5.1 |
| 1965 | 31.4 | 480,000 | 3,997 | 3,479 | 15,195 | 79,687 | 5.0 |

Sources: *U.N. Yearbook of National Account Statistics; U.N. Statistical Yearbook;*
AID, *Summary of Basic Data; Turkey;* OECD, *Economic Surveys; Turkey.*

West no alternative but to intervene on Turkey's behalf. In a nuclear confrontation Turkey would be among the first targets of Soviet retaliation because of the tactical nuclear weapons and radar installations on its territory. Given all these factors, Ülman concludes that Turkey would benefit by withdrawing from NATO. *(144)*

Another scholar from Ankara University, Professor Azmaoglu, suggests that Turkey's relations with the United States and NATO should become a secondary priority. The current policy of influence should be transformed into a flexible alliance based on common values instead of material interest, ridding Turkey of the unilateral dependence on American military and economic aid. *(145)* While he does not advocate withdrawal from NATO, he recommends a transformation of the Atlantic alliance into a true collective partnership:

> We sincerely believe that military ties between Turkey and the United States should develop within the framework of the collective partnership of NATO, not within the narrow limits of bilateral relations. On the other hand, we strongly oppose the complete elimination of bilateral military relations with the United States. *(146)*

Analyzing the same problem, Retired Admiral Sezai Orkunt writes in a series of articles that Turkish withdrawal from NATO would be advantageous both internally as well as externally. The disengagement from the United States would reduce the internal unrest fostered by the American economic and military presence. Turkish anxieties about exposure to Soviet nuclear retaliation would also subside with the removal of the strategic and tactical nuclear weapons. Neutrality would do away with Turkish resentment of dependency on the United States or any other nation. Finally, a neutral Turkey would not be pulled into war or a regional conflict.

In the admiral's view, these benefits did not outweigh the disadvantages to Turkey's economic and military well-being in leaving the alliance. First, Turkey would be deprived of large amounts of economic aid. This would kill the successful implementation of the second and third five-year plans. *(147)*

---

144  Váli, *op. cit.*, pp. 158-159, passim.
145  *Ibid.*, p. 158.
146  Quoted in *ibid.*
147  The second five year plan (1968-1972) was based on a seven percent growth rate of G.N.P. while Turkish imports and exports were to be increased by fifty and forty percent. The deficit on the balance of trade was expected to be met by the so-called invisible exports: growing tourist receipts and remittances from Turkish workers in Western Europe. Faced with a chronic balance of payments deficit, the objectives of the second five-year plan could only be realized if loans and grants were forthcoming. In other words, foreign aid was vital for the realization of the various development targets. Through the five-year plans (1963-1967, 1968-1972, 1973-1977) the Turkish government hoped to achieve a level of self-sufficiency

Disengagement would lead to the complete military isolation of Turkey, while the regional balance of power would be seriously affected by Greece's continued enjoyment of military support. The dismantling of American bases and installations would leave many Turks unemployed. Moreover, if Turkey were deprived of multilateral or bilateral military aid the Turkish army would have to be contracted, weakening Turkey's position in relation to Greece. Orkunt predicted that this prospect alone would precipitate an immediate reaction from the Turkish military. Finally, the Soviet Union would in one way or another try to exploit these disadvantages. In the end, the Russians would be the sole beneficiary of Turkey's withdrawal from the Atlantic alliance. On only one condition would Orkunt advise a Turkish withdrawal from NATO. If the forward strategy was not applied on NATO's southern wing and if the allies proposed to send only a token force, the Turkish government should seriously consider a neutral foreign policy. *(148)*

The report of the Republican People's party on Turkey's continued participation in NATO was very similar to Orkunt's evaluation. Turkey would suffer most in the economic and military fields, tipping the regional balance of power in favor of Greece. The connecting link between NATO and CENTO would disappear, to the advantage of the Soviet Union. The R.P.P. concluded that Turkey had no alternative but to remain a member of NATO, although it saw that a radical revision of the nation's international obligations was necessary. *(149)*

The government's evaluation of the situation was elaborated in several

while raising the Turkish economy from the developing stage to the industrial level. The corollary of this ambitious economic development program was the unavoidable dependence on foreign economic assistance, which the Turks realistically accept as a necessary evil. However, the long-range goal is to reach the stage where foreign aid on special terms is no longer needed. A sharp reduction in the American and O.E.C.D. foreign-aid programs would ruin the economic development program, especially in view of the insignificant Soviet assistance. Between 1962 and 1968, aid under the O.E.C.D. consortium amounted to $ 1,139,150. American economic assistance to Turkey, although decreasing since 1964, totaled the astronomical figure of $ 2,531.2 million in December 1968. The decreasing American economic aid is to some extent countered by the growing West German assistance.

148 *Ibid.*, pp. 159-160, passim, and information gathered during a personal interview.

149 These revisions, according to Váli, were almost identical with Admiral Orkunt's recommendations. Both Orkunt and the R.P.P. suggested that strategic nuclear weapons should be removed from Turkish territory and the use of tactical nuclear weapons entrusted to the Turkish military command. The NATO headquarters in Izmir should be removed and the Turkish forces placed under the Southern Europe Command in Italy. The R.P.P. leaders favored a radical change in Turkey's military structure in order to safeguard the country's national interest. This was of course an indirect reference to NATO's inability to solve problems or disputes between members. See *ibid.*, pp. 160-161, passim.

newspaper articles by Foreign Minister Çağlayangil. He pointed out that NATO had been conceived primarily as a defensive arrangement and as such had contributed to peace in Western Europe. He refused to believe the thesis of many revisionists who suggest that NATO is an obstacle to a real détente. NATO, he said, has been the most important instrument in the actual balance of power, and he warned those who for various reasons had been advocating fundamental changes in Turkey's foreign policy:

> To tie her security to the strongest safeguards, in the geopolitical situation she finds herself, is a matter of life and death for Turkey. In seeking its security, every country should use its judgement in the light of political and military realities by discarding sentimentalism, preconceptions, and academic speculations. The basic principle for this judgement should be not to leave national security, as much as possible, to chance. *(150)*

According to the foreign minister, the opponents of NATO underestimate the political and military realities their nation faces. The military factor indicates Turkey's weakness when faced with a potential aggressor, and although he did not name the Soviet Union, the thread of his argument leaves no doubt about the identity of the enemy. Turkey originally had sought its security through NATO because of this weakness, and the consideration remains valid. A return to neutralism would seriously impair either the work of economic development or the military effort, since Turkey is not in a position to have guns and butter at the same time:

> Another reality is that Turkey would have to make very big sacrifices, cutting down her development effort, if she wished to maintain her defense power alone. It is common knowledge that many countries following a neutralist policy feel the necessity of devoting a much greater slice of their national income to military expenses than does Turkey. *(151)*

The minister admitted that as a member of NATO Turkey had to make certain sacrifices, but he estimated that Turkey's burden sharing was not excessive.

> Turkey maintains a force of 15 divisions for the purposes of her NATO membership. Turkey's present level of armed forces is based on her needs as found after survey's and calculations. The dominating view holds that Turkey would have to increase and not reduce her forces should we have to leave NATO. *(152)*

150  *Ibid.*, p. 162.
151  Quoted in *ibid.*
152  Quoted in *ibid.* In 1970 the strength of Turkish armed forces was as follows:

| Army (Thousands) | Navy (Th.) | Air Force (Th.) | Submarines | Cruisers | Destroyers[s] Frigates | Total Ships |
|---|---|---|---|---|---|---|
| 390.0 | 37.0 | 50.0 | 10 | – | 10 | 20 |

| Fighter-Bombers | Fighters | Defense Expenditure as Percentage of G.N.P. |
|---|---|---|
| 100 | 180 | 4.6 |

Source: *Britannica, Book of the Year 1971, op. cit.*, p. 249.

The minister denied that NATO had relegated Turkey to a satellite of the U.S. On the contrary, Turkey pursued "her own national goals according to her own determination." *(153)* Foreign Minister Çağlayangil concluded his analysis:

> The Alliance aims today at creating an atmosphere conducive to easing political tension and to solving conflicts, all this in addition to the achievement of collective security. No matter what some people might say, peace is being safeguarded in Europe, thanks to the balance of power provided by the Alliance. *(154)*

A comparison of the various pro-NATO arguments leads us to conclude that neutrality would only benefit the Soviet Union, who would probably not hesitate to exploit Turkey's isolated position. National security and economic development remain the most powerful arguments for remaining an ally of the West. Regardless of the recent Turco-Soviet rapprochement, the Turks will always remain suspicious of the real intentions of the Soviet Union. *(155)* Ankara watches closely the growing Soviet presence in the Mediterranean and the Arab Middle East and the prospect of being sandwiched in by "this military power in her vicinity" remains the final argument for Turkey's place in the Atlantic alliance. *(156)*

## THE SOVIET NAVAL PRESENCE IN THE MEDITERRANEAN

The massive increase of Soviet naval power in the Mediterranean occured after the Six-Day War in June 1967. In May 1967 nine destroyers patrolled the area. During the short Arab-Israeli war Soviet naval strength rose to two cruisers, fifteen destroyers, twelve submarines, and fifteen auxiliaries. By July 1971 the Soviet fleet had increased to over fifty ships. The West naturally

---

153 Quoted in Váli, *op. cit.*, p. 162.
154 *Ibid.*, p. 163.
155 In spite of the stern measures taken by the Demirel, Erim, and Melen government toward the extreme left, Turco-Soviet relations were apparently not affected. The rapprochement between Moscow and Ankara continued, and even led to a joint declaration regarding the "principles of good neighborship". According to the *Neue Zürcher Zeitung*, the declaration was more or less a substitute for the Treaty of Friendship denounced by Stalin in 1945. As a matter of fact, the Soviet Union has officially proposed a treaty of friendship and cooperation. Trade between the two countries continued to rise, and totalled $ 80 million in 1971 as opposed to $ 15 million in 1964. See *Neue Zürcher Zeitung*, 25 April 1972, and *Keesing Historisch Archief*, 13 October 1972.
156 The sandwich position refers to the possibility of a Soviet attack on Turkey's northern and southern frontiers. The exposure of Turkey's southern border following the Soviet naval build-up in the Mediterranean is a matter of much anxiety in Turkey.

## The Soviet Naval Presence in the Mediterranean

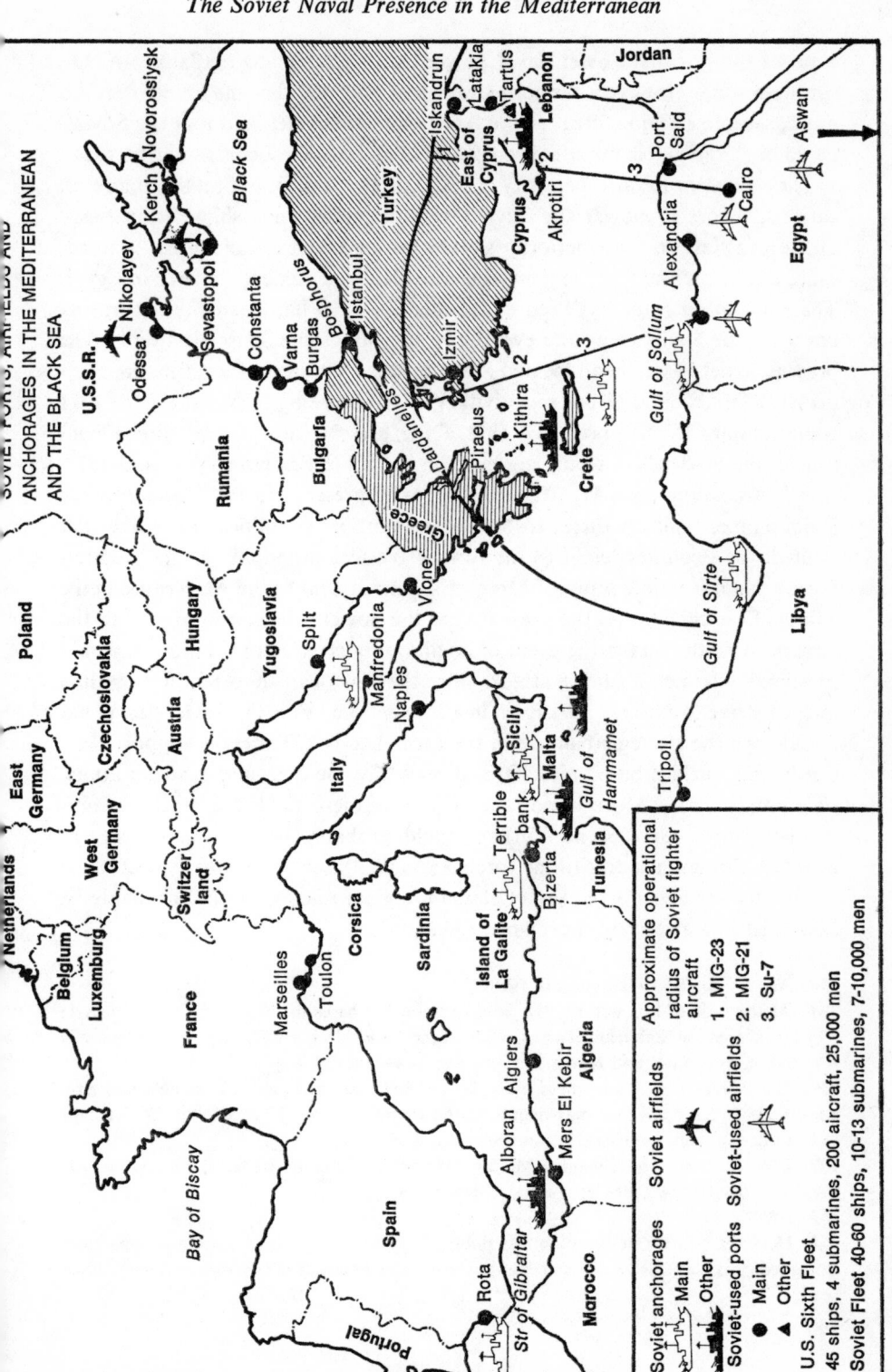

assesses the growing Soviet naval power as an attempt to outflank NATO's southern wing. However, Western strategists indicated that the Soviet fleet did not constitute a major threat to the American Sixth Fleet, and that the Soviets could be eliminated in minutes in the event of an East-West confrontation. *(157)*

Their claim to naval superiority is based on the American fleet's two aircraft carriers, whose firepower the Soviets cannot match on a ship-to-ship basis. However, Western air superiority should not be taken too much for granted, especially in the wake of the newly-installed Russian tactical air force in Egypt. The Russian air force has been entrenched into 200 hardened sites. It can fly cover for the Soviet ships and eventually also attack the Sixth Fleet units. The present Soviet bases are all located in the Eastern Mediterranean; their location explains Turkish and Greek sensitivity. *(158)* According to *Newsweek*, in 1971 some military experts predicted that if the present rate of deployment continued, the Soviet fleet would surpass the Sixth Fleet in potency by mid-1972. *(159)* According to L.W. Martin, the Soviet presence in the Mediterranean is not a direct military threat to NATO. Its purpose is political and somewhat limited. As a counterweight to the former Western monopoly in the Mediterranean Sea it is visible proof of Moscow's commitment to the Arab cause in the Middle East conflict. At the present time the Soviet fleet is still inferior to the American Sixth Fleet in the event of an all-out nuclear confrontation. It would presumably launch a suicide attack, since the American ships retain a residual nuclear strike capacity. *(160)* Even in a conventional war, the Soviet fleet could not change the strategic balance in the area. The NATO fleet is supported by Greek and Turkish-based aircraft, and probably could repulse a Soviet attack successfully. *(161)* More important on the southern flank are massive Communist armies. Greece and Turkey would probably be overrun by the far superior Communist territorial forces. Should this happen, the Soviet ships in the Mediterranean would only play a marginal role and would probably be destroyed in a relatively short time. *(162)*

157  *New York Times*, 11 February 1969.
158  At the time of this writing, the Soviet Union has bases in Syria and Egypt. In Syria they are located in Latakia and Tartus, south of the Turkish border. The bases in Egypt are in Alexandria, Port Said, and Mersa Matruh. See *Newsweek*, 19 July 1971.
159  *Ibid.*, 1971. This prediction is based on the fact that the Soviet Union now possesses guided-missile cruisers which may neutralize the aircraft carriers. Moreover, the Soviet ships seem to be far more modern compared with the U.S. ships.
160  L.W. Martin, "The Changing Military Balance", J.C. Hurewitz (ed.), *Soviet-American Rivalry in the Middle East* (New York, 1969), p. 64.
161  *Ibid.*
162  However, Martin's evaluation was published in 1969. The Soviet Union is apparently embarked on a painstaking drive to change the balance of power in the Mediterranean. Even

Although the Soviet naval presence serves a political and psychological objective, its political effects on NATO's southern wing should not be minimized. As a matter of fact, the conflict between Greece and Turkey over Cyprus has resulted in a fragmented NATO command structure. Greece and Turkey stand virtually alone, and the presence of Soviet ships has only accentuated their isolation. Both countries feel they are being gradually encircled; more importantly, they fear abandonment in case of an attack on the southern flank. At the roots of their uncertainty is the creeping atmosphere of détente and NATO's acceptance of the flexible response strategy. *(163)* One result of these feelings has been improved relations with Moscow. *(164)* The Soviet presence in the Mediterranean is no doubt part of a long-range strategy to cut off the Middle East, with its vast oil resources, from the West. What puzzles the Turkish leadership most are the Soviet arguments justifying their presence in the Mediterranean. The Kremlin argued:

> Our state, which is, as known, a Black Sea and consequently also a Mediterranean power, could not remain indifferent to the intrigues of those fond of military ventures organized directly adjacent to the borders of the U.S.S.R. and other socialist countries. No one can be allowed to turn the Mediterranean into a breeding ground of a war that could plunge mankind into the abyss of a worldwide nuclear missile catastrophe. The presence of Soviet vessels in the Mediterranean serves this lofty, noble aim. *(165)*

On another occasion a Soviet party newspaper said:

> Soviet ships entered the sea on the strength of the U.S.S.R.'s sovereign right to make free use of the open sea... As a Black Sea and, in this sense, a Mediterranean power, it is closely connected with all problems involving the interests of the peoples of this area of Europe, Africa and Asia. It is directly interested in insuring the security of its southern borders. *(166)*

This is the argument that raises second thoughts among the Turkish leaders when they begin speculating on the longe-range intentions of the Soviet Union. It means that Moscow considers the eastern Mediterranean its first line of defense. Under Soviet naval pressure to the north and to the south, Turkey

---

more important, it seems to me, is the present trend of neo-isolationism in the United States. In 1970 two American air force squadrons were pulled out of Europe; the European allies were not even forewarned of their departure. Moreover, the prospects of détente have created a climate in the West favoring a unilateral reduction of NATO forces. The gradual American disengagement and Western Europe's inability to offer a credible countervailing force may in fact mean that things will continue to go Moscow's way. See *Newsweek*, 19 July 1971.

163 Martin, *op. cit.*, p. 64.
164 *Newsweek*, 19 July 1971.
165 Quoted in Váli, *op. cit.*, p. 215.
166 Quoted in *ibid*.

could easily be surrounded. Although a direct Soviet-American confrontation seems remote, the entire Mediterranean area is prone to conflict. Its small area keeps in close proximity a number of heterogeneous and divisive peoples hostile to each other for centuries. Not only is the Arab-Israeli conflict unsettled, the even older enmity between Greece and Turkey, dramatized in the struggle over Cyprus, adds tension to the areas. The independence of Cyprus has been guaranteed by U.N. peace-keeping forces and a tacit U.S.-Soviet understanding that political union with Greece is out of the question. But the possibility of a local conflict, which could easily escalate into a confrontation between the two superpowers, cannot be excluded. *(167)* The increased Soviet presence has convinced many Turks that Moscow will one day reopen the issue of the straits. Váli says that Turks are constantly reminding the West that they "know the Soviets." *(168)* He remarks:

> They [the Turks] are aware of the realism of Soviet strategical thinking, their strong geopolitical approach to international affairs and... their belief in the necessity of con-tiguous land power. Under such circumstances it appears inconceivable that Moscow should feel anything but unhappy about being dependent on Turkey's control of the "umbilical cord" leading to its navy far out in the Mediterranean. *(169)*

Such considerations raise the question of whether the Soviet Union is really trustworthy. The Turks feel that their survival depends on a correct evaluation of this question. Relations with the Soviet Union are the only foreign policy issue where even the smallest risk may lead to a disaster. Moscow holds the key to neutrality in Turkey. As long as "the clouds in Soviet Turkish relations are not dispelled", Turkey seems to have no other alternative but the West in order to safeguard its national security and independence. *(170)*

---

*167* *The Jerusalem Post*, 25 April 1972.

*168* Váli, *op. cit.*, p. 216.

*169* *Ibid*.

*170* The recent developments in Turkey are not basically related to foreign policy and do not affect the relevance of the strategic and military evaluation. However, the similarities with the pre-1967 situation in Greece are striking. The growing political unrest and the ap-parent inability of the Demirel government to check the activities of leftist and rightist forces triggered the intervention of the Turkish military establishment. On March 12 Premier Demirel was forced to resign. In a memorandum signed by the chief of staff, General Tagmac, and the commanders of the army, navy, and air force, the military requested the formation of a government of national unity. On 19 March 1971, a new government was formed with Nihat Erim (R.P.P.) as prime minister. On April 26, the Erim government proclaimed martial law in eleven of the sixty-seven Turkish provinces, justifying this measure by pinpointing several antigovernment groups: an extreme right-wing Muslim organization apparently fomenting an atmosphere which might lead to a civil war; extreme leftist and Maoist move-ments purporting to break down the vested social and economic order; several separatist movements, for example, the Kurds and an Arab separatist group, supported by Iraq and Syria respectively. The attacks reached a climax when the Marxist Turkish Labor party and the extreme right National Order party were dissolved by the constitutional court The T.L.P. was accused of supporting separatist movements and the leading party members were arrested and imprisoned. Especially, although not exclusively, the leftist intellectual community became the victim of the government's purification campaign.

See *Nieuwe Rotterdamse Courant*, 20 March 1971, *Neue Zürcher Zeitung*, 2 October 1971, and *Keesing Historisch Archief*, 4 February 1972.

# CONCLUSION

The alignment process in Greece and Turkey contains striking similarities as well as various differences. After World War II both countries became spearheads of U.S. containment policy. American intervention through the Truman Doctrine determined the final victory of the Greek government forces in the civil war and prevented the absorption of the small Balkan country into the Soviet orbit. Internal and external Communist threats were without doubt the overriding factors leading to Greek alliance with the major Western powers, particularly the United States. A strong and subversive Communist movement was nonexistent in Turkey; on the other hand, the external Soviet danger was very real.

Although the Truman Doctrine did not constitute a formal alliance, it definitely institutionalized various economic and military ties between the two Mediterranean countries and the United States. For Greece, a close alliance was not a fundamental change in Greek foreign policy; bonds with the West and Great Britain in particular were traditional. The Turkish-American affiliation diverged sharply from Ankara's previous position of neutrality. The huge amounts of military and economic aid the U.S. offered its allies under the Truman Doctrine and the Marshall Plan were clearly designed to undercut the Communist appeal. To the Americans, political stability and economic recovery were prerequisites for a successful defense against the infiltration of Marxist ideology. In furthering these objectives both Greece and Turkey had to live with certain curtailments of their national sovereignty, especially in the economic field. Neither government seemed overly sensitive to these limitations, however, and the prospect of financial and military aid was definitely an incentive to encourage an American friendship.

The ideological factor was more visible in Turkey. The Turks' traditional emnity with Russia became a vigilant anti-Communism. Moreover, the democratization of Turkish society was accelerated as a result of alignment with the West. Neither Greece nor Turkey was among NATO's founding members. Although this was so for several reasons, it seems ironic, even contradictory, that the keystones of Washington's containment policy were absent from an organization meant to check the Soviet Union in the struggle of the immediate postwar years.

Nevertheless, the Truman Doctrine made Greece and Turkey America's allies. Both countries were certainly within the limits of the American defense perimeter. NATO was to offer little more in terms of security; it was the formalization of a *de facto* security guarantee. International prestige and the advantages of a multilateral structure more likely explain the two nations' determination to become full-fledged members of the North Atlantic alliance.

The Menderes administration's international policies synchronized perfectly with whatever the United States thought to be NATO interest. It accepted the presence of a large colony of American servicemen without hesitation, and was among the first to station middle-range nuclear missiles on its soil. Although Ankara received less military aid than Athens, the Turkish defense effort remained high. At least until 1956, Greece followed a similar course. The Papagos government accepted an American military presence and showed no reticence in accepting the limitations that accompanied it. American interventions in Greek internal affairs were numerous; occasionally foreign aid became an instrument in achieving American objectives. The center and conservative parties enjoyed a high level of agreement in their perception of NATO's advantages, and only the leftist and quasi-Communist E.D.A. party constantly attacked every aspect of Greek-American relationship. E.D.A. favored non-alignment and closer ties with the Communist countries.

The repercussions of the 1956 Cyprus crisis were particularly strong in Greece. Anti-American sentiments appeared for the first time since the Truman Doctrine. A wide range of foreign policy alternatives were suggested, including leaving NATO and formulating a neutral policy. Tendencies toward non-alignment were discernible in almost every Greek political party, although the conservative government categorically ruled them out. However, the events of 1956 led to a more independent, pragmatic, and versatile Greek foreign-policy, amply demonstrated by Karamanlis's refusal to station nuclear weapons in Greece.

An analogous development occured in Turkey during the mid-1960s; again Cyprus was the direct cause. Now the Turks were particularly outraged by a tactless and inappropriate action by the U.S. president, Lyndon Johnson. The most dramatic consequence of the change was Turkey's rapprochement with the Soviet Union and the East European countries. Rumors predicting that Turkey was leaving the Western bloc were certainly exaggerated, but the swiftness of Ankara's move baffled many observers. In fact, Turkey was merely doing what all other NATO countries had done, ameliorating its relations with the Soviet Union in a spirit of détente. The old suspicions about Moscow's ultimate intentions remain, but they could not be allowed to hinder the cultivation of normal relations with the Soviet Union.

Actually, the record of Soviet-Turkish trade and Soviet economic aid is modest, and there seems to be no sign that the situation will alter soon. The invasion of Czechoslovakia by the Warsaw Pact and the steadily growing Soviet presence in the Mediterranean were an indication, at least to the Turkish government, that the ultimate Soviet objectives remained unchanged. Moreover, the appearance of extreme leftist and rightist forces has recently led to stern and oppressive governmental measures. The Erim and Melen governments are cracking down on the leftist movement, and the Turkish Constitutional Court ordered the dissolution of the Turkish Labor Party on the grounds that it constituted a threat to national unity.

After the election victory of George Papandreou, Greece entered an era of liberalism which generated certain centrifugal forces. The Papandreou government was often very critical of U.S. policies, but it never contemplated leaving NATO, even though some leftist politicians from the Center Union actually advocated a policy of nonalignment. Papandreou s fall and King Constantine's direct intervention in internal politics paved the way for social unrest and growing political unstability. The 1967 coup and the military dictatorship that followed were certainly nothing new in the history of modern Greece. Proclaiming themselves strong NATO supporters, the colonels slowly but effectively consolidated their power. Some of their various stronger measures, such as dissolving the E.D.A. and attacking the left, are apparently being repeated in Turkey. As long as the military rulers remain in power, Greece's leaving NATO seems a remote possibility. However, if the majority of the Greeks decide that NATO and the U.S. have been instrumental in keeping a despised regime in power, a return to a democratic form of government might trigger a repudiation of Greece's continuance in the Atlantic alliance. Various indications show that Turkey is gradually following the Greek example. At this point NATO seems to be among the factors creating political and social instability in Turkey. Whether Turkey will end up as Greece has done remains an open question, but the available evidence tends toward a rather pessimistic conclusion.

# Part III

# DENMARK, NORWAY, AND ICELAND

By Herman De Fraye

# INTRODUCTION

An analysis of the security policies of Norway, Denmark, and Iceland would be incomplete if it failed to take into account the larger Scandinavian framework. The Scandinavian members of NATO cannot be studied as isolated countries. With Sweden and Finland, they constitute a whole bound together by geography, history, language, culture, and politics. To be sure, the widespread sense of Scandinavian solidarity has not precluded these countries' finding different solutions to their economic and security problems. This does not mean, however, that Scandinavian unity is an unattainable dream to which politicians pay only lip service. On the contrary, attempts for joint Scandinavian solutions to major problems have consistently been supported by a consensus both of the political leadership and of the public at large. For example, a fruitless attempt to conclude a Scandinavian defense pact was made in 1948-1949, and the idea resurfaced in the mid-sixties when the Atlantic crisis developed. If these joint Scandinavian solutions have failed to materialize, it is not for lack of popular support, but because the Scandinavian area to date has seemed too inadequate a power base to offer viable solutions to these pressing problems.

This study of the alignment policies of Norway, Denmark, and Iceland, then, while discussing the individual historical, geographic, and strategic situations of these countries, will at the same time continuously refer to the larger Scandinavian context. Only thus can the defense policies of these countries be understood and their membership in the Atlantic alliance properly evaluated.

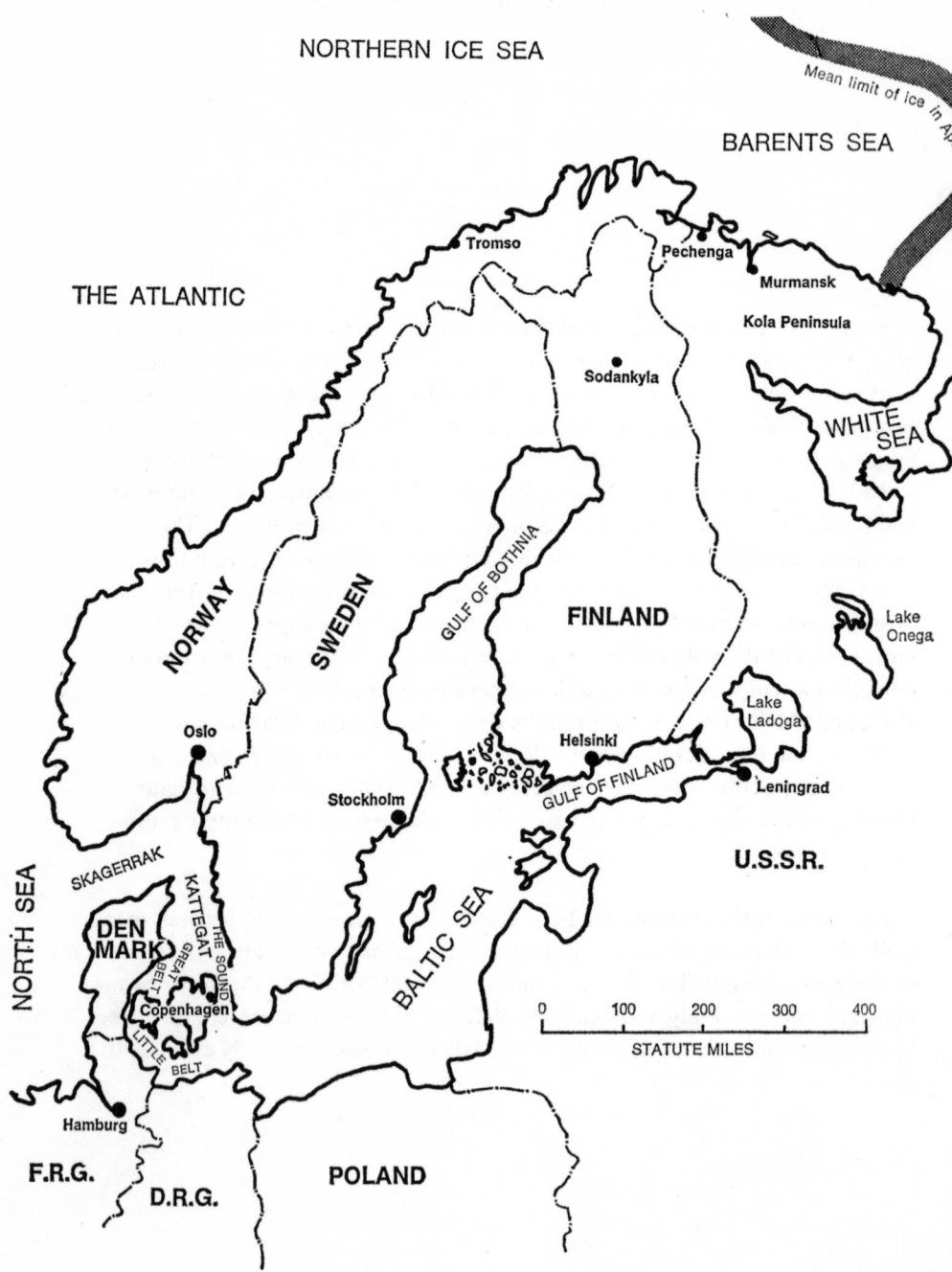

NORTHERN ICE SEA

Mean limit of ice in April

BARENTS SEA

THE ATLANTIC

Tromso

Pechenga

Murmansk

Kola Peninsula

Sodankyla

WHITE SEA

NORWAY

SWEDEN

GULF OF BOTHNIA

FINLAND

Lake Onega

Lake Ladoga

Oslo

Helsinki

Stockholm

GULF OF FINLAND

Leningrad

SKAGERRAK

U.S.S.R.

NORTH SEA

KATTEGAT

THE SOUND

GREAT BELT

DEN MARK

BALTIC SEA

LITTLE BELT

Copenhagen

| 0 | 100 | 200 | 300 | 400 |

STATUTE MILES

Hamburg

F.R.G.

D.R.G.

POLAND

# Chapter I

# DENMARK, NORWAY, AND ICELAND IN THE POSTWAR WORLD

## THE WARTIME EXPERIENCE OF THE SCANDINAVIAN COUNTRIES

The Scandinavian states emerged from World War II with their commitment to the concept of neutrality effectively shattered. Different security needs, plus certain unresolved psychological and territorial issues, had prevented them from joining efforts against the growing menace from Nazi Germany. Norway and Finland still harbored bitter memories of Swedish rule, Norway and Denmark disputed the title to eastern Greenland, and Sweden and Finland contested the status of the Aaland Islands. *(1)*

During the 1930s, there had been talk of a Scandinavian defense agreement, but it came to nothing because "the Scandinavian nations could not agree upon a common enemy: the Finns feared Russia, and the Danes feared Germany; the Swedes could not make up their mind which they ought to fear; the Norwegians believed themselves to be safe from both." *(2)*

German troops invading Denmark and Norway on 9 April 1940, found both countries almost completely defenseless. Denmark surrendered immediately, and only eight German divisions were able to clear Norway of all organized resistance in less than two months. The Scandinavians' failure to oppose the invading forces was due less to geographical accident *(3)* than to the prewar political climate prevailing in their countries.

In Denmark, the political posture was one of watchful noninvolvement. Since its crushing military defeat at the hands of the Prussians in 1864, Denmark had followed a strict policy of neutrality, continuously aware of its stra-

---

1 N.J. Padelford, "Regional Cooperation in Scandinavia", *International Organization*, XI (Autumn, 1957), 599.
2 M. Jakobson, *Finnish Neutrality* (London, 1968), 8.
3 Although Denmark is a flat, open, and ill-defensible land, this is by no means the case with Norway, a "very elongated and extremely rugged country, whose major population centers are located on its deeply indented coastline." J.A. Bassett, "The Invasion of Norway. An Example of Extended Strategy", *Military Review*, XXXIX (October, 1949), 3.

tegic position at the mouth of the Baltic Sea and its proximity to Germany. J.R. Wilkinson points out that in fact Denmark had no real alternative to such a position: the country could hardly rely on its own resources for defense, and, more important, prior to 1940 no other country offered to help "in view of the impossibility of the Danish position being guaranteed by any power other than Germany." (4)

After World War I Norway saw the creation of the League of Nations as a valuable supplement to an ongoing policy of neutrality. However, the League's inability to take effective action in the Ethiopian affair prompted the country to withdraw from its obligation to the organization's covenant in 1936 and revert to its prewar policy of strict neutrality. By the late 1930s the Norwegians could see the war approaching, but they assumed that, as before, a successful balancing of the economic and military demands of Germany and of England would keep them out of hostilities. Their inability to do so led to German invasion and occupation.

The second world war found England weak militarily, and in an attempt to strengthen its position, that nation initiated the economic blockade of Germany that had proved so successful during World War I. "Norway", Annette Baker-Fox says, "played a leading role in the initial stages of the Allies' economic warfare for many reasons, most notably because the Leads seemed the easiest place to stop the crucially important iron ore from reaching Germany." (5) Since the Germans believed this iron ore vital to their armament industry, keeping the British out of Norway was of the utmost importance to them. Likewise, control of the Danish Straits was the only way for Germany to prevent British interference with its Baltic shipping routes.

Purely strategic considerations were of even greater importance. Critics of German World War I naval strategy had suggested that one of the reasons Germany lost the war was its adherence to a "continental strategy", assigning only defensive tasks to the German navy instead of "allowing it to operate offensively on the high seas from positions in Denmark and Norway." (6) Although naval circles had pressured Hitler to adopt an offensive naval strategy, only when Allied demands upon the Norwegians -- first for control of Norway's overseas trade and the use of her merchant marine, later for the transit of an

---

4  J.R. Wilkinson, "Denmark and NATO: The Problem of a Small State in a Collective Security System", *International Organization*, X (August, 1956), 391.

5  A. Baker-Fox, *The Power of Small States; Diplomacy in World War II* (Chicago, 1959), 84. The Leads is the waterway between the Norwegian coast and a range of coastal islands through which Swedish iron was transported when the Baltic was frozen.

6  J.A. Bassett, *loc. cit.*, 9.

expeditionary force to Finland -- raised the spectre of Allied control over Scandinavia did Hitler decide to move. *(7)* In fact, an Allied military presence in Scandinavia would have endangered the German thrust to the Low Countries and France, and would have given them a favorable strategic position on the northern flank of Germany. To circumvent these dangers, the Germans attacked, marking the end of a century of neutrality for Norway and Denmark.

Ironically, the Allies made substantial demands on the Norwegians but took little action to support them, whereas the Germans' surprise attack was preceded only by minimal demands. The German success thus was diplomatic as well as military. In asking little, the Germans focused Norway's resistance on the more burdensome British demands, even though Great Britain had always been the ultimate guarantor of Norway's neutrality. After the German attack, British and a few French troops did take part in a counteroffensive, but they were too few and too late to be of any real help. Before their withdrawal on 9 June 1940, they succeeded only in reconquering Narvik.

And while some fighting continued in Norway, British forces landed in Iceland. Their action here was preventive; had the Germans seized the island, they would have gained a significant strategic advantage in the control of the North Atlantic sea routes. Although British occupation violated the permanent neutrality of Iceland established by the 1918 Act of Union with Denmark, and although the Icelandic government formally protested the action, both the population and the government apparently were pleased that their occupiers were British rather than German. *(8)* British intervention and a growing realization of their important location forced many Icelanders to rethink their concept of neutrality. Indeed, the prospective withdrawal of British forces to defend England against an expected German invasion motivated the conclusion of a defense agreement between the United States and Iceland on 1 July 1941 which provided for the stationing of U.S. forces on the island for the duration of the hostilities.

President Franklin D. Roosevelt discussed the agreement with Iceland in Congress on 7 July 1941, and his statement implies that the new alliance was made in the same spirit as the so-called destroyer-bases deal of a year earlier. At that time, the U.S. obtained ninety-nine year leases on naval and air bases on British territory in the West Indies, New Foundland, and Bermuda in

---

7 The British had begun mining Norwegian waters prior to the German attack. However, some argue that Germany had prepared its invasion before the "British violation of Norwegian neutrality". N. Andrén, *Power Blance and Non-Alignment. A Perspective on Swedish Foreign Policy* (Stockholm, 1967), 30.

8 D.E. Neuchterlein, *Iceland: Reluctant Ally* (Ithaca, 1961), 24.

exchange for fifty outmoded destroyers. The aim was twofold: to provide materiel for the British war effort and at the same time to help secure the Western Hemisphere. Although Iceland is not strictly a part of the Western Hemisphere as defined by the Monroe Doctrine, it could easily have served as an advance air and naval base for an attack there if it were under German control. Roosevelt outlined the threat as threefold: against Greenland and the northern portion of the North American continent, against all shipping in the North Atlantic, and against the steady flow of munitions to Britain. *(9)*

The Americans had already taken steps to secure the Western Hemisphere by signing an agreement on the defense of Greenland in Washington on 9 April 1941.

A complete picture of the situation in the North Atlantic at the beginning of World War II requires a word about Finland and Sweden. Like Norway and Denmark, Sweden had managed to stay out of World War I, and as a result had become a strong believer in the virtues of neutrality. Trust in the League of Nations, an increased sense of security due to the changed power structure in the Baltic, and the antimilitarist feeling of the Liberal-Socialist majority led the country to all but dismantle its defense apparatus in the 1920s. Yet in the mid-thirties the Germans' feverish rearmament program forced a reorganization of Sweden's defense. Whether Sweden managed to avoid the hostilities of World War II because it was militarily well prepared or because the Germans had little strategic interest in the country remains unclear. Probably a mixture of both saved Swedish neutrality.

Finland's situation was quite different. Since the time of Peter the Great, Finland's major political problem has been its relationship with Russia. After the former gained independence in 1917, mutual suspicion characterized their relations. Finland was afraid that the Soviet Union might attempt to recover the territories lost following its October Revolution. After Allied intervention in the Civil War, the U.S.S.R. feared that Finland once again might serve Germany or the Western powers as a base for an attack on Russia.

During the interwar period, the Finns wavered in their defense policy. In 1922 they signed a treaty of alliance with Poland and the Baltic states, but Parliament failed to ratify the treaty for fear that Finland would become involved in the French security system. After that date, Finland gradually adop-

---

9 Message of the President (Roosevelt) to the Congress, 7 July 1941, *Documents on American Foreign Relations*, Vol. IV, July 1941 - June 1942, ed. by L.M. Goodrich (Boston, 1942), 457-458.

ted a policy of neutrality and in 1935 associated itself with the Nordic group. *(10)*

As war grew imminent, the Soviets took a series of precautionary measures to increase their defensive strength. Particularly aware of the vulnerability of Leningrad, they asked the Finns to cede part of the Karelian Isthmus in exchange for some territory farther north. They also demanded the lease of the Hanko Peninsula for the establishment of a naval base. When the Finns rejected their ultimatum, the Soviets attacked on 30 November 1939. After initial successes the Finns where overwhelmed by the opposing forces, and yielded to Soviet demands in the Treaty of Moscow of March 1940. When the Germans attacked the U.S.S.R. the Finns joined them, hoping to recover the territories lost in the Treaty of Moscow. *(11)*

In this second Finnish-Soviet war, the so-called War of Continuation, the Finns fought as a cobelligerent, rather than an ally of Germany. This meant a refusal to participate in military actions that served only the Germans, for instance, the attacks on Murmansk and Leningrad. The Finns' status as a cobelligerent was honored both by the United States, which did not declare war upon them, and the Soviet Union, which negotiated an armistice in September 1944 instead of requiring an unconditional surrender. The peace treaty of 1947 confirmed and even increased Finland's 1941 territorial losses *(12)* and imposed a war idemnity of some $ 300 million to be paid over an eight-year period.

Its two consecutive defeats cost the Finns some 100,000 men (out of a population of 4,000,000) and one tenth of their territory. In analyzing these losses they concluded that Scandinavian cooperation had failed to provide security; the Western powers to whom they had appealed had proved incapable of extending their power to the eastern shores of the Baltic, and both the Germans in 1939 and the Western powers at Yalta had assigned their territory to the Soviet sphere of influence. These factors led to a reappraisal of Finland's foreign policy and to the adoption of the so-called Paasikivi line of friendly relations with the U.S.S.R.

---

*10* J.M. Jansson, "La neutralité Finlandaise. Ses Perspectives Européennes", *Politique Etrangère*, XXXVI (April, 1971), 363. See also Jakobson, *op. cit.*, 12-32.

*11* In addition to the loss of part of the Karelian Isthmus and the lease of the Hanko naval base, Finland also lost additional land north of Lake Ladoga and at the Arctic coast. The Soviet Union acquired a common frontier with Norway as a result of these transfers.

*12* One of the provisions of the 1944 armistice stipulated the lease of the naval base of Porkkala, near Helsinki, to the Soviets for a period of fifty years. The base was returned to the Finns in 1955 in exchange for a twenty-year extension of the Treaty of Friendship, Cooperation, and Mutual Assistance that Stalin had forced on them in 1948.

## NATIONAL INTEREST AND FOREIGN POLICY OBJECTIVES

World War II proved once again that small states can remain neutral only when their geographic location and their relationship to the larger powers around them are favorable. However, such a condition is often precarious. Small countries on the periphery of Europe, away from the center of conflicts, have sometimes succeeded in avoiding localized wars, but are often swept into hostilities on a continental or intercontinental arena in spite of a professed neutrality. As Denmark and Iceland in 1940, small countries were invaded and occupied not so much because they were of vital interest in themselves but because their aggressor sought to preempt its adversaries. Thus for the small nations of Europe the traditional concern has been twofold. First, they have worked to maintain a favorable, or at least a nonantagonistic relationship with the regional larger neighbor; if this proves impossible they try to insure that this potentially dangerous neighbor is checked by other powers operating on a larger scale than the regional one, either by tacit understanding or by a formal alliance. This is, of course, a two-edged sword. The security such an alliance may provide often means that the smaller member risks involvement in a conflict in which its interests are not at stake. Moreover, the sources of danger are not always readily apparent. This is illustrated by the dilemma which confronted the Norwegians in 1940. Should they enter an alliance with Germany to avoid pressing British demands, or ally themselves with the British against Germany, whom they did not see as imminently dangerous? As it was, by remaining neutral they laid their country open to invasion from either side, providing a premium to whichever might strike first.

A more favorable solution for the security problem of small states is of course a world order in which threatening and powerful neighbors can be dealt with not by compliance or an equally powerful counterbloc but by an international community that sets the norms of behavior and has the power to enforce them. Logically, therefore, efforts toward that goal are given first priority in the ongoing foreign policies of the Scandinavian countries. International organizations such as the League of Nations and the United Nations have always found active support there. It is probably significant that Norway and Sweden each provided one of the four secretaries general the U.N. has had to date, and that Scandinavian countries regularly make available personnel and equipment for the U.N. peace-keeping operations.

Concomitant with this universalist dimension of Scandinavian foreign policy stands a regionalist tendency which seeks to further Nordic cooperation and integration. This attitude expresses the strong "ties of ethnographic and cultural kinship" *(13)* which exist among these peoples, reinforced by common historical experience and a common body of social, commercial, and civil law. Until 1952, consultation and cooperation occured informally but in that year an intergovernmental body, the Nordic Council, was established. Its major task was to coordinate and centralize whatever cooperation then existed and to act as an advisory body to the governments on new proposals.

Although the list of measures aimed at integrating the Scandinavian countries is quite impressive, Scandinavian cooperation failed "on the great political-economic issues." *(14)* Negotiations for a Nordic Defense Union and a Scandinavian Common Market were both superseded by those for the North Atlantic Treaty Organization and the European Economic Community. "These failures", S. Henningsen writes, "seem to indicate that there have been and are limits to the scope of Scandinavian cooperation. Those limitations are the results of basic differences of interests and national approaches. It seems clear that since 1945 purely Scandinavian answers to the wider European and world issues are too narrow. Twenty million people and the Scandinavian resources are an insufficient basis for solving decisive military and economic problems." *(15)*

It may seem paradoxal that the deeply-felt sense of unity among the Scandinavian countries could successfully produce common policies in such matters as social security, education, and labor migration, and fail in such political concerns as defense. The forces which tend to make the rich and successful Sweden the focal point of any Scandinavian grouping are offset by equally strong economic, historical and defense-policy circumstances which tend to separate these countries on important issues.

Finland's delicate position as neighbor to the powerful and oversuspicious Russia leaves the smaller nation little room to maneuver; the Soviets tend to view cooperation with the other Scandinavian countries or with the rest of the Western world as a threat to a sensitive and vital interest zone. Finnish leaders now realize that the Soviet government had never found Finnish neutrality credible; on the contrary the U.S.S.R. continually feared that Finnish territory might be used as a base for German or Western aggression. Clearly mistaking cause for effect, the Soviets must have felt that their demands in 1939 were justified in the light of Finland's subsequent alignment with Germany. Under these circumstances, Finland's foreign policy must achieve a minimum level of

---

13  N. Padelford, *op. cit.*, 597.
14  S. Henningsen, "The Foreign Policy of Denmark", *Foreign Policy in a World of Change*, ed. J.E. Black and K.W. Thomsen (New York, 1963), 31.
15  *Ibid.*

Soviet trust to avoid complete satellization. Any cooperation with the West with political overtones likely to marr this trust must be ruled out.

Sweden is probably the country which most easily serves as a core area for the Scandinavian region, (16) and historically it has made some efforts in that direction, as has Denmark. However, two losses in power confrontations against Russia between 1700 and 1721, and 1788 and 1790 forced Sweden to settle for much less than big power status. With all of their former possessions but Finland gone, the Swedes blundered into the Napoleonic Wars and in 1809 lost Finland as well. In 1814 the acquisition of Norway compensated for that loss. From that date onward, Sweden has followed a highly successful policy of neutrality, and though, like the other Nordic countries, it has shown strong loyalties to the whole of Scandinavia this commitment has not altered the fact that national security problems have always received top priority. Since Sweden has no reason to fear any of her Scandinavian neighbors and is buffered from non-Nordic countries by the Baltic Sea and by Finland, neutrality has consistently proved the most successful line of defense.

Unique in the area for over a century Denmark has given strongest considabove-ration to Scandinavian regionalism. (17) This emphasis on Scandinavian unity dates back to the 1850s and 1860s when Denmark appealed to its neighbors for assistance in the face of the expanding and increasingly-menacing German states. In the 1864 war with Prussia for the possession of Schleswig and Holstein, help failed to materialize, and the end of the hostilities marked the beginning of Danish neutrality. Unlike Sweden, however, Denmark was not surrounded by friendly Scandinavian countries, nor was its population large enough to make armed neutrality credible. In its attempts to balance its own delicate position against the weight of Germany, Denmark continued to look north for help. This "search for Northern allies led the Danes to author almost every proposal for increased Scandinavian collaboration made in the last hundred years." (18)

In addition to the Nordic dimension, which reflects direct involvement with continental and, more specifically, German affairs, Danish foreign policy has a distinctly maritime aspect. Its political style and institutions as well as the traditional importance of the British market for its agricultural exports has brought Denmark closer to the United Kingdom than to the countries of the continent. (19) An appeal to Anglo-Saxon sea power when an enemy threa-

---

16   J. Frankel, "Compairing Foreign Policies. The case of Norway", *International Affairs* (London), XXXXIV, (July 1968), 483.
17   N. Andersen, *The Nordic Council. A Study of Scandinavian Regionalism* (Seattle, 1967), 9.
18   *Ibid.*
19   E. Bjøl, "Le Danemark et l'Europe", *Revue Danoise*, 37 (1971), 17.

tened the equilibrium in the Baltic or the independence of Denmark has customarily been a matter of course. Prior to World War I, however, Britain's capacity to provide effective aid was limited by the ease and speed with which the potential aggressor (Germany) could strike. Thus, from the 1860s until 1918, Danish neutrality was feasible only as far as it was acceptable to Germany, the strongest Baltic power.

After forty years of unarmed neutrality, in 1909 Denmark armed, arguing that no powerful nation would respect Danish neutrality unless it were effectively defended. Before this time Germany was the only country interested in Danish neutrality. As a continental land power, Germany's strategic theories anticipated that major conflicts would be fought in Central and Western Europe. Its interests in Scandinavia were restricted to keeping British sea power out of the Baltic, thus securing its northern flank and safeguarding the supply of raw materials from Norway and Sweden.

The decision to switch from unarmed to armed neutrality was also influenced by German hints that they would not violate a local and defended neutrality of Denmark. Although this policy was successful enough to enable Denmark to stay out of World War I, (20) a combination of factors led to a shift in strategy once the war was over, and Denmark once again disarmed. In the first place, with Germany and Russia defeated and a group of small Baltic powers newly created, big power rivalry disappeared in the Baltic area. The creation of the League of Nations promised a lasting peace, and against this background the Radical Liberals, who separately or in coalition with the Social Democrats had ruled the country throughout most of the interwar years, insisted on disarming. In fact, an independent Danish defense system had been one of the factors that had led to the pacifist Radical Liberals' secession from the Liberal party.

Norway's foreign policy is in some ways the same as Denmark's, in some ways different. Both are small countries whose defense policies have always had to adjust to the prevalent power constellation in the area. Yet because of its isolation in "Europe's quiet corner," (21) Norway is unique. Denmark is

---

20 The marked pro-German turn this neutrality was forced to take made its success relative. At the outbreak of World War I, the Germans began mining southern Danish waters, asking the Danes to mine the Great Belt. They threatened to do so themselves if the Danes failed to comply, and thereby establish defenses on Danish territory. After explaining its position to the British to the latter's satisfaction, Denmark complied. Thus Denmark protected Germany's northern flank against British intrusions in the Baltic, and at the same time avoided another war theater at its own doorstep. P. Haekkerup, *Danmarks Udenrigspolitik* (Aarhus, 1965), 26.

21 The term is P. Burgess's *Elite Images and Foreign Policy Outcomes. A Study of Norway* (Columbus, Ohio, 1967), 31.

only partly an Atlantic country. The lack of harbors on the west coast of Jutland and the concentration of population in the eastern part of the country have traditionally oriented the Danes toward the Baltic and the continent. Norway on the other hand has an Atlantic coast of over 2,100 miles (3,400 km) and its population is concentrated on the southwestern coast along the many fjords. As a major fishing and shipping country -- Norway's merchant fleet is the second largest in the world and its earnings cover about seventy percent of the country's trade deficit -- Norway is principally a maritime nation. The importance of the British market and dependence on the protection of the British navy (22) have accentuated Norway's Atlantic character, and reduced its need for Scandinavian cooperation. Its historical experience, dominance by its more populous neighbors, diminished its desire. Fairly recent national independence (since 1905) has made Norway wary of all forms of integration and any loss of national sovereignty. Neutrality is an overriding dimension of the country's foreign policy, based on its historical experience, geographic location, and economic structure. As a supplier of maritime transport it must maintain good relations with all possible customers. (23)

Despite repeated efforts Norwegian neutrality was never universally recognized, and in fact has always favored the nation which controlled the North Sea and the North Atlantic, Great Britain. This was not only because Norway counted on British help in case of danger, but also because it recognized Britain's vital interest in the area, an interest which originated in the British desire to avoid German control of Norway's strategic southern and western coasts in the event of war. (24) These were the conditions under which Norway avoided involvement in World War I, though in its last stages the Allies forced that country to grant a series of concessions. (25) After the war the Norwegians conceded only part of their policy of neutrality for membership in the League of Nations.

Only after the League failed to provide collective security and to develop into an instrument for the peaceful solution of disputes did the Norwegians withdraw from their obligations under the system and revert to complete noninvolvement. Their aversion to big power politics continued unabated even after World War II, even though during that conflict a neutral policy had disastrous consequences for their country.

Iceland, a country of 200,000 inhabitants located half-way between Europe

22   J. Frankel, *loc. cit.*, 483.
23   *Ibid.*, 484.
24   P. Burgess, *op. cit.*, 22.
25   J. Frankel, *loc. cit.*, 484.

and the American continent, remained aloof from European affairs until the beginning of the last world war. Only then did it realize its own strategic importance to any power seeking control over the Atlantic searoutes, and for the first time it gave serious consideration to a national defense posture. Prior to 1940 Icelandic foreign policy had focused exclusively on neutrality and the attainment of full independence. Indeed, the 1918 Act of Union concluded with Denmark had ended centuries-old Danish domination by extending home rule to the country. It stipulated that for the next twenty-five years, after which the agreement could be revised or even cancelled, Denmark was to administer Iceland's foreign affairs. At the same time Denmark was to notify all foreign powers that Iceland was a sovereign state that had declared itself permanently neutral. *(26)*

There was no doubt that at the conclusion of the twenty-five year period Iceland would cancel the Act of Union and become fully sovereign and independent. In 1937 the Icelandic Parliament (Althing) had already passed a resolution which authorized the government to begin preparations for accepting such responsibility. *(27)* But the country's permanent neutrality was to remain unchanged. The island's population hoped that powerful nations would show as little interest in the country as they had done in the past, *(28)* and would leave them to the business of survival in this bare and forbidding country.

## THE SCANDINAVIAN NATO COUNTRIES FROM 1945 TO 1948

Involvement in World War II marked a decisive turning in the foreign policies of the Scandinavian members of NATO, but this was not readily apparent in the immediate postwar period. Responsible leaders in Norway and Denmark recognized that the neutrality that had kept their countries out of World War I had in reality been heavily weighed in favor of their closest and most powerful neighbor. World War II had overwhelmed them despite their political position. Yet the geostrategic and political situation immediately after World War II was so like the post-World War I period that all three countries could easily have resumed their interwar policy, relying for security

---

26 C.S. Campbell, "The Influence of Domestic Politics on the Defense Policy of Iceland", *Naval War College Review* (December, 1970), 78.

27 *Ibid.*, 79.

28 The absence of raw materials and the remoteness and barrenness of the country has helped determine Iceland's isolation. They account for the fact that England, though undisputable master of the seas, never made an attempt to occupy the country. B. Benediktsson, "Islands Platz in der Welt", *Nato-Brief* (June, 1968), 6.

on the newly-created international United Nations Organization. Indeed, the traditional aggressor in the area, Germany, had once again been eliminated from the military picture. Of course, this time the eclipse of Germany had not been accompanied by a similar eclipse of the Soviet Union. On the contrary, the formidable advance of the Red Army, bringing Soviet power at the gates of Lübeck, more than filled whatever power vacuum the collapse of the Wehrmacht had created. Yet the military presence of the Soviet Union, however formidable and tangible, was initially considered less of an immediate threat than Germany had been previously. After all, Soviet forces had liberated parts of both Norwegian and Danish territory in Finnmark and the island of Bornholm. Moreover, both countries placed a great deal of faith in the continuation of big-power cooperation after the war, and the creation of the U.N., based on this very cooperation, certainly seemed to warrant their beliefs. Finally, the advance of the Red Army, deep into Central Europe, was considered a direct consequence of the military operations at the final stages of the war. The Soviet Government's reluctance to withdraw its troops after the defeat of Germany, and its insistence upon the creation of what it called friendly regimes in Eastern Europe met with understanding in many European quarters. This was because the weakness of East European governments in the interwar period had made German penetration easy. Later they had served as a base for the attack upon the Soviet Union. Under these circumstances it is not surprising that after 1945 Denmark again adopted a policy of neutrality, subject to its obligations to the U.N. The Danes clearly hoped to avoid involvement in bloc-building; their defense was to be realized in the collective security provided by the U.N.. *(29)* The foreign ministers' conferences in London in September, 1945, in Moscow in December, 1945, and in Paris in April, 1946 confirmed the deterioration of U.S.-Soviet relations already apparent at Potsdam in July-August, 1945. In fact, they marked the dissolution of the Great Alliance. Still, Denmark was firm in its policy of neutrality and cooperation with both East and West. *(30)*

29 To the Nordic Society in Oslo on 2 September 1945 and at a press conference on 18 September 1945, Danish Foreign Minister Christmas Moeller denied the possibility of Danish participation either in a Nordic Defense Union or a Western pact. Danish membership in the U.N. and the furtherance of a positive East-West relationship were the most important Danish foreign policy goals, Minister Moeller declared. Udenrigsministeriet, *Dansk Sikkerhedspolitik 1948-1966, II Bilag*, (Copenhagen, 1968), 26-27 [hereafter: *Dansk Sikkerhedspolitik, II*]. According to Henningsen, Danish trust in the promise of the U.N. was so great that the Parliament "decided to postpone its decision on new defense laws, until the U.N. Security Council was ready to negotiate an agreement about Danish military contributions to U.N. forces". Henningsen, *op. cit.*, 19.

30 In order to demonstrate its neutrality and at the same time rebuild its army between

The formation of a Social Democratic minority government under Hans Hedtoft on 28 October, 1947 made no difference in Danish foreign policy. Hedtoft was convinced that Denmark should avoid any power grouping, saying that it was not "in the Danish or Nordic interest to sharpen the already manifest antagonism between East and West." *(31)* Soviet intransigeance over the regimes in Eastern Europe and the growing American responce to their claims were to lead to the creation of a Western military alliance, and Denmark would become a member. Until then, Danish attention focused on three questions: South Schleswig, Bornholm, and Greenland.

Immediately after the second world war, an important Danish minority living in South Schleswig asked to return to the Danish state as a right of national self-determination. Denmark's dealings with Germany after World War I had been cautious and restrained, and this time it took a similarly moderate stand. The government and the Parliament refused to allow public opinion to push them into demanding the return of the province and they contented themselves with promoting Danish culture. *(32)* With the improvement of living conditions in Germany and the normalization of relations between Germany and Denmark, the problem gradually subsided from the political arena.

The Soviet liberation and subsequent occupation of the island of Bornholm posed another problem for Denmark. In the opinion of Mary Dau, *(33)* the move was related to wider Soviet attempts to gain control of the Baltic or at least insure that no other great power occupied a position of strength there. Apparently Field Marshals Montgomery and Rokossovsky instituted a race to liberate Lübeck at the end of the war for the same reason. By reaching Lübeck first, Montgomery succeeded in denying the Red Army entry into Schleswig-Holstein, and spared Denmark liberation by the Russians. On 9 May 1945, Soviet troops landed on Bornholm. They had promised to leave one day after the last German soldier, but in fact Soviet troops occupied the island for almost a year. Their withdrawal in 1946, simultaneous with that from positions in northern Norway and northern Persia, may have been the result of

---

1945 and 1947, the Danish government repeatedly tried to buy weapons from the Soviet Union. These attempts apparently aroused little Soviet interest. Udenrigsministeriet, *Dansk Sikkerhedspolitik, 1948-1966, I, Fremstilling,* (Copenhagen, 1968), 21-22, [Hereafter *Dansk Sikkerhedspolitik, I*].

31   *Ibid.,* 22.

32   Henningsen, *op. cit.,* 14.

33   M. Dau, "The Soviet Union and the Liberation of Denmark", *Survey* (Summer, 1970), 64-81.

pressure from the Western allies, *(34)* or a voluntary decision. The Soviets may have felt it necessary to retain portions of these countries to insure maximum leverage for their foreign policy objectives. Once they were reasonably confident that the territories would not be used against them, however, they were willing to withdraw.

The Greenland Defense Agreement of 9 April 1941 had provided for the installation of bases on Greenland, and American reluctance to dismantle them once the war was over caused some uneasiness between Denmark and the U.S. Article X of the agreement stipulates that "this agreement shall remain in force until it is agreed that the present dangers to the peace and security of the American Continent have passed." *(35)* It also provided compulsory consultation between governments and a termination notice of twelve months. In the climate of uncertainty that prevailed at the end of World War II, the U.S. preferred to retain the facilities. Growing antagonism with the Soviet Union coupled with the recognition of the new strategic importance of the Arctic region for the defense of America caused the Americans to temporize when the Danish government suggested terminating the agreement. A year and a half after an official request to start negotiations, the Danish foreign minister announced before Parliament on 18 November 1948, that Danish authorities had taken over control of all American stations on the east coast of Greenland although the U.S. continued to command five stations including two airfields on the west coast. The disagreement was eventually settled by Danish membership in the Atlantic Alliance. A letter from the Danish ambassador in Washington to his foreign minister dated 14 February 1949, indicated that American insistence on Greenland's and the Faroes' participation in the already negotiated North Atlantic defense system played a major role in gradually persuading Denmark to join the new organization. *(36)*

In Norway, disillusionment with neutrality came very early. Among officials of the Norwegian government-in-exile in London, the demand for a more active foreign policy based on cooperation with the Western democracies, resulted in a change in command. On 21 November 1940, Trygve Lie replaced Halvdan Koht, the main architect and supporter of Norwegian neutrality, as foreign minister. In a broadcast to the Norwegian people on 15 December

---

34 Suggested by B. Meissner, "Soviet Russia's Foreign Policy", *Western Integration and the Future of Eastern Europe*, eds. D.S. Collier and K. Glaser (Chicago, 1964), 89.
35 *Documents on International Affairs, 1939-1946. Vol. II Hitler's Europe*, published under the auspices of the Royal Institute of International Affairs (London, 1944), 218-219.
36 Udenrigsministeriet, *Dansk Sikkerhedspolitik, II*, 74-80.

1940, Lie rejected both Nordic unity and participation in a continental bloc as too small a base for a postwar Norwegian economic and security policy. As a seafaring nation and an old Atlantic people, Norway should seek closer ties with the West, particularly the United States and England. *(37)* Strategic considerations related to the protection of its long and vulnerable coast line increased the need for cooperation with the Atlantic powers, not only for the duration of the war but beyond, Lie added.

The re-orientation of Norwegian foreign policy toward the Atlantic was not particularly apparent in the immediate postwar world. A reluctance to give up neutralist aspirations was perhaps one reason for this. In the beginning Norway looked to the United Nations and continued cooperation among the big powers to ensure a safe and peaceful world. Also, probably more than Sweden or Denmark, Norway traditionally has been very sensitive to Soviet views on world politics and to Soviet interest in Northern Europe. Norwegian leaders after World War II were very much aware of the rise of new power centers, "Britain and America on the one side and Soviet Russia on the other", and that, because of new warfare techniques, especially strategic air power, Norway was situated right between them. *(38)*

Convinced that the founding of the U.N. paved the way for an indissoluable peace Norwegian Foreign Minister Lie told the first U.N. General Assembly that small nations were responsible for contributing to the mutual under-standing and confidence of the great powers. Ultimately peace rested with the ongoing cooperation of the big powers and their greater responsibility was reflected in their special status within the framework of the U.N. Lie's election as the organization's first secretary-general was interpreted as a vote of confi-dence in his, and hence in Norway's, foreign policy. "The Norwegian Govern-ment had been able to gain the trust of the Soviet Union without simultaneously forfeiting the confidence of the United States and the other Western powers." *(39)*

The basis for cooperation with the Western powers had been laid during World War II, when the Norwegian government-in-exile had worked closely with the Atlantic powers. Moreover, immediately after the war the Soviet Union enjoyed a great deal of goodwill in Norway. The Red Army had de-veloped into a decisive factor in the struggle against Nazi Germany and had actively participated in liberating northern Norway as well. These factors greatly facilitated cooperation with the U.S.S.R.

---

37  Burgess, *op. cit.*, 51.
38  *Ibid.*, 76.
39  *Ibid.*, 82.

The only issue troubling friendly relations was the status of the Spitzbergen Archipelago, which under the 1920 Convention of Paris had been placed under Norwegian sovereignty. *(40)* In October, 1944, a Norwegian delegation traveled to Moscow to discuss Soviet military operations begun in northern Norway, and Molotov brought up the matter of Spitzbergen. The convention, he said, was up for revision, and he proposed that article nine, which stipulated that the uses of the Archipelago were to be nonmilitary, be changed to allow a joint Russo-Norwegian defense of the islands. In an attempt to buy time until after the war, when they hoped to be in a better negotiating position, the Norwegians set up a committee to study the matter. The Soviets raised the question again in 1947, but the Norwegian government, backed by a 101 to 49 vote in the Storting, rejected their demands, and eventually the Soviets dropped the issue. This, coupled with their otherwise correct behavior in northern Norway, convinced the Norwegians that the Soviet Union was not a direct threat to their country. *(41)*

Norway's postwar defense policy assumed the efficacy of the U.N.'s collective security policy, which was dependent in turn on cooperation and mutual understanding among the big powers. Understandibly, Norwegians were reluctant to admit the developing hostility between East and West. Although he was not unaware of the tension provoked by Churchill's Iron Curtain speech, the Truman Doctrine, or the creation of the Cominform, Foreign Minister Lange said on 20 January 1949, that this was "more a post-war tension than a prelude to a new order." *(42)* As the next chapter discusses, only with the Czech coup and the Soviet-Finnish treaty of friendship would Norwegian public opinion accept the possibility of a Scandinavian Defense Union, and, later, of the North Atlantic treaty.

The situation was not much different in Iceland. The war had made it all too clear that a policy of neutrality was no guarantee of security to the country. Besides, the interest of England and the United States in denying control of the

---

40  Spitzbergen or Svalbard, as the Norwegians call it, is an archipelago of some 62,000 square kilometer, situated between the North Pole and Norway, 600 km off the Norwegian coast. Until the 1920 Convention of Paris, the archipelago was considered no man's land, most particularly by the Soviet Union, who had important economic interests in coal mining in the area. The Soviet Union had been excluded from the Paris negotiations and had not signed the convention.

41  Burgess, *op. cit.*, 80. Nor did they feel that the Soviet Union was a direct threat to world peace. Soviet actions in Eastern Europe were largely considered justifiable as security measures against Germany.

42  Quoted in *ibid.*, 85.

island to a rival for domination of the Atlantic was such that Iceland had to account for this new element in its foreign policy.

Immediately after the war, Icelanders sought a middle course between neutrality and a closer relationship with the United States. The Icelandic government insisted that the American forces withdraw from their bases, as stipulated by the 1941 defense agreement. They went in a rather short time. Pending further negotiations, American troops remained only on the Kéflavik airbase. On 1 October 1945, however, Washington asked the Icelandic government for leases on military bases for a period of ninety-nine years, possibly under the jurisdiction of the U.N. Security Council. When it was made public, the request caused a popular outcry against what was termed selling out Icelandic territory. *(43)* Hesitation within the government antagonized nationalist forces who wanted to exclude all foreign intervention and a return to neutrality. The eventual decision of the government to refuse the request met with no public opposition, although some felt that the way the decision was reached might harm the relations with a friendly nation *(44)* with whom a solution to the Kéflavik base still had to be found. Kéflavik was of the utmost importance to the Americans as a refuelling station for their transatlantic flights to various bases in Europe. As a port base for patrolling the sea lanes of the North Atlantic and as a center of anti-submarine warfare, Kéflavik had proven invaluable during World War II.

Secret negotiations eventually resulted in the Kéflavik agreement of 7 October 1947. The remaining American troops were to leave and Icelandic authorities would take over control of the base. Six hundred American civilians with various extraterritorial rights would remain at the base to service airplanes en route to American bases in Europe. *(45)* The battle for ratification in the Althing was tense and the agreement was approved only after some members of the opposition, belonging to the Progressive Party voted with the government. The Communists, who were partners in the coalition, voted against the agreement and left the government. They charged that they had not been consulted during the negotiations; moreover, the agreement was contrary to the Icelandic policy that denied military bases to foreign powers.

---

43  Campbell, *loc. cit.*, 81.
44  *Ibid.*
45  B. Gröndal, *Iceland: From Neutrality to NATO Membership* (Oslo, 1971), 39.

# Chapter II

# FROM NEUTRALITY TO NATO MEMBERSHIP

By 1948 the failure of Norway's and Denmark's attempts at mediation had become only too apparent. The Czech coup of February 1948 was but the last in a series of *Gleichschaltung* moves whereby the Soviet Union undertook to consolidate the political influence it had gained in Eastern Europe. The Soviets' policy of stabilization in an area which they considered indispensable as well as a legitimate security zone was the main source of friction between them and the Western allies. Scandinavian bridge-building efforts could not alleviate the growing antagonism between the U.S.S.R. and the United States, nor could it prevent the outbreak of the Cold War.

The subsequent rallying of the Western democracies, first in the Brussels Pact, later around the North Atlantic treaty, presented Norway and Denmark with a serious dilemma. Although they had foresaken nonalignment after World War II, they had done so very reluctantly. Both countries had conditioned their membership in the U.N. with the expressed wish to avoid power politics, and an active foreign policy within a universal organization was the limit of their interest in collective security. Once the U.N. was deadlocked by big-power antagonism and the regrouping of European nations into two opposing political-military blocs was gaining momentum, Norway and Denmark faced an important decision. Should they join the Western bloc, or return to the policy of neutrality which had proved fatal in World War II or should they accept the Swedish offer of a Nordic defense union, hopefully combining the virtues of neutrality with increased security?

The choice was not an easy one, nor was the ultimate outcome, NATO membership, a matter of course. A better understanding of why the two countries chose as they did, requires an overview of the political and military situation in Europe, especially in northern Europe.

## THE POLITICAL AND STRATEGIC SITUATION IN
## NORTHERN EUROPE IN 1948

With the Czech coup in 1948, the Soviet Union hoped to round off its sphere of political influence in the area liberated by the Red Army. The U.S.S.R. concluded bilateral treaties of friendship, cooperation, and mutual assistance with all the countries under its control, tying them firmly to itself for a period of twenty years. When Stalin proposed negotiations toward such a treaty with Finland in early 1948 he understandably provoked great emotion in Finland and in the rest of Scandinavia as well. The Finns were hardly in a position to turn down the proposal, however, and they signed the pact on 6 April 1948. Although the agreement was restricted in scope compared to those concluded with the People's Democracies, *(1)* its very conclusion so soon after the events in Czechoslovakia suggested that Stalin's expansionist policy had spread to Scandinavia. According to President J.K. Paasikivi of Finland history and geography taught the Finns that they had no choice but to sign. Still, he felt the Soviet Union had only limited goals in Northern Europe, centered on the defense of Leningrad and other vital sectors of Northwestern Europe. *(2)* Taking advantage of the defense negotiations going on in Western Europe, Finnish representatives in Moscow are said to have succeeded in wording the treaty so that it expressed neutrality more than submission to the U.S.S.R.. *(3)* The Soviets were persuaded that too much pressure on Finland would induce Norway and Denmark and perhaps Sweden to seek closer defense arrangements with the Western powers.

Despite Paasikivi's optimistic interpretation of the Soviet-Finnish treaty, other Scandinavian countries were unconvinced. On the contrary, the conclusion of the treaty provoked a serious crisis in Norway and Denmark, called the Easter Crisis, and induced Sweden to propose negotiations for a Scandinavian defense agreement. In January of 1948, Norwegian and Danish leaders still cherished the role of bridge-builder between East and West, and in consequence had approached the Marshall Plan negotiations in Paris cautiously.

---

*1* Whereas the U.S.S.R. and its Eastern European allies discuss all international problems which may affect their common interests, under the Finnish-Soviet pact only armed aggression or the threat of armed aggression against Finnish territory requires consultation. Moreover, in case of German attack the Eastern European allies would both receive help and be obliged to provide assistance to the Soviets. Finland, on the other hand, is compelled only to defend its own territory.
*2* Jansson, *loc. cit.*, 365.
*3* E. Bjøl, N.J. Haagerup, *et al.*, *Danmark og NATO* (Copenhagen, 1968), 163. For a detailed account of the negotiations, see Jakobson, *op. cit.*, 35-44.

Burgess skilfully analyzes the reasons for the decisive shift in Norway's foreign policy. *(4)* One reason was the events in Czechoslovakia, a country highly respected in Norway and considered an exponent of the bridge-building policy. After the coup, bridge-building seemed to have no future. Moreover, the signing of the Brussels Pact and the Berlin blockade sharpened tensions throughout Europe. Finally, the conclusion of the Soviet-Finnish Treaty of Friendship, Cooperation, and Mutual Assistance, says Lange, "showed that the Soviet Government was re-examining the question of securing itself militarily on its northern flank." *(5)* Rumors in Norway predicted that the Soviets would request a nonaggression pact with Norway; *(6)* the Norwegian Storting reacted by voting an extraordinary defense appropriation of twenty million dollars and appointing a Special Committee for Foreign Policy and Defense Preparedness in April. The committee was in fact to assume the decision-making functions of the regular Foreign Affairs Committee, *(7)* and Communist Parliamentarians were excluded from its deliberations. Iceland had exhibited a similar distrust of Communists previously when the Communist Ministers had not even been informed, let alone been invited to participate in the negotiations over the Kéflavik agreement.

In Denmark, alarm over the Czech coup and the Soviet treaty with Finland was reinforced by an undated dispatch from a counselor in the Danish Embassy at Washington, which reported the viewpoint of "official circles" in Washington on the new situation in Europe. *(8)* According to this man, Americans apparently believed that the basic goal of the Soviet Union was world domination. Seizure of power could be achieved indirectly from within a country either through organized terror or a military coup. However, direct methods, in the form of a military attack, were not to be excluded completely. Any overt action would have to be swift to present the U.S.A. with a *fait accompli*, and its consequences would have to be limited enough to discourage Congress from declaring war upon the U.S.S.R. The report concluded with the information that American officials considered Italy and Denmark the most likely victims of a direct Soviet attack. *(9)* Rear Admiral Thomas B. Inglis of the U.S. Naval

---

4 Burgess, *op. cit.*, 88-90, 98.

5 Quoted in *ibid.*, 90.

6 As with similar rumors circulating at the time in Denmark, they appear to have been partly the result of a misinterpretation of articles in *Pravda* and *Krasnaia Vezda* attacking Norway and Denmark, and partly due to American hints that high level American politicians had foreseen such a conclusion to the new situation in Europe.

7 Burgess, *op. cit.*, 89.

8 *Dansk Sikkerhedspolitik*, *I*, 23-25.

9 *Ibid.*, 23. Difficulties at Trieste seem relevant to this thesis.

Intelligence Service seems to have been privy to the same analysis. He sent the Swedish naval attaché similar information, asking him to inform his Norwegian colleague on the matter. *(10)* The Danish government took immediate measures; they drastically reduced the number of officers and soldiers on leave during the Easter holidays.

Once the Scandinavian countries perceived the Soviets as a threat, they saw how formidable the Soviet military position in the Baltic area had become after the defeat of Germany and how their own position in the area had suffered. The equilibrium between Russia and Germany that had existed in the Baltic for almost two centuries, had broken in the Russians' favor. During the interwar period the U.S.S.R. controlled less than sixty miles (100 km) of the Baltic coastlines and had no noteworthy naval capacity. For a brief period in the 1920s, Sweden had had the strongest naval force in the area. *(11)* After the war, the Soviet Union commanded 1,200 miles (2,000 km) along the Baltic shore and possessed an impressive naval force. World War II had enabled the U.S.S.R. to acquire a military position in the Baltic unlike that of any other power along the coast, with the possible exception of Germany during 1941-1943. *(12)*

As a flank theater for operations in Central Europe and as a means for transporting ammunition and food to the combatants at that front, the strategic position of the Baltic Sea is vital. Immediately after the war and well into the 1950s, the Soviet Union had at its disposal only five railways connecting with the rest of Europe. Four of these went through Poland, the fifth through Hungary, and they were all of different gauges than those in Russia. Moreover, the U.S.S.R. may have been wary of its East European allies from the start. *(13)* In any case a sustained effort in Central Europe continued to necessitate complete control over the Baltic and denial of access to non-Baltic powers. Domination of the Danish straits therefore became as important for the U.S.S.R. as it had been for Nazi Germany.

The development of air and submarine warfare has introduced the Baltic area into the larger strategic picture. For possible counterattacks against Soviet industrial areas, large cities, or air bases, the United States would have to rely on its strategic bombers, operating from bases in Iceland, Greenland, Great Britain or the U.S. Directed against Moscow, Leningrad or Murmansk,

10  *Ibid.*, 24.
11  H. Jung, "Strategische Probleme um die Ostsee", *Wehrkunde*, VII (March, 1961), 121.
12  *Ibid.*, 122.
13  G. Bindlingmaier, von, "Die Bedeutung der Ostsee für die NATO und die Aufgaben der Bundesmarine", *Wehrkunde*, VII (December, 1958), 678.

they would have to fly over Scandinavian territory. Geographical conditions had limited Soviet early warning systems but an advance to the North Sea and the Atlantic coast would improve this weakness considerably. *(14)* Furthermore, a Soviet offensive including a serious attempt at destroying or at least endangering the Atlantic searoutes so vital for the West, necessitated an easy exit for its important Baltic fleet as well as an easy reentrance for refuelling, repair, and bunkering. These factors make control of the Danish straits and of the Swedish and, or Norwegian shores of the Skagerrak essential.

The Germans had considered their capabilities for submarine warfare greatly enhanced by control of positions on the Norwegian coast. *(15)* In a major conflict with Western powers, the Soviet Union may feel the same. In addition to offering better shelter against air raids, such a move would increase the range of operations by reducing the attacking distance by 900 to 1,200 miles.

For all these reasons, the Scandinavians were very much alarmed at Stalin's demand for a pact with Finland. Considering the open and bitter antagonism between the two superpowers, it was easy to see Soviet policy as "maneuvering for position before offering battle." *(16)*

Had that been a realistic interpretation of the state of affairs, the news from Washington about an invasion of Denmark and a request for a treaty with Norway would have been serious. As it was, it provoked considerable alarm in the Scandinavian countries. It led to a drastic reappraisal of the neutralist policies of Norway and Denmark, and the search for some kind of regional security arrangement.

## DISCUSSIONS ON A NORDIC DEFENSE UNION

On 22 April 1948, the Swedish government officially proposed the start of negotiations to examine the possibilities of a cooperative defense system among the Scandinavian nations. The idea had been discussed before the war -- the press, for example, had offered several alternative plans -- but eventually all were abandoned when Sweden, necessarily the core of any defense union, showed little interest in any of them.

During and after the war, the Swedes reversed their opinion, and the concept of defense cooperation resurfaced. *(17)* This time, however, Norway refused

---

14 Jung, *loc. cit.*, 125.
15 F.C.U., "De Rol van de marine in de Noorse defensie", *Het Leger en de Natie*, XII (10), 23.
16 *Ibid.*
17 T. Greve, *Norway and Nato* (Oslo, 1968), p. 10.

to participate and the idea was shelved again. Persuant to its return to neutrality, the country preferred to entrust its security to the United Nations, whose success depended upon big-power cooperation, and Norway intended to serve as a communicating link among them. As a result it did not seriously consider the creation of a Scandinavian bloc because such a measure might antagonize the Soviet Union. As mentioned in the previous chapter, Norway felt that a Scandinavian bloc was too small a base to provide an effective safeguard.

The Swedish government made its proposal with some urgency; after the events in Czechoslovakia and the Finnish-Soviet Treaty it felt that Norway was leaning dangerously toward the West. On 12 February 1948, the Norwegian foreign minister disavowed any Norwegian support for the Swedish rejection of the Bevin plan, eventually to result in the creation of the West European Union.

In a speech before the Oslo Military Society on 19 April 1948, the Norwegian foreign minister analyzed the latest events, stressing that in the end, "there can be no doubt that we are a part of Western Europe, economically, geographically, and culturally, and we shall continue to be a Western European democracy." *(18)* Referring to the Brussels Pact, signed on 17 March 1948, he said, "we will not preclude for ourselves the possibility of discussing a closer relationship with the West". Although he added that only "very weighty reasons could cause us to choose a policy which can separate us from Denmark and Sweden or from one of them", he also pointed out that "the problems of military policy and security which face the three Scandinavian Countries are not identical, and this fact may create certain difficulties in the work to find a common solution." *(19)* Despite such differences, high-level talks began. They were to last for ten months, and to end with a *constat d'échec*. From the start, the goals of the participants were irreconcilable. Sweden's most important consideration was keeping the superpowers out of Scandinavia. The Swedes apparently felt that the Soviets had been relatively moderate in their relations with Finland. They had not demanded a joint Finnish-Soviet defense of the country nor the stationing of Soviet troops after the collapse of the Finnish army. They saw Soviet interests in the area as defensive, and therefore favored a position of neutrality. They certainly wanted to avoid Norwegian alignment with the Western powers. This raised the spectre of an armed U.S. presence in Norway, to which the Soviets might retaliate by insisting upon Soviet forces in Finland. Were this to happen, Sweden would be caught directly between the two. Neutrality had served the country well during two world wars, the Swedes

18  Quoted in Burgess, *op. cit.*, 90.
19  Quoted in Padelford, *op. cit.*, 601.

felt, and they were optimistic about the future. Their armed forces had been expanded and modernized during the war, and were one of the best in the world. For both reasons, Swedish policy was more intent on avoiding war than on creating favorable conditions for support once war began. *(20)*

The situation presented itself differently in Norway. As discussed above, the strategic geographic position of the country made it probable that in any conflict, one or both opponents would press for control of the country. Moreover, experience had shown that for a poorly-armed country, organizing support in case of attack was more important than trying to keep the area out of the hostilities. World War II had made it clear that a sufficient national mobilization was impossible for a small country. Security depended completely on friendly relations with more powerful states. The Norwegian leadership perceived the main threat as coming from the Soviet Union; in their minds, assistance was only possible in sufficient quantity from sources in the West.

The Danish position was somewhere between the other two. Poorly armed and difficult to defend, the country, like Norway, vitally needed assistance in case of an attack. On the other hand, the Danes saw themselves as having only a limited strategic value for the large powers. As a result, they felt it was more to their advantage to isolate their territory from outsiders' quarrels, rather than conclude security agreements that would only serve to involve the superpowers in northern Europe. In the interests of its own security as well as of Scandinavian unity, Denmark from the outset favored a cooperative program for defense. The Swedish government attached two preconditions to its proposal: participating countries must agree to remain neutral and keep out of any power bloc, and a policy of common armament and defense planning should be established among them. *(21)*

In a meeting at Oslo between Lange and the Swedish foreign minister Undén, and in Stockholm on 9-11 May 1948 among the prime and foreign ministers of the three countries, Lange said that the Norwegian government refused to accept neutrality as a precondition for Scandinavian defense cooperation. He repeated his structures in Malmö, Sweden, on 4 June and in a speech in Copenhagen the following day. Different historical experiences as well as differently-conceived current security needs precluded a defense policy common to Scandinavia. *(22)* The matter was deadlocked in the summer of 1948, although the Danish government actually attempted to rescue the plan, maybe because, as Erik Reske-Nielsen surmises, the Danes were aware that they

---

20  N. Andrén, *The Foreign Policy of Sweden* (Stockholm, 1967), 60.
21  *Dansk Sikkerhedspolitik, I*, 25.
22  Burgess, *op. cit.*, 103-105.

would be more of a liability than an asset, considering their exposed geographical position and their limited financial resources. *(23)* A few days before Lange spoke in Malmö, the Danish foreign and prime ministers emphasized in the Folketing their strong hope for a close collaboration on defense among Norway, Denmark, and Sweden. *(24)*

At a foreign ministers' conference in Stockholm on 8-9 September 1948, participants agreed that, despite their differing views, enough common ground existed to justify a serious inquiry into the possibilities of military cooperation among the three countries. A Scandinavian Defense Commission was established on 15 October to carry out the investigation. But time was running short; the Western powers had made considerable advances on the road to alignment. On 11 June 1948, the U.S. Senate had adopted the Vandenberg Resolution, a measure which opened the possibility for engagement in regional and collective security arrangements. On 6 July 1948, exploratory negotiations began in Washington on a Canadian proposal for a North Atlantic defense system, conducted by the U.S. Department of State and the ambassadors of the Brussels Pact states and of Canada. Two months later, on 9 September 1948, a report outlining the principles of a defense pact, was sent to the concerned governments, and representatives of the seven countries initiated formal negotiations based on that report in Washington on 10 December 1948.

Running almost parallel in time, the two sets of meetings were to a large degree mutually exclusive. Norwegian Foreign Minister Lange had stated repeatedly that he was willing to explore the possibility of Scandinavian defense, although he saw Norwegian security assured only within a politically and militarily strong Western grouping. He wanted to establish formal ties with the Western nations to avoid a power vacuum in the North, which would provoke tension, rather than alleviate it. Lange also faced the urgent problem of weapon deliveries, a question broached both by him and by the Danish foreign minister Gustav Rasmussen in their discussions with U.S. Secretary of State George Marshall in the U.N. General Assembly in Paris in early October 1948. The Scandinavians sought a clear and unequivocal stand from the Americans on their willingness to supply armaments and equipment, since the U.S. was almost the only possible source of these goods for Norway and Denmark if their investigatory committee established the need to acquire military supplies from outsiders. At its final session in Oslo from 11 to 14 January 1949 the Scandinavian Defense Commission concluded that such

23 E. Reske-Nielsen and E. Kragh, *Atlantpagten og Danmark, 1949-1962* (Copenhagen, 1962), 47.
24 *Dansk Sikkerhedspolitik, II*, 44-45.

foreign purchasing was necessary. The main findings of the commission were known a few days before their publication, and the prime ministers of the three countries, as well as their colleagues of foreign affairs and defense, discussed the defense situation at the Karlstad meeting of 5-6 January 1949. They set up a time table during which to determine a course of action on all pending questions.

The commission established first that a Scandinavian defense pact was possible, although such an arrangement required a substantial improvement in the Norwegian and Danish defense apparatus and a modernization of the Swedish one. In addition Sweden agreed to ally immediately with Norway and Denmark, regardless of the condition of their military equipment, stipulating only that all three countries renounce political-military ties with non-Nordic nations. Finally, Norway and Denmark were to sound out London and Washington on the matters of political support and priority in arms purchases. Both countries made inquiries although the Vandenberg Resolution had implied that American aid would go only to states cooperating closely with the United States. Any hopes they might have nourished were shattered on 14 January 1949, when the American government issued an official communique stating that military aid was available only to states allied with the United States, including Turkey and Greece under the Truman Doctrine. *(25)*

At Karlstad and at subsequent inter-Scandinavian meetings at Copenhagen on 22-24 January 1949 and at Oslo on 29-30 January 1949 officials discussed various schemes for a Scandinavian pact. All their proposals stipulated automatic assistance in case of an attack on one of the contracting parties, although not when aggression was directed at one of the outlying territories, such as Greenland, the Faroes, Jan Mayen Island, or Spitsbergen. They agreed that defense planning and armament production should be coordinated in peacetime, and that any state would be allowed to call in outside help in the event of hostilities.

The differences between Norway and Sweden remained irreconcilable, however. Throughout the meetings the Swedes attempted to convince the Norwegians that formal ties with the Western nations, rather than increasing the security of Norway, would on the contrary mean tension and big-power rivalry in Northern Europe. Even the proposed Scandinavian pact, they stressed, was a major departure from their policy of neutrality, and was attractive to them only to the extent that it was alliance free. They saw it as a sort of extended neutrality. The Norwegians, on the other hand, considering the increased strategic value new war techniques had imposed on their territory as

25  *Dansk Sikkerhedspolitik, I,* 27-28.

well as its position in the middle of two opposing powers, felt that the deterrence potential of a Scandinavian bloc was not sufficient to counter such a charged situation. The latest war had taught them the danger of isolation -- they had found themselves suddenly overrun by a powerful neighbor -- as well as the possibility of cooperation with the Atlantic powers, and it strengthened their belief that binding arrangements with those nations should be made in peacetime. The Scandinavian Defense Commission itself had stressed the necessity of outside help should an attack occur. However, for such aid to be effective, it had to be ready before it was needed. Perhaps the Swedes were willing to gamble on Western help on the assumption that Northern Europe was too vital to the United States to be lost to the other side, said the Norwegians; they were not. The question of armament supply, although central to the discussion, was really secondary to this overriding political consideration. At best it was another powerful argument to convince the Norwegians that the Nordic area was too limited a base to provide adequate security arrangements.

In a foreign policy debate in the Storting on 3 February 1949, Lange summarized the reasons why the negotiations had failed. Two days later, he flew to Washington to begin discussions with State Department officials. He inquired once more about possible U.S. support for a Scandinavian defense union; in reality he questioned top American policy makers about the implications of his country's membership in the Atlantic Alliance. Once home, Lange briefed the national conference of the Norwegian Labor party on the Nordic defense negotiations and his talks at Washington, and in response the group passed a unanimous resolution which concluded that "Norway must solve her security problems in joint and binding collaboration in the sphere of defense policy with the Western democracies." (26) The following day Swedish Prime Minister Erlander acknowledged that Scandinavian officials were divided on the question. Danish Prime Minister Hedtoft made a last attempt to save Scandinavian unity. He asked Erlander to consider the possibilities of a Danish-Swedish defense pact. On 23 February 1949, the Swedes refused, and, faced with isolation on the one hand and membership in the Atlantic pact on the other, the Danes eventually followed the Norwegian example. All hopes for a Scandinavian defense pact were dead, at least for the time being.

## CONDITIONAL ALIGNMENT

Lange's mission to Washington was primarily concerned with answering some pressing questions concerning Norwegian membership in the Atlantic

26   Greve, *op. cit.*, 18.

alliance. He wanted to know what economic responsibilities the Pact would entail, how the obligation to render aid would be interpreted, how the great powers perceived Norway's role, and how assistance would be rendered in the event of attack. *(27)*

From 7 February until 11 February 1949, he negotiated with U.S. Secretary of State Dean Acheson. On his way home, he saw British Foreign Minister Bevin as well. Their pledges to deliver weapons were made conditional to Norway's joining the organization, although for its part the country was not required to provide bases. This point was of the greatest importance, since the Norwegian government had promised the Soviets that it had no intention of putting any naval, land-, or air bases at the disposal of the U.S.

The Soviet Union followed the negotiations among the Scandinavian countries for a joint defense union closely. The Soviet press implied that Soviet leaders feared that Scandinavian cooperation would be only a stepping stone to an Atlantic pact. They already foresaw, with some justification, the presence of a U.S. naval and air force in Norway close to their own bases in the Kola Peninsula. *(28)* On 29 January 1949, the opening day of the Oslo conference of Scandinavian foreign ministers, the Soviet ambassador in Oslo delivered a note to the group warning against Norwegian adherence to the Atlantic pact, terming the alliance a group of powers pursuing aggressive aims by the establishment of military stations on the periphery of the Soviet Union. They reminded Norway of their common border, requesting information as to Norwegian intentions vis-à-vis the Pact, specifically with regard to the possible erection of naval and air bases on Norwegian territory. *(29)* The Norwegians replied promptly. In a note dated 1 February 1949, the Norwegian government refuted the Soviet charge that the new alliance was a violation of the U.N. Charter. Regional cooperation for mutual defense was expressly stipulated in the charter, they said, adding that the U.N. had failed as an instrument of security.

Then, in a desire to stress the defensive and nonprovocative character of its association with the Atlantic powers, the Norwegian government extended a guarantee which was to become Norwegian policy on foreign military stations. "The Norwegian Government", the note said, "requests the Soviet Government

27 *Ibid.*, 15.
28 Soviet leaders must have read with some alarm statements like that of Walter Lippmann in the *New York Herald Tribune* of 21 January, which said that "the Atlantic Pact would be more than a mere association, for to Denmark and Norway it would mean deliveries of weapons and... the development of Anglo-American sea and air installations in Scandinavia". Quoted in Burgess, *op. cit.*, 138, note.
29 Burgess, *op. cit.*, 126; see also Greve, *op. cit.*, 16.

to rest assured that Norway will never be a party to a policy with aggressive intentions. It will never permit Norwegian territory to be used in the service of a policy of this kind. The Norwegian Government will not be a party to any agreement with other states involving obligations on the part of Norway to make available for the armed forces of foreign powers bases on Norwegian territory as long as Norway is not attacked or subject to the threat of attack." (30) Although the response, delivered to Lange on 5 February 1949, found the Norwegian base declaration "unsatisfactory", commenting that all that was necessary for the establishment of bases was "a few provocative rumors or hastily concocted prevarications about Norway being threatened by attack", the Soviet Union was probably quite happy with Norwegian assurances. Of course, the Soviets probably would have preferred Norwegian refusal to accept a foreign force under any circumstances; making the decision dependent on Norwegian appraisal of the international situation made it subject to review at any time. But with prudence, the U.S.S.R. could avoid a direct American military presence at its northern border.

The Norwegians waited a month before answering the second Soviet note, first because Lange was heading a delegation to Washington to negotiate the terms of a Norwegian participation in NATO, but also because their response could only repeat previous statements. The recent Soviet offer of a nonaggression pact was refused on the grounds that as members of the U.N. both countries had already pledged themselves to nonaggression. (31)

Lange had briefed the Storting on his discussions with the American secretary of state on 24 February 1949. On 3 March, a secret session of the body gave him the permission to participate in the final preparations for the Atlantic pact. Parliamentarians argued that Norway should be able to exert its influence on the alliance's final form. Moreover, American planners had to know Norway's defense needs before drawing up their 1949-1950 aid program. (32) A bill sanctioning Norwegian alliance to the Atlantic nations was debated in the Storting on 29 March 1949, and approved by an overwhelming majority of 130 votes to thirteen. Those who opposed were the eleven Communists and two dissident members of the Social Democratic party.

Norway's decision to participate in the Atlantic pact was the final blow to a Scandinavian defense union. With this option gone, the Danes were left with choosing between a return to an isolated neutrality, or following the Norwegians into the Atlantic pact.

---

30 Quoted in Greve, *op. cit.*, 16. For the full text of the Soviet and Norwegian notes, see *ibid.*, appendix.
31 *Ibid.*, 19.
32 *Ibid.*

Neutrality posed two problems, however. First, the Americans had been very reluctant to evacuate the bases established on Greenland in 1941. Both for their early warning defense system and as a stop-over for the intercontinental flights of its strategic bombers, Greenland at this stage of the Cold War was of vital interest to the United States. Reports from the Danish ambassador in Washington, H. Kaufmann, indicated that, far from willing to negotiate the evacuation of their bases, the Americans were insisting on a longterm agreement for the defense of Greenland. *(33)* To acquiesce on this point, however, invited the possibility of a Soviet compensatory demand for bases on Bornholm or other parts of Danish territory. *(34)* An even more important problem concerned the American government's lack of interest in the Danish mainland. U.S. planners considered the country too exposed geographically to be defensible, and useful only in preventing the Soviets from breaking out of the Baltic, an object equally well achieved from the Norwegian shores of the Skagerrak. *(35)* Kauffmann considered it very unlikely that American guarantees for the integrity of Denmark would be forthcoming unless the Danes became members of the Atlantic alliance.

Under these circumstances, the response of the Danish government came as no surprise. On 27 February 1949, Prime Minister Hedtoft told officials of his Social Democratic party that the government *(36)* would not approve a policy that led to isolated neutrality. The same day his party, and a few days later the Foreign Relations Committee of the Folketing, extended the permission to investigate extended political and defense cooperation with other democratic nations. Foreign Minister G. Rasmussen left for Washington on 9 March 1949, for direct talks with Dean Acheson and State Department officials on the terms of Danish alliance. During the discussions the Americans emphasized that they expected no foreign bases in Denmark, and that their presence in Greenland would cease to be an issue once Denmark and the U.S. joined forces. On 17 March 1949, the Brussels Pact countries, Norway, the U.S., and Canada invited the Danish government to sign the Atlantic Treaty in Washington in early April. After extended debate in the Folketing, their offer was accepted by a vote of 119 to twenty-three. *(37)*

---

33  Letter from Ambassador H. Kauffmann to Foreign Minister G. Rasmussen, 14 February 1949, *Dansk Sikkerhedspolitik, II*, 79. The Americans clearly felt that the stipulation of the 1941 treaty extending U.S. rights until threats against the American continent had ceased had lost none of its importance. Henningsen, *op. cit.*, 26.
34  E. Bjøl, "NATO and Denmark", *Cooperation and Conflict*, III, 2 (1968), 95.
35  *Ibid.*
36  The Social Democrats then formed a minority government.
37  The Conservative and Liberal (Venstre) parties, who had always considered an Atlantic

Iceland greeted the failure of the Scandinavian defense union with much relief. Excluded from the proposed organization, Iceland had feared the union's succesful implementation would mean isolation for the outsider. Yet World War II and the tensions between East and West made it all too clear that the country would immediately be drawn into any conflict between the Soviet bloc and the West. Prime Minister S. Stefansson argued this way in a letter to his Norwegian counterpart informing him that on 7 December 1948 the U.S. ambassador had implied that Iceland would soon be invited to join the Atlantic alliance. *(38)* In view of Iceland's key position in the Atlantic, mid-way between Britain and America, the invitation was not unexpected. The formal offer was delivered in January 1949, and at the Oslo meeting of Scandinavian foreign ministers, Icelandic Foreign Minister Bjarni Benediktsson discussed the matter with his colleagues from Norway and Denmark, who by then had also received invitations.

On 12 March 1949, Benediktsson too left for Washington to obtain further information about the rights and obligations under the proposed treaty and to clarify the special position of Iceland, which had no military forces and was unwilling to station foreign troops on its territory in time of peace. *(39)*

Following discussions with Dean Acheson and State Department officials, a declaration was issued which contained the following points:

1) "In case of war the alliance would be granted a position in Iceland similar to that of Allies during the last war. Iceland alone would decide when such concessions should be given.
2) All other members of the Alliance have complete understanding of Iceland's special position.
3) It is recognized that Iceland has no armed forces and does not intend to establish any.
4) Iceland shall not be required to receive foreign troops or grant military bases in peacetime." *(40)*

C. Campbell suggests that the resolution *(41)* confirming Iceland's acceptance of the North Atlantic Treaty, passed the Althing easily because the Progressive party, after its electoral defeat in 1946 increasingly dominated by its

alliance the only rational solution if the Scandinavian option failed, consequently voted with the Social Democrats.
38  G. Gröndal, *op. cit.*, p. 43.
39  *Ibid.*
40  Quoted in *ibid.*, 44.
41  After the conclusion of the Kéflavik Agreement of October 1946 the Communists had left the coalition government -- other coalition partners included the Independence and Social Democratic parties -- provoking a government crisis which lasted until February 1947. A new coalition government was formed among the Social Democratic, Independence, and Progressive parties, representing 17.8, 39.4 and 23.1 percent of the electorate respectively.

nationalist-neutralist wing, was satisfied on the foreign troops issue and therefore willing to vote with its more pro-Western coalition partners. *(42)* And
in fact, the resolution was carried by thirty-seven votes to thirteen, with two
abstentions.

In this manner three of the Scandinavian countries became members of the
Atlantic alliance. Finland locked into a special and very delicate relationship
with the Soviet Union, only Sweden remained faithful to Scandinavian aspirations of neutrality. On the other hand, while committed to the Allied cause,
Norway, Denmark, and Iceland succeeded in antagonizing the Soviet Union
only minimally by avoiding the presence of allied forces on their territory. In
Iceland, the question of foreign troops was related to the preservation of national identity, language, and culture, whereas in Norway and Denmark *(43)*
it was an expression of the national desire to maintain as low an alliance
profile as possible to save what was left of their abandoned neutrality.

Eventually the Norwegian and Danish base policies would develop into
operational factors in the Scandinavian political-strategic picture later known
as the Nordic Balance. This will be treated in more detail in the next chapter.
Here it is sufficient to say that both Denmark and Norway realized the danger
inherent in alliance membership of being dragged into a conflict over issues of
interest only to the superpowers, and they hoped to minimize it by limiting the
tensions their alignment would generate in Northern Europe. Denying the
Americans bases on their territory was a means to that end. In doing so they
effectively reduced Soviet freedom of action in the North, a bonus they gladly
accepted even though they had not clearly foreseen it at the treaty's signing.

In addition, a low-key response was also an expression of the lack of enthusiasm with which they entered the alliance. Rather than seeing association with
the world's most powerful nation as an increase in international prestige, they
regretted the abandoned neutrality and forsaken Scandinavian unity security
considerations had forced them to concede.

---

42  Campbell, *loc. cit.*, 83-84.
43  In fact, Denmark never made as firm a commitment to the U.S.S.R. on foreign bases as
Norway did. On the contrary, when the vote on NATO membership was taken in the Folketing, an amendment introduced by the Communists to prohibit foreign bases got only nine
votes, all communist. After the outbreak of the Korean War, the U.S. asked both Iceland
and Denmark to receive an American air base. Iceland acquiesced but Denmark refused the
request, saying that the stationing of foreign troops might have adverse psychological effects
upon the population and that the allied deployment of forces south of Denmark was still
insufficient. In 1957 the Danes' prudent attitude on foreign bases was extended. The Danish
government, like the Norwegian, let it be known that "under the present circumstances" no
nuclear warheads would be allowed on Danish soil. The Danish governments have maintained
that policy ever since that time. Bjøl, Haagerup, *et al.*, *Danmark og NATO*, 33-35.

# Chapter III

# EVALUATION OF SCANDINAVIAN NATO MEMBERSHIP

## ASSETS FOR NATO

As discussed above, one of the key reasons for Scandinavian participation in NATO was the 1949 decision of the U.S. National Security Council not to supply arms to the proposed Scandinavian defense union. The Americans argued that priority belonged to countries allied or cooperating closely with the U.S. They hoped as well that if the Scandinavian scheme failed to materialize, at least Norway would enter the Atlantic alliance and thus provide the West with much needed air bases within striking distance of the Soviet Union. *(1)*

As it turned out, Norway, Denmark, and Iceland entered the alliance on limited terms by refusing foreign bases on their territory. In 1951 Iceland reversed that position and accepted American troops. Norway and Denmark, however, have continued to maintain their low profile. Iceland later repeatedly threatened to end the defense force agreement, most recently in 1973 but so far has not done so. Given the minimal contribution of these three countries, the question arises: what has the alliance gained from their participation?

At first glance, one might say that merely denying the Soviets domination of the Norwegian coast and the Danish Straits has been an asset for the West. For both offensive and defensive reasons, the Soviet Union obviously has a vital interest in controlling the routes to and from the Baltic Sea. Especially during the latter half of the 1940s and the 1950s, before the massive build up of Soviet naval forces on the Kola Peninsula, securing access to the Atlantic for their Baltic-based submarines and other warships must have been imperative. And, conversely, closing the area to enemy warships threatening to Soviet communication lines as well as to Soviet-controlled coastal areas was equally

---

*1* L. Burbank, "Scandinavian Integration and Western Defense", *Foreign Affairs*, XXXV (October, 1956), 150.

important. *(2)* On the other hand, the Norwegian coast and Iceland would probably be of value to the U.S.S.R. only in the case of a generalized conflict with the West, when control of these areas could cut dangerously into the communication channels between the U.S. and Europe and open the way for the Soviet navy to threaten America itself. In the international political atmosphere of the late 1940s, a generalized conflict may not have been imminent, but its possibility could not have been excluded. At the time, denying Soviet control over the Norwegian coast and Iceland meant a precious safeguard against Soviet interference with the communication lines between Western Europe and the United States.

The three countries certainly were not desirable for their military strength. Iceland had no army and intended to establish none. In 1948-1949 Norway and Denmark had little more than the nucleus of a force which had grown out of the resistance during the occupation. It was still being organized and was greatly in need of new and modern equipment. In terms of armed forces, Norway and Denmark were, at least initially, more a liability than an asset.

With allied, mainly American and Canadian, aid Norwegian and Danish military force eventually reached a level of strength sufficient to withstand a first wave of an enemy attack, before allied help arrived. The exposed location of both Denmark and Norway, and their refusal of foreign bases led alliance defense planners to design a balanced military structure for both Scandinavian members. Unlike Belgium, which can afford to accept special responsibilities such as a concentration of naval efforts on minesweeping, Norway and Denmark must be able to defend themselves in the initial stage of an attack. Unless they can hold out long enough for the allied forces to intervene, *(3)* their territory will be speedily occupied, and the larger powers would confront a *fait accompli.*

In both Norway and Denmark, trained and well-equipped local defense forces, or home guards, consisting of some 70,000 to 80,000 volunteers in each country *(4)* make the Danish and Norwegian defense effort credible. As sti-

2   E. Reske-Nielsen, "Danmarks Sikkerhedspolitik" (mimeographed paper prepared for the Gotlandseminar, 20-26 August 1967), 4.
3   Reske-Nielsen and Kragh, *Atlantpagten og Danmark*, 112-113.
4   In Denmark the local defense force, or Hjemmevaernet, has stabilized at around 70,000 since 1957. It consists of army, navy, and air force numbering 47,500, 3,000, and 10,500 men, and 6,600, 1,000, and 1,400 women respectively. Their duties range from direct combat activities to surveillance, sabotage, and sanitary and ordinance services. See Bjøl, Haagerup *et al., Danmark og NATO*, 29. See also X., "Denmark's New Territorial Army", *Military Review*, XXXII (April 1952), 92-95. The Norwegian home guard is comparable to its Danish counterpart in tasks and structure. Most of the 80,000 men, however, are recruits who are

pulated by the Defense Law of 1960, after mobilization the Danish army contains approximately 80,000 men, consisting of three tank infantry brigades, three motorized infantry brigades of 5,000 men each, a reduced infantry brigade on the island or Bornholm, fifteen local defense batallions and as many local defense batteries, and a series of supply and support units, among them two Honest John and one Nike rocket units. In peacetime, however, the standing forces of the Danish army number only four armoured infantry brigades, two in Jutland and two in Zealand, one batallion of Centurion tanks, and three artillery batallions, of which two are equipped with Honest John rockets and one with 203 mm. Howitzers. In addition to the various supply and support units, one infantry batallion is stationed on the island of Bornholm. In 1971, the peacetime strength of the Danish army was around 24,000 men, a figure well below the peak of the fifties and early sixties -- it reached 34,000 in 1964 -- due to the gradual reduction of the legth of military service. In 1952 service lasted eighteen months, in 1954 sixteen months, in 1964 fourteen months, in 1966 twelve months. *(5)*

Denmark's strategic importance lies in its capacity to control access to the Baltic Sea, and the Danish armed forces are responsible for preventing the enemy from utilizing the straits. The job mainly falls to the Danish navy, which maintains control over the Sound and the Belts and protects the country against invasion. In case of attack, maritime forces would blockade the straits and secure the mobility of the Danish land forces by using the inner waterways as supply and communication routes. *(6)*

A steady surveillance of adjacent waters is one of the conditions for preparedness as well as one of the services Denmark renders to the alliance. Keeping a close watch on the traffic in shipping among Eastern bloc countries helps greatly in assessing their military intentions. *(7)* The Danish Defense Law of 1960 therefore provided for an important naval build-up, designating eight large units, eighteen torpedo boats, six submarines, eight minelayers and twelve minesweepers, and nine patrol craft, plus a number of depot and other

allocated to the local defense force. For more details see *Ministry of Defense, Vårt Forsvar*, (Oslo, 1964), and E. Riggert, "Norwegische Heimwehr", *Wehrkunde*, VIII (February, 1959).

5  Another five field brigade groups supposedly can be activated within twenty hours, as the reservists live close to their mobilization depots and two of the reserve brigade groups are called up each year for three to four weeks of training. E. O'Ballance, "Defense Problems of Denmark", *Military Review*, XLII (June, 1962), 27-28.

6  E. Bjøl, Haagerup *et al., Danmark og NATO*, 26.

7  *Ibid.,* 27.

special units. Danish efforts with mainly American help *(8)* have largely realized this program. *(9)*

The Danish air force, mainly a tactical force, supports the land and naval
forces in their defense of the national territory and control of adjacent waters.
With some hundred fighter planes and fighterbombers, seventeen transport
planes and fifty training aircraft, *(10)* the air force closely approximates the
provisions of the law. *(11)* The Danish armed forces are relatively small and
designed to hold the first wave of an enemy attack. Yet conviction of the likelihood of such aggression has changed over the years, and in response the size
of their military and the amount the Danes have been willing to spend on it,
has gradually reduced. Danish defense expenditure has stabilized around three
percent of the gross national product (G.N.P.), one of the lowest in NATO.*(12)*

8  In 1959, a Danish-American shipbuilding program produced some twenty-three ships
for a total value of ± 300 million Danish kroner. The U.S. contributed fifty percent of the
construction costs. See Reske-Nielsen and Kragh, *Atlantpagten og Danmark*, 147.

9  In 1971 the Danish navy consisted of six submarines, two fast frigates and four other
frigates, four corvettes, four fleet minelayers and eight coastal minelayers, twelve minesweepers, nine seaward defense craft, sixteen torpedo boats, twelve patrol craft, and ten
other ships. In peacetime the Danish navy numbers some 7,000 men. Figures received from
F. Borberg, military affairs contributor of *Berlingske Tidende*. Also *The Military Balance*
(London, 1971).

10  These include three squadrons of fighter bombers two of which are equipped with
F-100/Fs and one which converted to the Swedish Draken F-35 XDs in 1971; three squadrons
of interceptors, one equipped with Hawker Hunters, the other two with F-104G starfighters;
one reconnaissance squadron with RF-84Fs and in the process of converting to Draken
RF-35s; one transport squadron of C-47s and C-54s; one air-sea rescue squadron equipped
with Catalinas, S-55, and S-61 helicopters. Finally, in 1968 four semimobile Hawk batteries
were installed to supplement the four Nike Ajax batteries located around Copenhagen.
Information from spokesmen of the Danish Ministry of Defense as well as *The Military
Balance*, 1960 through 1971.

11  It provided for three squadrons of fighter bombers, one squadron of reconnaissance
planes, three all-weather fighter squadrons, and two air defense rocket units. Bjøl, Haagerup,
*et al.*, *Danmark og NATO*, 4.

12  From 1949 until 1970 Danish defense expenditure as a percentage of the G.N.P. (at factor
cost, current prices) were as follows:

| 1949 | 1950 | 1951 | 1952 | 1953 | 1954 | 1955 | 1956 | 1957 | 1958 | 1959 |
|------|------|------|------|------|------|------|------|------|------|------|
| 2.1  | 1.8  | 2.3  | 3.0  | 3.7  | 3.6  | 3.6  | 3.4  | 3.5  | 3.3  | 2.9  |

| 1960 | 1961 | 1962 | 1963 | 1964 | 1965 | 1966 | 1967 | 1968 | 1969 | 1970 |
|------|------|------|------|------|------|------|------|------|------|------|
| 3.1  | 2.9  | 3.4  | 3.5  | 3.2  | 3.3  | 3.1  | 3.3  | 3.3  | 3.0  | 2.8  |

Source: NATO, *Facts and Figures* (Brussels, 1971), 226-227.

As in Denmark, the Norwegian armed forces assure an effective warning and surveillance service, prepare the strongest possible resistance against invasion, and create the conditions for best receiving allied help. *(13)* Not surprisingly, therefore, the Norwegian military effort is very much like the Danish one, with a low number of permanently active effectives and a highly developed system of territorial defense.

Norway is divided in two military regions, north and south. Because of its NATO membership, the country is able to concentrate its attention in the north, relying on Danish, German, and British forces for the defense of southern Norway. Thus, of a total armed strength of only one division, one brigade is stationed at Tromsö and one batallion in the northernmost province Finnmark. In the south, a royal guard batallion is stationed in Oslo, with smaller units at various airfields.

The province of Finnmark, of 48,650 km² and 72,000 inhabitants, shares a border with the Soviet Union of some 120 miles (200 km) and is badly defended. Against an estimated Soviet strength of four to five divisions, stationed in the Murmansk area, the Norwegians have positioned only one batallion. This unit is not really expected to counter the Soviet forces in the area, however. Its responsibilities include establishing that armed aggression has taken place and locating it, and symbolizing Norwegian defense will. *(14)*

Norway's real strength lies south in the Tromsö-Bardufoss area, some eight hundred miles (1,300 km) southwest of Murmansk. The area is extremely rugged and inaccessible, and excellently suited for defense purposes. Here a thoroughly trained and well-equipped brigade *(15)* has prepared a serious defense against a possible Soviet invasion. Because of the overwhelming superiority of the U.S.S.R., however, this brigade can only fight for time, so as to enable NATO forces to come to the rescue of Norway. *(16)* Norway's

---

13 *Vårt Forsvar, op. cit.,* 4-5.

14 L. Crollen, "Les Flancs de l'alliance Atlantique sont-ils menacés?" *La Revue Générale Belge,* n° spécial: *Pourquoi l'OTAN?* (September, 1969), 13.

15 Beginning in 1970, modern German Leopard tanks have gradually replaced the M-48 tanks. After mobilization the brigade can became a division almost overnight. In a very short timespan Norway can mobilize some 130,000 troops, not including a home guard of 70,000.

16 Crollen, *loc. cit.,* 14. To demonstrate allied solidarity and to insure the immediate dispatch of allied forces to threatened or vulnerable areas, a multinational mobile force (A.M.F. or Allied Command Europe's Mobile Force) was created in 1960. This task force, of one brigade, exercises almost exclusively on the flanks of NATO in northern Norway and in Turkey. It consists of infantry batallions from Canada, Italy, the United Kingdom, and the United States. In December 1967, a similar naval force was established under SACLANT, known as STANAVFORLANT (Standing Naval Force Atlantic). NATO, *Facts and Figures, op. cit.,* 64. Maneuvers such as the Northern Express (June 1965), Polar Express

policy not to alow foreign troops on its territory in peacetime, has created difficulties on the question of outside assistance. U.S. reinforcement would take an estimated ten days to two weeks to reach Norway, the British ten to twenty days, and thirty days for Canadian troops. *(17)* In order to speed their arrival, airfields and naval bases have been constructed with allied, mainly American, aid. In northern Norway, airfields are situated at Tromsö, Bodø, Bardufoss, Banak, and on the island of Andöya. A naval base is situated at Haakonsvern.

Securing allied access to these bases and keeping communication lines between the various airfields and ports intact are among the major responsibilities of the Norwegian navy and air force. The reconstruction of the Norwegian navy, which in the forties and fifties consisted of older British and American ships, was approved by parliament (Storting) in 1960. In 1968 the renewal program was for all practical purposes finished, thanks to a substantial American assistance in the estimated expense of 750 million crowns. Today, the navy consists of five frigates, fifteen submarines, four minelayers and ten minesweepers, two coastal escort ships, twenty-one gunboats, and twenty-five torpedo boats. Its personnel numbers 8,500, not including the 800 who man the coastal artillery. *(18)*

The Norwegian air force (R.N.O.A.F.) at present consists of 9,400 men and 121 combat aircraft. This is well below the peak in 1957, when the R.N.O.A.F. had over 200 modern fighter aircraft at its disposal following a feverish build-up begun in 1951. *(19)* The change is indicative of the gradual reduction in American aid, which resulted in the establishment of more realistic defense goals for the country. Yet the air force continues to enjoy a high priority since it is considered the most economic means of protecting long areas of coastline with a low manpower investment. *(20)*

(1968) and Strong Express (September 1972) have given a great deal of attention to the smooth cooperation of the Norwegian and A.C.E. Mobile Force troops and the efficiency of STANAVFORLANT.

17 "The Soviet Threat to NATO's Northern Flank", *Time*, 18 October 1971, 31.

18 *The Military Balance*, 1960 through 1971. Although the Norwegian coast is recognized as the weak spot of Norwegian defense, many coastal batteries left over from the German occupation have been dismantled for economic reasons. Today coastal artillery is concentrated in the Oslo Fjord and on vulnerable stretches of the coast in northern Norway. A. Haugan, "The Defense of Norway", *Military Review*, XLIV (January, 1964), 20.

19 This massive build-up was only possible through shared financing of the infrastructure and the delivery of aircraft and other technical equipment from the United States under the military aid program. T. Anderssen, "The Royal Norwegian Air Force", *The Royal Air Force Quarterly*, VII (Summer, 1968), 97.

20 W.C. Wettmore, "Norwegian Defense Posture gives Key Role to Air Force", *Aviation Week and Space Technology*, XC, 11, [no date provided] 40.

An analysis of the structure of the Danish and Norwegian armed forces reveals the importance placed on the navy and air force. Within both branches, surveillance and reconnaissance are emphasized, striking capacities deemphasized. This parallels the official expectations of the military capacity in both countries: stress on surveillance and participation in early warning systems, a reasonable amount of transport capability to enable small army units to move into threatened areas, and emphasis in the air force on fighterbombers, "in order that forceful attacks can be made without delay on an intruder" and "the strongest possible defense of selected air bases... in order that allied air and ground forces can be flown in for assistance." (21)

In the early years of NATO, the Norwegian and Danish refusal to allow foreign (meaning American) bases on their territory constituted a serious setback for the U.S., since it reduced the striking capabilities of the Strategic Air Command along the northern border of the U.S.S.R. Nevertheless, Norway and Denmark constituted a major asset to the alliance. They offered surveillance possibilities along the Soviet navy's route to the Atlantic, and were a vital link in the early warning system that protected the American continent against Soviet long-range bombers.

The development of intercontinental ballistic missiles dramatically reduced the need for forward bases. At the same time it increased the need for an extensive line of prewarning stations. Here the Scandinavian NATO partners continue to play an important role. Greenland, Iceland, and the Faroes are part of the D.E.W. line (22) which stretches from Alaska over northern Canada to the Norwegian Sea. Norway and Denmark contribute to N.A.D.G.E. (23) which covers NATO's air space from north to south, down through Italy, Greece, and Turkey. Greenland is also the site of one of three B.M.E.W.S. stations. (24) The island of Bornholm, more easterly than the Polish-East German border, houses a valuable base for early warning installations.

Their responsibilities in supervizing the movements of the Soviet navy and preparing serious obstacles to these movements in case of a conflict are also

---

21 Anderssen, *loc. cit.*, 100.
22 Distant Early Warning.
23 NATO Air Defense Ground Environment is a defensive shield that became operative in early 1972. An electronic network made up of high capacity, high speed computers, it introduced new giant radar systems, modernized existing facilities, and eliminated loopholes among the individual air defense stations. See E. Nouel, "NADGE: The Last Word in Computerised Air Defense", *NATO Review*, XIX (July-August, 1971), 8-12. See also NATO, *Facts and Figures*, op. cit., 122-123.
24 Ballistic Missile Early Warning System, which covers the whole of the Soviet bloc. The other sites are located in Alaska and in Scotland.

vital to the alliance. Denmark, of course, has been the historical gatekeeper of the Baltic. Until 1658, when it ceded the eastern coast of the Sound to Sweden, Denmark had absolute control over all the waterways connecting the Baltic with the Atlantic Ocean. After that date, and particularly following the construction of the Kiel Canal in the nineteenth century, the passage to and from the Baltic has ceased to be an exclusively Danish affair. *(25)* Still, of the 100,000 ships that every year move in and out of the area, something like 40,000 use the Danish straits. Approximately half of these fly a Soviet bloc flag. *(26)* Bound by the Sound Treaty of 1857, which declared the Danish Straits international waters, Denmark will not violate the right of passage of foreign ships, including warships, in time of peace. In accordance with international law, however, the Danes request submarines to pass the straits surfaced, giving them excellent opportunities to follow their movements. Of the three Danish Straits (Little Belt, Great Belt, and Sound), the Little Belt is of minimal importance as a transit route. Although its waters are sufficiently deep, a range of small islands divides it in a series of narrow passages where the current becomes very strong. The Sound is only navigable for ships with a draft of under twenty-six feet. The Great Belt alone can be used by larger ships. Even though in the 1950s and 1960s a great part of the Soviet naval strike capacity was transferred to the Arctic, the Soviet Baltic fleet remains quite impressive, as the table below illustrates.

The gradual relocation of the Soviet fleet was inspired by the ease with which the Danish straits can be closed blocking Soviet ships in the Baltic. However, the actual strength of the remaining force (seventy-seven submarines and 455 surface craft) suggests that the Soviets still regard the Baltic as a strategic area of the utmost importance.

A realistic assessment of the probable Soviet course in an international war revolves around several goals: thwarting a nuclear threat from NATO, iso-

---

25 Important to mention here is the so-called Stalin Canal, built by the U.S.S.R. between both world wars to overcome the naval difficulties it encountered as a result of the independence of the three Baltic republics. Their neutrality deprived the Soviets of a Baltic coast except for a small area around Leningrad, inside the Finnish Gulf. The Stalin Canal links the White Sea with Lake Onega, and, beyond Lake Ladoga with the Newa. Submarines and destroyers can move through the Canal from the Baltic to the Arctic. However, the passage is very vulnerable to air attack, and is ice-bound for at least six months a year.

26 H.M. Petersen, "Maritime Denmark", *US Naval Institute Proceedings*, XCIV, (January, 1968), 47. In a report to the Assembly of the West European Union, the present Dutch foreign minister Van der Stoel stated that in 1968 four hundred Soviet naval craft, including sixty submarines and some 15,000 Soviet bloc commercial and fishing ships, passed the Danish straits. M. Van der Stoel, "Le Flanc Nord de l'Alliance Atlantique", *Nouvelles de l'OTAN*, XVII (September, 1969), 16.

## TABLE I

The Soviet Navy: Number and Strength of the Northern and Baltic Fleets.

| Category of vessel | Total | Northern fleet | Baltic fleet |
|---|---|---|---|
| Helicopter carriers (cruisers) | 2 | — | — |
| Missile cruisers | 10 | 3 | 2 |
| Cruisers | 10 | 2 | 3 |
| Missile destroyers | 40 | 8 | 6 |
| Destroyers | 60 | 15 | 12 |
| Missile patrol boats | 140 | 20 | 40 |
| Ocean-going escorts | 105 | 35 | 20 |
| Coastal escorts | 250 | 40 | 70 |
| Fast patrol boats | 250 | 60 | 125 |
| Minesweepers | 300 | 60 | 120 |
| Landing ships | 105 | 25 | 42 |
| Landing craft | 120 | — | 15 |
| Missile submarines | | | |
| SLBM nuclear (Surface Lauched Ballistic Missiles) | 35 | 20 | — |
| SLBM diesel (Surface Launched Ballistic Missiles) | 28 | 15 | — |
| SSCM nuclear (Subsurface Launched Ballistic Missiles) | 35 | 20 | — |
| SSCM diesel (Subsurface Launched Ballistic Missiles) | 25 | 12 | 2 |
| Attack submarines | | | |
| Nuclear, long-range | 21 | 18 | — |
| Nuclear, short-range | 4 | — | — |
| Diesel, long-range | 60 | 30 | 15 |
| Diesel, middle-range | 140 | 50 | 50 |
| Diesel, short-range | 15 | — | 10 |

Note: Fleet size changes; the figures quoted are typical examples.
Source: Institute for Strategic Studies, *Strategic Survey*, 1971, 28.

lating Europe from the United States, and neutralizing NATO forces on the European continent. *(27)* Penetration into the Atlantic from positions on the Kola Peninsula is a matter of relative ease -- the concentration of the majority of Soviet submarines in the Murmansk area is a reminder of this -- and the destruction of the communication lines between the U.S.A. and Europe does

27  Petersen, *loc. cit.*, 48.

245

not require passage of the Soviet Baltic fleet through the Danish straits. On the other hand, of vital interest to the Soviets is denying NATO powers operation in the Baltic, where they would threaten extremely important Soviet industrial centers, many of their medium-range ballistic missile sites, and, finally, many ports, shipbuilding-, and repair centers between Leningrad and the Elbe River. Thus, the Soviet Baltic fleet would normally attempt to turn the Baltic into a *mare clausum. (28)* N. Örvik suggests that the gradual restructuring of the force from large conventional warships to smaller missile-bearing craft indicates that the Soviets are creating a local fleet designed for operations only in the Baltic. The rapid improvement in Soviet amphibious capacity and the accelerated training of marine infantry point in the same direction. *(29)* For solely defensive purposes, the Soviets would be vitally interested in occupying Denmark and securing control of the Danish straits. Such a move would at the same time improve their capacities for maritime warfare in the North Sea and the North Atlantic by liberating the still impressive number of ocean-going submarines and surface ships in the Baltic fleet. Danish and NATO strategy therefore centers around establishing zones of naval control, to be maintained behind "air, surface and subsurface [mine] barriers at the southern entrances of the straits." *(30)* Once functioning, such a barrier would allow neutral and allied traffic to pass in reasonable safety while denying the use of the straits to enemy ships. The composition and preparedness of the Danish naval and air forces and their institutionalized cooperation with West German counterparts through B.A.L.T.A.P. *(31)* are efforts in the realization of this strategy.

As noted above, the Soviet naval build-up has emphasized the Arctic fleet. If the Soviet navy has become "the super navy of a super power," *(32)* the Arctic has developed into the home base of its main deterrent component. Obviously this factor has given a dimension to Norwegian NATO membership completely lacking in 1949. At that time, the U.S.S.R. was far from being a sea power. Its naval apparatus was designed to be an extension of its stationary coastal defense. *(33)* Although "Stalin's twenty-year building program of 1946 envisaged the eventual creation of a balanced "fleet-in-being", writes J.J. Holst, research director of the Norwegian Institute for Foreign Affairs, "that fleet was apparently intended primarily for defending against seaborne

28  E. Bjøl, "A Soviet View on Northern Europe", *Cooperation and Conflict*, VI, (1967), 113.
29  N. Örvik, "Die Strategische Lage Skandinaviens und der NATO", *Wehrkunde*, XVII (May, 1968), 257.
30  Petersen, *loc. cit.*, 49.
31  Joint Danish-German command for the Baltic approaches, established in 1961.
32  *Jane's Fighting Ships*, (London) 1971-1972.
33  N. Örvik, *loc. cit.*, 259.

invasions." *(34)* Seen against the defensive nature of its navy, the strong Soviet reaction against the Norwegian and Danish alliance in NATO takes on additional meaning. The Soviets were primarily interested in preventing a rival (American) presence in the Baltic and on the North Cap that would threaten Leningrad and northcentral Russia, as Germany had done during World War II. The Norwegian rejection of foreign troops, Swedish neutrality, and the Finnish-Soviet Treaty of 1948 alleviated their concern. *(35)* However, the Norwegian base policy Holst notes, was formulated against the background of Anglo-American preeminence in the Atlantic. *(36)* This implied that in case of a Soviet attack allied help could reach Norwegian territory with relative ease, making the need for foreign bases on Norwegian soil secondary to the country's security, and allowing it the opportunity to play down the provocative character of its alliance.

In the late sixties and the early seventies, the strategic picture in Northern Europe changed completely. The Soviet Union developed a naval force second only to that of the United States, and concentrated most of its strike force on the North Cap. Effective naval parity between the superpowers has been established, clearly affecting the possibility of allied help in the event of localized aggression by the Soviets. For reasons developed below, such a move could occur only in northern Norway, an area of so small a population and so lacking in economic significance *(37)* that the allies might accept a *fait accompli* there. The primary reason why the Soviets would risk a test to allied solidarity, so the argument goes, is their inadequate facilities on the Kola Peninsula. They look with eagerness to the ice-free fjords on the Norwegian coast to support their expanding Arctic fleet. "What is new in the actual situation", writes Örvik, "is the existence of a Soviet naval capacity of such dimensions that it cannot be fully utilized without having at its disposal base and operation facilities that can only be obtained at the Norwegian coast. That means that the Soviets in case of war or in an intense crisis situation could have such a need to control these areas that they discard all objections against such a move." *(38)* Another Norwegian expert argues that in its composition and armaments as well as in its operational patterns, the Soviet fleet to a large extent reflects the altering Soviet assessment of the American naval threat. *(39)*

34  J.J. Holst, "The Soviet Build-Up in the North-East Atlantic", *NATO Review*, XIX (September-October, 1971), 21.
35  Örvik, *loc. cit.*, 259.
36  Holst, *loc. cit.*, 21.
37  Of the 72,000 inhabitants, nearly all are fishermen or farmers.
38  Örvik, *loc. cit.*, 260.
39  J.J. Holst, "The Soviet Union and Nordic Security", *Cooperation and Conflict*, VI, 3-4, (1971), 139.

*Soviet Naval activity in 1960 ...*

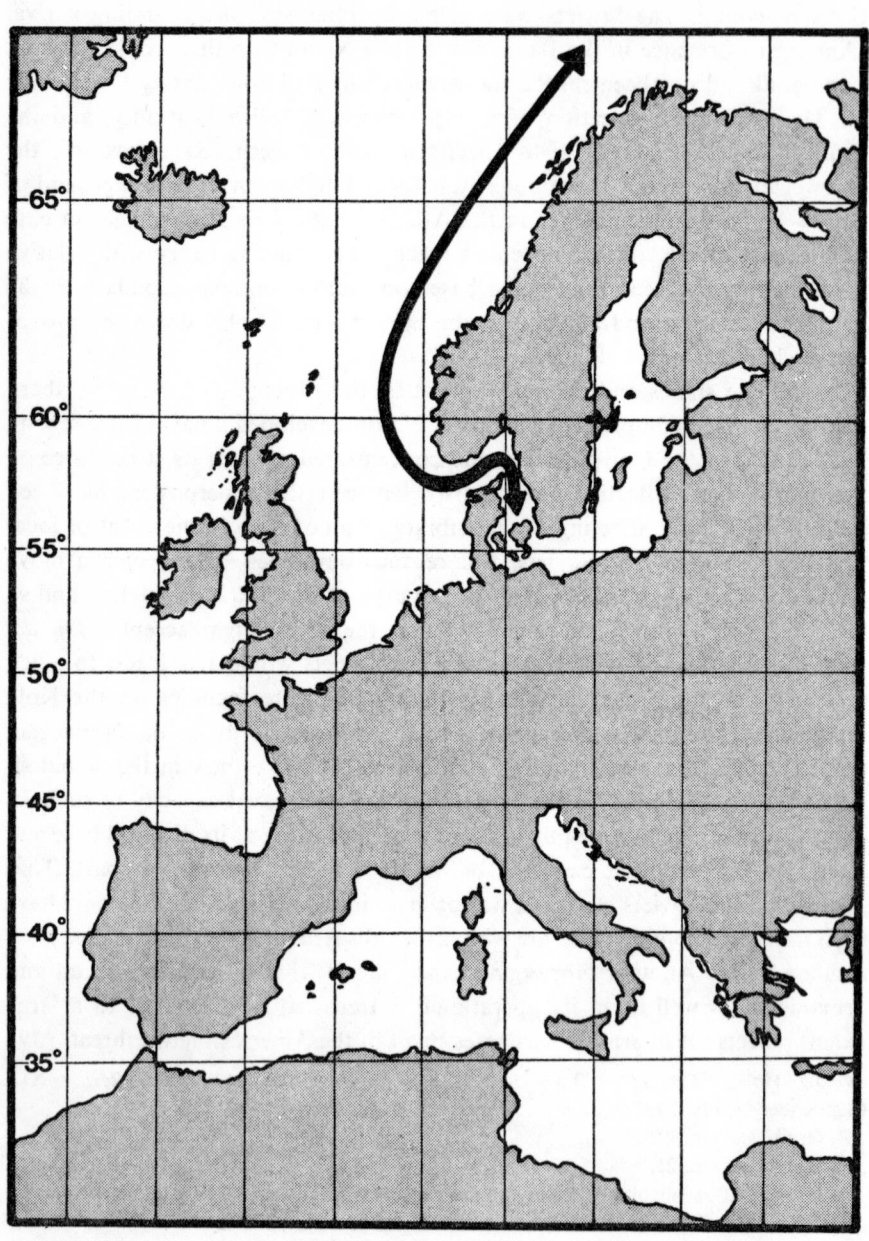

*... and in 1969*

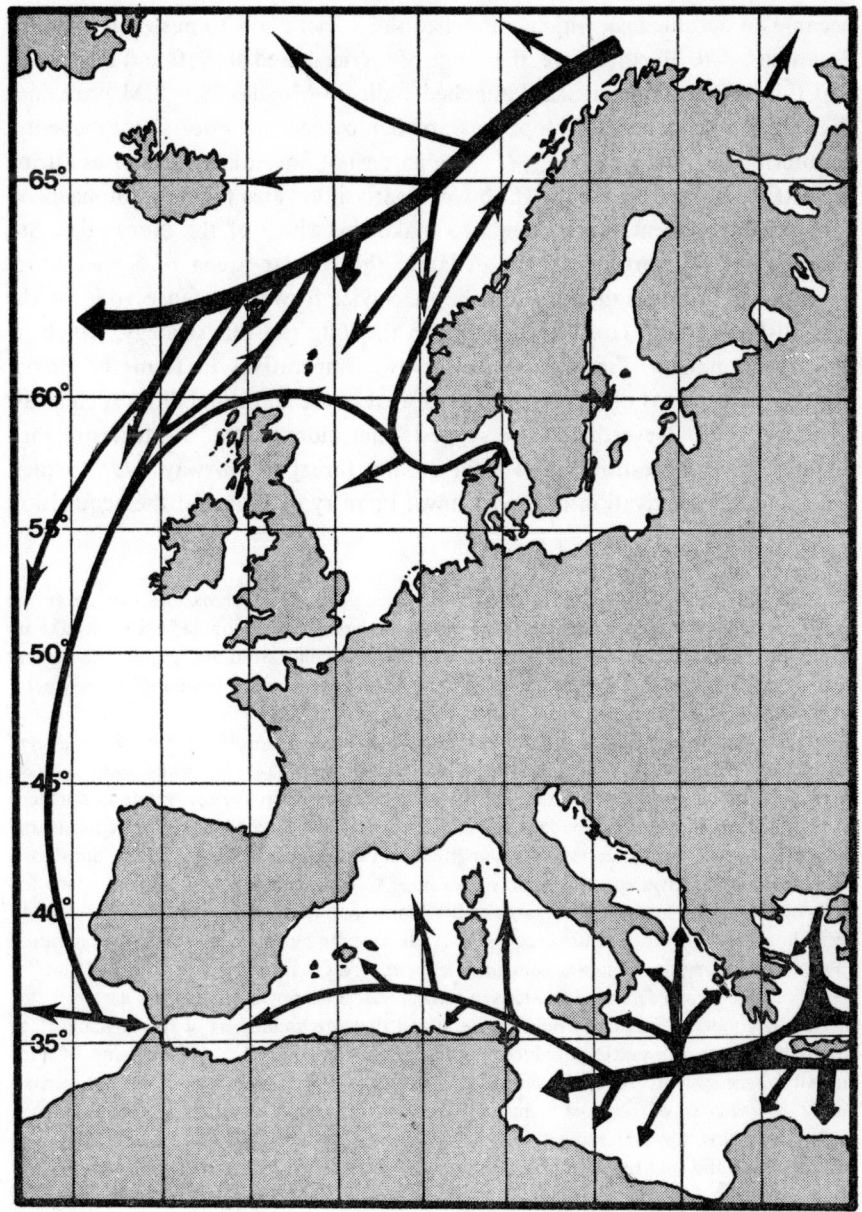

For example, the emergence of the Polaris in the sixties forced the Soviets to equip their surface ships with antisubmarine warfare missiles and to develop fast hunterkiller submarines. "The whole problem of anti-submarine warfare became an oceanic task which compelled the Soviet Navy to push out from the fleet areas. *(40)* Furthermore, the range of carrier-based aircraft and the second and third generation Surface Launched Ballistic Missiles (S.L.B.M.) are such that the Russians had to adopt forward deployment in order to implement a counterforce strategy at sea." *(41)* The pattern of Soviet naval exercises during the sixties, as seen on the chart above, clearly illustrates the new emphasis on forward deployment, which tends to make the whole of the Norwegian Sea and the central portions of the Atlantic the regular arena of Soviet naval operations. In addition, it establishes a Soviet forward defense zone in the Iceland-Faroes gap. Holst argues that in the long run this strategy, which he sees as permanent, "may generate its own imperatives in terms of Soviet military perceptions of the desirability of real estate and capabilities such as air coverage." *(42)* Nevertheless, he suggests that more subtle "strategies of inti-midation and suggestion" pose a far greater threat to Norway. *(43)* In fact, following the reactivation of Soviet naval infantry in 1964 and the acquisition

40   *Ibid.*, 140.
41   *Ibid.*, 142. Holst adds that whereas U.S. strategic nuclear submarines can cover the major portions of the Soviet Union from the Arctic basin, Soviet submarines must take up positions south of the Norwegian Sea to reach the major industrial and population centers of the United States, due to limitations in their missile range and a geographical assymetry which locates Canada in such a position as to afford the U.S. a certain protection.
42   *Ibid.* J. Klenberg makes a very incisive contribution to this problem in his *The Cap and the Straits -- Problems of Nordic Security*, Occasional Paper N° 18 (Cambridge, Mass., 1968). Among the more commonly advanced reasons for a Soviet desire for real estate in northern Norway, Klenberg mentions the lack of aircraft carriers, which confines the activities of the surface element of the Soviet navy in a war situation to their coastal waters, where land-based air support is also available. They may also hope to compensate for insufficient space for bases in the Kola Peninsula with bases in the Norwegian fjords. This would offer the addi-tional bonus of lessening the distance to the Atlantic shipping routes by some three hundred miles. Commenting on the first argument, Klenberg agrees that this may be true, but that "in operations other than defensive missions in coastal waters the Soviet submarines are the factor that really counts" (p. 26). He might have added that the limitations of the Soviet surface vessels have been substantially reduced by the acquisition of A.S.W. missiles and of anti-aircraft missile systems. As to the supposed crowding of Soviet bases on the narrow, perma-nently ice-free coast of the Kola Peninsula, Klenberg notes that the distance from Petshenga to Svayatov Nos, the easternmost year-round, ice-free point on the coast is still some 240 nautical miles and that the area is fairly suitable for hardened base construction (p. 39). All in all, Klenberg considers it "improbable that an issue like this would become significant enough to cause risky and costly political or military moves of a super power" (p. 41).
43   J.J. Holst, "The Soviet Union and Nordic Security", *loc. cit.*, 142.

of numerous amphibious and landing craft, the Soviet navy is well prepared for a rapid seizure of contiguous coastal areas. Maneuvers such as SEVER in 1968 and OKEAN in 1970, contrary to former practice, have been widely publicized, and in part consisted of rather ominous circumnavigations of the Norwegian coast by amphibious forces, with subsequent landing maneuvers on the coast of the Kola Peninsula. (44)

Norway's strategic value to the NATO alliance lies in its contribution to offer excellent sites for radar and communication installations in an area close to the main gateway of the Soviet naval deterrent forces. In case of attack, the few Norwegian troops stationed in the North would mount a delaying action, safeguarding airfields and naval bases until the arrival of allied reinforcements. The Soviets claim that such arrangements serve purposes other than the defense of Norway alone, (45) and even if official Norway refutes this thesis the accusation has some justification. For the airfields and naval bases in northern Norway, constructed at great cost through the NATO infrastructure program, to dispatch allied help to Norway alone, without countering the Soviet naval threat to Norway's allies, would be almost unimaginable.

Iceland and the Danish provinces of Greenland and the Faroes (46) are important to the alliance in the same ways as Norway and to a lesser extent Denmark. All these territories are vital links in a defensive arc that maintains surveillance of Soviet activities in the Atlantic and provides an early warning against missiles directed toward the United States and Canada. Iceland represents the keystone in the arc. Because of its geographical location, forces operating from its territory can detect and attack Soviet naval forces heading for the American continent through the Iceland-Faroes gap, or through the Denmark strait between Iceland and Greenland. Under the Kéflavik Agreement of 1946, American forces had been asked to evacuate the huge Kéflavik air base they had operated during World War II. Events in Korea changed the Icelandic perspective however and the government acquiesced to renewed American demands for bases. On 5 May 1951 Iceland signed a bilateral agreement with the United States which delivered the defense of the island into American hands on behalf of NATO. The treaty also stipulated that the com-

---

44  *Ibid.*, 141.

45  A.O. Brundtland criticized Klenberg's use of this argument in reviewing his paper in *Cooperation and Conflict*, IV, 4, (1968), 254.

46  Strictly speaking the Faroes Islands are not a Danish province but have been a self-governing region of the Danish Kingdom since home rule was instituted in 1948, flying its own flag and having its own Parliament, the Løgting. The Danish government and parliament continue to assume responsibility for foreign affairs and defense matters, however. The Faroes elect two members to the Danish Folketing.

position of U.S. forces on the island would be determined by the Icelandic government. Two days later, a first contingent of the Iceland defense force arrived at Kéflavik, where facilities had been maintained and partly used after 1946. Eventually, the personnel there numbered some 5,000 men, composed of elements of the army, the navy, and the air force. The army contributed tactical units for the defense of Iceland, the navy provided airborne early warning and patrol squadrons, and the air force maintained a fighter interceptor squadron and operated four radar stations at Kéflavik and the three other corners of the island. (47) In 1960, the army units were withdrawn, and eventually the size of the defense force fell to 3,000 men. (48)

The strategic importance of Greenland for the defense of the American continent has been discussed in a previous chapter, and U.S. reluctance to terminate the 1941 agreement establishing its involvement on the island was due primarily to uneasiness in Washington over a possible Soviet threat. Once Denmark was a member of the Alliance, the way was open for a continued American military presence on Greenland, formalized in the 1951 treaty. This time the Danes took great care to emphasize their sovereignty over the island, and contrary to the 1941 agreement, no bases were formally ceded to the Americans. Rather, the document created three separate defense areas -- Thule, Søndre Strømfjord and Narssarssuaq -- to be mutually controlled by both countries. (49) In 1958 Narssarssuaq was disbanded. The treaty also placed the American marine depot Grønnedal under Danish command. Although Greenland is part of the Allied Command Atlantic, in case of war the defense of the island would become the responsibility of a Danish admiral with his seat at Grønnedal, who would then function as island commander Greenland.

In fact, the Danish military presence in Greenland is restricted to some 125 men in Grønnedal and to the sledge patrol SIRIUS which consists of about twenty-five men who control the east coast of Greenland. The actual defense of the island has been assumed by the Americans, who in reality run the Thule and Søndre Strømfjord bases much as they wish. Greenland's real significance lies in its warning stations, which are part of the D.E.W. (Distant Early Warning) and B.M.E.W.S. (Ballistic Missiles Early Warning) systems. Thule,

---

47  Gröndal, *op. cit.*, 51, 68.

48  *Ibid.*, 68. The situation was somewhat paradoxical, since the U.S. presence was officially justified by the American commitment to defend the island. Global strategic considerations in the U.S. and its concern over growing Soviet naval activities in the Atlantic, inspired extensive changes in 1960, including a take-over in command of the Iceland Defense Force by the U.S. navy. In the process, the army tactical units were withdrawn, although they had been specifically earmarked for the defense of the island.

49  *Dansk Sikkerhedspolitik, I,* 69.

designed as a supply and logistics base for the American warning stations, has a runway of 2.1 miles (3,500 meter) and is able to receive the largest jet planes. Since Greenland is a part of the Danish Kingdom, which allows no nuclear weapons on its territory, the crash close to Thule in January 1968 of an American B-52 carrying four nuclear bombs provoked anger and resentment in Denmark. Apparently, the plane's attempted landing was not a regular occurence, however, and the bases on Greenland are not generally used for strategic purposes. In October 1957, Danish newspapers announced that the American government wanted to set up missile bases on Greenland: Danish Foreign Minister H.C. Hansen responded immediately with an unequivocal denial.

The Faroes have also been subject to Danish-American negotiation. In 1959 the allies agreed to establish a L.O.R.A.N. station (Long Range Navigation) at Ejde, on the west side of the main island of Stromø. The installation is controlled and operated by the American Coast Guard, and supplements a similar one built by the British during World War II. Under the NATO infrastructure program, a combined radar and radio station has also been constructed on Stromø as part of the NATO early warning line stretching from Alaska to the Norwegian Sea, where it joins N.A.D.G.E. As in Greenland in 1960 Denmark set up a Faroes Command, including a small naval detachment at Thorshavn and an air force unit that handles the early warning stations. In case of war, the Faroes commander also integrates into the NATO command system under the Allied Command Atlantic, where he becomes the island commander Faroes. *(50)*

## EFFECTS OF NATO MEMBERSHIP UPON NORWAY, DENMARK, AND ICELAND

Clearly and most importantly, membership in the North Atlantic Treaty Organization provides Norway, Denmark, and Iceland with increased security. In fact, the compelling factors behind discussions on a Nordic defense union and eventually behind alliance with the West were first and foremost security considerations, which centered around a perceived threat from the Soviet Union. Since the danger, although not immediate, was considered ubiquitous, a Nordic defense scheme seemed inadequate to the need. Neither the Danes nor the Norwegians found such a plan satisfactory, partly because Sweden, then the only noteworthy Scandinavian military power, could not guarantee the security of Greenland, Spitzbergen, the Faroes, or northern Norway, partly because the necessary supply of American military hardware was unobtainable.

50   *Ibid.*, 73, and Bjøl, Haagerup *et al.*, *Danmark og NATO*, *op. cit.*, 31.

The subject of security has been dealt with in the preceding pages, and will be touched again in next chapter, when Scandinavian perceptions of the altered relationship between East and West will be discussed. Consequently, this section will be limited to the question of economic and military assistance to the three countries, and to the strains NATO membership placed on their political leadership.

a) *Economic and Military Assistance*

From 1946 until 1965, Denmark accepted a total of $ 301.8 million in U.S. economic aid of which $ 54.3 were loans. Norway received $ 401.8 million, $ 238.4 million in grants, $ 163.4 million in loans. Iceland obtained $ 35.7 million in grants and $ 40.7 million in loans. Although these figures are unimpressive when compared with those describing assistance to other European countries, one must remember that such aid was basically aimed at reconstruction and that war damage in these countries generally was far less ruinous than elsewhere in Europe. Furthermore, all three nations are very prosperous, with Gross National Products per capita surpassing most of their European neighbors. Moreover, most economic assistance to Europe was dispensed in the immediate post war years, when Norway and Denmark were actively engaged in a policy of bridge building. As a result, they were inclined to take a cautious approach to the Marshall plan. Finally, Norway and Denmark were not essentially interested in economic aid. Their needs were more crucial in the area of military assistance; they welcomed weapon deliveries and the introduction of modern warfare technology.

By far the larger part of U.S. military assistance in the years between 1949 and 1952 and 1957 devolved to European countries. The figures reflect the American perception of Soviet expansionism, which led U.S. leaders to considerably expand and strengthen the defense posture of European countries in the belief that meeting the Soviet threat required such means. At the time, Central Europe was the presumed area of operations in a major conflict, and the most substantial part of American military assistance went to the countries that were to absorb a possible Soviet drive to the Atlantic, France, West Germany, and the Benelux countries. However, the West's vital interest in safeguarding its communication lines in the Mediterranean made help to Greece, Turkey and Italy important from the beginning, and NATO's southern boundary received extensive assistance throughout the fifties and the early sixties. After the Soviet-American confrontation over Cuba and the initiation of a feverish Soviet naval expansion program, the flanks of the alliance began to feel increasingly pressured by the Soviet threat. Military assistance to most

European countries began to decrease in the early sixties, ending by 1965. Only the allies located at the gateways of Soviet naval power continued to receive military assistance. This was especially true on NATO's southern border; Greece and Turkey, and to a lesser extent Portugal and Spain continued to receive substantial American aid. In the north, the flow of American military assistance to Denmark diminished more slowly than that to other countries, and military help to Norway extended beyond 1969 at a fairly high level.

In the period between 1951 and 1968, approximately 30 billion Norwegian kroner ($ 4.3 billion) were expended on Norway's defense. Some 6.5 billion kroner ($ 950 million) were in the form of direct help: 6.1 billion ($ 880 million) from the Americans, 400 million ($ 58 million) from Canada, and 1.5 billion kroner contributed by the allies through NATO's common infrastructure program. During this period, Norway paid only around seventy percent of its total defense costs. Military assistance allowed the country to spend an average of fifteen percent of its military budget on the purchase of materiel. The rest was concentrated on building programs, training, and maintenance. (51)

The major portion of American aid was used for the procurement of aircraft, ships, ammunition, and spare parts. NATO infrastructure funds helped construct eleven modern airfields, (52) bases for the fleet, communication systems, depots, and control and radar stations. Comparing the modest sum of 500 million kroner that Norway expended for equipment between 1951 and 1957 with the 7,300 million Norwegian kroner that Sweden paid for similar purchases, T. Greve concludes that NATO membership made a modern defense possible in Norway at no cost to the standard of living. (53) The importance of outside help was especially great in the early fifties, when the Norwegian armed forces were expanded and modernized. In 1952-1953, for instance, less than half of the 1,900 million kroner in defense costs were covered by the Norwegian defense budget; military aid amounted to 900 million and 100 million originated in the NATO infrastructure program. (54)

Between 1949 and 1969 Denmark accepted around 4.5 billion kroner ($ 640 million) in American military aid. More than three-quarters of it was extended in the 1949 to 1959 period and consisted of deliveries of supplies and equipment

51 J.J. Holst, *Norsk Sikkerhedspolitik i strategisk Perspektiv, II: Dokumentasjon* (Oslo, 1967), 23.
52 Gardermoen, Rygge, Torp, Lista, Flesland, Ørland, Vaernes, Bodø, Andøya, Bardufoss, and Banak.
53 Greve, *op. cit.*, 21.
54 "Forsvarsutgifterne og den økonomiske baereevne", *Internasjonal Politikk*, (1968), 2, 5.

to the army ($ 290 million), the navy ($ 70 million) and the air force ($ 290 million).

Canada provided assistance in the form of pilot training. *(55)* Under the infrastructure program, airfields and fleetbases including Korsør and Frederikshavn, fuel depots, and communication and warning stations have been built in Denmark. They represent a sum of approximately 650 million kroner ($ 90 million), an amount only slightly exceeding the Danish contributions to the infrastructure program between 1949 and 1969, ± 580 million kroner.

b) *Strains resulting from NATO Membership*

Even the most hostile Norwegian and Danish opponents of NATO will admit that a policy of armed neutrality similar to Sweden's would have represented an economic burden far in excess of their financial obligations within the Atlantic organization. Allied, mainly American, economic and military aid has seen to that. On the other hand, the staunchest defenders in all three nations can not deny that NATO has placed serious political and psychological strains on their populations.

In Iceland, the problems created by NATO membership can be condensed into one word, *Ueberfremdung,* the feeling that the physical presence of 3,500 to 5,000 men of the Iceland Defense Force poses a threat to the preservation of cultural and linguistic values on the island. Initially the poor recreational facilities at Kéflavik sent American servicemen flocking to nearby Reykjavik, where among other things they introduced prostitution, previously unknown in Iceland. *(56)* In an attempt to quell rising uneasiness, their movements were restricted by a ten o'clock curfew. In 1955, the American forces were granted permission to operate a television station at Kéflavik, a measure aimed at increasing their recreational possibilities and making life on the base more tolerable. It provoked an intense debate on the desirability of the American presence and its impact on the island's population. Thousands of Icelanders received the American transmission. No alternative Icelandic broadcoast existed, *(57)* and officials feared that Icelandic language and culture would be

55  *Dansk Sikkerhedspolitik, I,* 146.
56  Gröndal, *op. cit.,* 52.
57  The Icelandic Defense Force had originally received permission to operate a television station, with the proviso that transmission power do not exceed 50 watt and that the maximum radiation of the antenna be directed toward the radar site. In 1961, the defense force requested that it be allowed to install a 250-watt television transmitter, arguing that the old one was worn out and no modern transmitter was available with a power of less than 250 watt. The permission was granted; experience had shown the original limitations to have been useless, as the programs could be equally well received in Reykjavik and Kéflavik. *Ibid.,* 71.

adversely affected. Icelandic youth would become Americanized, and eventually the island would undergo the same cultural fate as had Hawaii. *(58)*

As early as 1956, under the impact of the spirit of Geneva and of lessening tension once the Korean War ended in stalemate, the Icelandic government attempted to renegotiate the 1951 defense agreement and end the stationing of foreign troops on Icelandic soil. The revised policy was an indirect result of the 1953 elections, which introduced a new party, the National Preservation party, whose program was contained in its name and who campaigned exclusively on a platform opposing the defense force. It polled six percent of the vote and won two seats in the Icelandic parliament, the Althing.

In March 1956 the Progressive party withdrew its support from the coalition government it had formed with the Independence party and with the Social Democrats and the Communists passed a resolution *(59)* requesting the departure of American troops. Following the elections of June 1956, the three parties supporting the resolution formed a leftist coalition which initiated negotiations on the issue with the U.S. However, the Soviet invasion of Hungary and the events in Suez dissuaded the government from pursuing the discussion, and the American presence continued. In December 1956 Foreign Minister G. Gudmundsson declared that in his opinion the world situation was now much more serious than it was in 1951, when the Defense Force was requested, and he did not believe that now was the time to discuss its withdrawal. *(60)*

Iceland also faced difficulties connected with trade. Following the successive extension of its fishing limits from three to four miles in 1952 to twelve miles in 1958 and to fifty miles in 1972, a very important part of its products *(61)* was sold on the Communist market (see Table 2).

---

58  *Ibid.*, 73.

59  The resolution reads: "The Althing resolves to declare: Iceland's foreign policy shall hereafter, as hitherto, aim to safeguard the independence and security of the country, foster friendly relations with all nations, and maintain cooperation between Iceland and her neighbors in security affairs, among other things by participation in the Atlantic Alliance.

In view of changed conditions since the Defense Treaty of 1951 was concluded, and in view of declarations that foreign troops shall not be stationed in Iceland in peacetime, revision of the system then adopted shall immediately be initiated with the purpose that the Defense Force be withdrawn, and Icelanders shall themselves undertake care and maintenance of the defensive installations, other than military duties. If an agreement to this effect is not reached, the Defense Treaty shall be terminated according to Article 7 thereof". Quoted in *Ibid.*, 56.

60  Quoted in *ibid.*, 58.

61  In 1970 fishery accounted for 20 percent of the G.N.P. and fishery exports for 72 percent of total exports, $ 113 million. *International Herald Tribune*, 3 August 1972, 6.

TABLE II
Percentage of Icelandic Exports to the U.S.S.R. and the Eastern Bloc.

|  | Percentage to the Soviet Union | Percentage to entire Eastern Bloc |
|---|---|---|
| 1948 | 0.2 | 8.6 |
| 1949 | 0 | 8.5 |
| 1950 | 0 | 9.6 |
| 1951 | 0 | 6.9 |
| 1952 | 0 | 6.6 |
| 1953 | 2.0 | 9.4 |
| 1954 | 11.7 | 18.3 |
| 1955 | 13.6 | 22.1 |
| 1956 | 16.5 | 26.4 |
| 1957 | 20.5 | 33.2 |
| 1958 | 17.5 | 32.4 |
| 1959 | 16.1 | 30.8 |
| 1960 | 13.9 | 23.2 |
| 1961 | 14.6 | 23.0 |
| 1962 | 11.6 | 19.3 |
| 1963 | 10.8 | 17.9 |
| 1964 | 8.5 | 16.3 |
| 1965 | 8.8 | 15.9 |
| 1966 | 6.9 | 11.3 |
| 1967 | 6.4 | 10.5 |

Source: Gröndal, *op. cit.*, 78.

Its rather heavy dependence on Eastern buyers may have made the island vulnerable to Soviet influence. Although to my knowledge no evidence of direct Soviet pressure exists, it seems hardly a coïncidence that the first serious attempt to evict the American military occurred in 1956 when exports to the Eastern Bloc were also reaching their peak. *(62)*

Possibly because of the obvious limitations to the barter system under which Icelandic-Eastern Bloc trade was conducted, *(63)* perhaps also due to the

62 L. Burbank states that in 1955-1956 the Soviets were clearly courting Icelanders and trying to create neutralist sentiments in Scandinavia. In October 1955 Moscow inaugurated a month of Soviet-Icelandic friendship. The evacuation of their base at Porkkala, Finland, a few months earlier gave the Soviets a powerful propaganda weapon in their efforts to induce the Icelanders to withdraw the American forces. L. Burbank, "Scandinavian Integration and Western Defense", *Foreign Affairs*, XXXV (October, 1956), 149.
63 In exchange for its frozen fish exports, Iceland imports almost all its oil products, lumber, iron and steel, grains, and automobiles from the U.S.S.R. Czechoslovakia, Poland, and Eastern Germany provide mostly consumer goods and machinery. Gröndal, *op. cit.*, 79. See also J. Nordal and V. Kristinsson, eds., *Iceland 1966*, handbook published by the Central Bank of England (Reykjavik, 1967), 203-229.

rapid growth of the Eastern Bloc's fishing fleets, Icelandic sales to that area have stagnated during the sixties. At present the sizeable increase of exports mainly to the European and African markets, have reduced exchange with Communist nations to between ten and fifteen percent of the islands total.

Parochial though the preservation of Iceland's cultural identity may seem to the outsider, at times of détente between East and West demands for American withdrawal have surfaced again and again. Within the Independence and Social Democratic parties, which have ruled the country from 1959 to 1971, as well as in the Progressive party, second largest after the Independents, anti-Americanism has never affected the conviction that Iceland's interests continue to be served by membership in the alliance. In fact, the Independence party has always considered the presence of American troops a necessity. Even before the Czech invasion, in February 1968, Premier B. Benediktsson of the Independence party declared that an American withdrawal would create "a dangerous vacuum... in the North Atlantic in which case the island would become a completely dismantled and isolated advance post." (64) However, the 1972 extension of Iceland's fishery limits to fifty miles created new and bitter hostilities, known as the Cod War II, between the island and some of its NATO allies, especially England. Nationalist and anti-NATO feelings rose when the alliance failed to force England's compliance with Icelandic wishes, and the conflict gradually became critical. An Icelandic gunboat sank an English trawler and the British navy began accompanying its fishermen into the fifty-mile zone. The Icelandic government refused British aircraft permission to land on the air base of Kéflavik, and later requested immediate negotiations on the termination of the 1951 defense agreement. Demands for a cancellation of NATO membership and a return to neutrality became increasingly intense. The second Cod War had propelled Iceland into the worst conflict in its experience with NATO.

In Norway and Denmark too, membership in the alliance has occasionaly provoked second thoughts and sometimes bitter feelings. One of the first conflicts was the 1950 proposal to transform the alliance into a tight military organization with a unified command, a measure inspired by the outbreak of the Korean War. Although both governments succeeded in obtaining parliamentary approval for a joint military command, (65) they had much more difficulty in passing two other proposals that grew out of the same session of the

---

64 Quoted in Campbell, *op. cit.*, 92.
65 However, a majority in the Danish Parliament insisted that in peacetime the command over Danish forces remain in Danish hands. In case of an attack, the Danish government was to decide when the command would transfer to the regional headquarters of SHAPE.

Atlantic council: the rearmament of Germany and the admission of Greece and Turkey into the alliance.

Emotions ran high on the German issue, especially in Denmark, where negative historical experience had been reinforced by the recent occupation. Fear of renewed German military strength, even if limited to a fifth of allied forces in Europe, *(66)* was unaffected by Danish Defense Minister Petersen's argument that the defense of Jutland would be greatly facilitated by a German military contribution. However, the French government's proposal for the creation of a European Defense Community (E.D.C.), the framework of which guaranteed a controlled rearmament program, significantly reduced tensions over the issue. *(67)*

The 1950 invitation to Greece and Turkey to become members of NATO met with even greater hostility in Denmark and Norway. Opponents argued that these countries had little in common with the Atlantic states, either socially, economically, or culturally. Their acceptance would aggravate Soviet anxieties about Western encirclement and increase the risk of war because it would extend alliance commitments and activities into the traditionally sensitive areas of the Balkans and the Dardanelles. *(68)* Danish and Norwegian representatives at the Ottawa council of ministers were instructed to discourage the measure by proposing as an alternative the creation of a Middle East pact which would cooperate closely with NATO but remain outside its automatic collective security provisions. *(69)* But the two ministers stood alone at Ottawa, and first Norway and later Denmark succumbed to the majority opinion rather than use their veto. As Danish Foreign Minister Kraft explained, to do so in a democratic organization would have been futile, and impolitic as well. *(70)*

Participants in the Lisbon meeting of 20-25 February 1952 had pressured both countries to increase their defense budget and raise military service from twelve to eighteen months. The same meeting had agreed on a jointly-financed infrastructure program, and gradually the question of common installations was coupled with a proposal to station American military personnel and 150

66  As the U.S. proposed at the NATO Defense Committee meeting at Washington, 28-31 October, 1950.
67  Invitations for the conference to discuss the French proposal were sent to those European states who were members of both the Council of Europe and of NATO, and to the Federal Republic of Germany. Only France, Germany, Italy, Belgium, and Luxembourg participated at the conference (the Netherlands joined later in 1951); with the exception of Iceland, the remaining NATO-members merely sent observers.
68  Wilkinson, *loc. cit.*, 395.
69  *Dansk Sikkerhedspolitik, I*, 44.
70  Reske-Nielsen and Kragh, *Atlantpagten og Danmark*, 213.

planes in Denmark and possibly in Norway to bolster a certain weakness in air defense. The Soviets charged the Norwegian government with opening the country to American military personnel, but Norway refuted their claims, citing its 1949 declaration not "to make available bases for the armed forces of foreign powers on Norwegian territory as long as Norway is not attacked or exposed to threats of attack. *(71)* In Denmark, the issue prompted widespread public debate which lasted for well over a year, and to which the Soviet Union contributed with various notes and maneuvers. Not until 6 October 1953, seven months after the death of Stalin, did the new Danish government formally reject under "present circumstances" the proposal for allied forces on its soil. Earlier, Prime Minister Hedtoft had discussed his reasons with members of his own party. He noted the unpleasantness Iceland, another small country, had experienced with foreign troops. He stressed that Norway had reaffirmed its 1949 commitment not to allow the establishment of foreign bases in peacetime, and that Danish policy on the matter paralleled the Norwegian one. Finally, he had rejected the proposal because he considered the stationing of allied troops of little military value as long as NATO lacked the strength to insuring an effective defense of Schleswig and Holstein. *(72)*

NATO's acquisition of such power, through the rearmament and integration of Germany into the European NATO command, posed even greater problems for the Danes. By 1954 the issue had become relatively urgent, since the Paris treaty of 27 May 1952 establishing the E.D.C. had not yet been ratified by its six signatories. On 29 August 1954 the French assembly refused to discuss the matter and the plan conceived by French foreign minister R. Pleven four years earlier was dead. Seeking an alternative to E.D.C. the subsequent London and Paris conferences of nine Western states held on 28 September and 20-22 October 1954 *(73)* invited the Federal Republic of Germany to join the Atlantic alliance. Neither Denmark nor Norway were able to oppose this decision. Danish Foreign Minister Hansen commented that the question was not one of preventing German rearmament, but of the forms and guarantees under which rearmament, in the long run considered inevitable, would take place. *(74)* When the three so-called Atlantic parties in Denmark, the Social Democrats, the Conservatives, and the Liberals and members of the Single Tax party (Danmarks Retsforbund) pushed Danish ratification through Parliament, the

---

71 Greve, *op. cit.*, 25.
72 Reske-Nielsen and Kragh, *Atlantpagten og Danmark*, 219-220.
73 Participating countries were France, Italy, Germany, the Benelux countries, the United Kingdom, the United States, and Canada.
74 Reske-Nielsen and Kragh, *Atlantpagten og Danmark*, 221.

Radical Liberals and the Communists demanded a referendum. Their request was rejected, Hansen explaining that a Danish veto not only would not prevent West German entrance into NATO, but would isolate Denmark and lead to its withdrawal from the Alliance. (75)

The German issue continued to stir passions, although with increasingly less dramatic effect. In the winter of 1958-1959, discussion arose in Norway over the so-called German bases, which were nothing more than supply depots built under the NATO infrastructure program to be used primarily by German naval forces. (76) In Denmark, the German issue resurfaced in 1961, when a joint Danish-German command was established, and in 1965, when common Danish-German maneuvers held in Denmark met with strong opposition from a small but highly vocal minority. (77)

Unpleasant as many of these incidents were to the Danish and Norwegian people, they failed to affect the basic conviction in both countries that their security needs were best served within the Atlantic alliance. The presence in NATO of non-Atlantic countries like Greece and Turkey or of a rearmed Germany also proved of lesser importance than the protection the alliance afforded. Even the B-52 accident near Thule in 1968 or the U-2 incident in 1960, (78) as much damage as they inflicted to the Scandinavians' trust in their American ally, again held little weight in the final analysis.

## THE NORDIC BALANCE

As a result of different security policies in the Scandinavian countries after 1945, a power structure has come into being there which differs considerably from the one in effect in Central Europe. Here the total defeat of Germany created a power vacuum that was quickly filled by the two superpowers. In Northern Europe, however, the presence of a militarily-ready and well-equipped

75  Henningsen, *loc. cit.*, 28.

76  Greve, *op. cit.*, 25-26.

77  According to a Gallup poll 63 percent of the people questioned felt that the presence of German soldiers in Denmark was necessary as long as Denmark was a member of NATO, 18 percent was opposed, and 19 percent did not know. K.E. Miller, *Government and Politics in Denmark* (Boston, 1968), 256.

78  In 1968 an American B-52 en route to the American operated base of Thule in Greenland crashed in the vicinity of that base. Contrary to the Danish-American agreement not to use facilities in Greenland for offensive purposes or for the stockpiling of nuclear weapons, the B-52 carried 4 nuclear bombs, which were never found. The well-documented U-2 incident, the direct cause for Khrushchev's abortion of the Paris summit of 1960, involved Norway. Many of the flights, which originated at airfields in Turkey, were destined for Norwegian airbases.

Sweden probably spared its Scandinavian neighbors the kind of "protection" imposed on the continental states. *(79)* Instead of confronting each other directly, as in Central Europe, the U.S.S.R. and the United States are separated in Scandinavia by the neutral buffer state Sweden and are not physically present in their respective client states. This particular model of power relations has been called the Nordic or Scandinavian Balance. Some see it merely as a description of an actual power relationship at a given time; *(80)* other ascribe to the concept an operational value, *(81)* and still others categorize it somewhere between these two extremes. Jakobson, for instance, accepts the proposition that "any change in the status or policy of one part of the area is bound to have a profound effect on all others", although he seriously doubts the implication that "a system of checks and balances [exists] that automatically tends to counteract any attempt to alter the existing balance." *(82)*

Among those who allow the theory an operational function, Holst feels that "the North European security zone is characterized first and foremost by a set of interdependent and interlocking commitments and restraints in the political orientation of the Nordic countries and the involvement of the Great Powers in the process of Nordic politics." *(83)* According to Brundtland, a Nordic Balance means "that [Soviet and NATO] engagements are mutually limited and not enlarged because there exist similar possibilities on both sides for adjustments making enlargement of the one party of no practical value. There is a balance in restraints." *(84)*

Whether the equilibrium of power in Northern Europe can be an instrument of policy for the Nordic countries and/or the superpowers, theorists and politicians are in full agreement on the factors that have created the situation. They include the Soviet Union's restraint toward Finland, Sweden's neutralist policy, made credible by a substantial defense effort, and the Norwegian and Danish low-key position in NATO, notably their refusal to allow foreign bases or nuclear weapons on their territory.

---

79 A. Schützsack, "Neutralität und Machtbalance in Nordeuropa", *Aussenpolitik*, XXII (September, 1971), 553.

80 N. Örvik, "Scandinavia, NATO, and Northern Security", *International Organization*, XX (Summer, 1966), 384.

81 Holst, "Soviet Union and Nordic Security", *loc. cit.*, 137-145; A.O. Brundtland, "The Nordic Balance", *Cooperation and Conflict*, I, 1, (1966), 30-63; and A.O. Brundtland, "The Nordic Countries as an Area of Peace", A. Schou and A.O. Brundtland, eds., *Small States in International Relations* (Stockholm, 1971), 129-145.

82 Jakobson, *op. cit.*, 92.

83 Holst, *lpc. cit.*, 138.

84 Brundtland, "Nordic Countries as an Area of Peace", *loc. cit.*, 141.

Observers have generally agreed that the Soviet Union has met only its defensive needs in Northern Europe. Only in the case of Finland, whom the Soviets considered untrustworthy, did they formulate clear demands. One was the cessation of certain territory around Leningrad to better protect the city against attack from the West, in particular Germany. After the second world war, the Soviets sought to guarantee that Finland would never again participate in an aggressive coalition directed against them. Obviously, they could have easily realized that objective by simply occupying and satellizing the country, which they had defeated during the war. Instead, they secured the area at less cost by formal treaty. Under Soviet pressure, Finland pledged to consult and eventually to take joint military action with the U.S.S.R. whenever the Soviets perceived a German threat approaching through Finnish territory. The treaty of 1948 provided the Soviet Union with reasonable defensive assurances and they did not press the matter further.

Even if Soviet concern with Finland is of a basically defensive nature, what matters to the smaller country is the fact of intervention rather than the reasons behind it. To the outside world the Soviet Union seems haunted by real or pretended defensive needs which give rise to recurrent attempts to aggrandize its sphere of influence. The occupation of Eastern Europe also was seen as a defensive move for the purpose of creating a buffer territory between the U.S.S.R. and the hostile West. But when the largest and secondmost powerful nation in the world is so insecure in its position that it must bully the smaller states around it, either its power base is weak, its expressed motives are suspect, or its perception of world affairs is faulty.

The argument that the Soviet ultimatum to Finland in 1939 or its imposition of a treaty in 1948 were defensive acts may be valid in the sense that the U.S.S.R. had no desire to possess the country physically or ideologically but was guided solely by strategic considerations. The net result for Finland, however, has been a severely restricted freedom of action in foreign affairs as well as a domestic political life hampered by Soviet interference. *(85)*

The second factor in the Nordic power relationship is the neutrality of Sweden. Unlike Swiss neutrality, which is guaranteed by powerful nations, constitutionally based and absolute, that of Sweden originates from a unilateral Swedish decision. It is neither permanent nor internationally guaranteed, and

---

85   As a result of Soviet pressure, an anti-Communist coalition was ousted in 1958 and replaced by a minority government led by Urho Kekkonen whom the Soviets trusted as the guarantor of Finland's post-war course. In 1961, Soviet interference again forced the Social Democratic presidential candidate, running against the same Kekkonen, to withdraw his candidacy "in the national interest". Jakobson, *op. cit.*, 76-78.

can be revoked at any time by a parliamentary decision. Swedish neutrality rests on a successful tradition of more than one hundred years, however, and has kept the country out of both world wars. On the basis of this record, Sweden will probably also be able to avoid any future conflicts, the Swedes assume.

After World War II, all the Nordic countries, including Sweden, shared the conviction that the U.S.S.R. posed the most important threat to their security. *(86)* Three of them chose to join NATO and one was forced into a special relationship with the Soviets; only Sweden preferred to remain neutral. Its reasons were fourfold. First, the Swedes were convinced that joining NATO would make their country an automatic target of a Soviet attack in the initial stages of a war between East and West. Second, by staying neutral as long as possible in a general war, the country could gain precious time for the mobilization of the armed forces and the evacuation of civilians. Third, the Swedes assumed that the strategic value of their territory for the West was great enough to insure that NATO would resist a Soviet attack on Sweden, even if it had no formal ties with the alliance. Fourth, and probably most important, Sweden believed that merely by serving as a buffer between two antagonist blocs, it would contribute to the effort to reduce tensions and encourage international peace. *(87)*

Despite its strong tradition and its acceptance by the population, Swedish neutrality is neither absolute nor permanent, as official consideration of a Scandinavian defense union in 1948 and 1949 proved. *(88)* Some have argued that Sweden's participation in the negotiations indicate its willingness to compromise its neutrality; others say that it was a last ditch effort to prevent its neighbors from joining NATO, offering as an alternative its own brand of nonalignment to the whole of Scandinavia. Neither point is important here. Swedish presence at the discussions meant that its neutrality was negotiable. Either directly or indirectly, the option to join NATO was open to Sweden, although "the only conceivable reason for the eventual Swedish use of this option would be serious Soviet aggressiveness in the Northern European area." *(89)*

---

86   There seems to be general agreement that Sweden, as a Western democracy, felt a lesser threat, if any, from the West than from the East. Brundtland, for example, writes that "even neutral Sweden has in her military planning put a higher priority on preparations for warding off a military attack from the East". Brundtland, "The Nordic Countries as an Area of Peace", *loc. cit.*, 140.
87   N. Lund, "Warum gehört Schweden nicht zum Atlantikpakt?" *Wehrkunde*, IX (August, 1960), 390.
88   Brundtland, "The Nordic Balance", *loc. cit.*, 32.
89   *Ibid.*, 33. In fact, the Soviets were aware of this possibility. Their main objection to the

The last factor in the paradigm representing the Nordic Balance is the Danish and Norwegian refusal to allow foreign military bases or nuclear weapons on their territory. As discussed earlier, *(90)* their decision was closely related to the kind of threat they saw emanating from the East. Both countries, but especially Norway, perceived the threat as direct and all encompassing, and justified membership in the Western alliance on this basis. On the other hand, they did not see the threat as so imminent that the military presence of a major ally was required to discourage aggression. In consequence, the Norwegians rejected the acceptance of foreign bases from the beginning and the Danes formalized an identical policy in 1953.

Like the Swedes, the Danes and the Norwegians have always been sensitive to Soviet defensive needs, acting with one eye to the East. The Swedes viewed membership in NATO or links between a Scandinavian alliance and the Western defense system as antagonizing to the Soviets. Placing the substantial Swedish military capacity "at the disposal of the Americans" would have represented a considerable increase in the Western war machine and probably would have resulted in a proportional Soviet expansion in the Baltic and the northwest. *(91)* Similarly, the Norwegians and the Danes have realized that accepting American protection might provoke a Soviet response. While the refusal of foreign forces might seem to make American protection less effective, Scandinavian policy on bases to a large degree reassured the Soviets that the smaller nations would not serve as a stepping stone for attack. In other words, "it was more important for the Soviets to avoid American bases in Norway than it was important for the Americans to have bases in Norway." *(92)*

The interdependence of these factors and their effect on one another have been the matter of much speculation. As mentioned earlier, *(93)* in 1948 the Soviets apparently realized that applying too much pressure to Finland would be counterproductive if it led the other Scandinavian countries into closer cooperation with the Western defense system then in the making. Whether Sweden or Norway and Denmark acted deliberately to promote Finnish in-

---

proposed Scandinavian Defense Pact, as their vigorous attacks against it show, was their fear that it would be linked to NATO at Norwegian insistence.

*90* See chapter II, pp. 32-37.

*91* Brundtland, "The Nordic Balance", *loc. cit.*, 33.

*92* *Ibid.*, 32. The author adds that on February 1951 in an official interpretation of the Norwegian base policy the Norwegian defense minister left open the possibility of brief visits for allied maneuvers. These would make the defense guarantee more credible, both to the Norwegian public and to the Soviet Union. *Ibid.*, 50.

*93* See chapter II.

terests is doubtful, however. More likely, each attempted to solve its own security problems each in its own way, without regard to Finland's fate.

In any case the fact that the Soviets connected their actions in Finland with the security options of the other Scandinavian countries is an argument in favor of the theory of the Nordic Balance. But the real test came in 1961, when the so-called Note Crisis exploded in Finland. It may be recalled that 1961 was a year of hightened tensions between the two superpowers. In early June in Vienna, Khrushchev had warned Kennedy that unless the West make West Berlin a free city before the end of the year, the Soviet government would sign a separate peace treaty with the German Democratic Republic. His warning was a challenge to Kennedy's statement confirming the U.S. commitment in West Berlin, and before and after August 13, the day the Berlin wall went up, both sides took steps to increase military preparedness, indicating the degree of tensions between the two states. Finally, in September, nuclear tests were resumed, the Geneva disarmament talks were disbanded and on October 30, the Soviets exploded a fifty megaton bomb.

On the same day, the Finnish ambassador in Moscow received a lengthy note from the Soviet government proposing consultations, in accordance with the Finnish-Soviet Treaty [...], on measures for the defense of the borders of the two countries against the threat of armed aggression on the part of West Germany and states allied with it." *(94)* The Soviets claimed that Germany, far from being under NATO control, was increasingly able to use NATO for its own aims because of the size of its contribution to the alliance. They were alarmed at the German "penetration" of Northern Europe, which they documented with a series of "facts" highlighted by the joint German-Danish Baltic command.

Initially, almost no one took Soviet accusations seriously. They were interpreted as a pretext for pressuring Finland and for influencing the presidential elections due in the summer of 1962. *(95)* Sweden, Norway, and Denmark responded to the note by confirming their security policies. Apparently they were convinced that the crisis was limited to Finland and the U.S.S.R., and could be resolved through internal Finnish measures. President Kekkonen

---

94 Quoted in Jakobson, *op. cit.*, 70.
95 Only the Communists and the Agrarians supported Kekkonen who belonged to the Agrarian party. All other parties, representing the larger part of the electorate, had united behind Mr. Honka, a Social Democrat. Although the Honka coalition had no intention of changing Finland's foreign policy and aimed only at ending Kekkonen's "corrupt regime", Soviet leaders had expressed concern over an alteration in Finland's policy of friendship with the Soviet Union.

disagreed, saying that the note was a reflection of the grave international crisis over Berlin; still, he thought he could handle the situation with a domestic political decision. On November 14, he dissolved the Parliament and ordered the new elections moved ahead, to early February 1962. In this way he shortened the period of uncertainty that Gromyko had complained about, and with the same move threw the opposition into a state of confusion. *(96)*

The Soviets were not overly impressed with the move, and on November 16 insisted on holding the staff talks they had requested. Hoping to persuade Khrushchev personally that neither the international situation nor the internal situation in Finland necessitated such measures Kekkonen met with the Soviet leader in Novosibirsk on November 23. He warned Khrushchev that Soviet-Finnish military consultations might "arouse a certain uneasiness and lead to war psychosis in the Scandinavian countries." *(97)* On the other hand, he implied that if Khrushchev withdrew his proposal, public anxiety in Scandinavia would diminish resulting in less need for military preparations, not only in Finland and Sweden, *(98)* but also in the two Scandinavian members of NATO, Denmark and Norway. *(99)* The Finnish president argued skillfully and his argument was bolstered by previous Norwegian statements on the matter. During a visit to Moscow a few days earlier, the Norwegian foreign minister had implied to Gromyko that the stability of Northern Europe might be disturbed if the existing balance of forces were changed. *(100)* In a public speech at Copenhagen, the Norwegian defense minister was more blunt. He accused Stalin and Molotov of "scaring Norway into NATO"; without their interference the country would never have joined the alliance. Continued pressure, he went on, rather than forcing Norway out, would merely serve to entrench it further into the Western power bloc. *(101)* Addressing Soviet concern in the presidential elections, Kekkonen informed Khrushchev that

---

96 Jakobson, *op. cit.*, 77. Because the parties supporting Honka had united only for the purposes of the presidential elections, and continued to oppose each other in the parliamentary race, they were forced to conduct two mutually-contradictory campaigns at the same time.

97 Quoted in Brundtland, "The Nordic Balance", *loc. cit.*, 46.

98 As early as October 31 the Swedish defense minister had ordered an increased alert of the various warning systems. On November 13 the Swedish prime minister remarked that Swedish defense had been strengthened during the last few months and that Sweden was prepared for both short-term and long-term increases in its defense budget, whenever this should be deemed necessary. *Ibid.*, 43.

99 Jakobson, *op. cit.*, 78.

100 Brundtland, "The Nordic Balance", *loc. cit.*, 45.

101 *Ibid.*

Honka had given up his candidacy in the national interest. As a result of the meeting, Khrushchev gave up insisting on staff talks. The crisis was over.

Jakobson emphasizes that Norwegian threats were not decisive in Khrushchev's decision to abandon military consultation. He suggests "that the note to Finland was part of a sustained Soviet campaign, designed [...] to frighten the Western Powers to come to their senses [...] on the question of Berlin". Khrushchev yielded either because he believed he had achieved his objective or because he had underestimated American firmness; in either case there was no longer any need to pressure the Finns. *(102)*

Brundtland concludes that:

> prospects for a change in the Finnish neutrality status were offset by the prospects of a similar change in the Norwegian and possibly the Danish security status, their policy on nuclear weapons and foreign bases, and generally by the risk of further arming of the four small states of Northern Europe. [...] It is an interesting example, he states, of small state power vis-à-vis a superpower in the field of security policy on a particular level of crises. *(103)*

Finally, Nils Örvik, who is generally critical of the balance theory, argues that both politically and strategically "it is very hard to see what the Soviet Union possibly could gain by taking a tighter control of Finland." *(104)* The Soviets already possessed all the strategic points they had originally demanded, and had included in their war gains the important nickel mines and ports in the Petsamo area. "The important strategic objective", he continues, "are in Norway rather than in Finland. [...] A balance mechanism designed for maintaining the neutrality of Finland would be ineffective and even harmful to Norway. If tensions increased in the North, the Soviets might keep the Norwegian government from reconsidering its base and nuclear reservations by threatening reprisals toward Finnish neutrality. The Balance theory might just as well be run in reverse." *(105)*

The mere fact that the Nordic balance might be "run in reverse" does not mean that it does not exist. On the contrary, Soviet leaders may have been aware of the mechanism of the paradigm from the beginning. Pressure on the Finns was bound to effect feelings of Scandinavian solidarity, yet the Soviets took great care to direct the brunt of their attack toward Norway and Denmark. *(106)* These were the countries, rather than Finland, that they hoped to

---

*102* Jakobson, *op. cit.*, 79-80.
*103* Brundtland, "The Nordic Countries as an Area of Peace", *loc. cit.*, 142.
*104* Örvik, "Scandinavia, NATO, and Northern Security", *loc. cit.*, 385.
*105* *Ibid.*
*106* See Jakobson, *op. cit.*, 71. "The Soviet note was an attack against West Germany and a warning to Norway and Denmark, and to a lesser degree to Sweden, against the consequences of cooperation with West Germany. It was not an attack against Finland".

move. Clearly they sought reassurance on the continuity of Finnish foreign policy, but in all likelihood, they were even more interested in the cancellation of the COMBALTAP plans and the coercion of Norway and Denmark into a renewed, possibly an unconditional pledge on their foreign base and nuclear weapons policies. But their pressure was miscalculated. Finland's Scandinavian neighbors saw it as a threat to the Nordic balance. Rather than disengagement with the West, they answered Soviet interference with hints at an even closer alignment.

# Chapter IV

# CONTINUED MEMBERSHIP IN THE 1970s

## PERCEPTION OF CHANGED EAST-WEST RELATIONS

Faced with the potential military threat emanating from the East-West confrontation, the Scandinavian countries were unable to find a common solution to their defense problems. Instead, divergent security policies developed in the late 1940s and early 1950s, out of the different ways in which each nation perceived its security needs. Each analysis rested largely on objective factors, such as the geographic location and the country's consequent exposure and on the size and quality of the available armed force. Influential as well were less material considerations, such as the weight of historical experience or the sense of community with the major Western powers. The structure of what Holst calls the Northern European security zone *(1)* had remained unaltered during the first two decades of the Atlantic alliance. But the changes that swept over the world in the 1960s increasingly confronted the Scandinavians with the question of reevaluating their security policies. The spirit and the policies of détente seemed to require a readjustment in alliance principles basically a product of the Cold War. Other factors stimulated and influenced Scandinavian thinking on their security policies. The American world power seemed to be in a state of moral crisis due to its involvement in Southeast Asia and its support for reactionary regimes in Portugal, Spain, and Greece. Finally, integration processes in both halves of Europe were developing rapidly. These could not help but influence deliberations on defense in Northern Europe.

But even if peace in Europa is indivisible, it is equally true that European security assumed different qualities depending on the European security zone one is considering. *(2)* In the initial stages of the Cold War the primary struggle

---

1 Holst, "The Soviet Union and Nordic Security", *loc. cit.*, 137.
2 *Ibid*. Holst differentiates three security zones: Northern Europe, Central Europe, and Mediterranean Europe. "One of the principal structural functions of the collective defense system of NATO", Holst writes, "has been to link the three zones by the application of American glue". *Ibid*.

between the U.S. and the U.S.S.R. took place in Central Europe, largely because the Soviet Union was essentially a land power. Having taken the initiative in the confrontation, the Soviets had also set its premises. With the consolidation of spheres of interest, however, Central Europe as a battlefield gradually took on blurred features. Moreover, the slow but continuous build-up of German strength diminished the maneuverability in the area. Instead of being an object of hostility between the Soviets and the Americans, Germany -- or perhaps I should say the two Germanies -- increasingly became an independent actor in the confrontation. In addition, the Soviet Union soon learned, especially after the Cuban missile crisis, that it would never equal the United States as a world power until it also became a full-fledged sea-going nation.

Probably a combination of these factors led to the gradual shift in attention from Central Europe to NATO's northern and southern borders in the 1960s. There security positions were increasingly influenced by Soviet-American maritime rivalry. The parallel appearance of a marked Soviet naval build-up in the Arctic and the stationing of a sizeable fleet in the eastern Mediterranean is striking. It seems to indicate that the Soviet Union has for the time being abandoned continental hegemony, if it ever nourished that aspiration, in favor of a truly global strategy. Grown a mature world power, the U.S.S.R. is no longer preoccupied only with its European back yard.

De Gaulle, of course, was the first Western statesman to perceive the political consequences of the changed situation in Europe. With the Soviet military threat sharply reduced, the time was ripe to reject American predominance and secure the opportunity for European nations to determine their own fate, presumably under French leadership.

In February and March 1966, De Gaulle initiated steps to effect his proposals but the move met with little enthusiasm among his NATO-partners. *(3)* Although they were willing to allow the justification of his arguments, *(4)* they were unable to concede that the measures he proposed grew automatically out

3  In a press conference on February 21, De Gaulle announced France's withdrawal from all integrated NATO commands and the expulsion of all NATO equipment and personnel from French soil. In memoranda to NATO partners he outlined the concrete measures he planned to take in that regard.

4  Basically he argued that the threat against the Western world, in particular against Europe, had changed since the establishment of the alliance; the European countries had recovered economically, politically, and militarily; nuclear parity between the U.S. and the U.S.S.R. had fundamentally altered the conditions for the defense of the West; and Europe was not any longer the centre of international crises -- the Third World, specifically, Asia, had become the more common battle-ground. Udenrigsministeriet, *Udviklingen inden for NATO, 1966-1967* (Copenhagen, 1968), 11.

of them. For one thing, although the Soviet military threat to Europe had been reduced, it had not vanished completely and France's decision to remain in the alliance after 1969 was interpreted as an indication that basically that nation felt the same way. Both in political and in financial terms, the insurance NATO provided cost little *(5)* and none of its European members, including France, saw any value in giving it up. The logical consequence of De Gaulle's motion, was the disintegration of NATO. Without NATO, Western Europe would suffer a power vacuum that could only serve to generate tension. Attempts to alleviate the dangers inherent in such a situation would result in a new power grouping, although on a smaller scale, with an ambitious France or Germany, or both at its head.

Rather than follow the French example, the other fourteen NATO members proposed the restructuring of the alliance, *(6)* adding new strength and new responsibilities to its traditional military character. They demanded a more active role in the pursuit of détente and the creation of a platform for joint political action to that end. In its 1966 winter session, the NATO ministerial council resolved to undertake a broad analysis of international developments since the signing of the North Atlantic treaty in 1949, the so-called Harmel exercise. A year later, the council approved the Harmel Report, which proposed that the alliance assume the dual function of providing military security and pursuing a policy of détente. The report noted the split of the monolithic Communist bloc, the Soviet doctrine of peaceful coexistence, and the fact that Europe had recovered and was on its way toward unity. In view of their previously mentioned concern to underemphasize the aggressive character to NATO membership, Norway and Denmark welcomed this new emphasis on détente. Yet restlessness under American domination and the fear that American involvement in Asia or the Middle East might drag them into conflicts outside their own sphere of interest continued to affect public opinion in both countries. The value of an American security guarantee in a state of nuclear

5 Defense appropriations have tended to level off or even to diminish, whereas the uneasiness and growing restlessness over U.S. policies have led America's smaller allies to become increasingly critical and independent. N. Örvik states: "NATO has become a comfortable backrest giving ample room for verbal adventurism with few, if any risks attached. Why hand in one's membership card when no one is pressing to collect the fee?" N. Örvik, "NATO, NAFTA, and the Smaller Allies", *Orbis*, XII (Summer, 1968), 460.
6 The Standing Group, composed of representatives from France, the U.K., and the U.S.A. and responsible for strategic planning, was abolished, and its functions taken over by the Defense Planning Committee. Nuclear planning, became the responsibility of two permanent bodies, the Nuclear Defense Affairs Committee, open to all member countries, and the Nuclear Planning Group, composed of seven members.

parity, even the necessity for a guarantee at all, became questionable. Danes and Norwegians increasingly came to regard the Soviet Union as a *status quo* power. Especially in Northern Europe, they felt, after the 1961 crisis over Berlin the U.S.S.R. had accomodated itself to the existing power relationships.

Their changed attitudes found limited expression in the voting patterns within the two nations. In 1965, Norwegian voters ended the thirty-year reign of the Social Democrats. Although the new coalition government headed by Center party leader Per Borten, was no less pro-NATO than its predecessor, the 3.6 percent loss of support the Social Democrats sustained accrued to the Socialist People's party (up from 2.4 percent in 1961 to 6.0 percent in 1965), strongly opposed to NATO membership. In 1966, a similar shift took place in Denmark. The Social Democrats, who had formed a minority government under J.O. Krag, lost seven of their seventy-six seats. The other traditional pro-NATO parties also lost, although less spectacularly. *(7)* The main beneficiaries where the Radical Liberals (up from ten to thirteen seats), and the Socialist People's party (up from ten to twenty seats). While the latter favored an immediate withdrawal from NATO, the Radical Liberals' platform was more complex.

In 1949 the Radical Liberals and the Communists had violently opposed Danish entry into the Atlantic alliance. Later the Radical Liberals compromised their position on neutrality and during their eleven years of coalition with the Social Democrats from 1953 until 1964, they served loyally as partners in the government. Returned to the opposition after 1964, the Radical Liberals reverted to their neutralist origins. In 1965 the former Radical education Minister, H. Petersen, declared that future Danish security problems suggested a reconsideration of a Scandinavian defense union.

This subtle shift toward anti-NATO parties was only temporary in Norway. but it assumed a more lasting character in Denmark. *(8)* This is undoubtedly

---

7  The Conservatives went down from thirty-six to thirty-four seats, the Liberals from thirty-eight to thirty-five.

8  In the September 1969 elections in Norway, the Socialist People's party lost its two seats in Parliament, and received 3.5 percent of the vote. The Social Democrats obtained seventy-four seats but only an extra 3.8 percent of the vote. In Denmark, the January 1968 elections confirmed the decline of the Social Democrats (they lost another seven seats). Although the Socialist People's party percentagewise lost even more heavily (with its splinter party, the Leftist Socialists, they went down from twenty to fifteen seats), the benefit of this shift, rather than accruing to the pro-NATO parties, went to the Radical Liberals, who went from thirteen to twenty-seven seats. Obviously these election results cannot be easily interpreted in terms of pro- or anti-NATO sentiments. Socioeconomic considerations were probably more important in determining the voting behavior of the electorate. Further, in Norway the debate on NATO membership had already been favorably concluded by election time. In Denmark, the popu-

because of the differing strategic situations developing in the sixties around both countries. As the preceding chapter describes, Soviet pressure had gradually subsided in Central Europe. On the other hand, NATO's flanks have increased in importance as the Soviet naval capacity developed. The Norwegians have been very sensitive to the vastly expanded military activities in the Arctic; in fact, they have never considered a basic change in their security policy. *(9)*

The Danes, on the other hand, have reacted to the same phenomenon in the opposite way. The concentration of Soviet naval strength on the Kola Peninsula has led them to conclude that the Soviets see the Baltic exits as having proportionately less strategic value. As a small appendix of continental Europe, they experienced the lessened tension in the larger area, and as a result they came to feel that much of the threat that existed in 1949 had disappeared. Finally, the German issue had lost much of its sharpness. The participation of Willy Brandt's Social Democrats in the coalition government in 1966 started Germany on a course that was gradually to destroy its reputation of revanchism. In the late sixties, the possibility of a conflict begun by or over Germany seemed more and more remote.

Not surprisingly, then, the first measures of the new bourgeois government, constituted after the 1968 elections and led by the Radical Liberal H. Baunsgaard, had some traditional radical overtones. The defense budget was cut, and foreign policy emphasized détente and disarmament. *(10)* In June 1968, officials decided to undertake a broad review of Danish security policy, and a committee of three ministers was set up for that purpose. They were instructed to examine Denmark's alternatives to a Western alliance or to justify continued NATO membership. *(11)* Even before the study got under way, a vast outpouring of pamphlets, brochures, analyses, and policy statements contributed to a public debate. *(12)*

lation apparently was motivated by its dissatisfaction with Krag's supposed red cabinet. Still, the disappearance of the Socialist People's party from the Norwegian Parliament and the relative survival of the Danish counterpart, coupled with the success of the Radical Liberals, does indicate a certain trend.

9  Although in 1967-1968 in Norway a public debate on NATO and Norwegian security also took place, it had nothing of the sharpness which characterized the Danish discussions. The vast majority of Norwegian politicians and experts saw no real alternative to continued NATO membership.

10  N.J. Haagerup, "Denmark's Security Policy", reprinted in *Survival* (May, 1971), 173.

11  *Ibid.*

12  Reference has already been made to some of these publications, including Bjøl, Haagerup, *et al.*, *Danmark og NATO*; the official documentary survey of Danish security policy, *Dansk*

Since the positions of the outspokenly pro-NATO parties, the Liberals and the Conservatives, and the anti-NATO parties, the Communists and the Socialist People's party did not change drastically during the period, a discussion of their views is not really necessary. A look at the arguments developed by the Radical Liberals and the Social Democrats should be revealing, however, since they are the critical variables in the development of Danish security policy.

The debate began in December 1965 with the publication of an essay by the former Radical Liberal minister H. Petersen entitled "Defense -- Viewpoints in a Debate." *(13)* Petersen proposed a rational scheme for Danish defense whose main objectives were stabilization and a reduction in defense spending. Central in his plan was lowering military service from twelve to eight months. Reaction was most intensely focused on his view on NATO's future, however. Anticipating France's decision in February 1966, Petersen warned that the alliance might be transformed into a grouping centered around an American-West German axis. This combined with the eclipse of the United Kingdom as a major power would secure for West Germany the foremost place in European politics. *(14)* He considered it a serious risk for Denmark to participate in a community in which West Germany had a dominant influence. Germany, he said, was the only nation in Europe having a potential border conflict on its hands and apparently it had not given up every thought about using force to bring about reunification. *(15)* Since the international situation was in a state of flux, Petersen went on, it would be dangerous not to keep all options open, including the Nordic one. Nordic cooperation, he felt, should have been enlarged to the economic and the defense spheres; only the political will to act had been lacking.

Comments on Petersen's essay were published in various Danish newspapers during the months following its publication. *(16)* Critics argued that the Nordic alternative was neither actual nor realistic because the strategic requirements of the Scandinavian countries continued to differ. Norway's options

---

*Sikkerhedspolitik, I and II* and *Udviklingen inden for NATO, 1966-1967* (Copenhagen, 1968). Further contributions were N.J. Haagerup, *NATO efter 1969* (Copenhagen, 1967); K.H. Petersen, *Debat om Forsvaret*, (Copenhagen, 1967); O.B. Henriksen, *Lille Land-Hvad nu?* (Aalborg, 1967); X, *NATO i 70'erne*, (Copenhagen, 1968); E. Kragh, *Focus på Danmarks Sikkerhedspolitik*, (Copenhagen, 1967); X., *9 om NATO*, (Copenhagen, 1969); X., *Danmarks Sikkerhedspolitik*, (Copenhagen, 1969).

13  Petersen, *Debat om Forsvaret, op. cit.*

14  *Ibid.*, 20.

15  *Ibid.*

16  They have been included in *ibid.*, as well as his remarks on these reactions.

rested with the Atlantic sea powers, Finland's fate depended upon the U.S.S.R., and Danmark had to consider vital German and Soviet interests in the Straits and the Baltic. Social Democratic Deputy P. Søgaard doubted that a Nordic defense pact would be feasible and wondered whether the Radicals would accept the economic consequences even if it were. Far from reducing defense expenditures, the integration and adaptation of the defense and weapon systems needed to match the Danish with that of the Swedes, would probably double them. *(17)* Søgaard saw neutrality as the only real alternative to NATO membership. But whether in or out of the Atlantic alliance a reduction of the Danish military potential would probably automatically mean German pressure as that country sought to effectively protect its northern flank. *(18)*

The Swedes were clearly pleased with the way Scandinavian security arrangements had developed after 1949, although they indicated their willingness to renew negotiations for a Scandinavian defense pact at their neighbors' request. *(19)* But after June 1968 the Nordic option ceased to be a central issue in the Danish security debate. By then the Norwegian Parliament had voted almost unanimously (144 to six votes) to remain in NATO after 1969. Curiously, even after that decision Radical Liberals had a hard time giving up their dreams of Nordic unity and neutrality. *(20)* In his analysis of the Danish security situation, the Radical N.H. Petersen argued that the Warsaw Pact and NATO had gradually lost both their coherence and rationale as a result of détente. "When today a Soviet-American showdown in Europe is among the least likely things to happen", he wrote in 1968, "then it is obvious that the basis of the respective alliances, fear, has gone. ...The goal of Danish security policy in this new situation must be to work for a European security system that will lead to the dissolution of the Pacts." *(21)* By leaving the alliance the Danes might contribute to détente, but he immediately added that the conditions for that move were not ripe. *(22)* He suggested that after 1969 withdrawal on one year's notice would provide members with a greater freedom of action.

17  P. Søgaard, in Petersen, *Debat om Forsvaret, op. cit.*, 84-85.
18  S. Vestergaard, in *ibid.*, 82.
19  N. Andrén, "Den rimeligste Løsning er NATO", *Fremtiden*, XXIII, 5 (1968), (special issue on NATO), 29-35. See Swedish Prime Minister Erlander's statement of 17 October 1965: "Today the question of Nordic defense cooperation does not arise for the Swedes... The Swedish government does not intend to take any initiative in the matter. It will be up to our Nordic neighbors themselves to decide what will best suit their vital security interests". Quoted in *Fremtiden*, XXIII, 5 (1968), 19.
20  For example the Radical Liberal Folketing member N.H. Petersen, "Alliance-systemernes Opløsning", *Fremtiden*, XXIII, 5 (1968). 17-21.
21  *Ibid.*, 17-19.
22  *Ibid.*, 19.

Social Democrats took a position remarkably similar to that of the Radical Liberals. They differed in their perception of a Nordic defense system, which they felt was unrealistic, and tended to envision a more distant future in which the alliance would be superfluous. They agreed that NATO was not an appropriate organ for furthering détente and other political goals, but suggested that each individual country was responsible for encouraging improvement in East-West relations. According to K. Olesen, the previous Social Democratic defense minister, Danish foreign policy should concentrate actively on promoting cooperation between the two power blocs and the creation of a European security system. *(23)*

Generally speaking, the Social Democrats have been much more sensitive to the argument that alignment with undemocratic countries like Portugal or Greece or with the U.S. following its involvement in Vietnam, has affected the moral integrity of the country. Their objections, although merely verbal protests, have been responsible for worsening relations between Denmark and the states in question. They have violently opposed the addition of Spain, another country whose government is unrepresentative, to the alliance, and have suggested a revision of the treaty's declarations about democracy and rule of law to correspond more closely with the character of some members. *(24)*

The occupation of Czechoslovakia seemed to end the debate on NATO. Indeed, even prior to the events there, the two parties had admitted that the process of détente had not yet reached the point where Danish NATO membership was unnecessary. *(25)* With the Warsaw Pact invasion of Czechoslovakia détente had encountered a serious drawback, and a continuation of the debate seemed a waste of time. *(26)*

By 1968, public opinion in the three Scandinavian NATO countries agreed that the national interest was best served by continued membership in the Atlantic alliance at least for the time being. Public opinion polls assessing Denmark in September 1968 recorded 54 percent of the population in favor of NATO, a high level matched only by 57 percent in August 1961, the time of the Finnish Note Crisis, and 66 percent in November 1957, when the first Sputnik was launched.

---

23  Olesen, "Der er opgaver for en aktiv Dansk Politik", *NATO i 70'erne, op. cit.*, 45.
24  *Ibid.*
25  The Congress of the Radical Liberal Party in early 1968 had in fact decided to postpone a "thorough, comprehensive debate" about continued membership until the coming election campaign of 1971-1972. S.B. Jerregaard, "Den étårige Opsigelse", *9 om NATO, op. cit.*, 7. In other words, until the results of the 1968 commissioned committee were available.
26  Haagerup, "NATO efter Czecoslovakiet", *Fremtiden*, XXIII, 5 (1968), 5.

In Iceland, a poll conducted in September 1968 indicated that 57 percent of the population not only approved extending the alliance, but even accepted the continuation of the controversial defense agreement. *(27)* On the other hand, the "Soviet assertion of imperial and pontifical authority in Czechoslovakia," *(28)* however much it increased doubts about Soviet decision making, was not considered an end to détente. After all, the occupation of a Warsaw-Pact state and armed aggression against a NATO member were two different things. *(29)* At most, Soviet intervention was a reminder that East-West détente was not synonymous with lessening restrictions within the East-European states. Once the process of détente had resumed, the revaluation of Scandinavian security policies would take up again.

## NORDIC COOPERATION, EUROPEAN INTEGRATION: IMPACT ON THE SECURITY OF NORWAY, DENMARK, AND ICELAND

As the Atlantic crisis in the mid-sixties developed, people on both sides of the ocean began to wonder whether the alliance had outlived its usefulness or whether a drastic overhaul could adapt it to the new circumstances. N. Örvik suggests that NATO faced increasing difficulties because it no longer answered certain basic conditions, necessary for an alliance's viability. These included a community of interests and common goals, reciprocal sharing of contributions to these goals, and unity of leadership. *(30)*

The breakdown of the third condition became apparent in the sixties. Not only De Gaulle but almost all America's allies began to question the accuracy of its perceptions and the wisdom of its decisions. Fear that the United States might not respond to aggression gradually gave way to fear that it might over-react. American leadership had become a serious drawback for many partners in the alliance.

Örvik contends *(31)* that some measure of reciprocity existed in the early years of the alliance. In return for American economic and military aid and a guarantee of safety, the allies placed their territory at American disposal and offered moral and political support in the international organizations. The theory is open to some argument. Whatever the importance of allied real

---

27 Campbell, *loc. cit.*, 88.
28 Holst, "A Norwegian Look into the Early Seventies", *International Journal*, XXIV (Spring, 1969), 356.
29 Haagerup, "NATO efter Czekoslovakiet", *loc. cit.*, 6.
30 Örvik, "NATO, NAFTA and the Smaller Allies", *Orbis*, XII (Summer, 1968), 456-460.
31 *Ibid.*, 456-457.

estate in the fifties, technological advances have reduced it to being valuable only in that it is denied to the Soviet Union. No wonder, then, that in the sixties the U.S. government increasingly felt unfairly committed and that its now-prosperous European partners should accept more responsibilities for the functioning of the organization.

Ideally, partners in NATO share an interest in preventing a military confrontation between East and West. But when perception about the possibility of such a conflict vary widely among the members, one can hardly speak of a commonality of purpose. The withdrawal of the French because they were afraid of being caught up in a conflict outside their own making, was symptomatic of a more general feeling among European states. Various plans to give the European NATO members a greater responsibility within the alliance have been forwarded, (32) but none has been successful in concealing the wide, and growing gap between European security needs and the American pursuit of their national interests in a global confrontation with the U.S.S.R.

Revitalized briefly after the Czech invasion in 1968, fear of a Soviet threat was still strong enough to influence members against resignation in 1969. But the Atlantic crisis may explode again in the seventies, even more seriously this time. In his article, Örvik suggests reorganization on a regional basis as a solution to NATO's problems. "The EEC is likely to pay increasing attention to security matters" and "the NATO members that remain outside the E.E.C. could merge economic and security goals on the basis of the recent proposals for a North Atlantic Free Trade Area (N.A.F.T.A.). (33) Writing as he was in 1968, before The Hague decision to enlarge the Common Market, his insights are interesting for the historical record. Central to his hypothesis is the assumption that a new and more viable community could be created on a restricted regional basis with the E.E.C. and an Anglo-Scandinavian "mini-NATO" serving as vehicles for their interests. (34)

Örvik's reasoning is flawed, however, by his failure to see that the present conditions of reduced tension minimize interest in the creation of regionalized security communities. As the past few years have shown, the E.E.C. is far from taking first steps in that direction. In the still more restricted area of Northern Europe each state is looking after its own problems. Yet a glance at the map

32 Such stillborne proposals as the multilateral force (M.L.F.) or Atlantic Nuclear Force (A.N.F.), or the creation of such institutions as the Atlantic Policy Advisory Group, the Political Committee, the Defense Planning Committee, or the Nuclear Planning Group, come to mind here.
33 Ibid., 462. NAFTA would include the U.S. and Canada, plus member countries of E.F.T.A.
34 Ibid., 463.

makes it clear that the defense interests of the Northern countries are so inter-woven that they form a strategic whole. The problems emanating from the North Cap concern not only Norway and Finland but perhaps Sweden as well, because land operations against Norway aimed at sealing off Finnmark would in all likelihood sweep over Swedish territory. Control of the Baltic exits in-volves Denmark, Sweden, and Norway. And finally, the fact that the confron-tation between the Americans and the Soviets has become a naval one is of particular importance to Norway, but must also affect Iceland and Denmark, with its Greenland and Faroes dependencies.

Yet the interconnectedness of their strategic interests has not led the Scan-dinavian countries to adopt regional policies coordinating their security needs with the cultural and economic integration process in Northern Europe. On the contrary, such matters have received such low priority, especially compared to economic ones, that Nordic cooperation and the proposed North European peace zone received a deadly blow in 1970 when Finland refused to participate in a Nordic economic organization (NORDEK).

Denmark proposed negotiations on the establishment of the Nordic Econo-mic Union at the February 1968 session of the Nordic Council. Partly a result of the dissillusionment at continued French resistance to enlarging the Com-mon Market, the initiative was also due to a more pronounced pro-Scandina-vian attitude in the new bourgeois government. As mentioned earlier, the Ra-dical Liberals, who had been the real winners in the January 1968 elections in Denmark, *(35)* had also been the strongest proponents of the Scandinavian defense league in the Danish security debate of 1966-1968. One of the first steps of the new government was the establishment of a commission to review Danish security policy and explore possible alternatives, including a Nordic defense union. *(36)*

However, in both economics and security affairs, the Scandinavian proposal was disadvantaged from the beginning. The invasion of Czechoslovakia served to remind the allies that the kind of protection offered by the Atlantic alliance might still be necessary. Moreover, a basic ambiguity in NORDEK's economic functions hung over the negotiations. Norway and Denmark had never con-

---

35  Their seats in the Folketing more than doubled, from thirteen to twenty-seven, and they named the new prime minister, H. Baunsgaard.

36  The report of the Commission, *Problemer omkring Dansk Sikkerhedspolitik. En Redegø-relse fra det sagkyndige Udvalg under Regeringsudvalget verdrørende Danmarks Sikkerhed-politik I-II*, (Copenhagen, 1970), was published in the autumn of 1970. In it, the hypothetical nature of the debate on a Nordic defense pact was stressed. A Scandinavian solution could become a real alternative, and an attractive one, only when the present alliance systems began to disintegrate. See Haagerup, "Denmark's Security Policy", *loc. cit.*, 174-175.

cealed their real preference for full membership in E.E.C. and they would not allow the creation of NORDEK to prevent their attaining that goal. Instead of an end in itself, Norway and Denmark considered NORDEK a vehicle to improve their starting position in future negotiations on an enlarged community.

Following the ministerial meeting in The Hague of December 1969, an extended E.E.C. became an imminent possibility. In consequence Finland which had already obtained a one-year resignation clause in case one of its partners joined the larger community, refused to sign the NORDEK treaty. The Soviets would have raised serious opposition to Finland's close association through NORDEK membership with the E.E.C. Even prior to The Hague conference, the Soviets had repeatedly voiced their concern over NORDEK which they feared would be drawn into the orbit of the E.E.C. Their response was an echo of their similar concern in 1948-1949 when they feared that a neutral Scandinavian defense pact would in fact be associated with the Western alliance. In Soviet eyes, the clear preference of Norway and Denmark for E.E.C. membership, coupled with Swedish hesitation about the terms of its affiliation with the Common Market, was an indication that NORDEK could only draw Finland closer to the Western camp. The Hague meeting made the possibility almost a certainty, (37) and consequently Finland, aware of Soviet antagonism toward the E.E.C., the "economic basis of NATO", refused membership.

The Finnish withdrawal from the NORDEK negotiations does not seem to have been the result of direct Soviet interference in their foreign policy. Rather, as G. Nielssen comments, it apparently was a case of "policy formulation on the basis of anticipation", anticipation, that is, of "the Soviet Government's refusal to accept Finnish participation in NORDEK when other members of NORDEK were simultaneously trying to become members of the European Common Market." (38) The outcome of the Finnish parliamentary elections of March 1970 provided President Kekkonen with another reason for the move. The Communists and Kekkonen's Center party, both willing to do "everything necessary to assure the U.S.S.R. of Finnish neutrality" (39) and therefore generally opposed to NORDEK, lost rather heavily, whereas the conservative parties and the Social Democrats, willing to explore "the possibility of turning

37 The preamble of the NORDEK Treaty stated for example that "the cooperation must be organized in a manner that will facilitate the four countries' participation in or cooperation with an enlarged European Market". Quoted in G.P. Nielssen, "The Nordic and the Continental European Dimensions in Scandinavian Integration: NORDEK as a Case Study", *Cooperation and Conflict*, VI, 3-4, (1971), 176.
38  *Ibid.*, 178.
39  *Ibid.*

more and more towards Scandinavia and the West" either lost nothing or pro-
gressed substantially. *(40)* Victories for the pro-Western parties *(41)* coming
at a time when Soviet suspicions were already aroused made Kekkonen's
position even more difficult and he set out to pacify his powerful neighbor. He
ended all speculations on NORDEK and in the summer of 1970 committed
Finland to a twenty year extension of the Treaty of Friendship and Mutual
Assistance, three years ahead of time. In a sense, his action precluded the kind
of change in the Nordic balance which the Soviets seemed to consider inevitable
and weighed in the West's favor if they allowed Finland to participate in a
Western-oriented organization.

Economically NORDEK would have benefitted all four Scandinavian
countries. *(42)* A rapid increase in intra-Nordic trade indicated a growing
regional division of labor, especially in the more advanced and technologically-
sophisticated industries. *(43)* In the decade between 1959 and 1968, intra-
Scandinavian trade grew in the following proportions.

TABLE III
Intra-Scandinavian Trade, 1959-1968

| | Scandinavia as percentage of total import | | Scandinavia as percentage of total export | |
|---|---|---|---|---|
| | 1959 | 1968 | 1959 | 1968 |
| Denmark | 14.3 | 22.0 | 17.3 | 24.7 |
| Finland | 12.3 | 19.7 | 6.6 | 16.7 |
| Norway | 21.2 | 27.7 | 17.6 | 24.1 |
| Sweden | 8.3 | 16.3 | 19.7 | 24.6 |

Source: Nielssen, *loc. cit.*, 176.

Important though the Nordic market might have been, an enlarged Common

40    The Communist party lost six of its previous forty-two seats; the Center party totalled
thirty-seven seats (against fifty in 1966); the Social Democratic party fifty-two down from
fifty-five; the National Coalition party thirty-seven up from twenty-six; the Smallholders
party of V. Vennamo eighteen up from one; and the Swedish People's party remained at
twelve.
41    The vote has been explained as a reaction of the Finns against communist participation
in the government and an expression of the fear among large sections of the electorate that
further socialist experiments might damage the improved standard of living.
42    Iceland was never a party to the negotiations. Although a member of the Nordic Council
it seems never to have shown any interest in a Nordic Economic Union.
43    Nielssen, *loc. cit.*, 176-177.

Market containing the United Kingdom but excluding Norway and Denmark would be of much greater significance to the region.

Nonparticipation in a European community of which England was a member would in fact mean facing trade barriers with a group of states which comprised roughly fifty percent of the Scandinavians' market. After considerable hesitation, Sweden eventually decided to pay the price for its neutrality and sought a bilateral agreement with the E.E.C. The Finns, of course, had little choice. In fact, even the limited agreement they concluded with the E.E.C. in July 1972 took quite some time before being signed, apparently because Brezhnev and Kosygin have expressed misgivings on the measure. *(44)* Saddled with fewer prohibitions, the Danish and Norwegian governments opted for full membership in the E.E.C. Iceland, whose trade is much less concentrated in Western Europe, has never applied for membership. Eventually, on 25 September 1972 the Norwegian held a referendum which rejected alignment with the European community. A week later, the Danes decided in its favor.

While the margin was slight in Norway (53.9 percent opposed vs 46.1 percent in favor), in Denmark an impressive 63.5 percent voted for entry into the Common Market. *(45)* In both cases, the main consideration was economic rather than political. As members of the E.E.C. Danish farmers hoped to avoid losing the English market and to recover the German one. In Norway, farmers and fishermen were afraid of competition from a more effective community. Political motivations behind the vote were probably not completely lacking in both countries. Those who approved the E.E.C. anticipated their country's consequent participation in the mainstream of European events. Those who opposed it feared it would mean the loss of national identity or the attainments of decades of welfare policy. In addition they were afraid of being drawn into the loathed *Grosspolitik* of a future European superpower.

Security had little or no part in the debate on the E.E.C. Proponents of Norwegian membership argued that Norway's survival and independence depended upon maintaining close ties with the Western countries. If and when Europe assumed responsibility for its own defense, they argued, outside the Common Market Norway would be left with only bilateral agreements with the Americans to safeguard its territory. In Denmark, the concept of a separate European military entity was given little credence. On the contrary, official

---

44  At least so the Swedish newspaper *Dagens Nyheter* revealed at the end of October 1972. The article resulted directly in a reversal of Kekkonen's decision of April 1972 to run for the presidency in 1974. Eventually, Kekkonen changed his mind again, saying he would be available for a fourth term after all.

45  Haagerup, "Denmark's Security Policy", *loc. cit.*, 176.

approval of the Davignon report on political cooperation in Western Europe was accompanied by a reservation on military questions which assumed that these would continue in the purview of NATO.

Norway, now isolated from an integrating Europe, could not count on its neighbors as an alternative were NATO to disintegrate in the seventies. Denmark and Iceland do not seem overly concerned about such a possibility, however. Rather, the optimistic view prevailing in today's Denmark on the chances of a lasting détente have led the former Social Democratic minority government to introduce defense reforms that further reduce the Danish defense capacity. *(46)*

In Iceland, the new leftist coalition formed after parliamentary elections in June 1971, made a policy statement asking the American government to gradually withdraw the forces stationed there over a period of four years. The Icelanders reaffirmed their membership in NATO, but said that with the current prospects for improved détente, especially in connection with the European Security conference, the presence of the defense force has become an unnecessary vestige of the Cold War. The renewed demand to terminate the defense agreement of 1951 was the logical consequence of the entry of the Communists into the Icelandic government. Even more than that of their coalition partners -- the Leftist Liberals and the Progressive party -- their election campaign had emphasized immediate and unilateral extension of the fishery limits and expulsion of the American presence on the island. In the steadily worsening climate of the second Cod War, the Communists might have succeeded in convincing their coalition partners that withdrawal from the Atlantic alliance is the next appropriate response to the changing international political situation. However, as a result of the government crisis that broke out over the departure of the Minister of Social Affairs, itself a sequel to measures aimed at curbing an extremely high inflation rate (over 30% in 1973), new elections will be held

---

46  The reforms include a reduction in the number of military personnel, the liquidation of heavy naval units (frigates), and the disbandment of the naval base of Korsör. Military service is reduced from twelve to nine months but compensation is sought in the creation of a volunteer corps for the Army. The reforms are less drastic than those initially proposed by the Social Democratic Defense Minister Kjell Olesen. The Social Democrats had to compromise as they needed the support of another party to pass them and the Leftist Socialists, who normally voted with them, were not willing to do so on the defense issue because their goal was to leave NATO and to cancel the defense budget and not merely to reduce it. After long negotiations among the four traditional parties (the Social Democrats, the Conservatives, the Liberals and the Radical Liberals), a compromise was found and the bill was voted with an overwhelming majority of 120 to sixteen votes. In its original form, the proposal has been openly criticized in American and NATO circles.

fairly soon. It is very unlikely that the present coalition with the Communists will be continued which may well have an effect on the emotional Kéflavik issue to which a new government might have a more sober approach.

# CONCLUSION

Their experience during the second world war left the Scandinavian countries with two important convictions. One was that, with the exception of Sweden, a policy of neutrality had not prevented involvement in the conflict or occupation by one or the other of the major antagonists. The other was that their defense perimeters clearly differed, even though their geographic positions were aligned. Finland and Denmark both neighbored a major continental power, Russia and Germany, and represented an undeniable strategic interest in each case. Their territory was useful to an enemy of the larger state as a base for attack on its northern flank. In addition, Denmark controlled the gateways to and from the Baltic, and as a result was of vital importance to the continental powers for both offensive and defensive measures. Norway's importance essentially lay in its long Atlantic coast, which was (and is) excellently suited for naval, especially submarine, warfare. Iceland was particularly valuable to belligerents because of its location halfway between America and Europe. Under control of a major power, the island constitutes an ideal base for disrupting the lines of communication between the two continents.

Sweden was the only Scandinavian country to be spared hostilities and occupation during World War II. The country bordered none of the antagonists and its strategic interest to them was only marginal. Moreover, the Swedes were militarily well-prepared, and equipped with the most modern weaponry. In these ways they constituted enough deterrent to secure their nation from the damages of war.

In 1947 and 1948, the great wartime alliance collapsed and the Cold War broke out, but the political and strategic situation in the Scandinavian countries did not change drastically from what it had been in the late 1930s. Politically the Nordic countries all but completely identified with the Western world, much as they had in 1939. Their distaste for Communist ideology matched their onetime distrust of fascism, and their fear of Soviet expansionism that of the earlier German drive for hegemony. And once again, the East-West conflict centered around a major continental power and a group of states tied to the Anglo-American sea powers.

Not surprisingly under these circumstances, Sweden hoped to continue its successful policy of armed neutrality. In Norway, Denmark, and Iceland, on the other hand, nonalignment had failed, and these nations understandingly sought outside insurance for their safety. Only to prevent Norway from finalizing binding arrangements with the West did Sweden propose negotiations in 1948 for a Scandinavian defense pact. Denmark fully supported the Swedish proposal because it combined the advantages of Scandinavian unity and increased security with the preservation of some measure of neutrality but Norway entered the negotiations halfheartedly. The Norwegians insisted that in order to be credible the proposed Scandinavian Defense Union should formally join forces with the Western powers. Sweden refused the condition and discussions faltered. Another, although less important reason for the breakdown in negotiations was Sweden's inability to insure the necessary delivery of modern military equipment to Norway and Denmark. This was particularly vital since the United States had stated clearly that priority for weapon deliveries would go to its own allies.

With the death of the Nordic Union, Denmark and Norway were left no alternative to the Atlantic alliance then in the making. Iceland greeted their decision to join NATO with much relief; that country would not have been included in the proposed Scandinavian defense community and in its isolated position it would have found resisting American demands for stationing troops on the island very difficult to sustain.

The three Scandinavian countries joined NATO on minimal terms by refusing to allow foreign bases or nuclear warheads on their soil. This was as much an expression of their desire to limit great-power rivalry in Northern Europe as a proof to the Soviets of the basically defensive nature of their alliance membership.

Thanks to substantial allied, mainly American, help, Norway and Denmark succeeded in expanding and modernizing their armed forces at very little expense to themselves. Even so, membership in the alliance never has been very popular, especially in Denmark where large sections of the population opposed the inclusion into NATO of Greece, Turkey, and Western Germany, the involvement of the United States in Vietnam, Portuguese colonial wars in Africa, or the establishment of a military dictatorship in Greece. In Iceland, uneasiness centered around the presence of an American defense force, which the island had been coerced into accepting after the outbreak of the Korean War. But nowhere did anti-Americanism or hostility toward NATO lead to withdrawal from the alliance.

288

One reason was that the conflict between East and West, although submerged in nuclear stalemate, was still very much a fact of life. In that context, the Warsaw Pact invasion of Czechoslovakia was important as a reminder of the instability of détente. Furthermore, with the build-up of Soviet naval power, especially in the Arctic and in the Mediterranean, the locus of the main confrontation between the superpowers has gradually shifted from Central Europe to the northern and southern flanks. The move obviously affected Norway more than it did Denmark, but even the latter was insure enough about the Soviets' ulterior motives to remain a member of the alliance after 1969, at least for the time being.

# Part IV

# BELGIUM, HOLLAND, and LUXEMBOURG

By Frans Govaerts

# INTRODUCTION

In the political calculations of the larger European powers, the Benelux countries have traditionally occupied a more important place than might normally be expected from nations of their size. Their strategic location among great powers and their proximity to the North Sea have been largely responsible for this. The area has been drawn into conflicts on the European chessboard so many times that security has become an extremely important factor in their policies, and they have tested several courses with security in mind. Alignment has been only the most recent of them.

Belgium and Luxembourg have been neutralized since their independence, and Holland from the second half of the nineteenth century. However, Belgium's bitter experience of the German invasion in 1914 made it clear that neutrality did not necessarily keep a country out of conflict. After the war it tried to guarantee its safety through collective security on both a universal and a regional level. It became a member of the League of Nations, it signed the Locarnopact, and it concluded a military agreement with France. After World War I, Holland and Luxembourg also joined the League of Nations, although with some reservations, and pursued an independent policy until the outbreak of World War II. From 1936 onward Belgium did the same, since both the League of Nations and the regional agreements very quickly proved unreliable means for safeguarding its vital interests. Unfortunately, this could not avert the brutal attack by the German forces on the Low Countries in May 1940, the beginning of almost half a decade of Nazi occupation and the end of excessive reliance on noninvolvement.

This study, then, will investigate the motives that drove the Benelux nations toward alignment after 1945 and those that made them stay in NATO even after 1969, when the treaty offered them the chance to leave. In addition, it focuses on the role the Low Countries have played within the alliance and on the important influence they have had on NATO decision making, particularly on questions of political consultation and cooperation in the Atlantic organization, European integration and Atlantic partnership, and relations with Eastern Europe in a period of détente.

# Chapter I

# THE ROAD TOWARD ALIGNMENT

## PLANNING FOR THE POSTWAR PERIOD

After the German invasion of May 1940, most European governments fled to London, continuing the struggle against the Axis powers from there. For Holland, Belgium, and Luxembourg this dramatic new experience contained two important lessons: first, neutrality or independence could never again be the basis of security; second, if some new international institution for peace and security was organized after the war, it would have to be both more universal and more efficient than the League of Nations. Since collective security could only be effective with permanent cooperation among the larger powers, many hoped that the wartime alliance of the U.S.S.R., the U.S., and Britain would survive to provide the basis for a new international security system.

Others were doubtful from the beginning. They thought it more realistic to seek security in a more tangible regional defense organization. This was more particularly the case in the wartime planning of the Dutch, Belgian, and Luxembourg governments in London. Although they supported a universal organization for peace and security in theory, practical politics strongly inclined them to a regional solution. Their small size, restricted resources, and the recent experience of two German invasions were responsible for this, at least in Belgium and Luxembourg. Moreover, they were afraid that the wartime alliance among the larger powers might be hard to maintain once the binding element of the common struggle against Germany was lost and strong differences of interest again became paramount. As early as 25 November 1942, Mr. van Kleffens, the Dutch foreign minister, expressed his preference for regionalism in a London radio broadcast: "I would be surprised, if an organization based on regions, not neglecting however, the universal element of the indivisible peace, would not perhaps be more effective. Such an organization can only be achieved by the collaboration of like-minded states." *(1)* In 1941,

1 Quoted in A. Vandenbosch, *Dutch Foreign Policy since 1815. A Study in Small Power Politics* (The Hague, 1959), p. 289.

the Belgian foreign minister, P.H. Spaak, had noted similar ideas to Irene Ward, Conservative member of Parliament:

> What has happened in Europe for 20 months proves that it is indispensable for the European nations to unite. Their security clearly proves to be interdependent. The countries of Europe will be ready, after the war, to unite closely under the leadership of victorious England. ...The ideal would evidently be a universal organization, or, for lack of this, an all-European organization. The ideal, however, is generally not compatible with political realities. ...Belgium, evidently, is essentially pre-occupied with the security and prosperity of Western Europe. Western Europe shows these particular charac-teristics, that among the composing nations, there is no territorial competition and that, on the contrary, there is a community of political, legal and moral principles and a social level that is comparable. ...It is essentially on this united or federated Western Europe, which must be the core of postwar politics and postwar reconstruction, that England will have to rely. *(2)*

Such official points of view clearly show how intensely both countries thought in terms of a Western European organization from the very beginning. On the other hand, the struggle between regionalism and a universalist approach to security continued for the rest of the war, and even intensified in the postwar period. In September 1944 Belgium, Holland, and Luxembourg set a first example of regionalism by signing the Benelux treaty that was to create a customs union among them. Their action continued a long tradition of econ-omic cooperation between Belgium and Luxembourg begun with the creation of the Belgium-Luxembourg Economic Union (BLEU) in 1921. *(3)* The concept of Western European cooperation had benefitted to an exceptional degree from the close personal wartime collaboration among the foreign ministers of Holland, Belgium, and Luxembourg in London, particularly between van Kleffens and Spaak, both strong supporters of Western European unity and of maintaining close ties with Great Britain. In London on 25 November 1943, South African Prime Minister General Jan Smuts had suggested that the na-tions of Western Europe create a larger European state in close union with England. *(4)* Minister van Kleffens broadcast a reply on 28 December 1943: "In modern times no nation can be militarily strong without having at its disposal an enormous industrial organization." *(5)* He described as an ideal the development of a

> strong formation in the West with America, Canada and other British Dominions as an

---

2  P.H. Spaak, *Combats inachevés. De l'Indépendance à l'Alliance* (Paris, 1969), p. 148.
3  Closer cooperation between the BLEU and Holland was initiated on 21 October 1943, when the official rate between the Dutch guilder and the Belgian franc was fixed.
4  Vandenbosch, *op. cit.*, p. 290.
5  Quoted in *ibid.*, p. 291.

arsenal and a vast reservoir of power, with England as a base, especially for air-power, and the West European mainland – by which I mean the Netherlands, Belgium and France – as a bridgehead. A development of this nature would indeed compel us to rely on the Western powers, but conversely they would also need us. It is difficult to imagine a stronger position for our country. This formidable western bloc would find its eastern counterpart in Russia. *(6)*

It was an important speech, clearly emphasizing that Holland's national interests required an Atlantic as well as a Western European framework. But both the Belgian and the Dutch governments qualified those kinds of statements by adding that they had no intention of organizing Western Europe against the Soviet Union. On many occasions they spoke of the possibility of the resurgence of German expansionism once Germany was reorganized after the war.

From 1942-1943 onward, if not earlier, European postwar security plans were defined in terms of two separate blocs, although the ideal of a world organization and the desire for friendly relations with all nations were regularly mentioned. *(7)* The first concrete plan for the creation of a European community after the war originated with General Sikorski, the Polish prime minister, who proposed in the fall of 1941 the organization of a postwar community among the eight European nations based in London at the time. Several commissions examined his proposal in 1942, but an agreement was never reached. In 1943 this kind of planning ended, partly because of General Sikorski's death, partly because of obvious hesitation on the part of the Czechs, who feared Soviet objections to an all-European organization that excluded Russia. The Dutch and Norwegians were more interested in an Atlantic alliance, and the Belgians also showed some reluctance. *(8)* In fact, Belgium had never been greatly enthusiastic about an alliance incorporating all of Europe. To the Belgian government, Western and Eastern European countries lacked a community of interests sufficient to create a lasting sense of solidarity. *(9)* On 16 October 1942 Van Langenhove wrote an important note *(10)* reflecting

---

6   *Ibid.*

7   The best historical work discussing Belgian and Dutch wartime planning for the postwar period is F. Van Langenhove, *La Sécurité de la Belgique. Contribution à l'histoire de la période 1940-1950* (Brussels, 1971). As former secretary general of the Foreign Ministry, principally under Spaak, Van Langenhove offers a mass of nonofficial documents with comments. They are the best source now available on this period, since official diplomatic documents have not been published.

8   Spaak, *op. cit.*, p. 156.

9   Van Langenhove, *op. cit.*, p. 74.

10   *Ibid.*, pp. 82-84.

official Belgian thinking on those vague schemes for a European federation. From a short analysis he drew the following conclusions. First, European unity could hardly be realized in the very near future unless the continent came under the control of a dominant power. Second, a European federation would endanger Belgium's independence, since it implied the need for an imperialist power to exercise a hegemonial influence over it. This would make efforts to destroy German oppression idle. Finally, such an organization would be contrary to Belgian overseas interests. *(11)* In the second part of his note Van Langenhove stated that Belgium should not loosen ties with the other allied nations, especially in the West, for it was particularly with Britain, Holland, the U.S., and France that it shared a real community of interests. With them, too, his country could always find support. So as early as 1942 the orientation of Belgian foreign policy was clear. Spaak notes in his memoirs: "If my diplomatic activity in 1942 was particularly focused on this idea of a European entente, in 1943, 1944, and 1945, my efforts turned toward the organization of Western Europe under the leadership of England." *(12)*

A clearer insight into the part the Low Countries have had in the creation of a Western European bloc requires a consideration of the reactions of the larger European powers. British Prime Minister Winston Churchill was much too occupied with wartime planning to pay serious attention to Benelux efforts to organize postwar Europe. On the other hand, Foreign Minister Anthony Eden told Spaak in July 1944 that he was convinced that out of the conference then being prepared in Washington *(13)* would come some future universal organization for the maintenance of peace. Eden had kept Spaak and van Kleffens waiting for some time for his answer to their regionalist proposals, and he had told Spaak earlier that he had been waiting because he felt it preferable to begin discussions on a world organization before considering alliances in Western Europe. He hoped in this way to avoid hindering American efforts to reach a universal agreement, and to counteract any isolationist reactions in the U.S. to the idea that Europe planned to be independent of American support. However, Eden felt that a universal organization needed an underpinning of regional alliances; the time was nearing, he said, when Great Britain, Belgium, Holland, Norway, and France could begin negotiations of their own. Moreover, the Soviet Union had already accepted the idea of a regional organization for Western Europe; he and Joseph Stalin had examined the question as early

---

11  *Ibid.*
12  Spaak, *op. cit.*, p. 157.
13  This conference eventually resulted in the United Nations Organization.

as 1941. *(14)* A few months later, at the end of 1944, Eden told Spaak that from his conversations with the Soviets and the Americans he was sure that

> Stalin, anxious to create, between Germany and Russia, a sort of "glacis" of more or less independent states that would absorb the shock of any new German aggression, was not against the fact that England would create an analogous system and would agree with Belgium, Holland, Luxembourg, Norway, and possibly France, to create a barrier against any sudden attack, which was always possible from Germany. *(15)*

On the other hand, Spaak's efforts to convince Prime Minister Churchill remained unsuccessful. In addition, the new British Labour government, headed by Attlee, preferred to wait until the United Nations system was functioning before preparing a similar structure in Western Europe. But in principle at least, Foreign Minister Bevin agreed with Spaak's proposals, which by that time included a treaty of friendship between the Soviet Union and Belgium similar to the Anglo-Russian pact of 1942 and the Franco-Russian pact of 1944. *(16)*

French official reactions remained ambiguous in the last years of the war. On the one hand, the French felt inclined to a Western European grouping for reasons of security; on the other, they wanted to keep the way open for a European settlement with the other large powers.

In sharp contrast with Eden's 1944 reports to Spaak that the Soviets did not oppose the formation of a regional organization, the Soviet press launched heavy attacks on Belgium in October 1944, representing this country as the "instigator and the champion of a Western bloc." *(17)* Spaak presided over the first UN assembly in London on 8 February 1946, and used the occasion to reassure the U.S.S.R. of Belgium's good intentions and to defend his foreign policy line. He told Soviet Ambassador Vychinsky that Belgian policy essentially aimed at avoiding war. The best way to do this was to maintain the wartime alliance among the big powers, and Belgium would never do anything to endanger this alliance. On the other hand, Spaak said that Belgium was op-

---

14   Spaak, *op. cit.*, p. 158.
15   *Ibid.*, p. 159.
16   *Ibid.*, p. 164.
17   Van Langenhove, *op. cit.*, p. 138. Moreover, in December 1944 Belgium sold Congolese uranium to the Anglo-Saxons, thus facilitating the production of nuclear weapons by 1945. The Belgian government had first been contacted in this connection on 23 March 1944. Spaak notes this in his memoirs: "We have thus contributed in an important way to their war efforts. We made it possible for them to take a lead in the field of nuclear weapons over the rest of the world and thus we helped them to maintain peace during the following years, when Russian politics in Europe were so menacing". Spaak, *op. cit.*, pp. 177-178.

posed to a Western bloc if it meant a political alliance against Russia, but in his view certain problems, such as defense, could only be settled in a regional framework. He ended his meeting with the Soviet representative by proposing a Belgian-Soviet treaty of friendship. Spaak's memoirs indicate clearly that the U.S.S.R. was given every assurance that Belgium opposed an anti-Soviet alliance in Western Europe. *(18)* The important question, of course, is whether Spaak's words convinced the U.S.S.R. and eliminated the impression that during the war Belgium had taken the lead of an anti-Soviet campaign. Were his words not interpreted as a pure lipservice, while at the same time he went on to press for a Western European bloc?

The French and the British waited until 4 March 1947 to take the first concrete step toward regionalism, when they signed the Treaty of Dunkirk, a real alliance for mutual assistance. Only under the pressure of events in Europe after the war had they changed policies. "Until then [1947] England and France had accepted only reservedly and with prudence the idea of an entente among Western European democracies which, for Belgium, Mr. Spaak had repeatedly advocated to them. They did not want to rebuff the Soviet Union, who had not been hiding her distrust, if not hostility, toward what she called a western bloc. *(19)*

## THE UNIVERSALIST OPTION:
## THE BENELUX COUNTRIES AND THE UNITED NATIONS

The wartime planning of the Low Countries for a postwar security organization had been dominated by a regionalist approach; by the end of the war they shifted markedly toward universalism. Big power cooperation in the creation of the UN, the hope that the wartime alliance among them would continue, and the general euphoria of victory undoubtedly contributed to Benelux support of the United Nations. To a certain extent U.S. pressure may also have influenced Belgium's positive attitude. *(20)* The Benelux countries accepted

---

18   Spaak, *op. cit.*, pp. 165-166. Belgian-Russian relations during the war had been difficult. From May 1941 to May 1943, the U.S.S.R. suspended its diplomatic relations with Belgium because it could no longer regard Belgium as a sovereign state. T. Luykx, *Politieke Geschiedenis van België* (Brussels, 1964), p. 400.

19   Van Langenhove, *op. cit.*, p. 205.

20   This is implied in a note written by Charles De Visscher, Belgian representative at the San Francisco Conference, dated 11 June 1945, in which he said: "We will nevertheless sign the Charter: 1) First of all, because it seems politically impossible to do otherwise. U.S. support for an eventual defense of our country has been offered on the condition of our acceptance of the Charter". Quoted in Van Langenhove, *op. cit.*, p. 164. Though this source specifies only Belgium this was probably also the case for the two othercountries.

the UN Charter without much enthusiasm, well aware of its imperfections. The privileged position the larger powers were claiming for themselves and the growing opposition among them strengthened small-power scepticism initially the result of the failure of the League of Nations. *(21)*

In a speech to the Belgian Parliament *(22)* on 6 December 1944, Foreign Minister Spaak expressed his government's support for universal collective security. However, he strongly hoped that the new system would be free of the deficiencies and contradictions that had made the League of Nations so ineffective, and he stressed the need for a corresponding European alliance and a regional entente, saying that any future world security system would have to be built upon these three complementary stages. The proper functioning of a European alliance required "big particular treaties" like the Anglo-Russian treaty, whereas regional ententes could serve as a sort of executive for collective security policies. *(23)* The same belief in the advantages of regionalism appeared in a "Memorandum of the Belgian Government to the Governments of the Allied Powers" on 5 February 1945. In this document, the Belgian government criticized particularly the principles on which decisions in the United Nations Organization were to be made, as well as the planned relationship between great and small powers. *(24)* Similar criticism was expressed in the "Suggestions of the Dutch Government on the Dumbarton Oaks Proposals" of January 1945. *(25)* The Belgian document approved of regional ententes' dependence on the new international organization. On the other hand, Belgium suggested that coercive measures in the framework of an immediate action and prepared by a special regional arrangement should not be

---

21  For Belgian and Dutch foreign policies in the interwar period, see O. De Raeymaeker, *België's internationaal beleid 1919-1939* (Brussels, 1945); P. Van Zuylen, *Les Mains Libres. Politique extérieure de la Belgique, 1914-1940* (Brussels, 1950); J.K. Miller, *Belgian Foreign Policy between Two Wars 1919-1940* (New York, 1951); D.O. Kieft, *Belgium's Return to Neutrality. An Essay in the Frustrations of Small Power Diplomacy* (London, 1972); and A. Vandenbosch, *op. cit.*

22  Belgium, *Parlementaire Handelingen, Kamer,* 1944-45, 6 December 1944, pp. 90-93 [Hereafter *Parl. Hand., Kamer*].

23  *Ibid.*

24  *La Belgique et les Nations Unies,* Study by a commission of the Royal Institute for International Relations for the Carnegie Endowment for International Peace (New York, 1958), pp. 33-34.

25  Vandenbosch, *op. cit.,* pp. 293-294.
See also S.I.P. Van Campen, *The Quest for Security – Some Aspects of Netherlands Foreign Policy, 1945-1950* (The Hague, 1958), pp. 15-22.

suspended without the Security Council's authorization. *(26)* With this suggestion the Belgian government sought guarantees for direct action on a regional level. At the San Francisco Conference Belgium had tried to modify the veto system accepted at Yalta. *(27)* Although the Belgian amendment was not accepted, the small states saw the right of legitimate individual and collective defense recognized under Article 51 of the charter.

At the San Francisco Conference Holland also submitted several amendments to the proposals arising from the four powers' conference at Dumbarton Oaks. Traditionally, a legalistic and moral approach has characterized Dutch foreign policy and, true to form, the Dutch delegation insisted on inserting a reference to international law as a standard of conduct in international affairs into the charter. An independent body of eminent men from different countries would oversee the law's application. *(28)* Holland also insisted on suitable representation in the Security Council of smaller powers, who "are in a position to make a substantial contribution to the success of the organization." *(29)* Moreover, the right of veto had to be restricted to those cases which involved coercion by force. *(30)* Later, when ratification of the charter was discussed in the Dutch Parliament, the government once again stressed its readiness to "support the principle of universal cooperation to the fullest possible extent." *(31)* On the other hand, it was very cautious on the question of regional groupings. "It was considered that such groupings would be placed under the Charter and as regards a Western European Alliance or Bloc, a non-committal attitude was adopted. An alliance with one great power in any circumstances was rejected; a certain freedom for manoeuvring was obviously considered essential." *(32)* In contrast to Spaak's ideas on the necessity of regional ententes, Holland's cautious position, at least by 1945, seemed more committed to the UN than Belgium's. Perhaps this difference in emphasis can be explained

---

26 *La Belgique et Les Nations Unies*, p. 35. See also O. De Raeymaeker, "Regionale accoorden en wettige zelfverdediging", *Politica*, Tijdschrift voor Staatkunde en Sociologie (Louvain), VII, 3 (July, 1957), 193-213.

27 By amending the text with the following paragraph: "Dissident votes of permanent members of the Security Council who are no party to such arrangements or bodies, will not be an obstacle to the value of a Council-decision on this matter". Source "Amendements présentés par la délégation belge aux propositions de Dumbarton Oaks, relatives à l'établissement d'une Organisation générale", *UNCIO*, Vol. 4, Doc. 2 (French), G/7 (kl) (5 May 1945), p. 481. *Arrangements* or *bodies* here mean regional ententes.

28 Van Campen, *op. cit.*, p. 16.

29 *Ibid.*, p. 17.

30 *Ibid.*, p. 18.

31 *Ibid.*, p. 22.

32 *Ibid.*

by the fact that Belgium was experienced in the field of regional security arrangements through its membership in the Locarnopact and the Franco-Belgian military agreement of 1921.

The Luxembourg government was anxious that the new organization avoid the deficiencies of the older League of Nations. It suggested a more universal orientation, founded on a solid base and possessing more effective ways of taking action than the Geneva organization. *(33)* Despite these criticisms, in official Luxembourg the UN system was seen as the only possible guarantee for the smaller nations, at least under prevailing conditions. On the other hand, ratification of the charter caused some difficulties in this country. Although the consultative assembly had unanimously approved it on 9 August 1945, some had questioned its conformity to the Luxembourg constitution. In fact, ratification by right belonged to the House of Representatives, but in the middle of 1945 the first legislative elections had not yet been held. The government expressed the opinion that the procedure was constitutionally valid, however, and a grand-ducal decree on 10 August 1945 approved the UN Charter. Since the charter was considered incompatible with the country's neutral status, ratification formally ended Luxembourg's neutrality. *(34)* All political parties supported this new orientation to their country's foreign policy. In fact, it was a logical continuation of one begun before World War II with membership in the League of Nations and pursued during the war.

Dutch and Belgian Parliaments ratified the charter with a very similar mixture of realism, self-deception, and lack of enthusiasm, in a spirit of loyalty to the common cause. Spaak expressed the opinion of the majority on 31 October 1945:

> When I ask you to ratify the charter, to take part in the UN, I do not do this with great enthusiasm, but with the will to participate loyally in the effort that begins, the authors of which have had the wisdom to say that it had not its final form, but, on the contrary, that it could be improved. *(35)*

## FROM UNIVERSALISM TO REGIONALISM

Benelux support for the United Nations did not mean that hope for regional ententes to complement a world-wide organization had been abandoned, nor that confidence in the UN was very strong. On the contrary, when the evolution

33 L. Schaus, "Les fondements du statut international du Luxembourg. 1944-1957, "*Le Conseil d'Etat du Grand-Duché de Luxembourg, Livre jubilaire* (Luxembourg, 1957), 243.
34 In fact, neutrality had ended by May 1940.
35 *Parl. Hand., Kamer,* 1944-1945, 31 October 1945, p. 1210.

of international politics after the war led quickly to the emergence of two opposing powerblocs, the Benelux countries were among the first and most active promotors of a regional security organization in Western Europe. If they seemed to temporarily abandon an areal focus in the years between 1945 and 1947, this was so for several reasons. The first was the strong desire of the Benelux governments to give collective security a fair chance. An essential condition to this scheme was a permanent agreement and mutual understanding among the larger powers, and the small nations sought an equal relationship with all of them. *(36)* In addition, Benelux Parliaments contained an unusually strong Communist presence. In Belgium and Luxembourg Communists had shared government responsibilities for some time, and they undoubtedly constituted an obstacle to every attempt at regional solidarity. *(37)* And finally, in 1945 and 1946 both France and Britain refused to participate in a Western European alliance.

These factors were insufficient to stop the growing support for a regional organization binding first Western Europe and later all the West, however. The increasing fear of Soviet expansionism in Western Europe, the failure of the UN, almost paralyzed by the Soviets' frequent use of the veto right, and the tightening web of Western economic cooperation under the Marshall Plan led quickly to the Brussels Pact and NATO.

In fact, the first and most important factor influencing the foreign policy course of the Benelux nations has been the fear of the Soviets. The immediate

36 The Dutch government's declaration of 1946 shows a strong preference for a policy of universal cooperation. See Vandenbosch, *op. cit.*, pp. 301-302. On 31 October 1945 in the Belgian Parliament, Foreign Minister Spaak had pledged that Belgium would never play one big power against another, and rather it would use every means to be "a hyphen" among them. *Parl. Hand., Kamer*, 1944-1945, 31 October 1945, p. 1208. See also *La Belgique et les Nations Unies*, pp. 158-195; and De Raeymaeker, *loc. cit.*, 193-213. Some twenty-five years later, in an interview with the Belgian newspaper *La Libre Belgique* of 10 April 1969 P.H. Spaak reaffirmed the Belgian attitude at that time: "What I want to stress is, that right after the second World War, the Western countries did not want blocs to be built in Europe. They wanted to maintain their alliance with the U.S.S.R., and in their minds, Yalta was not the division of the world in spheres of influence. ...I too, at that time being foreign minister, when meeting Vichinsky in London, insisted on the wish of Belgium to avoid the creation of a Western bloc and to maintain the collaboration with Moscow". This statement is somewhat difficult to understand when contrasted with the following testimony in Spaak's memoirs: "If my diplomatic activity in 1942 was particularly focused on this idea of a European entente, in 1943, 1944 and 1945, my efforts turned towards the organization of Western Europe under the leadership of England". Spaak, *op. cit.*, p. 157.
37 In 1946 the Belgian Parliament, for example, numbered twenty-three Communist representatives and seventeen senators, more than the number of Liberals in both houses.

postwar years were a time of great uncertainty among the larger powers, as each tried to decipher and predict the others' behavior. It was a time of exaggerations and misperceptions as well. How far Western countries were correct in their views of Soviet threats, military as well as political, and how far their attitudes were influenced by the Americans is beyond the scope of this study. Sufficient literature from both traditionalist and revisionist historians is available on the emergence and the development of the Cold War. *(38)* What is of concern to us is how political leaders in the Benelux countries perceived the European situation in those days. An analysis of parliamentary debates and ministerial declarations makes it clear that all the Western European countries felt threatened by Soviet power. *(39)* The UN system failed to relieve such situations as the disagreement on Germany and Austria, or Soviet pressure on Iran, Turkey, and Greece. The consolidation of Soviet power over their zone of occupation in Germany, and over Poland, Hungary, Rumania, Bulgaria, Albania, and later Czechoslovakia were all frightening experiences for the weakened Western European democracies. Moreover, the U.S.S.R. refused proffered U.S. aid, counteracting with the Cominform, which was followed by the announcement of an economic aid plan for Eastern Europe later to result in Comecon. The Communist coup in Prague and the Berlin blockade were the most dramatic events in the whole series of Communist postwar actions in Eastern Europe.

Secondly, Western European apprehension of the U.S.S.R. included a widespread fear of communist ideology. For people only very recently free of Nazi occupation, the prospect of subjugation to another authoritarian political system was terrifying. Stalin's iron-hand policy and the atrocities committed in the name of Communist ideology were only too well known in the West. Many political leaders singled out France and Italy, where powerful Communist parties played an extensive role in national affairs, as possible new targets for Soviet expansionism. In fact, immediately after the war the French Com-

---

38 For traditional views on the Cold War, see, for example, L.J. Halle, *The Cold War as History* (London, 1967); A. Fontaine, *Histoire de la Guerre Froide* (Paris, 1965, 1967); N.A. Graebner, *Cold War Diplomacy, 1945-1960* (Princeton, 1962). For a revisionist approach, see, for example, D.F. Fleming, *The Cold War and Its Origins* (New York, 1961); D. Horowitz, *The Free World Colossus* (New York, 1965); and G. Alperowitz, *Atomic Diplomacy: Hiroshima and Potsdam* (New York, 1965).
Interesting views on this problem can also be found in R. Hunter, *Security in Europe* (London, 1969); G.F. Kennan, *Memoirs* (New York, 1967); R. Steel, *Pax Americana* (London, 1968), and R. Aron, *République Impériale. Les Etats-Unis dans le monde 1945-1972* (Paris, 1973).
39 Even if the U.S.S.R. harbored no direct military expansionist intentions, its doctrine was perceived as a threat.

munist party was the largest group in the Assemblée Nationale. In both France and Italy, as in many Western European countries at that time, Communists shared government responsibility until May 1947. *(40)* Events in Eastern Europe and the strong Communist presence in France and Italy were alarming factors for the weak Benelux countries. *(41)* Moreover, during the war and the liberation, Communists had been influential in the resistance groups of these three nations. The social and economic chaos of 1945 and 1946 provided an excellent opportunity for a Communist coup, but these groups were quickly disbanded, and a Communist presence in the Belgian and Luxembourg governments *(42)* had disappeared by February-March, 1947. Communist representation in Benelux Parliaments was unusually strong compared to the two next decades, although they remained one of the smaller political parties. In the Dutch elections of 1946 only ten out of one hundred Second Chamber seats went to Communists; in 1948 the number was reduced to eight, and in 1952 they won just six seats. In the Belgian House of Representatives the situation was similar. In 1946 Communists occupied twenty-three of the 202 seats, in 1949 twelve out of 212, and in 1950 only seven out of 212. *(43)* In Luxembourg their presence was limited to ten percent of the House of Representatives, six out of fifty-one seats. *(44)* As these statistics show, the Communist threat to government stability and the vested interests of the majority has never been great; in 1948 and 1949, the years when the Benelux countries finally turned toward alignment, it was no longer real.

A third factor uniting most European countries that had escaped Soviet occupation or Communist rule, making them largely if not totally dependent on the U.S., was the urgent need for economic aid and cooperation. When the war ended in Europe the economic activity in most countries had almost stopped completely. War damage was particularly high in Greece, Holland, France, Italy, Austria, and of course in the war's major protagonist, Germany. *(45)* Among the Low Countries, Holland in particular faced serious recon-

40  F. Goguel and A. Grosser, *La Politique en France* (Paris, 1964), pp. 110-111 and 273-275 and F.R. Willis, *Italy chooses Europe* (New York, 1971), pp. 14-15.

41  Belgian Foreign Minister Spaak dramatically articulated their feelings in his famous speech before the UN General Assembly in Paris on 28 September 1948. Spaak, *op. cit.*, p. 216.

42  Holland has never known a Communist presence in its government.

43  G.L. Weil, *The Benelux Nations. The Politics of Small Country Democracies* (New York, 1970), pp. 95 and 111.

44  Luxembourg, *Compte Rendu des Séances de la Chambre des Députés du Grand-Duché de Luxembourg*, 1948-1949 (9/11/1948 until 26/7/1949), volume unique, p. V-XI [Hereafter *C.R. Chambre*].

45  J.F. Dewhurst, J.O. Coppock, P. Lamartine Yates, *et al.*, *Europe's Needs and Resources*.

struction problems. In the last eight months of Nazi occupation Holland had been largely devastated. Thanks to a quick liberation, Belgium had escaped Holland's fate. Luxembourg had been liberated with Belgium in September 1944, but the von Rundstedt offensive of 16 December 1944 to 23 January 1945 had left its northern, eastern, and central sectors in ruins. *(46)* The damage to Holland and Luxembourg was so extensive that the implementation of the convention to create a Benelux Customs Union, signed by the three governments in London on 5 September 1944, became impossible. At that time each country hoped that more or less the same amount of damage would enable parallel reconstruction policies and facilitate the establishment of a customs union. Their plans would never materialize. Belgium and Luxembourg, both under the same economic and monetary system, took a reconstruction route different from Holland's. The magnitude of war damage to the Benelux countries is illustrated by the following figures:

TABLE I

War Damage to the Benelux Countries

|  | Destruction (in million $ of 1938) | Damage value per inhabitant ($ of 1938) | Damage value per worker ($ of 1938) |
|---|---|---|---|
| Belgium *(47)* | 2,274 | 274 | 522 |
| Luxembourg | 179 | 597 | 1,422 |
| Holland | 3,947 | 418 | 1,062 |

Source: J. Van Der Mensbrugghe, *Les Unions Economiques. Réalisations et Perspectives* (Brussels, 1949), p. 40.

Because of the good situation of its industrial equipment, Belgium was able to rapidly reorganize its production system in the fall of 1944 and immediately start the production of goods under the reverse lend lease arrangements. "The goods and services thus provided were paid for in foreign currencies, mostly in

*Trends and Prospects in Eighteen Countries* (New York, 1961), p. 6.
46 J. Anders, "L'Evolution économique du Grand-Duché de Luxembourg depuis la Libération", *Bulletin d'Information et de Documentation*, ed. Banque nationale de Belgique, XXIII, II, 1 August 1948, 3.
47 For an interesting analysis of Belgian postwar social and economic problems, see F. Baudhouin, *Histoire Economique de la Belgique, 1945-1956* (Brussels, 1958). For Dutch and Luxembourg postwar recovery problems, see respectively: Persdienst van het Ministerie van Economische Zaken, *Nederlands Economisch Herstel*, (n.p., 1952) and Anders, *loc. cit.*

dollars. Thus, at the close of hostilities, Belgium enjoyed the tremendous advantages of having her production potential to a large extent restored and of having already accumulated substantial foreign exchange reserves." *(48)* Not only because of the lesser war damage it had suffered, but also in terms of production, export capacities, and monetary situation, Belgium was far better off than Holland at the end of the war. In a fight against inflation, the Belgian government had taken monetary measures *(49)* as early as October 1944 to strictly limit the amount of money in circulation in order to adapt it to the amount of goods available. *(50)* In Holland, similar measures were possible only in September 1945. *(51)* With the growing availability of goods in the following years, these measures were gradually abolished. The Belgian balance of payments was also better than the Dutch one. Belgium had suffered less damage, and so had less to import for reconstruction. Moreover, it could immediately start production, and its exports provided much of the necessary foreign capital it needed to pay for its own imports. *(52)* The BLEU saw only a very short period of strict government control, and the two countries rapidly returned to a liberal economic policy, a policy of abundance. Emphasis lay on consumption, and wages and prices were high. *(53)* The Dutch recovery program stressed investment *(54)* and production, *(55)* understandable in view of the "pressing needs of reconstruction and industrialization." *(56)* But such a policy was "almost bound to maintain inflationary pressure in the economy." *(57)* As a result, the Dutch government kept both wages and prices under strict control, and maintained rationing for a long time. *(58)*

Although by 1948 the economies of the BLEU had almost returned to a

---

48  L. Camu, "The Postwar Monetary Policy of the Benelux Countries in its Effect on Foreign Trade", *International Banking and Foreign Trade* (Lectures delivered at the Eighth International Banking Summer School, Christ Church, Oxford, September, 1955), published for the Institute of Bankers (London, 1955), 73. These reverse lend lease arrangements concerned prestations for the U.S. government by countries that had accepted U.S. aid under the 1941 Land Lease Act, such as the U.K., Belgium, and Holland. See H. Zoetewey, *De Dollarschaarste in West-Europa* (Leiden, 1949), p. 9.
49  The so-called Gutt measures, named after the Belgian minister of finance, C. Gutt.
50  Van Der Mensbrugghe, *op. cit.*, p. 68.
51  Persdienst van het Ministerie van Economische Zaken, *op. cit.*, p. 13.
52  Van Der Mensbrugghe, *op. cit.*, pp. 71-73.
53  Camu, *loc. cit.*, 76.
54  *Ibid.*, 82.
55  Persdienst van het Ministerie van Economische Zaken, *op. cit.*, p. 15.
56  Camu, *loc. cit.*, 82.
57  *Ibid.*
58  *Ibid.*, 73.

peacetime pattern, *(59)* the economic situation was still far from perfect. Thanks to its active investment policy, Holland was able to outstrip its partners in industrial and, to a lesser extent, agricultural output. But in the end Dutch recovery policy would lead to serious balance of payments difficulties. The BLEU had been able to sell a substantial amount abroad, whereas Holland's imports remained very high, as the following table shows:

TABLE II

Benelux Foreign Trade Balance

|  | BLEU | | | %<br>covered | | Holland | | %<br>covered |
|---|---|---|---|---|---|---|---|---|
|  | imports[a] | exports[a] | saldo[a] | | imports[b] | exports[b] | saldo[b] | |
| 1938 | 23,069 | 21,670 | — 1,399 | 93.94 | 1,414 | 1,038 | — 376 | 73 |
| 1946 | 57,184 | 29,836 | —27,348 | 52.18 | 2,145 | 785 | —1,360 | 37 |
| 1947 | 85,599 | 61,655 | —23,904 | 72.06 | 4,253 | 1,859 | —2,394 | 44 |
| 1948 | 87,518 | 74,121 | —13,397 | 84.69 | 4,921 | 2,670 | —2,251 | 54 |
| 1949 | 81,858 | 80,092 | — 1,766 | 97.84 | 5,297 | 3,794 | —1,503 | 72 |

a. In 1,000,000 Francs          b. In 1,000,000 Guilders

Source: For the BLEU see Belgium, Belgisch Ministerie van Economische Zaken en Energie, Nationaal Instituut voor de Statistiek, *Handel-Toerisme-Verkeer en Vervoer 1900-1961* (Brussels, n.d.), pp. 20-21; for Holland: Centraal Bureau voor de statistiek, quoted in: Belgium, Ministère des Affaires Economiques et des Classes Moyennes, *L'Economie Belge en 1948* (Brussels, 1949), p. 238, and *L'Economie Belge en 1949* (Brussels, 1950), p. 329.

Holland's massive imports for both reconstruction and consumption negatively influenced its balance of payments:

TABLE III

Balance of Payments Deficit (million dollars)

|  | Belgium and Luxembourg | Holland |
|---|---|---|
| 1946 | n.a. | 489 |
| 1947 | 295 | 587 |
| 1948 | 40 | 359 |

Source: OECE, *Rapport sur l'amélioration de la situation économique en Europe Occidentale* (n.p., June, 1949), p. 75.

59   *Ibid.*, 76; and Anders, *loc. cit.*, 17.

Moreover, the extremely cold winter of 1946-1947 caused a dramatic shortage of foodstuffs, fuel, and coal in all European countries, still in their first phase of recovery. Emergency conditions placed a new and unexpected burden upon very limited amounts of foreign currencies and gold holdings, and the balance of payments was stretched even further. The situation was particularly favorable to Communist agitation, especially in Greece, France, and Italy.

The seriousness of conditions made the U.S. aid program proposed by Secretary of State G. Marshall in his historic speech at Harvard University on 5 June 1947 of vital importance, particularly for Holland, and to a lesser extend for Belgium and Luxembourg. Following the Truman Doctrine, announced on 12 March 1947, the Marshall Plan constituted the second step in the new policy of containment the U.S. had adopted toward the Communist threat in Europe. *(60)* Marshall's speech laid the basis for the European Recovery Program, as his plan came to be known in Europe. In it, he offered U.S. cooperation and economic aid to any government that wanted to assist in the recovery task. However, he asked that the European governments collectively delimit their needs and the part of the responsibility they could assume themselves. *(61)* The Europeans responded quickly. A meeting of sixteen European states held on 12 July 1947 led to the creation of the Comité de Coopération Economique Européenne (CCEE), which was to prepare a proposal to the U.S. government outlining a recovery program, the means available, and the foreign aid required. The committee's response reached the U.S. on 22 September 1947, and by 3 April 1948 the Americans had passed the Economic Cooperation Act (ECA), the legal basis for the Marshall Plan. *(62)* On the

---

60 The Marshall offer, however, was not the first sign of U.S. preparedness to help Europe after the end of the war. Indeed, in the first postwar years European countries had received substantial American economic aid under Lend Lease Act arrangements, through U.S. funds for the UNRRA, through U.S. Export-Import Bank loans, and through other American loan agreements and economic programs. In the so-called postwar relief period (1946-1948), Europe had received a total U.S. economic aid of $ 10,445.8 million, of which $ 7,055.5 million were in the form of loans and $ 3,390.3 million as grants. U.S., Congress, House, *U.S. Overseas Loans and Grants and Assistance from International Organizations. Obligations and Loan Authorizations July 1, 1945 - June 30, 1965*, Special report prepared for the House Foreign Affairs Committee (Washington D.C.), p. 114 [Hereafter *U.S. Overseas Loans and Grants*].

61 For an authoritative analysis of the origins of the Marshall Plan, see D. Acheson, *Present at the Creation. My Years in the State Department* (New York, 1969), pp. 226-235 and Kennan, *op. cit.*, pp. 342-372.

62 M.A.G. Van Meerhaeghe, *Internationale Economische Betrekkingen en Instellingen* (Leiden, 1964), pp. 216-217. For an analysis of the Economic Cooperation Act of 1948, see: Zoetewey, *op. cit.*, pp. 29-41.

European end, the implementation of the program ultimately became the responsibility of the Organization for European Economic Cooperation (OEEC), created on 16 April 1948. The Benelux countries were among the OEEC's original members. Of the total amount of economic and military aid that poured into Europe from the U.S. during the Marshall Plan period, $ 15,378.1 million *(63)* over four years, the Benelux countries received the following share:

TABLE IV

U.S. Economic and Military Aid to the Benelux Countries in the Marshall Aid Period
(1949-1952) (in million dollars)

|  | Belgium and Luxembourg | Holland |
|---|---|---|
| *AID and Predecessor Agencies — Total:* | *559.3* | *982.1* |
| Loans | 68.0 | 149.5 |
| Grants | 491.3 | 832.6 |
| *Export-Import Bank Long-Term Loans:* | 6.8 | — |
| *Other U.S. Economic Programs:* | 0.7 | — |
| *Total Economic:* | *566.8* | *982.1* |
| Loans | 75.5 | 149.5 |
| Grants | 491.3 | 832.6 |
| *Military Assistance Program:* | *174.1* | *139.5* |
| Credit Assistance | — | — |
| Grants | 174.1 | 139.5 |
| (Additional Grants From Excess Stocks): | (14.3) | (35.5) |
| *Total Military:* | *174.1* | *139.5* |
| *Total Economic and Military:* | *740.9* | *1,121.6* |
| Loans | 75.5 | 149.5 |
| Grants | 665.4 | 972.1 |

Source: *U.S. Overseas Loans and Grants*, pp. 117 and 129.

This table clearly shows that Holland, whose economic need and dollar shortage were much larger than that of either Belgium or Luxembourg, received by far the greatest share. The dollar shortage particularly hampered Holland in 1947, but in Belgium and Luxembourg this was not the case. The

63  *U.S. Overseas Loans and Grants*, p. 114. Of this global sum, $ 13,443.8 million were grants, only $ 1,934.3 were loans. *Ibid.*

311

latter two countries found it impossible to sell their goods on the customary European market because their traditional clients lacked the necessary foreign currency for payment. To enable the European countries to buy again on the BLEU market, the greatest part of U.S. aid to Belgium and Luxembourg in this period came in the form of conditional aid. (64) Belgium and Luxembourg were to transfer the equivalent of the received sums in Belgian and Luxembourg francs to other European countries. (65) The results of this measure were twofold. The BLEU was able to continue its normal trading activities, while the European countries receiving help furthered their reconstruction policies.

Thus, the effects of the Marshall Plan were different in each of the three Benelux countries. Belgium and Luxembourg felt them for the greatest part indirectly (66). Of the 26,753.77 million Belgian francs that the BLEU received on 31 December 1953, 21,888.33 million was categorized as conditional aid.(67) For Holland the Marshall Plan was vitally important: "The Dutch policy has one single moment been in grave danger, namely, in the spring of 1948, when the available dollar-reserves were exhausted and one had to face the possibility of a brutal reversal. At that moment, the U.S.-aid, whose importance for the Dutch economy can not be sufficiently stressed, has come to help." (68)

Although the importance and the effects of the U.S. aid were different in Holland and the BLEU countries, all the governments concerned fully supported the Marshall Plan and membership of the OEEC. In the parliamentary debate on the treaty establishing OEEC membership and the bilateral agreements with the U.S. on economic cooperation, the only opposition came from the Communist representatives. In Belgium one Socialist representative and one independent senator abstained. (69)

Such were the circumstances under which the Benelux countries came to

---

64 Baudhouin, op. cit., p. 93. See also M. Cordemans, "België en de Mogendheden", De Gids op Maatschappelijk Gebied, 3-4 (March-April, 1949), 506-507.

65 In the form of drawing rights.

66 See Baudhouin, op. cit., p. 93 and Schaus, loc. cit., 270.

67 Belgium, Ministère des Affaires Economiques, L'Economie Belge en 1953, (Brussels, 1954), p. 379.

68 F.A.G. Keesing, "Le Développement économique des Pays-Bas depuis la libération", Bulletin d'Information et de Documentation, ed. Banque Nationale de Belgique, XXIV, I, 6 (June, 1949), 274.

69 See C.R. Chambre, 1948-1949, 17 March 1949, pp. 1072-1074; Holland, Handelingen van de Staten-Generaal, Tweede Kamer, 1947-1948, 1 July 1948, p. 2062 [Hereafter Hand. Stat., Gen., Tweede Kamer]; Parl. Hand., Kamer, 1947-1948, 29 July 1948, pp. 8-9; and Belgium, Parlementaire Handelingen, Senaat, 1947-1948, 27 July 1948, pp. 1831-1832 [Hereafter Parl. Hand. Senaat].

depend on U.S. support. This was especially the case with Holland, but in general the Marshall program, the Soviet threat and the fear of Communist ideology were important factors in the gradual process of alignment with the U.S. Countries with such limited capabilities (small territory, limited manpower and economic resources), so important a geographic situation, and facing enormous costs for economic recovery and defense in the turbulent postwar years, had very restricted policy options. Cooperation and alignment, even at the expense of some independence, were preferable to remaining weak and exposed to any external threat, especially when that threat emanated from the strongest European power, whose armies lingered in Central and Eastern Europe and whose ideology was totally antagonistic to Western ideals. As L.G.M. Jaquet puts it:

> In those circumstances the United States were the natural and by all West European powers unquestionably accepted leader of the Western alliance. They had the glamour of being the main victor in World War II; they had a nuclear monopoly and superior economic and financial resources; all the allies were dependent on the United States for their most vital interests. *(70)*

Unfortunately, dependence on one of the two superpowers meant an inevitable involvement in the sharply antagonistic relationships of the Cold War.


## BENELUX AND THE BRUSSELS PACT

By the end of 1947 the atmosphere in Western Europe had become increasingly favorable to a regional grouping. The first concrete step in the rapid process leading to the Treaty of Brussels was British Foreign Minister A. Bevin's speech to the House of Commons on 22 January 1948. In fact, Bevin had informed the U.S. as early as 13 January 1948 that Britain intended proposing to France and the Benelux nations bilateral defense agreements on the pattern of the Dunkirk Treaty. President Truman fully supported his plan, and with U.S. backing Bevin broached the subject. *(71)* In his speech he described the danger that threatened Western Europe from the East. He reminded Parliament of all the Western democracies had in common, and urged France and the Benelux countries to unite with England against the common danger in a multilateral defense organization. It was a very important speech for, as Spaak wrote, "It marked the beginning of a new European policy and foreshadowed

---

70  L.G.M. Jaquet, "The Role of Small State within Alliance Systems", *Small States in International Relations*, ed. A. Schou and A.O. Brundtland (Stockholm, 1971), 67.
71  H.S. Truman, *Memoirs. Years of Trial and Hope* (New York, 1956), p. 243.

the Atlantic policy." *(72)* Bevin had expressed the fears that beset all Western European countries at that moment, and the reaction of the small Benelux nations was immediate. It was an initiative Mr. Spaak had long been waiting for: "The reaction in Belgium was immediate and favorable. On 23 January 1948, a few hours after Bevin's speech, I had a communiqué issued that stressed our interest in the British foreign minister's declarations and my intention to consult without delay my colleagues from Holland and Luxembourg." *(73)* The three Benelux foreign ministers met at Luxembourg from 29 to 31 January 1948 to work out the principles of a common stance. *(74)* On 19 February 1948 memoranda were exchanged between the Benelux nations and France and Britain. The French and British documents were very similar, but they strongly differed from the Benelux proposals. The two greater powers wanted a treaty identical to the Treaty of Dunkirk of 1947, one that was bilateral and in which mutual assistance in case of German attack was guaranteed. France and Britain noted their fear that the U.S.S.R. would regard a Western European alliance as a provocation of hostility; *(75)* for this reason they directed their defense measures against Germany. But these conditions were too narrow for the Benelux countries, and too unrealistic. Danger to Western Europe lay not in a divided and occupied Germany but in an expansionist Soviet Union, and a defense treaty should acknowledge this fact. Moreover, they especially stressed the socioeconomic aspects of future cooperation. *(76)* Instead of the British and French proposals, the Benelux nations wanted a regional organization within the framework of the UN Charter. *(77)* They explicitly referred to Article 51 and cited the Rio Pact of September 1947 as precedent. *(78)* They wanted a "concerted action in case of a renewal of an aggressive policy by Germany or by whatever nation that would directly or indirectly act together with this country, and, eventually, the automatic rendering of mutual aid. A system of regular and periodical consultations on all problems of common interest had to be organized." *(79)* France and Britain were clearly hesitating, but the smaller nations were ready to accept the consequences of the choice

---

72 Spaak, *op. cit.*, p. 252.
73 *Ibid.*, p. 255.
74 *Ibid.*
75 Van Langenhove, *op. cit.*, p. 208.
76 van Campen, *op. cit.*, p. 60.
77 Especially to the Dutch government this reference to the UN Charter seems to have been extremely important. See van Campen, *op. cit.*, p. 60.
78 Van Langenhove, *op. cit.*, p. 209.
79 *Ibid.*

they had made. Rather than a traditional alliance, they envisioned a real community. *(80)* As President Truman noted:

> It was from the three small nations that a counterproposal came for one regional arrangement rather than a series of two-party treaties. Mr. Spaak, the Belgian Foreign Minister was largely responsible for this change and it was in this form that the treaty was made. I think to Spaak goes the credit for lining up the Europeans for the treaty. *(81)*

The British and French proposals included a warning against excessive haste in signing a mutual defense treaty, in case the U.S. used the five-nation mutual-support pact as a pretext to withdraw its forces from Europe. At the time both nations hoped for U.S. participation in the defense of Western Europe as well as an Atlantic pact for mutual defense. Therefore, they wanted to limit themselves to simple bilateral agreements. *(82)* The Benelux nations found this argument unconvincing. In their view, a limited regional agreement would serve as an incentive to wider American cooperation with Western Europe. *(83)*

On the basis of these mutual proposals, the five governments began talks in Brussels on 4 March 1948. By March 17 the Brussels Treaty was completed and signed. A political and psychological factor that hastened the agreement was the Communist coup in Czechoslovakia in February 1948. Especially the form of the treaty, which was based on strong multilateral, regional cooperation rather than the bilateral framework the British and the French preferred, was probably influenced by events in Prague. The pact is a kind of compromise between universalism and regionalism, although it is heavily weighed in favor of the latter. In order not to hamper great power cooperation, the treaty explicitly mentions its intentions against a possible German aggression, although all the signators took this to mean Soviet aggression. To the Benelux countries, membership in this pact was a first concrete, formal guarantee of their security within the framework of a regional defensive alliance. In its invitation to other states to join, the Brussels Treaty laid the basis for a broader alliance. It would lead directly to the North Atlantic Treaty, for the U.S. immediately reacted favorably to this European initiative. *(84)* On the other hand, it was the first important landmark on the road toward European unification, combining five countries not only militarily or politically, but also economically, socially, and culturally. The influence the Benelux nations managed to exert over the content

---

80  Spaak, *op. cit.*, p. 257.
81  Truman, *op. cit.*, p. 243.
82  Spaak, *op. cit.*, p. 257.
83  Van Langenhove, *op. cit.*, p. 210.
84  See M.M. Ball, *NATO and the European Union Movement* (London, 1959), p. 11.

of the treaty, was an important expression of the possibilities for small-power control despite the limited scope. As a result they laid the basis for stronger cooperation and a growing unity that would have been impossible under the bilateral agreements the French and British had proposed. The treaty's conformity to UN principles and its similarity to the Rio Pact must also have made American support for it more attainable. Thus it helped facilitate U.S. participation in the North Atlantic alliance. In fact, the Benelux countries had provided a definitive orientation for the agreement.

Ratification was achieved without difficulty in the three Benelux Parliaments. The only opposition came from the Communist parties. In Luxembourg the treaty was ratified on 29 April 1948 by a majority of forty-six against five Communist votes. (85) The Belgian House of Representatives approved it on 28 April 1948, with a large majority of 150 to twenty-one (all Communists) votes, and the Senate did the same on 24 March 1948 by 138 to fifteen Communist votes. (86) In Holland, the Second Chamber voted in favor of the Brussels Pact on 28 April 1948; again the Communists were the only opponents. (87)

## A LOGICAL CONSEQUENCE: THE NORTH ATLANTIC TREATY

The link between the Brussels Treaty and NATO is a direct one. European initiative and the treaty's invitation to any other state "inspired by the same ideals and animated by the like determination" (88) provoked immediate American reaction. On 17 March 1948, the very day the pact was signed, President Truman commended the action of the five European countries in an address to Congress:

> This development deserves our full support. I am confident that the United States will, by appropriate means, extend to the free nations the support which the situation requires. I am sure that the determination of the free countries of Europe to protect themselves will be matched by an equal determination on our part to help them do so. (89)

In fact, the Brussels agreement had not caused American isolationism or a

---

85  C.R. Chambre, 1947-1948, 29 April 1948, p. 1124. The Communists had also voted against the constitutional revision of 15 April 1948 that ended the country's neutrality.

86  Parl. Hand., Kamer, 1947-1948, 28 April 1948, pp. 21-22 and Parl. Hand., Senaat, 1947-1948, 24 March 1948, p. 781.

87  Hand. Stat.-Gen., Tweede Kamer, 1947-1948, 28 April 1948, p. 1648. For a most interesting analysis of the Dutch position with regard to the Brussels Pact, see Van Campen, op. cit., pp. 59-87.

88  Introductory words of the text of the Brussels Pact. NATO Facts and Figures (Brussels, 1969), p. 234.

89  U.S., Congressional Record, Vol. XCIV, Part 3, p. 2997, quoted in Ball, op. cit., p. 11.

further withdrawal from Europe, as France and Britain had feared. On the contrary, it strengthened the American commitment to the defense of Western Europe. Harmonized fairly well with the philosophy of American policies applied in the Truman Doctrine and the Marshall aid program, *(90)* the treaty fulfilled the hopes of many European political leaders who during and immediately after the war wanted the U.S. and Canada to unite in a common defense system. Canada had also reacted very favorably to the new alliance. According to the Canadian Secretary of State for Foreign Affairs, Mr. St. Laurent, the organization ought to be widened to an Atlantic defense system, with the United States and Canada as members. *(91)* In the United States, the chairman of the Senate Foreign Relations Committee, Senator Vandenberg, proposed the arrangement later called the Vandenberg Resolution of 11 June 1948, which opened the way to "Association of the United States, by constitutional process, with such regional and other collective security arrangements as are based on continuous and effective self-help and mutual aid, and as affect its national security." *(92)*

Once this decisive step had been taken, the first meeting on an Atlantic level followed quickly. As early as July 1948 conversations began between the five Brussels Pact countries and American and Canadian representatives. During these negotiations the Dutch representative, Ambassador van Kleffens, played an important role, as President Truman testifies in his memoirs:

> Next to Lovett, Dr. van Kleffens, the Netherlands Ambassador, was the outstanding member of the group. He seemed to have a remarkable grasp of the thing that mattered and was always able to supply the right word at the right time. It was he who first expressed the hope that the association which the Vandenberg Resolution had envisaged would take the form of a "North Atlantic Pact." *(93)*

As a result of these meetings, the North Atlantic Treaty was signed in Washington on 4 April 1949. The document laid the foundations for the organization of collective defense and mutual assistance within the North Atlantic area in accordance with the provisions of the UN Charter. To effect a military build-up, on 5 April 1949 the five powers of the Brussels Treaty asked for military and financial aid from the U.S. On 27 January 1950 the requests were granted by bilateral agreements between the U.S. and the by now eight European NATO

---

*90* This occurred under the influence of the different orientation the Benelux countries had given to it.
*91* Ball, *op. cit.*, p. 14.
*92* *NATO Facts and Figures*, p. 237. U.S. Senate Resolution 239, 80th Congress, 2nd Session, 11 June 1948.
*93* Truman, *op. cit.*, p. 248.

members. The North Atlantic Treaty was a logical consequence of the efforts for Western European defense begun under the Brussels Treaty; *(94)* both agreements in large part served the same security purposes. As members of both alliances, the Brussels Pact countries possessed defense capabilities strong enough to credibly deter a possible aggressor. *(95)* U.S. prestige and particularly U.S. nuclear power were indisputable counterweights to Soviet force. When Soviet Ambassador Vychinsky asked why five European countries had united under the Brussels Pact, Spaak answered him in the General Assembly meeting in Paris on 28 September 1948. The first reason was fear, he said. "Fear of the U.S.S.R., fear of its government, fear of its policy." *(96)* The second was the obvious failure of the UN, as the Dutch foreign minister, D. Stikker, said in his Washington speech on 4 April 1949:

> The treaty we are about to sign marks the end of an illusion: the hope that the United Nations would, by itself, ensure international peace. Regretfully, we were driven to the conclusion that the Charter, though essential, is not enough in the world as it is, to protect those vital principles for which we of the Western world who have gathered here, stand. Therefore, we felt it our duty to make this Treaty. *(97)*

The experiences of the past decade made such a response natural, especially for the Benelux countries. Except for the Communist members, their Parliaments and executives concurred.

## NATO PROS AND CONS

The Belgian government saw the North Atlantic Pact as a necessity once it became clear that the UN would not be able to function in the ways its creators had intended, *(98)* mainly because of Soviet obstructionism in the organization. Moreover, Soviet expansionist policies formed an obvious threat to security and peace on the European continent. The Brussels Pact, signed as a

---

94 In order to avoid duplication of the NATO and Brussels Treaty structures, a gradual merger of the latter into NATO took place between late 1949 and April 1951, when General Eisenhower, appointed SACEUR at that time, "was authorized by the Brussels Treaty Powers to take over the responsibilities of the Western Union Commanders in Chief Committee, and the staff and facilities of the land, air and sea commands of Western Union were placed at his disposal". B. Burrows and C. Irwin, *The Security of Western Europe. Towards a Common Defense Policy* (London, 1972), p. 33.

95 "The powers who have signed the Brussels Pact represented too weak a force really to assure the defense of peace". Spaak, *Parl. Hand., Senaat,* 1948-1949, 11 May 1949, p. 1401.

96 Spaak, *op. cit.,* p. 216.

97 Quoted in van Campen, *op. cit.,* p. 109.

98 Spaak, *Parl. Hand., Senaat,* 1948-1949, 11 May 1949, p. 1400.

first defense measure against this threat, seemed too weak to protect the smaller Western democracies, *(99)* and to them a larger alliance appeared to be the only solution. The Belgian government repeatedly pointed to the defensive character of NATO, *(100)* which it said constituted an important tool for the maintenance and promotion of peace, particularly through its deterrent influence. It created "a grand defensive alliance which unites almost 350 million men and lines up against a possible aggressor such important forces and would create such difficult problems to solve, that it is almost certain that all this would lead him to a serious reconsideration and would make him hesitate to declare war." *(101)* Nearly the same arguments sprinkled the parliamentary debate on ratification of the North Atlantic Treaty. To most of the Belgian political parties, security was the first justification for signing the pact. In their eyes the security of Western Europe and the world was threatened by Soviet policies. As the report of the Foreign Affairs Committee of the House of Representatives on the North Atlantic Treaty put it:

> ...the Soviet Government should be aware of the fact that, though we have their assurance, we have the right to be anxious and that we have the duty to take care of our security. And because, considering the technique of modern wars, the defense of one country alone can no longer be imagined, we are obliged to organize our defense in a collective way, according to article 51 of the Charter. Our anxiousness is justified by the Soviet attitude. *(102)*

At the same time, Belgian representatives stressed the defensive character of the treaty, *(103)* calling it a complement to their collaboration with the U.S. in the economic field, by which they meant the Marshall plan. *(104)* Moreover, the agreement recognized the existence of an Atlantic culture, with shared social and political philosophies. *(105)* But all parties to the treaty emphasized that it should not obstruct détente policies nor lead to the building of opposing

---

99  *Ibid.*, p. 1401.
100  *Parl. Hand., Kamer*, 1948-1949, 3 May 1949, p. 16.
101  *Ibid.*, p. 18. Interestingly, in the period of the signing of the Brussels and the North Atlantic pacts, Spaak was both prime minister and minister of foreign affairs in the coalition government of Christian Democrats and Socialists. He headed a first cabinet from 19 March 1947 to 19 November 1948, and a second from 27 November 1948 to 27 June 1949. Thus at a decisive moment he was in an excellent position to influence Belgian foreign policy making.
102  Belgium, *Parlementaire Documenten, Kamer*, 1948-1949, No. 403, 19 April 1949, p. 8 [Hereafter *Parl. Doc., Kamer*].
103  See, for example, Mr. Piérard (Socialist), *Parl. Hand., Kamer*, 1948-1949, 3 May 1949, p. 4.
104  Mr. Fayat (Socialist), *ibid.*, pp. 6-8.
105  *Ibid.*

power blocs. *(106)* Understandably, the Communist representatives rejected the treaty for two main reasons. First, it was an aggressive pact directed against the Soviet Union, and second, it was not in accordance with the UN Charter. *(107)* Although all parties except the Communists in both houses supported the treaty, they did so as they had in the case of the Brussels Pact, with a certain reluctance, regarding it as a bitter necessity. *(108)* The government was more enthusiastic. Nevertheless, as Spaak testifies in his memoirs, he had "no difficulties in having the Washington Treaty accepted by the Belgian Houses. Important majorities, with the exception of the communists, showed their agreement nearly without reserve on this policy which was new for Belgium and so different from the one pursued before the war." *(109)* The North Atlantic Treaty was ratified by the Belgian House of Representatives on 4 May 1949 by a majority of 139 votes against twenty-two, with one abstention (Socialist). The Senate's vote on 12 May 1949 resulted in 127 votes in support of the treaty and thirteen against. In both houses only Communists opposed it. *(110)*

In Holland, as in the other Brussels Pact countries, membership of the Atlantic alliance should not, as van Campen notes,

> be regarded as a turning-point in Holland's foreign policy: it was rather the logical continuation of the reorientation which was decided upon, or at any rate brought about at the time of the Brussels Pact in 1948. The Netherlands... had always desired this wider association which included the United States and Canada; the identity of fundamental interests between Western Europe and North America, which economically found its expression in ERP, *(111)* made such an association possible, and indeed necessary; the Atlantic Treaty served the same ends as the Brussels Pact. *(112)*

In support of Holland's signature to the Atlantic Treaty, the Dutch government, a coalition of four parties, *(113)* explained in a memorandum *(114)* to

---

*106* Mr. Van Zeeland (Christian Democrat), *Parl. Hand.*, *Senaat*, 1948-1949, 11 May 1949, p. 1391; Mr. Rey (Liberal), *Parl. Hand.*, *Kamer*, 1948-1949, 3 May 1949, p. 13 and Mr. Fayat (Socialist), *ibid.*, pp. 6-8.

*107* Mr. Taillard (Communist), *Parl. Hand.*, *Senaat*, 1948-1949, 11 May 1949, pp. 1383-1384.

*108* Mr. d'Aspremont Lynden (Christian Democrat), *Parl. Hand.*, *Senaat*, 1948-1949, 11 May 1949, p. 1393; Mr. Vos (Socialist), *ibid.*, 10 May 1949, p. 1362 and Mr. Rey (Liberal), *Parl. Hand.*, *Kamer*, 1948-1949, 18 January 1949, p. 11.

*109* Spaak, *op. cit.*, p. 266.

*110* See *Parl. Hand.*, *Kamer*, 1948-1949, 4 May 1949, p. 13 and *Parl. Hand.*, *Senaat*, 1948-1949, 12 May 1949, p. 1448.

*111* European Recovery Program.

*112* van Campen, *op. cit.*, p. 109.

*113* Namely, the Liberal Volkspartij voor Vrijheid en Democratie (VVD), the Socialist Partij van de Arbeid (PvdA), the Katholieke Volkspartij (KVP), and the Protestant Christelijk-Historische Unie (CHU), under the leadership of Minister Drees. R.C. Bone, "Dynamics

the Dutch Second Chamber the considerations that had led to this important political step. It listed the main reasons as the failure of the United Nations collective security system and growing East-West opposition in 1947 and 1948. The new pact grew out of the Brussels Pact, whose implementation was to have been an example to other states to whom Western European independence was of vital importance, especially the U.S. and Canada. The Dutch government also emphasized the agreement's purely defensive character and its conception as a reinforcement to the UN. Among the Benelux countries Holland had probably had the greatest hope in the UN; it paralleled so neatly the Dutch tradition of deference to international law. The UN's failure, which showed the obvious weakness of international law, seemed to have been a greater shock there than in Belgium or Luxembourg.

The great majority in Parliament agreed with the government's policy on NATO and its arguments in its defense, though on certain points differences of stress emerged. The interim report *(115)* of the committee in the Second Chamber investigating the treaty provides a revealing overview of opinions of both supporters and opponents. *(116)* Those in favor of the treaty listed four arguments. First, it complemented the UN. Second, it was a reaction to Russian expansionism and power politics. Third, it hoped to maintain the common values of the Atlantic powers, not only militarily but through better social and economic conditions. Fourth, it would discourage aggression. Opponents, on the other hand, attacked the treaty because it surrendered national independence and committed the country to war. They even feared that secret clauses were connected to it. Second, it constituted an aggressive act against the U.S.S.R. Third, it undermined UN principles, and fourth, it was an expression of bloc politics and showed the imperialist tendencies of the U.S. Last, it would raise military expenses considerably and worsen the social and economic position of the working class. Arguments for and against the treaty largely coincided with those of the Belgian and Luxembourg Parliaments.

Questions on the government position on the membership of Spain and Portugal and to what extent Turkey and Greece shared a common heritage with other members were also common to parliamentary debates in the three countries. *(117)* In Holland specific questions on the government's reaction to

of Dutch Politics", *The Journal of Politics* (February, 1962), 40.

*114* Memorie van toelichting door de Nederlandse regering bij de ondertekening van het NAVO-verdrag, *Hand. Stat.-Gen., Tweede Kamer*, 1948-1949, 1237, 3, pp. 7 ff.

*115* *Hand. Stat.-Gen., Tweede Kamer*, Appendix 1948-1949, 1237, 5, pp. 13-16.

*116* As in Belgium and Luxembourg, these were all Communists.

*117* See the contribution on Greece and Turkey by W. Andries.

American congressional criticism of Dutch policy in Indonesia also arose. Would American and British restrictions on arms' supplies for use in the Indonesia struggle not contradict the treaty provisions? Finally, the overseas territories had not been consulted about signing the pact. Arguments of this kind were present in the parliament's debate on ratification. *(118)* On 19 July 1949 the Dutch Second Chamber approved the treaty by an overwhelming majority of 65 against seven votes, the latter all Communist. Some weeks later, on 3 August 1949, the First Chamber, which is less important in political decision making than, for example, the Belgian Senate, approved the treaty with twenty-nine positive and two negative votes. *(119)*

In Luxembourg the North Atlantic Treaty received large parliamentary support; three political parties voted unanimously in favor of ratification, and only the Communists opposed Luxembourg membership. At the time the country was governed by a coalition of Christian Democrats and Liberals (Groupement patriotique et démocratique), with the Socialists and the Communists in the opposition. In this case debate was extremely limited, and agreement by an overwhelming majority was reached in a very short time without serious attack from the Communists. *(120)* Although the Dutch and Belgian Parliaments had ratified the treaty without difficulty, Luxembourg surpassed them in the ease of its acceptance. The debate lasted one day, 31 May 1949. "One has the impression", says J.-C. Wolter, "that neither the Government, nor the leaders of the majority-parties wanted to stress too explicitly the consequences of the pact." *(121)* In his view, Foreign Minister J. Bech minimized the consequences of Luxembourg's membership. *(122)* Bech particularly stressed that it was not "our fault" *(123)* that political events after 1945 had shaken confidence in the UN and that insecurity and fear had led to regional pacts. Nevertheless, he affirmed the principles of collective security embodied in the UN and deplored the international tensions "which have made necessary the conclusion of the treaty submitted to your approval." *(124)* On the other hand, Bech predicted that NATO would facilitate economic and social growth

---

118  See *Hand. Stat.-Gen., Tweede Kamer*, 1948-1949, 1237, 15 July 1949, pp. 1681-1701, and 19 July 1949, pp. 1703-1718.
119  Holland, *Handelingen van de Staten-Generaal, Eerste Kamer*, 1948-1949, 3 August 1949, pp. 767 ff. [Hereafter *Hand. Stat.-Gen., Eerste Kamer*].
120  For a Communist view on NATO and the implications for Luxembourg, see J. Kill, *1000-jähriges Luxemburg-Woher? - Wohin?* (Luxembourg, 1963).
121  J.-C. Wolter, *Le Luxembourg et l'OTAN* (mimeo; Luxembourg, 1963), p. 18.
122  *Ibid.*, pp. 18-19.
123  *C.R. Chambre*, 1948-1949, 31 May 1949, p. 1976.
124  *Ibid.*, p. 1980.

through newfound security. *(125)* During the parliamentary debate on ratification, Christian Democrats, Liberals, and Socialists repeated similar arguments in defense of the treaty. Supporters in the two other Benelux countries used them as well. A point that all Luxembourg parties particularly emphasized as in the treaty's favor was the existence of pacts between the U.S.S.R. and its neighbors. Although these were economic pacts, they were intended not to increase the standard of living but to create the basis for a military union among these nations. *(126)* Why should the West not do the same? Luxembourg Socialists responded by describing the limited possibilities of such pacts. On their own they did not solve anything. They were not an end in themselves, nor the only means of maintaining peace. Other means to worldwide security had to be sought in a reorganization of the UN, the solution of the German question, and disarmament. *(127)*

The treaty was ratified by a majority of forty-six, with five Communists opposed, showing unanimous agreement among the three major parties. *(128)* Just as in Holland and Belgium, Luxembourg had no other alternatives to a viable security. Awareness of this fact to a great extent explains the ease with which this country adopted the policy.

The evolution of Benelux foreign policies between 1945 and 1949 leads us to the following conclusions. First of all, the realization of proposals for a regional grouping in the West, as well as for cooperation among Holland, Belgium, and Luxembourg in both periods shows a remarkable continuity between wartime planning and postwar policies. Indeed, the scope and structure of both the Brussels and the North Atlantic pacts closely resemble the organizations Spaak and van Kleffens were outlining during the war. Of course, continuity in government leadership is in large part responsible for this fact; in the postwar period Spaak and Bech continued to shape foreign policy, and although van Kleffens had been replaced, he had strongly influenced the talks on the North Atlantic Treaty. Moreover, strong cooperation in economic, political, and military fields that had marked the London years continued after the war.

Second, Benelux postwar policies show that in spite of their restricted power small nations can exert pressure in international politics, albeit to a limited degree and within a limited range of alternatives. The influence of the Benelux countries on the content of the Brussels Treaty had been decisive. Instead of a

---

125    *Ibid.*
126    *Ibid.*, p. 1974.
127    *Ibid.*, p. 1975.
128    *Ibid.*, p. 1981.

set of bilateral agreements proposed by France and Britain, they formed a truly regional defensive community. With the Rio Pact as an example and the UN Charter as a framework American enthusiasm for the Brussels Pact was guaranteed, and the way for U.S. participation was opened. Although Bevin's original plan had already won President Truman's support, the pact's new orientation made an American commitment to an Atlantic alliance much easier. This shows the almost direct link between the Brussels and the Washington pacts.

Third, the similarity of political and economic conditions in the early postwar years led to similar reactions in the three countries. Confronted with the same problems, sharing the same values and similar historical experience, with like possibilities and the same geographic situation, it was not surprising that the Benelux governments reacted to the issue in the same way and with a strong sense of cooperation. Moreover, except for the Communists, their Parliaments supported them unanimously.

Fourth, these small nations had grasped at alignment initially out of fear of Soviet policies and the need for greater security. In addition they sought closer economic cooperation and aid. A last element in their strife for a formal political-military alliance in 1949 was their fear of Communist ideology.

# Chapter II

# THE PRICE OF SECURITY:
# BENELUX DEFENSE EFFORTS

## A SHORT HISTORY

Benelux defense efforts since 1949 have been determined by both internal and external demands. This has necessarily led to several adaptations and readjustments, always, of course, within the framework of NATO strategy and international politics. External demands, those resulting from NATO membership and the international political situation, have conflicted with internal factors, such as restricted manpower and financial resources, growing demands for the realization of welfare policies, and party politics, electoral promises, and a public opinion that shows a diminishing interest in defense matters, particularly among the younger generation. If alignment has provided greater security, what has it cost? The answer is closely tied to the division of labor within the alliance, and requires an analysis of what these countries have been willing to contribute to its common defense capability.

The most relevant indicator of a country's preparedness to spend for defense seems to be that amount as a percentage of its gross national product (GNP):

TABLE V
Benelux military expenditure as a percentage of GNP (1949-1971)

|            | 1949 | 1950 | 1951 | 1952 | 1953 | 1954 | 1955 | 1956 | 1957 |
|------------|------|------|------|------|------|------|------|------|------|
| BELGIUM    | 2.5  | 2.6  | 3.7  | 5.4  | 5.2  | 5.0  | 4.1  | 3.8  | 3.9  |
| HOLLAND    | 4.5  | 5.4  | 5.5  | 6.2  | 6.2  | 6.6  | 6.2  | 6.3  | 5.7  |
| LUXEMBOURG | 1.0  | 1.5  | 1.7  | 2.6  | 3.2  | 3.6  | 3.6  | 2.1  | 2.2  |

|            | 1958 | 1959 | 1960 | 1961 | 1962 | 1963 | 1964 | 1965 | 1966 |
|------------|------|------|------|------|------|------|------|------|------|
| BELGIUM    | 3.9  | 3.9  | 3.7  | 3.6  | 3.7  | 3.6  | 3.6  | 3.3  | 3.3  |
| HOLLAND    | 5.0  | 4.3  | 4.4  | 4.9  | 5.0  | 4.8  | 4.7  | 4.3  | 4.1  |
| LUXEMBOURG | 2.1  | 1.9  | 1.1  | 1.2  | 1.5  | 1.4  | 1.6  | 1.6  | 1.6  |

|  | 1967 | 1968(1) | 1969(1) | 1970(1) | 1971(1) |
|---|---|---|---|---|---|
| BELGIUM | 3.3 | 3.3 | 3.2 | 3.2 | 3.2 |
| HOLLAND | 4.2 | 4.0 | 4.0 | 3.8 | 3.6 |
| LUXEMBOURG | 1.4 | 1.0(3) | 0.9(3) | 1.1(2) | n.a. |

Source: *NATO Facts and Figures*, pp. 226-227.

However, these figures can only be meaningful if seen in the general context of international politics and of national defense policies and their related problems. For the Benelux countries the first postwar years were a period of military reorganization and reconstruction. In this respect Great Britain played a vital role, one that had an increasingly strong influence on rearmament policies until the end of the forties. For Luxembourg and Holland, building military strength was particularly hard. In fact, from 1867 Luxembourg had enjoyed an internationally guaranteed unarmed neutrality, and was totally unprepared when the government-in-exile in London decided to introduce compulsory military service on 14 June 1944. Limited economic and man-power resources in this tiny nation, as well as a lack of any military tradition, made the task almost impossible at the beginning. The Netherlands suffered from the expense of their intervention in Indonesia, which was exacerbated by American and British embargoes on arms' supplies to that region. The signing of the Brussels and Washington pacts was to ease the situation considerably, however. Defense ended to be a purely national responsibility and from then onward the global deterrent power of the alliance helped each country econo-mize to a certain extent on its national defense budget. On the other hand, pro-visions under Article 3 of the NATO treaty, which established "continuous and

1 Figures for Belgium and Holland from Belgium, Ministerie van Landsverdediging, *De Landsverdediging in cijfertaal* (Brussels, 1971), T 1 [Hereafter *De Landsverdediging in Cijfer-taal*].

2 *NATO Information Service.* The *Military Balance* figure indicates only 0.9 for 1970-1971. The *Military Balance* figures for 1967-1968-1969-1970 were:

|  | 1967 | 1968 | 1969 | 1970 |
|---|---|---|---|---|
| Belgium | 2.9 | 2.9 | 3.0 | 2.8 |
| Holland | 3.8 | 3.6 | 3.6 | 3.5 |
| Luxembourg | 1.2 | 1.0 | 0.9 | 0.9 |

Source: *The Military Balance*, 1971-1972 (London, 1972), p. 60.

3 Both figures (from *Military Balance*) must certainly be raised by 0.1 or 0.2 when comparing NATO figures with those from the *Military Balance*. The difference between NATO and *Military Balance* figures is due to the fact that certain items on the national defense budgets which are not of a purely military kind are not taken into account by the *Military Balance*.

effective self-help and mutual aid" as the proper means for developing and maintaining an individual and collective defense capacity, put national defense efforts within the framework of alliance burdensharing. But in 1949 only two countries, the U.S. and Canada, were able to provide the mutual aid the treaty described. In fact, the five Brussels Pact countries had already asked the American government for such help in the form of military equipment. On 27 January 1950 bilateral treaties were signed in Washington between the U.S. and each of the following countries: Great Britain, France, Norway, Denmark, Belgium, Luxembourg, Italy, and Holland. Although the Mutual Defense Aid Program (MDAP), as these treaties were called, was not a program designed specifically to execute treaty stipulations, in fact it provided for the kind of mutual aid the treaty described. Canadian aid to Western Europe has been channeled through NATO's Standing Group, particularly arms' supplies, vehicles, electronic equipment, and pilots' training programs. U.S. aid has been particularly substantial. Between 1946 and 1965, the Netherlands received U.S. military aid totaling $ 1,240.3 million plus economic aid worth $ 817.1 million. During the same period, Belgium and Luxembourg together received military aid from the U.S. amounting to $ 1,247.1 million and economic aid of $ 510.3 million. *(4)* U.S. military aid was particularly high in the 1949 to 1957 period, *(5)* when the Netherlands received $ 968.2 million (or seventy-eight percent of the amount the U.S. contributed in military aid to the Dutch between 1949 and 1965), and Belgium and Luxembourg $ 1,064.5 million (or eighty-five percent of the total military aid they received in those years). The decline in American aid after 1957 parallels the decline in Benelux defense expenditure, which peaked broadly between 1952 and 1955-1956, reflecting the international tension caused by the Korean War and the high point of the Cold War. The decline in Belgian defense spending set in as early as 1955; Luxembourg followed in 1956 and Holland in 1957. Indeed, over the whole period Holland shows a greater stability in defense expenditure than its two Benelux partners, and in this context the fact that Holland began in 1949 at a much higher point as a result of its special defense effort in Indonesia is important. The defense policies of the Benelux countries during their years of membership in NATO can be divided into three periods: a time of general rearmament from 1950 to 1954, a period of maintenance or slight regression in the defense effort between

---

4  *U.S. Overseas Loans and Grants*, pp. 117 and 129.
5  One of its forms were the so-called off-shore arrangements, a U.S.-financed weapons' production program outside the U.S., which helped to develop European armaments industries and was at the same time of effective economic and financial aid in the recovery of the European economies.

1955 and 1959, followed by years of reorganization and modernization in the last decade. *(6)*

## 1. *1950-1954*

As a result of decisions taken at the September 1950 meeting of the NATO council in New York, the Benelux countries had to increase their defense efforts considerably. In response to the growing threat of the Korean War NATO adopted a forward strategy which demanded a much greater military capability. "Military strength would have to be built up and defense plans revised." *(7)* The Korean War had made a strong impression on public opinion in Western European countries. Fear of further Communist aggression possibly against Western Europe was very real, making acceptance and support of the rearmament program easier to attain.

In March 1951, the Christian-Democrats, then in control of the Belgian government, decided to extend military service from twelve months (its level since 1945) to twenty-four, the longest extension in Belgium in the postwar period. The move was heavily attacked by the Communists, the Socialists, and the Liberals, although the latter were critical for different reasons than the leftist parties. Leftist agitation aroused public opinion, and after demonstrations and riots, even on military bases, the requirement was cut back to twenty-one months in August 1952. At the same time military expenditure was raised considerably, from 8,256 million BF in 1950 to 13,387 million in 1951; in 1952 it reached an unprecedented 19,965 million, a rise in percentage of the gross national product from 2.6 in 1950 to 3.7 in 1951 and 5.4 in 1952. *(8)* An important factor in the realization of this effort was foreign military and economic aid, especially that provided by the U.S. under MDAP. *(9)* At that time, Belgium had 145,000 men under arms. The air force numbered 450 planes and the navy forty-three vessels. *(10)* Once the Korean War was over *(11)* and a

---

6  Concerning this division, see for Belgium G. Brasseur, *La politique militaire de la Belgique depuis la fin de la seconde guerre mondiale*, (Brussels, March 1968), mimeo.; for Holland H.F. Enkelaar, "Naar een doelmatig bedrijfseconomisch beheer bij de Koninklijke Luchtmacht", *Militaire Spectator*, (September, 1968), 425. For Luxembourg see Wolter, *op. cit.*, pp. 20-29.

7  *NATO Facts and Figures*, p. 30.

8  *Ibid.*, pp. 224-225, 226-227.

9  Belgium, *Landsverdediging 1961-1965* (Brussels, November, 1964), pp. 11-12 [Hereafter *Landsverdediging 1961-1965*].

10  *Ibid.*

11  Belgium sent a volunteer corps to Korea.

thaw in the international situation had set in, military service was reduced to eighteen months in 1954. The financial effort had been especially hard on Belgium and Luxembourg. Of the smaller NATO partners their defense expenditure alone had more than doubled in terms of percentage of GNP between 1949 and 1955. *(12)*

On 17 March 1951 the Dutch Second Chamber *(13)* accepted a new far-reaching defense program that was to become the basis for Dutch defense policy until 1957. The "Army plan", initially scheduled for completion by the end of 1954, for lack of financial and manpower resources had to be realized in two phases, the first ending in October 1954, the second in the middle of 1957. *(14)* Military service was raised in 1951 to eighteen months and in the fall of 1952 to twenty. The air force program for the period between 1951 and 1955 outlined an operational force of fifteen Hunter squadrons, six tactical squadrons, one transport, two reconnaissance, and four artillery-observation squadrons. The air force had 20,730 men under arms. A further build-up of the Navy took place over five years between 1951 and 1956. It provided for 117 ships, ten air squadrons, marine units, armament, new bases, and some 23,000 personnel. Allied aid had subsidized navy rearmament to a very considerable extent: some fifty-seven ships, five air squadrons, and three helicopters were provided, for the most part by the U.S. It is important to remember that, unlike its Benelux-partners, until 1963 Holland had no troops in Germany. The Indonesian activities of the Dutch army made its introduction there impossible. Afterward, NATO authorities increasingly demanded a Dutch military presence in Germany, particularly once the new forward strategy was effected. However, only in 1963 were troops exchanged; a Dutch brigade was stationed at Seedorf and German units were stationed in the south of Holland, despite sharp criticism from certain groups. Holland's financial effort in the realization of its rearmament program in the early fifties was smoother than either Belgium's or Luxembourg's, since involvement in Indonesia had forced the country to maintain a high defense expenditure since the end of the forties.

In June 1952 the Luxembourg Parliament voted a new law on military organization. Although the program it contained dated from October 1950, approval had been delayed by a government crisis until 1952. It was supported by the three major parties, the Christian-Democrats, the Socialists, and the

---

12  Using 1949 as a basis. *NATO Facts and Figures*, pp. 226-227.
13  For a good analysis of Dutch defense policy see H. von Zitzewitz, "Der NATO Beitrag und die nationale Verteidigung der Niederlande", *Wehrkunde*, XIV (Munich, November 1965), 580-586.
14  Holland, *Nota inzake het Defensiebeleid* (The Hague, 1954), p. 108.

Liberals, *(15)* and provided for the construction of military buildings and the creation and equipment of intervention units which had been promised at the Ottawa NATO conference. These intervention units, *groupement tactique régimentaire* (GTR), included one light artillery battalion, three infantry battalions, and five companies, among them ones for mortar, medicine, transport and transmission, and in wartime numbered 4,718 men. In addition to the GTR a territorial force of 2,421 men was included. However, the planned total of 10,340 men under arms never materialized for lack of manpower and limited financial resources. *(16)* From 1952 till 1958 this program remained the basis of the country's part in NATO's burden-sharing. The financial cost to Luxembourg in these years was important. Defense expenditure rose from one percent of the GNP in 1949 to 1.5 in 1950, 2.6 in 1952, and 3.6 in 1954. Except for Canada, it made the strongest effort of all NATO members in this respect. *(17)* Nevertheless, Luxembourg public opinion was critical of obligatory military service and of the improvisation that characterized the creation of the Luxembourg army. Critics questioned the effectiveness of the Luxembourg military effort for the alliance and constantly protested rising defense costs. Successive governments had difficulty in maintaining the military service. Public opinion and the opposition parties (alternately the Liberals and the Socialists, and of course the Communists, traditionally in the opposition) demanded the end of obligatory service and the reintroduction of a volunteer army, a demand which grew stronger at every election.

## 2. *1954-1960*

Belgian defense efforts slacked off after 1954, when military service was reduced from twenty-one to eighteen months; in 1957 a new reduction brought it to fifteen months and finally to twelve months in 1959, where it continues to the present. In terms of percentage of GNP defense costs fell from five percent in 1954 to 4.1 in 1955 and 3.8 in 1956, a level which was gradually reduced to 3.6 in 1964. Several factors were responsible for this downward trend. First was the positive influence of a certain détente in East-West relations, the result of the end of the Stalin era, the Geneva agreements on Indochina in 1954, and the beginning of the peaceful coexistence policy of the Soviet Union. Second,

---

15 The Liberals and the Communists were in the opposition.
16 Wolter, *op. cit.*, pp. 43-44.
17 Although raising the defense effort from one to three percent of the GNP is still easier than raising it, for example, from four to eight percent. It should also be noted that Luxembourg troops were stationed in Germany from 11 November 1945 until 9 July 1955.

in 1955 the Federal Republic of Germany had become a NATO partner and was gradually rearmed. Third, growing internal demands for welfare policies and electoral promises on a reduction of the military service increased. At the same time U.S. aid was reduced. In the Mutual Security Act period between 1953 and 1961, total economic aid to the BLEU reached only $ 2 million; from 1949 to 1952, on the other hand, it had received $ 566.8 million. After 1957 military aid was also reduced considerably. From 1953 to 1957 Belgium and Luxembourg had received $ 890.4 million or an average of some 222 million per year, but in the period from 1957 to 1961 this figure was reduced to $ 111.5 million or an average of 27.8 million per year. *(18)* Of course, the substantial American aid of the early 1950s was intended for quick rearmament. After 1954 this could be considered a relative success, and new efforts were needed to cover constantly rising costs for maintenance of equipment and for ever-increasing personnel expenses. The government cited the costs of stationing Belgian forces in Germany as responsible for the fifteen-percent increase in the defense budget between 1956 and 1959. *(19)* Under these circumstances both the Belgian government and Parliament thought a reorganization of Belgian defense policy necessary. *(20)* On 14 January 1959 Parliament asked for a general reorganization of the Ministry of Defense, and a redistribution of the army according to the MC 70 plan (also called Plan 1960-1964). Belgian forces would consist of one infantry and one tank division, two reserve divisions, 214 airplanes, a few minesweepers, and the units necessary for defense of the ports. Along with the other NATO members, alliance officials asked the country to effect the modernization of its armaments and equipment as far as possible. *(21)* In fact, since the end of the fifties modernization and reorganization seem to have been magic terms for a gradual reduction of defense efforts, the tone of which has been: let us create a well trained and well-equipped force that will cost us as little as possible and still be acceptable to our allies.

18   *U.S. Overseas Loans and Grants*, p. 117.
19   *Parl. Doc.*, *Kamer*, 4-X (1958-1959), N.3, 24 February 1959, p. 2.
20   On the whole, in its 1959 report concerning the defense budget the defense committee of the Belgian House of Representatives, thought that four factors required a reorganization. First, economic and financial resources were limited by the needs for investment in other sectors. Moreover, Belgium is not a great arms producer and the costs of maintaining forces in Germany are substantial. Secondly, the defense effort suffered from a relative shortage of manpower. Thirdly, demands for NATO defense were growing. And finally, the structure of the Belgian army itself was not up to optimum efficiency.
21   *Parl. Doc.*, *Kamer*, 4-X (1959-1960), N. 6, 29 June 1960, p. 2.

Similar changes in the international situation, the rapid evolution in arms technology, and rising costs for equipment and personnel had an impact on Dutch military thinking. Here, too, demands for reviewing the defense effort came from the country itself and not from NATO authorities, although the latter were certainly aware that the Lisbon program of 1952 had been too ambitious. The reorganization Dutch political parties demanded was effected in 1957, much earlier than in Belgium or Luxembourg. The division force was reduced and the number of army-corps units limited, making possible a reduction of the five existing divisions to two active ones and two standing ready to be mobilized. *(22)* Priority was given to combat-ready NATO forces, but in addition important units for territorial defense remained. In comparison with their neighbors, the Dutch maintained a high level of expenditure in terms of the GNP, yet Dutch military efforts in the years between 1957 and 1960 show a decrease in absolute terms as well as in percentage of GNP:

TABLE VI
Dutch Military Expenditure, 1956-1960.

|  | 1956 | 1957 | 1958 | 1959 | 1960 |
|---|---|---|---|---|---|
| million guilders | 1,854 | 1,845 | 1,656 | 1,505 | 1,728 |
| percentage of GNP | 6.3 | 5.7 | 5.0 | 4.3 | 4.4 |

Source: *NATO Facts and Figures*, pp. 224-225, 226-227.

In the same period Belgian defense efforts stabilized, and Luxembourg, after a few years at the same level, strongly reduced its efforts in 1960: *(23)*

TABLE VII
Belgian and Luxembourg Military Expenditure

|  | 1956 | 1957 | 1958 | 1959 | 1960 |
|---|---|---|---|---|---|
| *Belgium* | | | | | |
| million BF: | 17,065 | 18,356 | 18,312 | 18,686 | 19,161 |
| percentage of GNP: | 3.8 | 3.9 | 3.9 | 3.9 | 3.7 |
| *Luxembourg* | | | | | |
| million LF: | 395 | 439 | 429 | 402 | 263 |
| percentage of GNP: | 2.1 | 2.2 | 2.1 | 1.9 | 1.1 |

Source: *NATO Facts and Figures*, pp. 224-225, 226-227.

22  M.J.J. Fens, "L'Organisation de la défense aux Pays-Bas", *La Revue Politique*, 2 July, 1957, 192-193.
23  However, the decline in the Belgian defense effort began as early as 1955; the fall year for Luxembourg was 1956, whereas for Holland it came still a year later.

The reduction in U.S. military and economic aid after 1957 reflected these changes in the military budget. While total military aid to Holland in the rearmament years from 1953 to 1957 reached $ 828.7 million (an average of 270 million per year), in the period from 1958 to 1961 it fell to 175.3 million (an average of only 43.8 per year). *(24)*

### 3. *1960-1970 (25)*

A similar tendency toward reorganization had appeared in Luxembourg by the end of the fifties. The changed international situation, the introduction of highly sophisticated new weapons systems, and rising costs for equipment and personnel lay behind the new approach, but the immediate cause was the 11 March 1958 statement of the Liberal representative, E. Schaus who after consultation with the NATO partners asked for a reorganization of Luxembourg defense and a reduction of military service to six months. *(26)* Legislative elections took place in February 1959, and on March 10 the new coalition government of Christian Democrats and Liberals announced its new defense policy. Referring to the traditionally mentioned limited economic and demographic resources of the country, the government decided to propose to its allies a structural reorganization of the army to be effected within Luxembourg's NATO obligations. Just as in Belgium, this move was meant to reach higher efficacy at lower costs, especially in the number of men under arms. Although several allies had expressed reservations on the proposed reduction of military service to nine months, *(27)* a resolution of the NATO council of 24 February 1960 authorized the reorganization. Through administrative measures, the government had shortened military service to nine months by 1959; nevertheless, it was three years before the House of Representatives approved the new military program on 23 July 1963. Both the Socialists and the Communists thought the results too small and opposed it strongly. Under the new system, the GTR was replaced by one light artillery battalion which was kept ready for M-day and was made up of both volunteers and conscripts, a total of 450 men. Operationally and logistically it was attached to the Eighth U.S. Army Division stationed in Germany by an agreement in August 1963. In addition to the NATO intervention unit, a small territorial defense force

---

24   *U.S. Overseas Loans and Grants*, p. 129.
25   For the actual situation of Benelux defense efforts in terms of numbers, budget, and equipment and their share of NATO's common defense, see: *Military Balance*.
26   Wolter, *op. cit.*, p. 23. Mr. Schaus' party was then in the opposition.
27   *Ibid.*, p. 25.

was maintained numbering some 3,200 men in wartime (from reserve units). *(28)* However, the following years placed additional strains on Luxembourg's defense policy. The Socialist party specified reduction of the military service from nine to six months as a condition for participation in a coalition government with the Christian Democrats in 1964, *(29)* and the measure was approved by Parliament on 17 December 1965. After a new cabinet crisis *(30)* in November 1966, compulsory service was totally abolished in July 1967. In fact, all political parties had supported the move; the only conflict between the coalition parties, the Christian Democrats and the Socialists, concerned the date on which it would be effected. *(31)* Once this was resolved, the measure was passed on 1 July 1967 by a vote of fifty to five, with one abstention. *(32)* From then onward the small Luxembourg army would consist only of volunteers, and the total military force reduced to 560 men, thirty officers, one hundred non commissioned officers and 430 volunteer soldiers forming a light infantry battalion comprising four companies, two of which are earmarked for the ACE Mobile Land Force of NATO. *(33)* At the same time the country's financial effort has been influenced by a continuous reduction of U.S. military aid, by growing costs in reorganization, new equipment, and personnel. The defense budget, 263 million LF in 1960, peaked at 497 in 1966 *(34)* in a manner similar to Belgium and Holland and almost the whole of NATO. The last decade, especially the later years, was a time of stabilization. Military expenditure in terms of percentage of GNP had fluctuated between 1.1 in 1960 and 1.6 in 1964, 1965 and 1966, 1.4 in 1967 *(35)* and 1 in 1970. *Military Balance* figures for these years indicate only 1.2 for 1967, 1.0 for 1968, and 0.9 for 1969 and 1970. *(36)* In 1967 and 1968, Luxembourg spent only 208 million francs, a figure which rose to 370 in 1968-1969, 401 in 1969-1970 and 402.8 in 1970-1971. *(37)*

For the Netherlands the decade between 1960 and 1970 has also been a time of reorganization, modernization of military equipment, and a gradual reduction of the defense budget, at least in terms of percentage of GNP. As in

28   *Ibid.*, pp. 44-48.
29   *Keesing's Historisch Archief*, 1965, 840.
30   *C.R. Chambre*, 1966-1967, 24 November 1966, pp. 782-806.
31   See Chapter IV.
32   *Keesing's Historisch Archief*, 1967, 550.
33   *Military Balance*, 1966-1967; 1967-1968; 1968-1969; 1969-1970 (London, 1966-).
34   *NATO Facts and Figures*, p. 225.
35   *Ibid.*, p. 227.
36   *Military Balance*, 1967-1971.
37   *Ibid.*

Belgium and Luxembourg, the number of men under arms has been gradually reduced, as the following table shows:

TABLE VIII
Number of Troops 1961-1971

|  | 1961-1962 | 1963-1964 | 1965-1966 | 1967-1968 | 1969-1970 | 1970-1971 |
|---|---|---|---|---|---|---|
| Luxembourg | 5,500 | 5,500 | 5,500 | 800 | 560 | 600** |
| Belgium | 110,000 | 110,000 | 108,365* | 108,961* | 99,014* | 97,904* |
| Netherlands | 142,000 | 141,000 | 135,000 | 130,000 | 124,000 | 121,250 |

Source: *Military Balance*. Figures marked with * are taken from *De Landsverdediging in Cijfertaal*; the one marked with ** was taken from NATO Information Service material.

In 1961 and 1962 military service still lasted from twenty to twenty-two months in the army and twenty-one to twenty-four in the navy and the air force; this was reduced in 1965-1966 to eighteen to twenty months for the army and in 1966-1967 to sixteen to eighteen. In 1968-1969 the two other forces were cut back to eighteen to twenty months. Whereas in absolute terms, as in most other countries, the defense budget has been constantly rising in the last decade, as a percentage of the country's GNP it has gradually fallen from 4.9 in 1961 to 4.1 in 1970, according to NATO figures. The *Military Balance* even speaks of 3.5 in 1970, an account closer to those mentioned in Dutch sources: 3.6 for 1970 as well as for 1971. *(38)* An analysis of the share of the defense budget in the national expenditure for each year in each country shows the same trend of reduction: in 1963-1964 Holland spent nineteen percent of its global budget on defense, Belgium sixteen percent and Luxembourg only five percent. In 1965-1966 these amounts were sixteen percent, twelve percent, and five percent respectively, *(39)* and in 1971 they were lowered even more to 12.8 for Holland, *(40)* 11.9 for Belgium *(41)* and 3.5 for Luxembourg. *(42)* In absolute terms Holland actually spends more than twice as much as Belgium: in 1971 the country's defense expenditure in million dollars amounted to 1,161, whereas Belgium spent only $ 594 million. In the same year Luxembourg spent just $ 9 million, which represents one percent of the country's GNP. *(43)* A look

38  *Elseviers Magazine*, Amsterdam (29 May 1971), 17; and *ibid.* (24 October 1970), 32.
39  *Military Balance*, 1963-1964, 1965-1966.
40  *Elseviers Magazine* (29 May 1971), 76.
41  *De Landsverdediging in Cijfertaal*, Table 2.
42  Figure mentioned by a Luxembourg official.
43  Figures from *Military Balance*, 1971-1972, 60.

at each country's per capita expenditure on defense shows that in 1970 Holland's expenses amounted to $ 85, Belgium's to $ 71, and Luxembourg's to only $ 24. *(44)* Dutch and Belgian GNP per capita in U.S. dollars amount to 1,951 and 2,160 respectively, according to 1970 NATO figures. Luxembourg's defense effort is extremely low both as a percentage of the GNP and as a share of the global national budget, respectively one percent and 3.5 percent compared with the country's GNP per capita of $ 2,220 in 1970.

Just as in the two other Benelux countries, in the last decade Dutch defense policy has stressed the qualitative improvement of personnel and equipment to strengthen the army's readiness. U.S. military aid to Holland no longer plays a substantial role in this improvement program. The Americans contributed $ 49.7 million in 1965, less than $ 50,000 in 1966, $ 2.8 million in 1967, and nothing in 1968 and 1969. *(45)* After 1964 new efforts were made specifically to increase the maximum combat value of NATO-assigned forces. Replacement of old equipment became an urgent task. For example, 415 new Leopard tanks were ordered for the army to replace the old Centurions; *(46)* the air force received 105 Northrop F-5 planes in 1967, *(47)* and similar replacement programs have affected the navy. *(48)*

In Belgium *(49)* the 1960s were years of reorganization and modernization of equipment. In relation to the GNP the defense budget was stable. Belgian defense policy in this period was based on solidarity with the NATO partners, a probable demand by NATO for some four percent of the country's GNP, and a very careful investment policy in the framework of the modernization plan. *(50)* The first defense program established for the 1960 to 1964 period had to be spread over a longer period for lack of financial resources. In fact, the implementation of defense plans was strongly hindered by limited finances and by uncertainties caused by the Atlantic crisis and the rethinking of NATO doctrine in the second half of the decade. For some time the Belgian government

44  *Ibid.*

45  U.S., *Military Assistance and Foreign Military Sales Facts*, Office of the Assistant Secretary of Defense (Washington D.C., March 1970), p. 12 [Hereafter *Military Assistance and Foreign Military Sales Facts*].

46  Holland, *Nota inzake het Navo- en het defensiebeleid 1968* (The Hague, June 1968), pp. 61 and 64-67. [Hereafter *Nota inzake het Navo- en het defensiebeleid 1968*].

47  *Ibid.*, pp. 77-78.

48  *Ibid.*, pp. 49-54.

49  For a short analysis of Belgian defense policy, see E. O'Ballance "The Armed Forces of Belgium", *Revue Militaire Générale* (Paris, January 1967), 54-71.

50  Report of the Defense Committee on the 1965 Defense Budget, *Parl. Doc.*, *Kamer*, 1964-1965, N. 2, p. 4.

waited for a general review of its obligations to NATO. In 1967, for example, the level of forces and the budget were regarded by government and Parliament as typically transitional. *(51)* The following outlines Belgian defense spending from 1960 to 1971:

TABLE IX
Belgian Defense Budget 1960-1971 (in million BF)

| 1960 | 1961 | 1962 | 1963 | 1964 | 1965 | 1966 |
|------|------|------|------|------|------|------|
| 19,161 | 19,561 | 21,111 | 22,230 | 24,853 | 25,036 | 26,313 |

| 1967 | 1968* | 1969* | 1970* | 1971* | | |
|------|-------|-------|-------|-------|--|--|
| 27,774 | 30,100 | 31,500 | 34,400 | 36,900 | | |

Source: *NATO Facts and Figures*, pp. 224-225 for 1960-1967; those marked with * were taken from *De Landsverdediging in cijfertaal*, Table I, and were figured on the basis of the NATO definition.

TABLE X
Belgian Defense Expenditure as a Percentage of GNP 1960-1971

| 1960 | 1961 | 1962 | 1963 | 1964 | 1965 | 1966 | 1967 | 1968* | 1969* | 1970* | 1971* |
|------|------|------|------|------|------|------|------|-------|-------|-------|-------|
| 3.7 | 3.6 | 3.7 | 3.6 | 3.6 | 3.3 | 3.3 | 3.3 | 3.3 | 3.2 | 3.2 | 3.2 |

Source: *NATO Facts and Figures*, pp. 226-227; for 1968-1971: *De Landsverdediging in cijfertaal*, Table I.

These tables demonstrate an obvious rise in absolute terms throughout the decade, with even a sharper rise in recent years and a gradual reduction of cost as a percentage of GNP, with a marked fall since 1965. According to the *Military Balance*, Belgian defense expenditure as a percentage of GNP amounts only to 2.9 in 1967 and 1968, 3.0 in 1969, and 2.8 in 1970. In comparison with the global national budgets, Belgian defense budgets show a much slower rise and their share of the national budget is continuously decreasing. Down from sixteen percent of the national budget in 1963, they have stabilized since 1965 at around twelve percent. *(52)* In 1968, the new government, a coalition of Christian Democrats and Socialists, announced the continuation of the reorga-

*51* Report of the Defense Committee on the 1967 Defense Budget, *Parl. Doc.*, *Kamer*, 1966-1967, N. 2, p. 2.
*52* See p. 335 and *De Landsverdediging in cijfertaal*, Table 2, for the years 1968-1971.

nization and efficiency program in accordance with a five-year plan scheduled from 1968 to 1973 and approved by NATO. Qualitative and structural improvements would compensate for a reduction in the number of men under arms. *(53)* Both the intervention force and territorial defense forces were affected by the changes. *(54)* The new program planned the dissolution of the sixteenth and eighteenth brigades, some units of which would be transferred to territorial defense, and the recruitment of new volunteers. The purchase of new equipment included Leopard tanks for the army, Mirage planes for the air force, and four new escort vessels. *(55)* As did its two Benelux partners, in December 1970 Belgium accepted new obligations amounting to 1,700 million BF as its share of the European Defense Improvement Program. *(56)* Part of it, 700 million BF, will be spent on participation in NATO's common infrastructure program to be financed by the European partners, and the rest, 1 billion BF, will be used to replace the old C-119 transport planes. In March 1971, the Belgian government decided to buy twelve new C-130 Hercules planes in the United States. On 10 November 1972, the Belgian government announced a new reorganization plan with four major goals. It hoped first to increase the operational or combat power of the Belgian forces through the establishment of a sixth armored battalion, an eighth battalion supporting ground-to-air Nike rockets, and armored units for the infantry battalions, all to be stationed on the other side of the Rhine. Second, it attempted to consolidate the global defense of the territory through the extension of the military responsibility of the gendarmerie *(57)* and the establishment of a regionally recruited reserve of light-armed units. Third, it hoped to effect rationalization through the abolishment of all special organizations and staffs. Fourth, it planned to decrease considerably the military obligations of Belgian youth through a shortening of the active first service, limiting recruitment to one conscript per family, gradually cancelling deferments for students, organizing a general civil

---

53 Between 1966 and 1970 some 10,000 men, mainly in the army.

54 Report of the Defense committee on the 1969 Defense Budget, *Parl. Doc.*, *Kamer*, 4-IX (1968-1969), N. 2, pp. 2-4.

55 General Explanatory Statement on the 1970 Defense Budget, *Parl. Doc.*, *Kamer*, 4, 1969-1970, p. 90, and *De Landsverdediging in Cijfertaal* which offers a global overview of Belgian forces and the new equipment program. In December 1972, NATO's Defense Planning Committee accepted the Belgian plan for the transfer of two Belgian brigades from Germany to Belgium, according to a rotation program. As a compensation, Belgium promised to station certain units on the other side of the Rhine to increase the manpower of its brigades in Germany from the actual 70 to 80 percent to 100 percent, and not to lower military expenditure. See *De Standaard* (5 and 7 December 1972).

56 See p. 342.

57 The Belgian National Guard.

338

conscription, and introducing a solidarity tax for those freed from military service *(58)*. This point was heavily criticized by Belgian youth.

Importantly, the modernization programs in all three Benelux countries in the years between 1960 and 1970 were partly facilitated by continued U.S. military aid, as the following figures show:

TABLE XI
U.S. Military Aid 1960-1969 (in million dollars)

|  | 1960 | 1961 | 1962 | 1963 | 1964 |
|---|---|---|---|---|---|
| Belgium + Luxembourg | 22.4 | 9.8 | 18.8 | 7.3 | 39.6 |
| Netherlands | 49.5 | 30.5 | 14.7 | 18.9 | 10.7 |

|  | 1965 | 1966 | 1967 | 1968 | 1969 |
|---|---|---|---|---|---|
| Belgium + Luxembourg | 8.1 | 1.6 | .1 | 1.9 | less than 50,000 |
| Netherlands | 49.7 | less than 50,000 | 2.8 | — | — |

Source: *U.S. Overseas Loans and Grants and Assistance*, pp. 117 and 129 and *Military Assistance and Foreign Military Sales Facts*, p. 12.

What then, is the place of the Benelux forces in the framework of the allied defense system? The Belgian army corps, the greatest part of which is stationed in Germany, belongs to the Northern Army Group (NORTHAG) and defends one of its sectors. The Belgian air force is almost entirely incorporated into the Second Allied Tactical Air Force (ATAF) with headquarters at Mönchen-Gladbach (Germany). The navy watches over a section of the North Sea and Belgian territorial waters under the Allied Command Channel. *(59)* Luxembourg contributes a light infantry battalion of two companies (320 men) earmarked for the ACE Mobile Land Force. The Dutch First Army Corps participates in NATO's defense in the Northern Army Group. Like Belgium, the Dutch air force defends one of the sectors covered by NATO's second ATAF. Here both Belgian and Dutch forces share the same responsibilities,

58  See *De Standaard* (13 November 1972).
59  *Landsverdediging 1961-1965*, pp. 7-8.
See also G.B. Howard, "The Role of Belgium in NATO", *Military Review* (July, 1971), 17-22. With Holland and Great Britain, Belgium takes part in the special mine-sweeping NATO unit, the Standing Naval Force Channel, that was created in May 1973.

but Holland plays a more important role in naval defense. The Dutch Royal Navy is attached to two allied naval commands: the Allied Command Channel and the Allied Command Atlantic. *(60)*

Benelux countries also participate in programs for the cooperative production of armaments and NATO's common infrastructure, to the advantage of their defense-related industries. As early as 1949 Belgium and Holland jointly manufactured British aircraft and engines under license. Later they cooperated in the production of the Hunter fighter planes, and between 1957 and 1962 they participated with France and Germany in the joint production of a modern maritime patrol aircraft, the French Bréguet 1150 (Atlantic). At the beginning of 1958, Belgium, Holland, France, Germany, and Italy co-sponsored a program to construct HAWK ground-to-air missiles. Begun by U.S. initiative and aided by U.S. technology, this program was an attempt on the part of the Americans to involve their European allies in NATO arms production. In 1959 a second project, this one for the manufacture of Sidewinder air-to-air missiles was implemented by Belgium, Holland, Denmark, Norway, Greece, Turkey, and Portugal. A year later the most important of these cooperative actions, involving Holland, Belgium, Germany, and Italy, began the production of the F 104 G Starfighter. Since July 1963 Holland, Norway, and Canada have produced the U.S. light antitank weapon known as the M-12. *(61)* At the moment, Belgium and Britain jointly manufacture a light reconnaissance vehicle, CVRT.

In addition to cooperation in arms production, the Benelux countries have also participated actively in the implementation of NATO's infrastructure, each paying a substantial share of the construction of airfields, pipelines, and communication systems situated both on their territories and on those of other allies. The creation of NATO's new early warning system (NATO Air Defense Ground Environment, or NADGE), and of NATO's Integrated Communication System (NICS) have also been in part Benelux responsibility.

In his study *Defense, Technology and the Western Alliance, (62)* C.J.E. Harlow offers a very interesting comparative analysis of Benelux defense procurement on a national and international scale. He concludes that neither

---

60  Both the Belgian and the Dutch armies are equipped and trained for delivery of tactical nuclear weapons, which are held under U.S. custody and can only be released by decision of the American president.
61  *NATO Facts and Figures*, pp. 103-114.
62  Published by the London Institute for Strategic Studies, 1967.

Holland nor Belgium has developed an independent arms industry of any importance. Since the end of the 1940s the U.S. has almost entirely assumed the role of supplier of arms to a Benelux market that traditionally belonged to Great Britain and France. However, unlike Belgium, Holland entered the Brussels Pact and the Atlantic alliance with "considerable industrial and technological assets to bring to an interdependent system of European defence" *(63)* (a.o. shipyards, Philips). From 1946 to the early 1960s, Belgian defense procurement figures have been rather low. Harlow explains this, at least for the earliest period, by a "low overall defense expenditure." *(64)* The first postwar years were a time of reorganization and all available resources went into this effort. The rearmament phase in the early fifties, which was characterized by a substantial increase in defense expenditure and length of military service left no money for investments in military hardware. *(65)* But even if Belgium had had sufficient financial resources by that time, it would have been obliged to buy its arms abroad since it had no companies of its own manufacturing modern weapons. *(66)* In the early sixties this situation changed, however. Participation in common production programs created Belgian firms experienced in the manufacture of sophisticated material, and since the beginning of the last decade the percentage of the defense budget spent on weapons procurement has risen constantly. *(67)*

Holland's defense expenditure, higher than Belgium's, parallels a higher level of defense procurement. Harlow suggests that this is because Holland has more armament manufacturers than Belgium to absorb government spending. *(68)* Nevertheless, while a great many Dutch firms are defense related and the Dutch procurement level is high, the significance of these figures should not be exaggerated. Dutch firms do not depend solely on defense orders, an inclination which Harlow sees as a "deliberate decision not to build an independent arms base [which] must be seen as an essential characteristic of Dutch defense policy." *(69)*

NATO's defense effort in the decade between 1970 and 1980, which includes an attempt to better balance burden-sharing between the U.S. and the countries

63  C.J.E. Harlow, *Defense, Technology and the Western Alliance* (London, 1967) p. 51.
64  *Ibid.*, p. 2.
65  *Ibid.*
66  *Ibid.* See also E. Coppieters, "Economische en sociale gevolgen voor België van een eventuele ontwapening", *Internationale Spectator* (8 July 1971), 1277-1296.
67  Harlow, *op. cit.*, p. 5.
68  *Ibid.*, p. 51. He mentions Fokker, Daf, Philips, and large shipyards.
69  *Ibid.*, p. 52.

forming what is called the Eurogroup, has been outlined in a new defense plan titled AD-70. *(70)* Under its auspices the Benelux countries are currently participating in the five-year European Defense Improvement Program *(71)* announced in 1970 by the countries composing the Eurogroup as their contribution to the AD-70. Within the framework of the Eurogroup, Belgium pilots the working group on medical cooperation (Euromed) and the one on armaments (Eurosched), and Holland supervises the working group on telecommunications on the battlefield (Eurocom). *(72)* Toward the end of 1969, NATO expanded into a new field, the study of the problems and challenges of modern society. Belgium administers a program that conducts research in sea pollution with the assistance of Portugal.

The evolution of Benelux defense efforts in the decade between 1960 and 1970 leads to the following conclusions. First, the length of military service and the number of men under arms generally fell. Second, defense spending as part of the total government expenditure decreased. A remark which also accounts for defense expenditure as a percentage of the GNP. Third, the country with the highest GNP per capita spends the least on defense per capita and as a percentage of its GNP; the one with the smallest GNP per capita spends the most per capita and as percentage of its GNP. Fourth, the Benelux countries have paralleled a general trend in NATO toward qualitative improvement and greater efficiency of men and equipment, and an active participation in common production programs of armaments and infrastructure construction and maintenance. Fifth, both Belgium and Holland are strongly dependent on foreign defense procurement, although in recent years international cooperation among European countries has stimulated Belgian and Dutch industries

---

70  Allied Defense 1970.

71  In fact, EDIP consists of three different parts: (1) a special contribution to NATO's infrastructure fund; (2) several special and totally new initiatives to improve the quality of national military forces; (3) a German initiative through which this country put sixteen C.160 Transall tactical transport-planes at the disposal of Turkey. The contribution to the infrastructure fund was more specifically directed towards financing the construction of aircraft shelters and the NATO Integrated Communication System (NICS). EDIP's total costs have been estimated at $ 1 billion. In addition to this, the Eurogroup countries decided to make an extra common defense expenditure of $ 1 billion in 1972 (decision of December 1971), and in 1973 there would be a new increase of $ 1½ billion over the 1972 expenditure. See: *NAVO-Kroniek* (November-December 1972), 8-12, and *De Standaard* (6 December 1972).

72  These are all working groups of the Eurogroup. See Chapter III. Moreover, both Belgium and Holland are members of the study group on logistics (Eurolog), together with Germany and under the chairmanship of the United Kingdom. The work of this group is concentrated on logistics in NORTHAG.

in this field. An independent national defense industry was not developed with the possible exception of the Belgian Fabrique Nationale d'Armes de Guerre at Herstal, which supplies NATO as well as other countries with its famous FN rifles and ammunition.

## HOLDING THE BALANCE: A CONSTANT PROBLEM

The essential characteristic of Benelux defense policy in the last decade has undoubtedly been the gradual but continuous decrease in the defense effort. In fact, over the last fifteen years the number of men under arms has steadily fallen. In 1954, high point of the Cold War, Belgium, for example, had 150,000 men under arms. Today Belgian forces number some 100,000. The same has been true for Holland and Luxembourg; Luxembourg's army has included 560 men since 1967. Every year more potential soldiers are excused from service for social reasons; others substitute by a two-year service in developing countries; a third group is granted student deferment. Moreover, length of stay in the military has always been an election issue, at least in Belgium and Luxembourg. As part of a political platform, it is an issue designed to appeal to most voters, especially the young. (73) Financial efforts show similar trends, both in percentages of GNP and of the global budget. In absolute terms defense budgets are rising, but this is due mainly to loan and cost inflation, which has increased considerably, particularly in later years, and to the acquisition of new, more expensive defense equipment. However, governments are obliged to keep their countries' defense efforts level with their alliance commitments, and they try to compensate for shortcomings by attracting volunteers and professionals and by reorganizing the army structure for maximum efficiency. The Luxembourg army, for example, is totally volunteer and professional. Some suggest a similar structure in Belgium, but most responsible leaders see the notion as unrealistic, at least in the near future. (74) Instead they have attempted a well-organized, well-trained, and well-equipped smaller force, filling in the gaps in their NATO obligations by periodically recalling part of the reservists for two or three weeks.

73 In Belgium in 1971 the new governmental coalition of Christian Democrats and Socialists promised a shorter military service in the near future. This promise was repeated in the governmental agreement among the three coalition parties of the Belgian government formed in January 1973 of Christian Democrats, Socialists, and Liberals. For a comparison of party programs and the government's intentions with regard to defense in 1970-1971, see *CEPESS-documenten*, 3-4 (Brussels, 1971).

74 Defense Minister P. Vanden Boeynants thought it would cost the country an additional expenditure of 10 billion BF. In his view a professional army is also disputable on political grounds. See *De Standaard* (22 June 1972).

The underlying reasons for these changed defense policies are several. First is the growing feeling of security and general openness to détente that has grown with the diminishing of East-West tensions. Since the Harmel proposal of 1967 détente has even become one of the pillars on which NATO policy is based. Secondly, demands for social and economic improvements mount. Very often the military budget becomes the balancing item of the global budget, while for electoral reasons political parties try to reduce military service. A third reason is the small countries' growing awareness of their powerlessness in a world where power has been monopolized by a few. Under the American nuclear umbrella they enjoy relative security, and are willing to assume their share, a very small one, of the burden of the alliance in payment. U.S. promises of intervention in case of attack are nowhere seriously doubted in the Benelux countries at present. (75) Moreover, in a nuclear age, national defense policies become practically impossible, a fact which has also led to a further loss of prestige for the army and to growing antimilitarism, particularly in Belgium and Luxembourg, which lack a strong military tradition. Defense policies in the three countries seem to be generally concerned with achieving the greatest security from the allies, mainly the U.S., at the cheapest price, and often become a matter of seeking a permanent balance between national efforts and the preparedness of the major power. However, this seems to be more obviously the case for Belgium and Luxembourg than for the Netherlands. A fourth factor is the growth of antimilitarism, pacifism, and some anti-Americanism in public opinion. In particular, the younger generation has long forgotten the Cold War and the Communist threat. Its priorities make it reluctant to think in the same terms as the older generations, and sceptical of the army as a part of the establishment. It disapproves of power politics and is more interested in social problems both on a national and an international level. Pacifism has increased noticeably in recent years and NATO is criticized for including such undemocratic regimes as Portugal and Greece. U.S. policy in Vietnam has been another source of conflict with the alliance. Though at first glance only small minorities seem responsible for the propagation of such ideas, they clearly have a strong influence on the younger generation. (76) Moreover, Benelux countries traditionally lack enthusiasm for military matters. (77) Repeated war and invasion and the fact that foreign powers have almost always guaranteed their

75 However, in recent years doubts have increased in Europe that the U.S. would release nuclear weapons as part of their obligation to their allies.
76 See pp. 385-386.
77 On Belgium, see General Vivario "La Défense de la Belgique", *Eeuwfeest Krijgsschool – Centenaire Ecole de Guerre 1870-1970* (Brussels, 1971), 173. The same remarks apply to the two other Benelux countries.

344

security has led to a certain reluctance to assume military efforts, and in general only direct confrontation with a serious external threat can induce them to undertake a serious military effort. In addition, internal affairs have customarily dominated foreign policy matters. Moreover, in a small country an army may be less prestigious than in larger nations. Finally, in the nuclear age, a small country's conventional force is often seen as useless.

In a more theoretical framework, B.M. Russett *(78)* links small power defense efforts in an alliance to the economic theory of collective goods. *(79)* He concludes that

> to the degree the alliance provides a collective good, the smaller allies will lack incentive to raise armed forces of their own and instead will rely largely upon the great power member(s). Thus the failure of smaller NATO and Warsaw allies to match their protectors' proportionate exertions could be explained in very general rather than ad hoc terms. It would be seen as a "normal" consequence of alliance rather than a lack of ideological fervor or, as has sometimes been alleged, a common European preference to shirk burdens and rely upon others wherever possible. *(80)*

Finally, the question of the differing levels of defense expenditure among the three Benelux countries, particularly that between Holland and Belgium, is of concern here. Luxembourg's extremely low expenditure, a mere one percent of the highest GNP per capita among the three countries and 3.5 percent of the national global budget, is the result of trust in the security of the alliance, weak military tradition, and lack of political will. *(81)* Earlier comments about the reasons for the decrease in defense efforts in the 1960s also apply here. Harlow

78  B.M. Russett, *What Price Vigilance? The Burdens of National Defense* (London, 1970).

79  An economic theory first set forth by P. Samuelson and applied to alliances by M. Olson and R. Zeckhauser in their study, "An Economic Theory of Alliances", *Review of Economics and Statistics*, 48, 3 (August, 1966), 266-279. Public goods are "produced by organizations whose function is to advance the common interest of members" (Russett, *op. cit.*, p. 93). They have two characteristics: "external economy" or "benefits that are made equally available to all members of a group" and "non-rivalness" or "jointness of supply", which means that "each individual's consumption leads to no subtraction from the supply available to others" Russett, *op. cit.*, p. 94.

80  *Ibid.*, pp. 98-99.

81  The Luxembourg government offers two different reasons for the country's very low defense expenditure. They cite first the weakness of the Luxembourg economy due to its largely monolithic structure, in other words, its heavy dependence on the steel industry. This makes, so the argument goes, maintenance of the GNP at its actual level uncertain. Secondly, Luxembourg is the sole NATO country that has no armaments industry of its own, and it draws no financial benefits from its armament efforts. The first reason is, of course, very weak, since in terms of GNP per capita Luxembourg is a rich country. It should normally be able to make a much greater defense effort than it has so far. The second argument is more acceptable. The investment of a defense expenditure to a certain degree in the national economy makes the expense politically more acceptable.

has suggested that differences in Belgian and Dutch defense efforts *(82)* occur because "Holland takes her NATO responsibilities seriously." *(83)* It is possible, of course, that Holland accepts its role as an ally with a greater sense of duty than does the more pragmatic Belgium and that its high defense expenditure is explained by the great esteem for international agreements that is part of the legalistic bent in Dutch foreign policy. Or would Holland make a greater effort in order to enhance its role in the alliance? *(84)* Even if the Dutch do work to appear a most loyal ally, Belgium's smaller effort might offer more advantages for communicating with the East, where outspoken loyalty expressed by high defense efforts might be suspect. In this sense Belgium can operate on a more systemic level between both blocs, whereas Holland's role is carried out on the subsystemic level, within the Western alliance.

Yet more concrete explanations are those that refer to the considerable costs of the Dutch naval force or to the fact that a different budgeting method might be used. The second explanation is admittedly weak since although NATO figures are based on the same standard, it could be applied to every country. On the other hand, the greater defense effort might reflect Holland's tradition as a trading nation, a great colonial power, and successful resister of Spanish hegemony. Whether by tradition or not, even today Holland does not see itself as a small power: "although Dutch people are often tempted to overrate the importance of their country's position, it can hardly be disputed that Holland maintains a position that is by far outreaching its geographical size." *(85)*

The problem of burden sharing within the alliance grew more pressing at the end of the 1960s and the beginning of the 1970s. By that time Europe had gathered enough economic strength to become a serious competitor to American economic power. At the same time the U.S. engaged in a seemingly endless

---

*82* According to the *Military Balance 1971-1972*, Dutch defense efforts as a percentage of GNP for 1970 (3.5) were higher than those of Belgium (2.8), Luxembourg (0.9), Canada (2.5), Denmark (2.3), Germany (3.3), Italy (2.8), and Norway (2.9). Only Belgium and Italy surpass Luxembourg, Denmark, and Canada. In absolute terms the Dutch defense budget for 1971 was more than twice that of Belgium. In terms of defense expenditure per capita, Holland, with $ 85, expends more than Belgium, Luxembourg, Denmark, Greece, Italy, Portugal, and Turkey.

*83* Harlow, *op. cit.*, p. 51.

*84* R.W. Russell, "The Atlantic Alliance in Dutch Foreign Policy", *Internationale Spectator* (8 July 1969), 1206. Also, L.G.M. Jaquet thinks that Holland is "prepared to pay a considerable economic price to be considered as a most loyal member of the alliance", in order to enhance its role within NATO. Jaquet, *loc. cit.*, 66.

*85* *Ibid.*, 58.

war in Southeast Asia and was struggling with heavy balance of payments difficulties. These conditions naturally prompted requests in the American Congress that prospering European partners assume a greater share of NATO's common defense obligations. Some even threatened U.S. withdrawal from Germany. *(86)* By the end of 1970 NATO had concluded a new defense agreement for the seventies which stipulated that European members would assume a greater part of the common burden, especially for NATO's infrastructure and further improvements in national forces (EDIP). Their *geste* does not make the share more proportionate at the moment, however. *(87)* Although it might have assuaged American uneasiness only temporarily, it has certainly helped the American government answer congressional criticism. President Nixon seems to have decided to maintain all U.S. forces in Germany for the nearest future. European reaction to a substantial decrease in U.S. forces in Europe remains an open question. *(88)* Much, of course, depends on the success of détente efforts between East and West. *(89)* Under today's conditions, a considerable increase in European defense efforts seems very unlikely. The same reasons mentioned earlier for low defense efforts would remain valid and Western Europe would continue to feel sufficiently vital to the United States to justify the Americans' willingness to provide deterrence and defense. And even if the credibility gap widens, growing détente might compensate proportionately. On the other hand, changes in the U.S.-European political, military, and economic relations may occur soon. *(90)* How will Europe answer possible American pressure? Will it yield militarily or in trade and finance, or both? Will American demands lead to new common European efforts with regard to defense? How will the Benelux countries react? One thing is certain, these are the questions the future promises, and to which Europe must find an answer.

86 Senator Mansfield's proposal.

87 It is of course true that such programs "are usually a little suspect in that some of the items consist of not making reductions which would otherwise have been made, or bringing forward equipment programs which would in any case have been implemented in later years" Burrows and Irwin, *op. cit.*, p. 112.

88 *The Economist* might eventually be right in stating that "The probability must be accepted that American withdrawals from Europe would be accompanied or followed by cuts in some other allies' forces, rather than by any strenuous effort by all the other allies to fill the gap". *The Economist* (28 April 1973), 15.

89 Particularly, possible positive results from a European security conference or from talks on MBFR.

90 See pp. 383-386.

# Chapter III

# BENELUX IN NATO

Belgium, Holland, and Luxembourg have been faithful members of NATO for more than twenty years; their governments as well as most of their political parties have consistently supported the alliance. Moreover, the largest part of the populous has also reacted favorably; the only dissenters have been the Communists, the extreme left, and the pacifists. Dangerous tensions between East and West have insured that at no time either in the alliance as a whole or between the Benelux nations and the U.S. have there been serious differences on the nature, structure, or relevance of the organization. (1) This was especially true until the beginning of the 1960s. Since then East-West tension has decreased, especially after the Cuban missile crisis; growing internal demands for social action have led to a constant decline in defense efforts by many European members and to resultant American criticism on burden-sharing; American uneasiness over the development of the Common Market in the last decade, European fear of American-Russian unilateral deals, all these factors have put serious strains on the alliance. In addition, the U.S. resented European criticism of the Vietnamese War and European demands for nuclear sharing and more political consultation. Although the Atlantic crisis found its most dramatic expression in the French withdrawal from the military organization in 1966, in Benelux Parliaments and later in NATO itself it prompted a reconsideration of the relevance of the present alliance to present needs and future tasks. The French example was not followed by other countries however. After 1967, emphasis was placed on both defense and détente and the organization assumed new roles in the field of international cooperation, in particular environmental studies.

*1* Except for the effects of the Suez crisis on U.S. relations with the U.K. and France, the desintegrative effects of the Cyprus problem on NATO's southern flank (Turkey, Greece and the U.K.-1956), and the strained relations between Belgium and several NATO-partners with regard to Belgian policies in the Congo in 1960-1961. Nevertheless, the effects of the Congo crisis have never been so divisive as to jeopardize Belgium's NATO membership.

Benelux nations have shared these changes and influences and none but the traditional critics such as the Communists, leftists, pacifists, and the youth, have contested their country's membership of the alliance. However, difficulties have risen from the necessity of maintaining a sufficient defense-effort level, and from tensions with the leading power over consultation, nuclear sharing, and the general crisis affecting the alliance in the sixties. As in the creation of the alliance, Benelux countries played a rather important role in adjusting the alliance to the needs of the late sixties, helping to find a suitable solution to the crisis left in the wake of the French withdrawal. During the twenty-five years of NATO's existence, the Benelux nations have participated actively in several attempts to form a European grouping within the framework of the alliance, beginning with the European Defense Community (EDC), the *relance* of the Brussels pact through the Western European Union (WEU), and during the past decade a European caucus. Of course, their size has kept their influence from being decisive, and some divergence among them has appeared when choices between Atlantic and European priorities have been necessary. On the whole, however, their policies toward NATO can best be described as follows: "The Benelux nations have demonstrated a continuing commitment to the alliance, based on an acute recognition of their own weaknesses as small nations. But they do not appear to favor a status quo." *(2)*

A more systematic analysis of all the matters particularly relevant to Benelux countries during their twenty-five years of NATO membership includes the problems connected with the simultaneous realization of the Atlantic and the European Communities, the question of consultation and equal membership, and finally, Benelux attitudes toward détente. The last point is especially interesting, since after 1967 it became one of the political objectives of the organization.

Logically the question of continued NATO membership after 1969 and Benelux reactions to the Atlantic crisis, especially to French withdrawal, should also be discussed in this chapter. However, I consider the national debates on continued membership important enough to this study to require separate appraisal in a final chapter. Specific defense matters were considered in chapter II.

## THE EUROPEAN AND THE ATLANTIC COMMUNITY

Western Europe's most important experience since the end of World War II has undoubtedly been the gradual emergence of the European community.

2  Weil, *op. cit.*, p. 247.

Its greatest realization has been the Common Market. This evolution has been possible through permanent, substantial American support that has not only given a strong financial and economic impetus to postwar Europe but has offered through its military and political commitments the kind of security Europe needed. The creation of a strong Western Europe was one of the main objectives of U.S. foreign policy after 1945, based on the premise that Europe is vital to American security and prosperity. *(3)* Ironically, however, a renewed Europe showed itself unwilling to enter into the kind of Atlantic community the U.S. had hoped for. In fact, during the first fifteen postwar years Europe had been weak and easily accepting American leadership, even dominance. The last decade, however, has seen a different sort of unity, mainly because Europe has grown stronger economically and has regained enough self-confidence no longer to accept U.S. leadership in the same passive way as it has done before. Western Europe has begun to realize that American and European interests do not necessarily coincide on all points at every moment. Despite American efforts to solve the disaffection of their allies, for example, Kennedy's equal partnership proposal, the creation of a multilateral nuclear force, and the extension of political consultation, the situation has devolved into a vicious circle in which the U.S. denies Western Europe the role and influence it demands because of its unwillingness to assume its military and political responsibilities in the alliance, and Europe says that it cannot take up these responsibilities unless its influence in alliance decisions increases. A satisfactory solution to this problem has yet to be found; until it is the crisis in Atlantic relations will continue.

The simultaneous emergence of the European and the Atlantic communities has at times given rise to conflicts in priorities among NATO's European members. The three Benelux countries have tried constantly to pursue both policies simultaneously, as did the rest of the Six, except for France since 1966. They tried to realize European unity within the framework of the Atlantic community. However, the growing divergence of interests in the last decade has sometimes made compatibility between European and Atlantic policies difficult. Faced with these problems of choice, European nations have been led to question whether a viable and satisfactory alternative to the Atlantic alliance is available in the immediate future. *(4)* The present situation in Europe makes a renewal of neutrality or nonalignment almost wholly impractical. An alliance

---

3  On the evolution of postwar relations between the U.S. and Western Europe, see E.H. van der Beugel, *From Marshall Aid to Atlantic Partnership* (Amsterdam, 1966).

4  See E.H. van der Beugel, "Defensie-Aspecten in het Europa van morgen", *Centenaire Ecole de Guerre — Eeuwfeest Krijgsschool 1870-1970* (Brussels, 1971), 203-214.

with one or more of the larger European powers, France or the United Kingdom, for example, is likewise impossible; particularly for the smaller nations it would mean an insufficient security guarantee combined with an at least equally great loss of independence. Only a strong European political community could be the condition for an acceptable alternative: a European defense community, with a supranational executive, where small powers could guarantee their security and the protection of their interests. Political unity in Western Europe is still far from realization, however. Moreover, many Europeans do not even see it as a desirable solution because it would be more expensive than alliance with the Americans, others because it would hasten the European integration process and still others because they fear that cooperation with European middle powers might result in a domination much stronger than that of the U.S. *(5)*

In fact, NATO has rivaled a strictly European alternative since its origin. The French Pléven plan for a European Defense Community in 1950 was the first concrete expression. The EDC would have been a decisive step toward a united Europe, even though it was conceived within the NATO framework. How did Benelux countries react to this first possibility to create some kind of Eurogroup within NATO?

The Dutch were the most reluctant of the three, saying they felt it necessary "for a considerable period of time, to attend the discussions on the EDC plan merely as an observer." *(6)* Nevertheless, they signed the treaty in 1952 with their five partners of the European Coal and Steel Community (ECSC), and their Parliament ratified it on 23 July 1953 with a majority of seventy-five votes in the Second Chamber. Six of the eleven negative votes were cast by Communist representatives. The discrepancy between the obvious haste with which the Dutch government promoted ratification and its initially reluctant position, expressed by sending merely an observer to the negotiations, requires some consideration. It has been suggested, although the Dutch government has emphatically denied this, that from the side of the U.S. and the German Federal Republic pressure had been exerted on Holland. *(7)* However, another explanation for the sudden change could be the appointment of a strong supporter of the European cause as minister of foreign affairs. In the middle of 1952 J.W. Beyen became foreign minister together with Mr. J. Luns, the secre-

---

5 For a most revealing analysis of European security problems, see Burrows and Irwin, *op. cit.*

6 I. Samkalden, "A Dutch Retrospective View on European and Atlantic Cooperation", *Internationale Spectator* (8 April 1965), 635.

7 *Keesings Historisch Archief*, No. 1153 (19-25 July 1953), 10751.

tary general of NATO; Beyen was responsible for European affairs. During the parliamentary debate, the Dutch government stressed that the EDC could not be treated separately from NATO. The central theme seems to have been German participation in the common defense effort, *(8)* which many saw as a necessity and others feared. In the end, an overwhelming majority were ready to take the risk.

In Belgium the treaty was ratified on 26 November 1953, some eighteen months after its signing. On 22 January 1952, the Belgian government, headed by Van Houtte, declared its enthusiastic support for EDC membership, saying that it helped realize several fundamental policy objectives: the creation of a more effective military force, the integration of Germany into the Western community, and a unification of Western Europe that respected the proper character of each nation. *(9)* In both Belgium and Holland, there was an obvious contradiction between the government's determination to have the treaty ratified and the slowness with which Parliament approached ratification. The House of Representatives ignored the government's request for quick action, and moved only after a long waiting period, "the result of the confusion in public opinion. The idea of rearming Germany in whatever way was far from meeting general support. In both the parties of the governmental majority as well as in those of the opposition ... the hesitators and the adversaries were numerous." *(10)* Ultimately, the Belgian House of Representatives ratified the treaty by a vote of 148 to 49, with three abstentions. Those opposed were the Communist representatives as well as several members of the three so-called national parties. In the Belgian Senate opposition was even greater: the agreement won 125 votes, with forty opposed and two abstentions.

The third Benelux partner, Luxembourg, ratified the treaty very late, on 7 April 1954, by a majority of forty-six, with four dissenting votes, all Communists. Fear of German rearmament was a central problem here, but other issues specific to Luxembourg's situation rose during the debate. In fact, membership in EDC without other guarantee would have caused Luxembourg serious difficulties because of the country's limited demographic and economic resources. Therefore, the same day a special protocol established that the "volume of Luxembourg military forces, their organization, the modalities of their eventual integration, and of their use would be settled by an agreement to be concluded between the Community and the Grand-Duchy, with the

8   *Ibid.* See also Holland, *Jaarboek Ministerie van Buitenlandse Zaken, Nederland, 1953-1954,* p. 8 [Hereafter *Jaarboek Min. B.Z.*].
9   *Parl. Hand., Kamer,* 1951-1952, 22 January 1952, p. 4.
10   Spaak, *op. cit.,* p. 271.

approval of NATO's Supreme Commander." *(11)* The arguments Foreign Minister J. Bech used to defend the treaty in the House of Representatives on 27 February 1951 were generally the same as those of his Belgian and Dutch colleagues. He saw the EDC as important to the Atlantic defense system and to the European unification process. German participation in the EDC was no menace to Europe's security; on the contrary, it was the best way to prevent a recurrence of German national militarism. *(12)*

Although their own Parliaments had criticized aspects of the EDC, the French National Assembly's rejection of the proposal on 30 August 1954 was a serious shock to the Benelux countries. *(13)* France's nationalistic reaction was a direct threat to the supranational Europe the smaller countries urged in all fields, military as well as economic and political. The Dutch apparently suffered the greatest disappointment. In fact, Holland and its foreign minister, Beyen, were more strongly committed to the EDC than Belgium or Luxembourg. The parliamentary majority that approved the EDC treaty was also much larger in Holland than in Belgium.

The Western European Union plan which British Foreign Minister A. Eden proposed in 1954 was an alternative to the EDC only in a very limited sense. However, the Benelux countries gave their full support to the British initiative that led to the important Paris Agreement of 1954, to German rearmament and membership in the revised Brussels Pact, retitled the Western European Union. The WEU has never proved an alternative to NATO in matters of defense, serving instead a more limited role as intergovernmental and inter-parliamentary contact point of the seven member countries. *(14)*

Since 1949 the Atlantic alliance has remained, numerous official statements proclaimed, the cornerstone of Benelux foreign policies and Benelux security. This was apparently more stressed in Holland than in the two other countries, and is a feature of the explicitly Atlantic bent of Dutch foreign policy. This country has also reacted more strongly than the others against any European group-building in the field of defense that would cut them off from the Atlantic community, as witnessed by their response to EDC, the WEU, and the present Eurogroup in NATO. *(15)* Holland's official pro-U.S. and pro-NATO policy

*11* Schaus, *loc. cit.*, 252.
*12* Luxembourg, *Bulletin d'Information du Grand-Duché du Luxembourg*, (Luxembourg, 28 February, 1951), 12.
*13* M.T., "The Benelux countries and NATO", *The World Today*, 15, 5 (May, 1959), 200.
*14* Belgium, Holland, Luxembourg, France, Germany, Italy, and the United Kingdom.
*15* As early as 1954 the Dutch government thought that "a strengthening of cooperation in the political, economic, cultural and military fields among the countries of the Atlantic Community, has to stay one of the basic principles of foreign policy. Therefore it is necessary

"is based on the conviction that Dutch interests are best guaranteed by a world power that is at the same time strong and unbiased in European affairs as well as on the kind of suspicion small countries – taught by history – usually have of their big neighbors." *(16)*

After the failure of the EDC and the European Political Community it would have fostered, and after the establishment of the WEU, the European integration process directed its attention away from the global political and defense arenas. The functionalists turned instead toward the economic field and very quickly achieved great successes in the creation of the European Economic Community (EEC) and Euratom. The first new initiative for political community among the Six was the Fouchet negotiations, which took place early in the 1960s. Unfortunately they led to no results, but during the negotiations Holland and later Belgium strongly opposed General de Gaulle's projections for European political cooperation as detrimental to NATO and the EEC. *(17)* The next step in this direction was only taken at The Hague in December 1969, when the Six *(18)* agreed to reopen talks on political cooperation. In fact, political cooperation only meant a gradual harmonization of their foreign policies. This became the task of the Davignon committee *(19)* and of the regular meetings of the foreign ministers of the six countries since 1971. At the European Summit Conference of October 1972, participants agreed to intensify political cooperation and to offer concrete proposals for a European Political Union by 1975. Except for a limited degree of cooperation in the production of armaments, no new initiative was taken in the field of defense until 1968, when the foreign ministers of several European NATO members first met separately in the framework of the alliance. From then onward, regular meetings have been held in which all European NATO members except France, Portugal, and Iceland, now take part. However, this "Eurogroup" is still far

that the European powers of the Atlantic Alliance refrain from cutting themselves off as a group, but that they maintain an openness towards the overseas Atlantic powers as great as is possible". The government warned that "the WEU should not behave as a bloc within NATO. Such bloc-building would have very undesirable repercussions in Europe as well as for the transatlantic NATO-partners". *Jaarboek Min. B.Z.*, 1954-1955, p. 5.

16   Jaquet, *loc. cit.*, 65.

17   For more details on this question, see *ibid.*, 62-65; Spaak, *Combats inachevés, De l'espoir aux déceptions* (Paris, 1969), pp. 357-380; R. Bloes, *Le Plan Fouchet et le problème de l'Europe politique* (Bruges, 1970); S. Bodenheimer, *Political Union: A Microcosm of European Politics. 1960-1966* (Leiden, 1967), pp. 76-99; D.W. van Lynden, "Perspectieven voor de Europese politieke samenwerking", *Internationale Spectator* (8 October 1972), 1651-1667.

18   The Benelux countries plus Germany, France, and Italy.

19   Mr. Davignon is the director of the Political Division in the Belgian Ministry for Foreign Affairs.

from realizing that sort of community that the EDC would have formed. From the beginning the Benelux countries have actively participated in these gradually formalized meetings, (20) which gave birth to the European Defense Improvement Program (EDIP) in the second half of 1970. The Dutch defense minister, Den Toom, has played an important role in establishing the project. It has been suggested, however, that Holland uses its membership of the Eurogroup primarily as a means to influence decisions and to have some control on trends toward group building within NATO that might be contrary to Dutch interests. Dutch decision makers think that these are best served by a truly Atlantic alliance in which the U.S. remains the dominating power holding the monopoly on nuclear weapons. This attitude would be in line with Holland's traditional position against group building within the alliance.

Until now neither the Eurogroup nor the political consultations among the Six, and even the Nine (21) of the Common Market has threatened political cohesion within NATO, although Secretary General J. Luns found it necessary at the end of March 1972 to warn against common European foreign policy decisions too divertent from NATO policies, which might split the alliance over important problems.

## CONSULTATION AND EQUAL MEMBERSHIP

As small powers the Benelux countries have a personal interest in the principles of political consultation and equal treatment. They insist on being heard on all questions and on participating in every possible discussion and decision. Not surprisingly, therefore, they fully supported the 1956 Commission of the Three Wise Men, which investigated the possibility of increasing consultation and cooperation in nonmilitary fields among the allies. Even more than Belgium or Luxembourg, however, Holland has explicitly emphasized the need for consultation, for example, in its efforts to include some small powers in NATO's nuclear planning.

Another basic principle strongly supported by the Benelux countries was the

20   In a recent article, Carl Damm and Philip Goodhart discuss the impact that both Belgium and Holland have had on the development of the Eurogroup: "The dynamics which the Eurogroup has developed so far are largely due to the considerable 'engagement' shown by the governments of Britain, the FRG, Holland and Belgium. They have taken initiatives and have been prepared to accept the burden of presiding a subgroup or to put institutions for common ventures at the disposal of the Eurogroup". C. Damm and Ph. Goodhart, "Die Euro-Gruppe im Atlantischen Bündnis", Europa-Archiv, 4 (1973), 142.
21   The six original EEC members plus the three new ones, Great Britain, Ireland, and Denmark.

concept of equal partnership. The most dramatic instance was their reaction to General de Gaulle's memorandum of 17 September 1958 to Eisenhower and Macmillan. De Gaulle had noted that the international situation had altered considerably since 1949, and suggested that NATO's structure be adapted to the changed conditions. He proposed the creation of a directorate or triumvirate among the West's three leading nations, the U.S., Britain, and France, where each would share an "overall responsibility for major questions facing the alliance." *(22)* De Gaulle's plan was an open threat to the principles of consultation and decision making among equal partners that was the basis of NATO structure. More particularly, it was a direct attack against the position of the smaller powers. *(23)* Therefore the Benelux countries decisively rejected the scheme, at the same time outlining once again the need for equal consultation among partners. *(24)* Fortunately, under strong opposition from other partners and in the atmosphere surrounding NATO's tenth anniversary, the plan was dropped. The position of the small nations was safe for the moment, but the attack on NATO's structure would not be the last, nor the least severe.

The importance of political consultation and equal membership to the Benelux countries, especially to Holland, was particularly apparent in the discussions about nuclear sharing and nuclear planning in NATO. The attitudes of the Benelux countries on nuclear sharing are very similar in many ways, although some differences are obvious. On the whole, the question is one of emphasis rather than principle. In keeping with the general Atlantic inclination of the Dutch, their nuclear policy is the most pro-Atlantic of the three countries, and they link this attitude directly with their efforts to safeguard their position and that of other small powers in the alliance. Holland reacted more decidedly than Belgium or Luxembourg in its support of the maintenance of a U.S. nuclear monopoly, while on the other hand it tried to guarantee a substantial participation for smaller, nonnuclear allies in NATO's nuclear planning. The question of nuclear sharing became most acute with John F. Kennedy's proposal for a multilateral force as part of his grand design for an equal partnership between the two pillars of the alliance, the U.S. and Europe. *(25)* The term

22   Weil, *op. cit.*, p. 246.
23   M.T., *loc. cit.*, 203.
24   See: *Jaarboek Min. B.Z.*, 1958-1959, p. 5 and *Parl. Doc.*, *Kamer*, 1959-1960, 13 January 1960, 4, No. 3, pp. 4-5.
25   For a thorough discussion of the MLF and the problems of nuclear control see H. Kissinger, *The Troubled Partnership* (New York, 1966), pp. 129-184 and H. van B. Cleveland, *The Atlantic Idea and its European Rivals*, (New York, 1966), pp. 37-64.

*nuclear sharing*, as H. van B. Cleveland says, can apply in different contexts. We will use it here to mean within the MLF proposal and the nuclear committees set up to discuss the improvement of allied participation as a result of the McNamara committee, created in 1965, and known as Nuclear Defense Affairs Committee (NDAC) and Nuclear Planning Group (NPG). An analysis of the MLF proposal is outside the scope of this study. Moreover, the works of H. Kissinger and H. van B. Cleveland discuss the subject in detail. Benelux reactions to the Kennedy idea are of concern here, however.

The Belgian government made a clear statement on the matter as early as 27 February 1963, when its foreign minister declared that Belgium had decided on principle not to take part in the creation of a nuclear multilateral force. Nevertheless, Belgium was present on 11 October 1963 at the first session of a special working group that met in Paris to discuss the American MLF plan, along with the U.S. the U.K., Germany, Italy, Turkey, and Greece. A few months later, on 16 January 1964, Defense Minister P.W. Segers announced Belgian withdrawal from the proposal for financial reasons. Participation in the MLF would cost at least two billion Belgian francs, and other expenses had priority, he said. For example, the expenditure of such huge funds would only make the planned reorganization of the Belgian forces and the modernization of equipment more difficult than it already was. The defense minister told Parliament: "The means available are hardly sufficient to maintain conventional forces in a sufficient state of efficacy." *(26)*

Luxembourg declined for similar reasons. On 12 March 1963, Foreign Minister E. Schaus explained that for "evident" economic reasons Luxembourg was unable to participate in a nuclear force, although it would follow the discussions on the proposal with great interest. *(27)* As the Belgian defense minister had done, Schaus also pointed to his country's specific role in the common defense policy, which lay in the maintenance of well-equipped and well-trained conventional forces. Although both countries refused participation for similar reasons, neither had objections to the creation of such a force.

Holland committed itself a little more fully than its two neighbors to the scheme, although limited financial resources were a consideration here as well. On the whole, in parliamentary debates and in published discussion, the problem of nuclear sharing received more attention in Holland than in the two other countries. At the beginning of 1963 the Dutch officially stated that they

26 Report of the Belgian House Defense Committee on the 1965 defense budget, *Parl. Doc., Kamer*, 1964-1965, N. 2, p. 25.
27 Luxembourg, *Bulletin de Documentation du Grand Duché du Luxembourg*, 15 March 1963, p. 2 [Hereafter *Bulletin de Documentation*].

had no objections to the maintenance of U.S. nuclear monopoly within NATO, but that at the same time they were ready to approach positively any attempt to further a stronger integration of the defense efforts among the member countries. They also declared their serious reservations about the cost of the MLF project, especially considering the need to strengthen their conventional forces. *(28)* The difference between Holland and the two other countries lay in the fact that Holland stated positively that it had no objections to the maintenance of the American nuclear monopoly, while Belgium and Luxembourg did not object to the creation of the MLF. This differing emphasis was important. On the other hand, Holland was not interested in being cut off from the discussions on the matter, and therefore the government declared itself prepared "to investigate with the allies the political opportunity and practical possibilities for the realization of the project." *(29)* Holland did not participate in the Paris talks of 11 October 1963, but Foreign Minister J. Luns announced on 12 December 1963 in the Second Chamber that his government had decided to take part in the MLF discussions. He added, however, that this action did not mean that Holland was going to take part in the MLF. Two months later, on 20 February 1964, he announced Holland's decision to participate in an experiment with a mix-manned *(30)* U.S. ship, in order to investigate the practicality of a multilateral nuclear force. *(31)* The Dutch attitude on this particular point must be seen in the wider framework of the country's global nuclear policy. An interesting report on this subject was published in January 1972 by J.H. Leurdijk. *(32)* His conclusions are important enough to warrant inclusion in some detail. Leurdijk lists the basic factors of Dutch policy on NATO's use of nuclear power:

1. Holland relies for its security totally on the nuclear guarantee provided by the U.S' in the framework of NATO,
2. Holland does not aim at national nuclear arms and feels no need for participation in forms of collective ownership of nuclear arms,
3. Neither does Holland strive for autonomous decision power or participation in decisions on the use of nuclear weapons; the decision to use nuclear arms of the alliance should totally rest with the President of the U.S., which implies also that Holland would like to see disappear autonomous national nuclear forces in Europe,
4. Holland opposes the creation of an autonomous European nuclear force, but does

28  *Jaarboek Min. B.Z.*, 1962-1963, pp. 5-6.
29  *Ibid.*, p. 3.
30  From different nationalities.
31  *Keesings Historisch Archief*, 1964, 117.
32  J.H. Leurdijk, "De Nederlandse buitenlandse politiek en de nucleaire bewapening", *Internationale Spectator* (8 January 1972), 21-41.

not want to exclude the possibility that an in due time united Europe disposes of an own nuclear force in cooperation with the U.S.,

5. However, for political reasons, Holland considers consultation and participation in nuclear planning desirable, as this was worked out in the Nuclear Defense Affairs Committee (NDAC) and the Nuclear Planning Group (NPG) of NATO,

6. Holland rejects further proliferation of nuclear weapons and thinks measures to prevent proliferation very urgent. *(33)*

Thus, while Holland showed more interest in the MLF than either Belgium or Luxembourg, it was never enthusiastic about the project. R.W. Russell's explanation, that Holland probably cooperated in discussions on the plan from "a desire to limit the damage the plan might cause to Dutch interests in NATO, rather than a desire to share nuclear forces with the United States" *(34)* is most likely the correct one.

This desire to be present on all levels of decision making in the alliance again became apparent in 1965, when the Dutch tried to be represented with other small powers in NATO's nuclear affairs and planning committees (NDAC and NPG). They realized that participation in such committees could provide a wealth of information as well as the opportunity to exert a certain influence on planning and perhaps on decisions. When the U.S. Secretary of Defense McNamara proposed on 31 May 1965, that a committee of five defense ministers be set up to consider ways of facilitating consultation on nuclear affairs within NATO, the Dutch together with other small countries sharply reacted against this sort of discrimination, despite the fact that the U.S. had considered Holland one of the five members. *(35)* Holland in this case fought for the principle of nondiscrimination and was opposed to any sort of exclusive group building. Moreover, smaller nations clearly had greater possibilities for influence in a larger group than in a limited one, where probably four of the members would be great or middle powers. Thanks partly to Dutch intransigence on this point, a committee of ten was created that later led to the NDAC and NPG. *(36)* The NDAC is open to all members, and both Belgium and Holland belong, but the NPG was originally to contain only five members, one of them a smaller country chosen from the NDAC. Again Holland successfully pressed its demands for larger membership, and a seat for a Benelux country was incorporated. The original five seats of the NPG were enlarged to seven, one of which is occupied alternately by Belgium and Holland. *(37)*

33  *Ibid.*, 29-30.
34  Russell, *loc. cit.*, 1189-1208.
35  *Ibid.*, 1194.
36  Nuclear Defense Affairs Committee and Nuclear Planning Group.
37  Holland occupied the seat from 1 January 1967, to 30 June 1968, and Belgium from that

Holland pursued a similar policy in the Fouchet negotiations, insisting on either a supranational political community structure or the entry of Great Britain into the discussions to insure the consideration of its national interests in a group dominated by a Paris-Bonn axis or by Paris alone. In 1959 the same thinking led to strong opposition to de Gaulle's triumvirate proposal.

In general, Holland's vigilance has done more to include the smaller non-nuclear powers in joint nuclear planning and consultation than the actions of any of its Benelux partners. The influence of all three within the alliance has been enhanced as a result. On the other hand, R.W. Russell's statement that Dutch policy has helped America maintain its position of primacy in the nuclear defense system, relegating all other NATO members to the second rank, with the result that the Dutch position "vis-à-vis the United States becomes equivalent to that of Germany, France and Britain," *(38)* surely is an exaggerated if not a wrong conclusion.

## BENELUX AND DETENTE *(39)*

The search for increased political consultation and participation in nuclear planning, the creation of the Eurogroup, the adoption of EDIP by the European partners, and the Harmel exercise on the future tasks of the alliance were in fact all efforts to adjust the alliance to the internal needs and changes that had created the Atlantic crisis. However, the Harmel exercise was also of significance for the outside world, especially in terms of the relations with the countries of Eastern Europe, and in this respect Belgium played an important role. Détente became official NATO policy in response to both internal demands in several countries and to a changed international situation. And even as the Harmel proposal was being implemented, many allies had already established bilateral contacts with Eastern Europe. Belgium had been particularly active on this point. The promotion of international cooperation, especially with European countries, is one of the traditional foreign-policy objectives of this country. To an export or transit nation such as Belgium, economic cooperation is vital, and from a political and military standpoint this country has every interest in working closely together with several nations, particularly the smaller ones.

---

date to 1 January 1970, etc. On NPG see also W.F. Van Eekelen, "Nucleaire wapenen en de Westelijke verdediging" *Internationale Spectator* (8 July 1970), 1211-1230.

38  Russell, *loc. cit.*, 1197.

39  This section will not deal with Luxembourg, since its significance in this respect is only marginal. It does not pursue an active détente policy and most of its contacts with Eastern Europe occur through Benelux or BLEU channels.

Belgium has pursued this policy through its bilateral contacts as well as through the international organizations of which it is a member. *(40)* And though international cooperation has been traditional policy for Belgium, it gained new impetus from the advent of détente into NATO policy in 1967. NATO's investigation of the future tasks of the alliance, which resulted in a strong emphasis on détente, was undertaken at the suggestion of the Belgian Foreign Minister P. Harmel at the end of 1966. *(41)* The final communiqué of the ministerial meeting of the NATO council from 7 to 8 June 1966 had conceded that "From now onwards, the member-countries want to further improve the relations between Eastern European and Western European countries, and to reduce between them distrust and fear. They are convinced that new tangible results can now be obtained in the cultural, economic, scientific and technical fields." *(42)* A few weeks later, the Warsaw Pact countries also issued an important declaration on the reestablishment of peace and security in Europe during the Bucarest Conference of 4-6 July 1966. Since 1965-1966 Minister Harmel has been following his détente policy carefully but persistently. Although he distinguishes three areas where détente policies could effect substantial changes, military, economic and, political, *(43)* in Belgian politics the widening of cultural, technological, commercial, and economic contacts has been given first priority. Belgium is well aware that détente can succeed only through the cooperation of all members of the Western alliance. Of all the NATO members, Belgium was in the best position to play an important role in the field of détente. In addition to its traditional links with Eastern Europe, it was one of the members of the UN group of nine, *(44)* established on 21 December 1965 to further contacts between East and West. Belgium is also a small NATO partner with a very low defense effort. These factors must make it more acceptable to the countries of Eastern Europe. On the other hand, its loyalty to the alliance is unquestionable. While its commitment is more visible than Denmark's, it is apparently not as fervent as Holland's. It proved its reliability by accepting NATO installations at Casteau and Evere when they had to be repositioned after France's withdrawal in 1966. Of course, housing NATO installations offers certain economic advantages and increases a country's international prestige. Thus, the Belgian action must be viewed in a

---

40 L. Colot, "La Politique Belge en matière de détente et de coopération en Europe", *Chronique de Politique Etrangère* (January, 1969), 53-128.
41 At the ministerial NATO council meeting at Paris on 15-16 December 1966.
42 Colot, *loc. cit.*, Doc. 3, 92.
43 *Parl. Hand.*, *Senaat*, 1966-1967, N. 18, 17 January 1967, p. 416.
44 Later the UN group of ten when Holland became a member.

larger perspective than that of pure alliance loyalty. *(45)* This balance between active alliance involvement and a marginal defense effort on the one hand, the search for early contacts with Eastern Europe and the limited national interests of the country on the other, has placed Belgium in a favorable position to be, to a certain extent and within the overall possibilities East-West relations offer, an outpost of NATO's détente policy.

The Dutch approach to détente, on the other hand, was very cautious at the beginning. *(46)* Although internal demands for détente, disarmament, and attention to the Third World seem much stronger in Holland *(47)* than in Belgium, *(48)* this has not led to a substantial change in the foreign-policy line of the Government, but has certainly stimulated interest in Eastern Europe.*(49)* The Dutch realize the possibilities a policy of détente offers the smaller Western European countries, and since 1967 contacts between Holland and Eastern Europe have multiplied. In 1967 Holland also joined the UN-group of ten which promoted links between East and West. Composed of Holland, Austria, Finland, Sweden, Yugoslavia, Rumania, Bulgaria, Hungary, Denmark, and Belgium, the group offered opportunities for direct contacts with smaller countries of Eastern Europe.

In fact, Belgium and Holland pursue their détente policies through similar channels: first through bilateral cultural, commercial, technological, *(50)* and even political and military cooperation, and second, through international organizations such as the UN Economic Commission for Europe, the UN group of ten and other organizations of the UN. They have also supported initiatives toward Eastern Europe by GATT, the Council of Europe, the OECD, and even the Common Market in certain respects. From 31 January 1973 onward, the Benelux countries have also participated in the talks on MBFR, together with the U.S., the United Kingdom, Western Germany, and Canada and with all the European countries in the European Security Conference.

45   Housing NATO installations was expected to stimulate economic activity in a disadvantaged area, bring in foreign capital, and increase the international prestige of the country.
46   H.N. Boon, "What is Détente?" *Internationale Spectator* (8 July 1968), 1074. Mr. Boon has been Holland's ambassador to NATO.
47   F.C. Spits, "Nederlandse gedachten over vrede en veiligheid, ontspanning en neutraliteit", *Militaire Spectator* (December 1969), 545-553.
48   See also M. Hayoul, "L'Europe de l'Est, le groupe des "neuf" et M.P. Harmel", *La Revue Nouvelle*, 6 (15 June 1967).
49   Boon, *loc. cit.*, 1075-1076.
50   Some of these agreements are even signed in the name of all the Benelux nations by one country.

Nevertheless, slight differences between Belgium and Holland are apparent. For instance, Belgium made its first move to the East as early as 1965. Holland's was a year later. Belgium was part of the UN group of ten from the beginning, Holland only later. Belgium originated the proposal on exploring the future tasks of the alliance of which détente was an important part. *(51)* Of all NATO countries it was Belgium that made the first official contact with Moscow after the Czech crisis of 1968, a move that many observers and the press saw as a NATO mission to reopen contacts with Eastern Europe. More recently, Belgium was the first NATO country to officially recognize the German Democratic Republic, followed a few days later by Holland and Luxembourg. *(52)* Although the NATO conference of early December 1972 had opened the way for the establishment of diplomatic relations with Eastern Germany once the basic treaty between the two German states was signed, Bonn had asked its NATO partners not to do so before ratification of the treaty in Parliament. The early action of the Benelux countries was therefore somewhat surprising. *(53)*

On the other hand, the differences between the two countries should certainly not be overestimated, since they are more a question of emphasis and timing than of essence. Just as Holland plays a more important role in the discouragement of group building in NATO or in the promotion of consultation on the basis of equality, in the field of détente and of cooperation with the East Belgium seems the more active of the two. Nevertheless, Belgium's policy has promoted an image of a country actively seeking détente. With détente a particular function of its foreign policy, Belgium fulfills a proper role on a more systemic level, namely that of relations between the two ideologically-opposed European subsystems. *(54)* Once the Western alliance made

51  It is, of course, possible that the U.S. asked Belgium to play this role, but there is no evidence on this point.
52  On 27 December 1972 and 5 January 1973 respectively.
53  Explaining Belgium's lead in this recognition-process, a spokesman of the Belgian Foreign Ministry said that this country was the first invited to do so by East Germany. Harmel's leading role in the process of détente between East and West has undoubtedly contributed to this. But the prospects of favorable treatment in future commercial relations must have influenced the quick Belgian decision. Indeed, East German officials had often suggested that the first Western countries to recognize the GDR would receive favorable treatment in trade relations. Holland and Luxembourg must also have been attracted by this incentive. See *De Standaard* (29 December 1972).
54  Borrowing two terms for role description used in a recent article by R.A.H. Schipper, A. van Staden, C.A. Tazelaar, W.J. Wassen, and J.W. Wesseldijk, and applying them to Dutch and Belgian foreign policies in the late 1960s in the framework of East-West relations, we might say that Belgium is more the "bridge-builder" whereas Holland is more the "faith-

détente an objective of its security policy, Belgium's role took on a special relevance as NATO's outpost as well.

The possibilities for détente have certainly been favored by growing contacts between the two superpowers and by nuclear parity. These contacts not only set an example for the smaller nations on both sides, but a growing tendency toward disintegration in both the Western and Eastern blocs has created some space for small power initiatives. Although détente is still essentially determined by superpower relations, the European Security Conference may bring about more changes in this field.

ful ally". See R.A.H. Schipper et al., "Rolopvattingen in de na-oorlogse buitenlandse politiek van Nederland", *Internationale Spectator* (8 January 1973), 21-30, in which the authors apply K.J. Holsti's approach to national role conceptions in foreign policy to Dutch postwar foreign policy. See K.J. Holsti, "National Role Conceptions in the Study of Foreign Policy, *International Studies Quaterly*, XIV, 3 (September, 1970), 233-309.

Perhaps this difference between Belgian and Dutch détente policies is to a limited extent also a question of personalities. The fact that the outspoken Atlanticist J. Luns has been Holland's foreign minister for almost two decades has undoubtedly helped to keep Dutch foreign policy truly pro-Atlantic and pro-NATO. If Belgium, on the other hand, has been the bridge-builder since the middle of the 1960s, this has partly been due to P. Harmel's presence at the head of the Belgian foreign service from that time. In a cautious and pragmatic way Harmel has continually furthered a policy of détente and cooperation with the Eastern European countries without neglecting Belgium's Atlantic ties.

# Chapter IV

# THE FAITHFUL ALLIES

## BENELUX AND NATO AT THE END OF THE 1960s

Partly under the influence of the Atlantic crisis, partly with the possibility in view of leaving NATO by 1969, the three Benelux countries at different points in the second half of the last decade organized a parliamentary debate on further commitment to the alliance. Since the immediate cause of the national debate was different for each, each will be discussed separately and in chronological order.

Belgian reconsideration of its NATO membership was a direct reaction to General de Gaulle's announcement on 22 February 1966 that he intended to withdraw France from the military organization of the North Atlantic alliance. On March 12, Foreign Minister Harmel published a communiqué on Belgium's position on the newest French initiative. It stressed Belgium's loyalty to the alliance and to all obligations contracted in its framework, calling the alliance an essential element of the political and military cooperation among the Western nations as it had been organized after the war. Particularly for smaller countries the alliance and the military integration that had resulted from it constituted the basis of their defense organization. *(1)* However, the French decision had direct consequences for Belgium, since immediately after de Gaulle's press conference rumors circulating in diplomatic circles suggested that Belgium would replace France as a possible recipient of the NATO installations. The other Benelux countries were also drawn into the debate, and a series of consultations among them followed. On 4 April 1966, their foreign ministers, meeting in Brussels, created a study group to investigate the possibilities of transferring certain NATO installations to the Benelux territory. *(2)* The

---

1  *Le Soir* (16 March 1966).
2  See *Parl. Hand.*, *Kamer*, 1965-1966, 26 April 1966, p. 25; for an extensive analysis of the Belgian attitude on the NATO transfer: M. Vincineau "Le Parlement Belge devant la crise de l'alliance atlantique", *Chronique de politique étrangère* (January, 1968) 89-164, on which this part of Chapter IV is based to a large extent.

Belgian government *(3)* acted with great care on the question of whether Belgium would offer its own land to this end. In Parliament and in interviews, Harmel continuously stressed during the first weeks that no decision had been taken on this point, that NATO had made no official demand, and that in any case Parliament would be consulted before the government accepted new commitments. *(4)* Nevertheless, premature forecasts of a positive answer in foreign newspapers, at the same time caused doubt and confusion in both public opinion and in Parliament, in spite of the fact that on June 1 Minister Harmel had repeated in Parliament that this body would be the first informed and that it would be able to discuss the matter "in such a way that each can assume his part of the responsibility under these circumstances: the government who assumes the burden of the responsibility to decide, and Parliament which approves or disapproves." *(5)* However, relations between Parliament and government became strained when Harmel told a Belgian newspaper that in fact the government felt no obligation to consult Parliament on the subject of the transfer, since the latter had ratified the North Atlantic Treaty and was obliged to accept all consequences of it as a result. *(6)* P. Struye, president of the Belgian Senate, reacted sharply. If the NATO transfer involved new financial burdens or would cause certain parts of the country to become extra-territorial, *(7)* Parliament, he said, had the right to be consulted. Finally on 6 June 1966, after long negotiations among the fourteen NATO partners, and particularly with the Benelux governments, Belgium, Holland, and Germany accepted the transfer of certain NATO installations to their territories, at least in principle. Four days later, after new Senate insistence on being informed before a decision was taken, the government announced that it had to assume its part of this task and that it would completely inform Parliament during the following week. *(8)*

Parliament began a general debate on this statement on 14 June 1966. The discussion revolved aroung whether the alliance was still relevant to the present situation, and on a definition of its future tasks and structure. *(9)* As to the actual relevance of the alliance, the government felt that a collective and inte-grated defense, in peacetime as well as in times of serious crisis or war, could

---

3 A coalition of Christian-Democrats (CVP-PSC) and the Partij voor Vrijheid en Vooruit-gang (PVV-PLP). The latter has replaced the old Liberal party.

4 See Vincineau, *loc. cit.*, 96-97.

5 *Parl. Hand., Senaat*, 1965-1966, 1 June 1966, pp. 1056-1057.

6 M. Vincineau, *loc. cit.*, 101-102.

7 *Ibid.*, 102.

8 *Ibid.*, 103.

9 *Ibid.*, 105. I follow Vincineau's division.

still be justified in 1966. Aside from the fact that Belgium had committed itself under Article 3 of the treaty, *(10)* the alliance meant an important saving on the military budget. Moreover, it provided a deterrent to aggression by guaranteeing direct American, British, and Canadian intervention in case of an attack from Eastern Europe. Integration of this kind prevented nationalism, Minister Harmel argued, and finally, a small power in particular could no longer afford a sufficient defense effort on its own, since the area needed for an efficient defense had become larger and larger. *(11)*

The government was generally supported in its opinion by the Christian Democrats and the PVV-PLP, the Flemish federalist party, Volksunie, and a majority of the Socialists, *(12)* although the last put more emphasis on the necessity for adapting NATO to the changing world situation. They wanted Belgian membership conditioned by the active pursuit of a policy of negotiation, détente, and controlled disarmament, leading eventually to a state where the abolition of both military blocs would be possible. *(13)* In fact, the Socialists were divided on the question of NATO's present relevance. Some were strong defenders, for example Mr. Spaak; others took a stand very close to the Communist viewpoint. *(14)* The Communist party simply refused to accept the thesis that NATO had maintained peace. Stability had been the result of nuclear parity achieved by an arms' race. This should be stopped and all military blocs dissolved. Moreover, they accused Germany of using NATO for the promotion of revanchist policies. *(15)* Similar opposition came from the smaller Brussels and Walloon parties, the Front Démocratique des Bruxel-

---

*10* Though this was mentioned by Mr. Harmel, it can hardly be called a reason for the actual relevance of the alliance.

*11* *Parl. Hand.*, *Kamer*, 1965-1966, 14 June 1966, pp. 13-15, and *Parl. Hand.*, *Senaat*, 1965-1966, 14 June 1966, pp. 1236-1239.

*12* See Mr. Tindemans (Chr.-Dem.), *Parl. Hand.*, *Kamer*, 1965-1966, 16 June 1966, pp. 19-23; Mr. Gilson (PVV-PLP), *Parl. Hand.*, *Senaat*, 1965-1966, 21 June 1966, p. 1370; Mr. Schilz (Volksunie), *Parl. Hand.*, *Kamer*, 1965-1966, 16 June 1966, pp. 43-46; Mr. Larock (Soc.), *ibid.*, pp. 7-8.

*13* Though the other parties also in one way or another stressed the need for negotiation and détente, they did so less explicitly than the Socialist party.

*14* See Mr. Spaak, *Parl. Hand.*, *Kamer*, 1965-1966, 16 June 1966, pp. 19-29, and Mr. Glinne, *ibid.*, pp. 31-35. The latter severely attacked NATO and the U.S., which by its aggressive policies had turned the organization into something quite different from the originally defensive alliance. He saw NATO as a product of the Cold War myth. Only a policy of détente could "liberate" the countries of Central and Eastern Europe. Finally, in his view, Portuguese and Belgian membership were incompatible.

*15* Mr. Drumaux, *Parl. Hand.*, *Kamer*, 1965-1966, 16 June 1966, pp. 24-25, and Mr. Terfve, *Parl. Hand.*, *Senaat*, 1965-1966, 21 June 1966, pp. 1362-1364.

lois Francophones, and the Parti Wallon, who both proposed at least an adaptation of NATO to changed circumstances. The Front Démocratique recommended the parallel reduction and dissolution of both blocs; *(16)* the Parti Wallon went so far as to call for an immediate dissolution of NATO. *(17)*

In addressing the second point of the debate in the Belgian Parliament, the future tasks of the alliance, Foreign Minister Harmel asked for an organization dynamic in its attempts to solve existing political problems. His government thought that

> as long as measures of real disarmament cannot be found and as long as on both sides the armaments' level remains what it is now, it [the Belgian government] will not give up the security that is offered by NATO. But, we are convinced that the efforts for détente and peace are more important than the defense effort... *(18)*

This attitude in particular would become the basis of Belgium's détente policy, and could also be recognized in the Belgian initiative that led to what is called the Harmel exercise. All political parties supported the government's position, although some differences on the ways to reach détente did arise. *(19)*

Parliament then turned to a discussion of the restructuring of NATO, followed by a consideration of future relations among the allies. Finally, an evaluation of the pros and cons of the transfer of the NATO installations to Belgium was made, and the government declaration on this point. The opposition parties attacked the government heavily for the way it had handled the issue, despite the fact that two days before *(20)* Harmel had emphasized that Parliament would make the final decision. In his view the transfer involved no additional danger for Belgian security, since in case of war attack was unavoidable. The importance of the port of Antwerp and the country's role as a center of communications almost guaranteed that Belgium would immediately

---

16  Mr. Defosset, *Parl. Hand.*, *Kamer*, 1965-1966, 16 June 1966, pp. 42-47, and Mr. Lagasse, *Parl. Hand.*, *Senaat*, 1965-1966, 21 June 1966, pp. 1361-1362.

17  Mr. Perin, *Parl. Hand.*, *Kamer*, 1965-1966, 16 June 1966, pp. 49-50.

18  *Parl. Hand.*, *Kamer*, 1965-1966, 14 June 1966, pp. 13-15.

19  The Communists wanted concrete proposals for détente and a simultaneous dissolution of both blocs. The Front Démocratique des Bruxellois asked for more independence from the U.S., and the Parti Wallon saw European unification as the only alternative. See Mr. Drumaux, *Parl. Hand.*, *Kamer*, 1965-1966, 16 June 1966, pp. 23-26; Mr. Terfve, *Parl. Hand.*, *Senaat*, 1965-1966, 21 June 1966, pp. 1362-1364; Mr. Defosset, *Parl. Hand.*, *Kamer*, 1965-1966, 16 June 1966, pp. 46-47; and Mr. Perin, *ibid.*, pp. 49-50.

20  *Parl. Hand.*, *Kamer*, 1965-1966, 14 June 1966, pp. 13-15, and *Parl. Hand.*, *Senaat*, 1965-1966, 14 June 1966, pp. 1236-1239.

become directly involved in the hostilities. The housing of the installations involved no additional costs, Harmel said, since Belgium was obliged to pay its share in any case. Moreover, the construction of new buildings and houses would benefit the Belgian economy. Harmel was supported by the Christian Democrats and the Liberals, but the Socialists reproached the government for providing insufficient information on the costs of the transfer and thought that England would be a better choice from a technical standpoint. They also questioned the length of time Belgium would be committed and whether the move anticipated continued membership after 1969. If it did they would not accept the transfer. *(21)* The Communist party rejected the government's policy because the transfer would mean inflation and increased insecurity.

The spokesman of the Volksunie expressed the same objections, saying that in his mind the worst result of the move would be the lessening of potential to play an active role in the establishment of détente. The smaller French-speaking parties largely coincided with the other opposition parties. In both the House of Representatives and the Senate, this discussion resulted in the submission of two motions by the governing coalition parties which basically reflected the government's position on NATO, détente, and the consequences of the transfer for Belgium. The motion submitted to the House of Representatives stressed Belgium's continuing loyalty to the alliance, as well as its commitment to a policy of international cooperation and détente. It noted further that the transfer would involve no excessive expenses for Belgium, since all partners would help meet the costs. Finally, it sanctioned the move as an indication of Belgium's solidarity with the alliance. The issue came to a vote on 21 June 1966; it was passed by 118 votes, with sixty-one opposed and sixteen abstentions *(22)*. All Christian Democrats and Liberals approved the measure, as did two Socialists, Mr. Spaak and Mr. Spinoy. A majority of Socialists, all Communists, the Front Démocratique des Francophones, the Parti Wallon, and one member of the Union de la Gauche Socialiste opposed it. The Volksunie abstained along with five Socialists, who supported NATO but not the government's policy on the transfer. *(23)*

The motion submitted to the Senate *(24)* stated that Belgium's duty and

---

21  *Parl. Hand., Senaat*, 1965-1966, 21 June 1966, pp. 1364-1386. Again Mr. Spaak alone of his party defended the transfer.

22  *Parl. Hand., Kamer*, 1965-1966, 21 June 1966, pp. 22-23.

23  After this positive result, another motion submitted the same day by two Socialist representatives, Mr. Cools and Mr. Terwagne, which stated that the House could not support the government in its policy to accept NATO installations on the Belgian territory, had no chance.

24  *Parl. Hand., Senaat*, 1965-1966, 22 June 1966, pp. 1410-1413.

interests demanded loyalty to NATO, whose purely defensive character and effective contribution to security and world peace was unquestionable. Solidarity among allies required the acceptance of NATO installations on Belgian territory, although on the following conditions: a fair repartition of the costs among all allies, a rationalization and simplification of Atlantic organisms; a limitation of the system of diplomatic immunities and fiscal exemptions; and a new investigation on the ways Belgian troops were stationed in Germany. Finally, the motion described this new responsibility as totally compatible with Belgian intentions to encourage détente with the East. The vote on this motion produced ninety-six in favor, thirty-three opposed, and twenty-two abstentions. Those who favored the measure included all Christian Democrats except one, all the Liberals, and one Socialist. Twenty-three Socialists, the Volksunie, the Communists, and one FDF senator cast negative votes. Twenty-one Socialists and one Christian Democrat abstained. (25)

The importance of détente in this debate is illustrated by the result of a special preliminary vote on the last paragraph of the motion submitted to the Senate, concerning the compatibility of the transfer with Belgian détente policy. Of the 151 senators present, 140 approved the passage, five did not, and six abstained. (26) Some observers have postulated a special connection between Belgium's special interest in détente and the transfer of NATO installations to this country. More particularly they said that Harmel's détente policy was initiated specifically to appease internal opposition to the move. However, their assertions are incorrect. Belgium's overtures to the East began as early as 1965, and in fact from 1956 onward officials have enjoyed numerous contacts with the U.S.S.R., Poland, and Yugoslavia. (27) Minister Harmel touched on this question in a speech to the Belgian Senate on 16 March 1971:

> In a recent work of an American diplomat who has been living with us for a long time, I have read that Belgium about the year 1967 would have pursued this policy (of détente) as a sort of psychological counterweight of our loyalty to the alliance, when this organization located its general secretariat and SHAPE in Belgium. In my opinion, this is a wanton appreciation! We have rather thought that for peace, at the same time, at least as many diplomatic as military risks should be taken. (28)

---

25 This left no room for another motion, submitted by two Volksunie senators, which declared itself in favor of NATO but against the transfer, since it would hinder the country from assuming its role of mediator in the détente policy.

26 See *ibid*.

27 Colot, *loc. cit.*, 107-109.

28 Persdienst Ministerie van Buitenlandse Zaken, *Rede van Minister P. Harmel n.a.v. de bespreking van de begroting van het Ministerie van Buitenlandse Zaken in de Senaat* (Brussels, 16 March 1971), pp. 18-19.

Thus by 1966 the majority parties and part of the opposition in the Belgian Parliament considered NATO relevant to Belgian security. All speakers stressed the need for cooperation with Eastern Europe. On the question of housing the NATO installations, however, opinion divided sharply. Only the parties then in power were willing to commit themselves to the new responsibility, indicating that a certain amount of parliamentary objection must have been the result of political maneuvering and oppositional tactics.

Unlike Belgium and Holland, Luxembourg accepted no major NATO installations. On 26 April 1966, Prime Minister P. Werner admitted that the Benelux area was well situated to this end and that, in view of the departure of the ECSC's High Authority to Brussels, the arrival of NATO installations might be welcome in Luxembourg. *(29)* However, his statement was not an indication that Luxembourg would automatically accept installations on its territory. On May 25, Werner spoke before Parliament on his government's attitude *(30)* toward the transfer problems and the alliance as such. Werner saw the existence of NATO as well as the presence of American and British forces on the continent as vital, an essential guarantee of security for small and middle powers. *(31)* Security through an integrated defense system in peacetime had been the basic reason why Luxembourg had made NATO membership the cornerstone of its foreign policy. Security remained its prime motivation for continued alignment. *(32)* Premier Werner admitted that the international situation had changed a good deal since 1949. But as long as the potential for hostility between East and West remained, he argued, NATO was indispensable for Western defense and irreplacable for Luxembourg security. Coming at the peak of the Atlantic crisis, Werner's speech was a clear expression of Luxembourg's loyalty to NATO, although he stressed at the same time the need to make NATO an active instrument for a more dynamic and constructive policy toward Eastern Europe. *(33)* Up to this point the Luxembourg view on the relevance and future tasks of NATO, at least on the government level, largely coincided with the official Belgian view. However, the similarity ended on the question of the installations. On the same day Premier Werner told Parliament that his government had informed its allies that "for evident reasons, and particularly with regard to the European vocation which our

---

29  Vincineau, *loc. cit.*, 94.
30  A coalition of Christian Democrats and Socialists.
31  *Bulletin de Documentation*, 26 May 1966, 6, p. 3.
32  *Ibid.*, p. 4.
33  *Ibid.*

country has already accepted, the installation in the Grand-Duchy of a major organization, as for instance a great integrated command, would meet almost insurmountable practical difficulties." *(34)* On the other hand, his country was ready to examine proposals for accepting a less important or less extensive organization. In the end, Luxembourg would receive only one smaller NATO installation. *(35)* Unlike Belgium and to some extent Holland, the transfer matter created no problems in Luxembourg. On the other hand, that country's defense effort, also essential to its membership in NATO, gave rise to certain difficulties.

On 16 November 1966, the Luxembourg Parliament unanimously requested the abolition of obligatory military service and the return to a volunteer army. *(36)* On November 24, Werner adressed Parliament on military policy and agreed to the motion of November 16, promising to contact NATO authorities in December to discuss the abolition of military service. Within the first months, he said, two measures would be submitted to the House to provide a legal basis for this important alteration in the military organization of the country. Werner asked the House of Representatives for confidence.

At this point, the leader of the Socialist fraction, Mr. Fandel, *(37)* expressed his party's feeling on the matter. In the first place, Luxembourg's military contribution had been purely symbolic from the start. Second, the absence of any military tradition and a nationwide desire for world peace explained the distaste the Luxembourg people had always shown toward compulsory service. Besides, the country's limited geographic and demographic resources clearly made people realize that all military efforts were useless. Third, since 1946 all professional and youth organizations as well as all but one political party had urged abolition of military service. Fourth, although the Socialist party did not wish to question the country's NATO membership, it recommended that the

---

34    *Ibid.*, p. 5.

35    NAMSO (NATO Maintenance and Supply Organization) at Capellen (Luxembourg). A Luxembourg official postulated that one of the reasons why the housing of NAMSO caused no difficulties (except for Communist criticism) was because it created many new jobs for Luxembourg citizens.

36    "The House of Representatives, considering the evolution of the international situation, together with the economic and demographic difficulties of our country, invites the Government to start again, within the nearest future, negotiations with NATO-authorities in order to obtain a new conception of our contribution to the defense of the territory, on the basis of a formula that enables the abolition of the obligatory military service". *C.R. Chambre*, 1966-1967, 24 November 1966, pp. 785-786.

37    *Ibid.*, pp. 783-784.

alliance adapt its structure and its objectives to correspond with the changed world situation. And finally, Luxembourg was incapable of providing a valuable contribution to the defense of the West. For all these reasons, Mr. Fandel wanted the November 16 motion to be turned into law. He submitted a bill to the House which, without questioning the country's loyalty to NATO, pursued only one objective: a formal modification of Luxembourg's NATO contribution. The text of the proposal abolished all obligatory military service from 1 January 1967 onward. *(38)*

Extensive debate on Fandel's proposal between Socialists and Communists on the one hand and Liberals and Christian Democrats on the other ended with Premier Werner's announcement that he was dissatisfied with the Socialists' responses to the question. He was forced to declare the government's abdication. *(39)* A new government was formed *(40)* and on 1 July 1967 military service in Luxembourg was finally cancelled by a parliamentary vote taken on 23 June 1967 of fifty to five, the latter Communist, and one abstention. *(41)*

Luxembourg's reaction to the Atlantic crisis was twofold. The government and the major political parties declared themselves clearly in favor of continued NATO membership, although all stressed the need for change and adaptation, particularly in relation to Eastern Europe. For solidarity reasons Luxembourg was prepared to consider the acceptance of some smaller NATO installations on its territory if asked to do so. On the other hand, the French withdrawal and the ensuing period of uncertainty created the opportunity for the realization of a long-standing objective, the abolition of military service, and Parliament made use of it for several reasons. First, public opinion through many organizations demanded it, making the issue a political one. When the Socialists pressed strongly for abolition on 1 January 1967, they did so with the electorate in mind. On the other hand, this substantial reduction in the country's defense effort was probably also in part caused, as one Luxembourg official said, by a certain uneasiness about the country's economic situation at the time. Finally, increasing prospects for détente facilitated the move. Political loyalty to the alliance coupled with an extremely low defense effort has characterized Luxembourg's position in NATO to the present day. Some might argue that loyalty and a marginal defense effort are contradictory factors. On the other hand,

---

38   *Ibid.*, pp. 787-788.
39   Mr. Fandel had stated that he no longer trusted certain members of the government.
40   A new coalition of Christian Democrats and Socialists.
41   *Keesings Historisch Archief*, 1967, 550.

given the smallness of the country, whether a different policy is possible remains an open question.

In terms of defense effort, Holland is obviously the most faithful ally of the Benelux group and has proven to be very loyal politically as well. From 1949 to the present, all official statements on foreign or defense policy have labelled NATO the cornerstone of Dutch foreign policy. *(42)* During the Atlantic crisis, the Dutch again demonstrated their reliability, maintaining a comparatively high level of defense expenditure and accepting a fair share of the burden of the NATO transfer. In fact, in the period immediately following the French decision to withdraw, they cooperated intensely with their Benelux partners on the question of transfer. On 12 October 1966, NATO accepted a Dutch proposal to transfer AFCENT to South Limburg, *(43)* and from the middle of 1967 it has been operative at Brunssum. Its presence has never caused any serious difficulties, except for some sharp though limited criticism from leftist groups, the Socialist party (PvdA), and the Communists on the arrival of General von Kielmannsegg as commander-in-chief of AFCENT. They objected particularly to publications of the general that had appeared during World War II. For example, the Socialist party issued a note on 31 August 1966 saying that it had no quarrel with a NATO base in Brunssum, "on the condition that the NATO-concept would not be undermined by the maintenance of general von Kielmannsegg as commander of the headquarters in case." *(44)* With regard to the possibility of leaving NATO by 1969, the Dutch government repeated on several occasions that the alliance, adapted to changed circumstances, remained as indispensable after 1969 as before both for security in the West and for East-West détente. *(45)* Rapprochement between East and West was only possible, in the Dutch view, within the framework of a strong political cooperation among NATO allies and a military effort adequate to maintain an equilibrium. *(46)*

Although Holland has consistently shown itself a faithful ally, the publication in 1968 of a white paper on the country's NATO and defense policy *(47)* and

---

42  See the yearly *Jaarboek van het Ministerie van Buitenlandse Zaken* (The Hague),the yearly *Memorie van toelichting* on the defense budget or the foreign affairs budget, and *Parlement en Kiezer*, published yearly at The Hague.

43  *Keesings Historisch Archief*, 1966, 501.

44  *Ibid.*

45  The queen's speech on 19 September 1967, quoted in P. Goossen, *"Parlement en Kiezer"*, 1967-1968 (1968), p. 293.

46  *Jaarboek Min. B.Z.*, 1968-1969, p. 4.

the announcement of an increase of the defense budget by 225 million guilders *(48)* led to extensive discussion in the Second Chamber on Dutch NATO commitments, the future tasks of the alliance, and even to the submission of a motion to denounce the North Atlantic Treaty. Arguments began on 20 November 1968 with a motion submitted by Representative van der Spek and others of the Pacifist Socialist Party (PSP), a group which included the most radical Socialists. It ran as follows:

> The Chamber, thinking that the North Atlantic Treaty perpetuates the division of the world in military-economic power-blocs; thinking, that this division's attendant arms' race on the one hand continuously puts at stake the existence of mankind, and on the other withdraws enormous amounts of capital from constructive objectives, invites the Government to denounce this treaty. *(49)*

The proposal, which was even more radical than the French withdrawal from the military organization of the alliance, was not the first one of its kind in Holland. As early as 1962 the Dutch Communist party had proposed leaving NATO and pursuing a policy of neutrality. Opposition from the Communists was traditional, however, and never a serious threat. In fact, neither was the van der Spek motion. But at a moment when one major ally had left, with the prospect of further détente, and the possibility to leave NATO in 1969, this action was clearly more dangerous than any previous attempt. It certainly gave rise to a thorough discussion on alliance membership and the future role of NATO. Defending his motion, Mr. van der Spek sharply attacked the government's policy, especially the announced increase of 225 million guilders in defense spending. In response to the additional expenditure, he introduced a second motion in which the Chamber called for the government to abandon its plans as contradictory to détente. *(50)* In general, van der Spek was also critical of U.S. interventionist foreign policy and the Dutch government's traditional Cold War view of NATO and defense. The alliance supported capitalist economies and the undemocratic regimes in Greece and Portugal, and supplied NATO weapons at least in the case of Portugal for suppression of colonial liberation movements. These alone were sufficient reasons for withdrawal.

The Catholic People's Party (Katholieke Volkspartij) *(51)* expressed a different opinion on the matter. It shared van der Spek's desire for an active

---

47  *Nota inzake het NAVO- en Defensiebeleid 1968.*
48  In order to meet NATO demands for greater defense efforts after the Czech crisis in the summer of 1968.
49  *Hand. Stat.-Gen., Tweede Kamer*, 1968-1969, 20 November 1968, p. 642.
50  *Ibid.*, p. 643.
51  *Ibid.*, pp. 643-648.

policy of peace, but recommended that this be realized through continued NATO membership. Since 1949 NATO had provided stability and enabled a war-damaged Europe to rebuild socially, economically, and politically without hindrance. In guaranteeing stability NATO also guaranteed peace, and therefore should remain the cornerstone of Holland's foreign policy. With regard to the membership of undemocratic regimes, the KVP *(52)* suggested they be pressured to conform more with the treaty's ideals. Ties with the U.S. were of a fundamental importance for Europe and thus for Dutch security, without needing a more formally organized atlantic community. Nevertheless, more political consultation, as well as the development of a European component within the alliance, would be most welcome. Finally, the KVP approved additional defense spending; not to do so would diminish the credibility of the alliance and its internal cohesion. In addition, Holland's influence on détente policies and in shaping NATO's political function would also decrease and U.S.-European relations would suffer.

Like the Belgian Socialists, the Dutch Socialist party (Partij van de Arbeid) emphasized détente. *(53)* It argued that dissolving the alliance would cause instability in Europe and thus be a menace to peace. On the other hand, it did not see NATO as the final aim of Dutch foreign policy. Rather, the alliance should merely be a tool for the realization of East-West détente, for example, through a new European security system. Dutch defense policy should stress mobility and quality, even if this involved new expenses. Finally, it recommended that the central idea of the Harmel proposal that military security and détente policy are complementary should become NATO's basic principle. In a motion which summarized the party's attitude, submitted to the Second Chamber by Mr. van der Stoel, the Socialists stressed the need to strengthen the political role of the alliance by coordinating efforts toward détente, arms control, and mutually controlled disarmament, and by intensifying consultation on preventing crises in Europe and the Mediterranean. Moreover, regular meetings among democratic European partners on political questions of common interest would be most welcome. In addition, the North Atlantic Assembly ought to be given a greater role. Finally, van der Stoel urged the government to begin talks with Greece and Portugal on political differences and to stop all military aid to those nations.

With the exception of the Communists, all smaller political parties *(54)* also

---

52 Katholieke Volkspartij.

53 *Hand. Stat.-Gen., Tweede Kamer*, pp. 648-653.

54 Democraten '66 (D'66), Volkspartij voor Vrijheid en Democratie (VVD), Christelijk Historische Unie (CHU), Anti-Revolutionaire Partij (ARP), Gereformeerd Politiek Verbond (GVP), Staatkundig Gereformeerde Partij (SGP).

favored continued membership in NATO. The Communists used traditional arguments to criticize the alliance, German generals and German forces on Dutch soil, the membership of undemocratic régimes, and the fact that large industrial monopolies such as Philips and Daf were earning fortunes through NATO and Dutch defense efforts. The new demands to increase the military budget directly attacked the standard of living of the working class. The Communist party accused NATO of undermining Dutch independence and the people's democratic rights. These could only be restored through a return to political neutrality and the withdrawal of Holland from NATO. In the end, Mr. Van der Stoel's motion was adopted by a large majority. The country declared itself in favor of continued NATO membership, promotion of détente, and more consultation among allies, a commitment totally compatible with NATO's official policy since acceptance of the Harmel proposal.

Parliamentary debates show clearly that in the second half of the previous decade NATO still continued to enjoy the full support of the great majority of political parties in the three Benelux nations. Only a few groups, the Dutch PSP, the Communists in all three countries, some smaller federalist parties in Belgium, and a few Belgian Socialists, urged immediate withdrawal from NATO or a gradual dissolution of both power blocs.

The debates indicate that the main reasons for maintaining the alliance after 1969 were security and stability in Europe, although most parties and all governments stressed the need for an active détente policy for which the alliance provided the necessary background. This main motive totally reflected NATO's official opinion on its primary functions as expressed in the Harmel Report of 1967. *(55)* In comparison with the security motive of 1949, this meant a clear change of emphasis, if not of concept. In 1949 defense was the key concept. In 1966-1968 both defense and détente were important. In fact, this was the only motive stressed by everyone in the three Benelux countries who favored NATO membership after 1969. A second, although much less common motive, was the potential of the alliance to serve to protect "the common values of Western civilization and society". Third, several NATO supporters also referred to the alliance as the only way small powers could effectively and at a reasonable cost organize their defense and security policies. Economically, the alliance is clearly the most pragmatic solution as long as the armaments level remains the same on both sides. Finally, some Benelux representatives saw the organization as offering important opportunities for international cooperation and consultation among the allies by which the influence, particularly of small

55  See NATO, *NATO Handbook* (Brussels, 1969), pp. 42-45, particularly point 5.

powers was considerably increased. Dialogue such as this indicated clearly that the Benelux nations would remain the faithful allies they had been for almost twenty years. The invasion of Czechoslovakia by the Warsaw Pact only reinforced the decision. Initially alarmed, the West quickly accepted this invasion as some sort of internal readjustment within the Communist bloc, although the event certainly had an effect on the public, especially the older generations, for whom an occupation of Czechoslovakia was no novelty.

In general, Benelux public opinion *(56)* supported the decision makers in their willingness to remain part of the Atlantic alliance at the end of the 1960s and the beginning of the 1970s. An opinion poll taken by the Nederlands Instituut voor de Publieke Opinie en het Marktonderzoek (NIPO) in May 1969 *(57)* produced the following results to the question, "Holland has been a member of NATO since its creation. Should our country remain a member or withdraw?":

TABLE XII

Opinion on Dutch membership in NATO (Percentage)

|  | *Total* | *Men* | *Women* |
|---|---|---|---|
| Should stay | 65 | 70 | 60 |
| Should withdraw | 13 | 14 | 13 |
| Don't know | 22 | 16 | 27 |
|  | (100) | (100) | (100) |

Source: *NIPO-Bericht nr. 1285.*

More recent data are available from a national public opinion poll held in connection with the Dutch general elections of 1971 *(58)*. Responses on the question of continued NATO membership were as follows:

56 Information on Luxembourg public opinion is lacking.
57 NIPO, *Bericht nr. 1285*, Nederland moet lid blijven van de NATO, (Amsterdam, 1 May 1969). From a sample of 1,079 Dutch inhabitants of twenty-one years old or more.
58 A. van Staden, "Oordelen over het Nederlands buitenlands beleid", *Acta Politica* (January, 1972), 112-132.

TABLE XIII

Opinion on Dutch NATO membership by political party preference (Percentages)

| | should stay member | should not stay | don't know | no answer | totals |
|---|---|---|---|---|---|
| total of interviews | 70 | 11 | 16 | 4 | 100 |
| PvdA | 63 | 15 | 19 | 2 | 100 |
| KVP | 76 | 4 | 17 | 3 | 100 |
| VVD | 87 | 8 | 4 | 1 | 100 |
| ARP | 79 | 5 | 16 | 0 | 100 |
| D'66 | 76 | 10 | 11 | 3 | 100 |
| CHU | 76 | 5 | 16 | 3 | 100 |
| DS'70 *(59)* | 95 | 4 | 1 | 0 | 100 |
| CPN *(60)* | 48 | 42 | 2 | 2 | 100 |
| PPR *(61)* | 67 | 21 | 12 | 0 | 100 |
| PSP | 23 | 71 | 0 | 6 | 100 |

Source: van Staden, *loc. cit.*, 119.

DS'70 and VVD indicated the strongest support for the alliance; the PSP, the CPN and the PPR were most opposed. Among the larger political parties the Socialist party (PvdA) was the strongest opponent. Very curiously, more Communists wanted Holland to remain part of NATO than to leave it.

Belgian public opinion at the critical moment of the installations transfer was reflected in the results of a public opinion poll by International Research Associates held between 18 March and 20 April 1967. *(62)* It seemed to indicate that, first of all, Belgians were poorly informed on NATO's nature and function. Some 65.9 percent of those interviewed were unable to define NATO or SHAPE at all, and only 8.9 percent gave the correct answer. *(63)* On the other hand, most of the responses the poll gathered on NATO itself were positive. *(64)* The Belgian public was asked:

---

*59* A recent political grouping, the right wing of the PvdA.
*60* Communist party of the Netherlands.
*61* Politieke Partij Radikalen, the progressive wing of the KVP that formed its own party.
*62* International Research Associates, *L'implantation de l'OTAN et du SHAPE en Belgique, Rapport des résultats d'une enquête concernant les attitudes du public belge à l'égard de l'implantation de l'OTAN et du SHAPE en Belgique* (Brussels, 19 May 1967) [Hereafter *INRA Report*]
*63* See *INRA Report*, Table 1.1.
*64* *INRA Report*, Table 1.8.

"These are some measures that might possibly contribute to a better under-
standing between non-communist and communist countries. Which one do
you prefer,
- Try to conclude political and economic agreements with the Communist
  countries without dissolving NATO.
- Organize a common defense in a new organization containing only non-
  Communist European states.
- Immediately reduce the military potential of the non-Communist countries
  without waiting for a similar move by the Communists.
- Dissolve NATO".

An overwhelming 61.7 percent preferred the first solution. The second was
favored by 9.6 percent, the third by 10.7 percent, and the fourth one by just
5.3 percent. The rest (12.8 percent) had no answer.

The transfer of the NATO installations to Belgium was the crucial question
at the time the poll was taken and the Belgian public was again positive:

TABLE XIV

General Opinion on the Transfer of SHAPE in Belgium (Percentage)

|  | (N = 3,066) |
| --- | --- |
| – strongly in favor | 6.2 |
| – relatively in favor | 25.1 |
| – relatively opposed | 11.0 |
| – strongly opposed | 3.5 |
| – no opinion | 46.6 |
| – don't know; no answer | 7.6 |
|  | 100 |

Source: *INRA Report*, Table 1.6.

Nevertheless, the number of those who favored the transfer was much smaller
than those who supported NATO in general. *(65)* Table 1.5 of the *INRA
Report* mentions the "most valuable arguments pro and contra the transfer

---

65  See: *INRA Report*, Table 1.8. See also conclusion 2.2 on p. 11 of the report.

of SHAPE to Belgium." *(66)* Remarkably, purely commercial interests played a very important role in the arguments in favor of the alliance. Material concerns are behind the largest number of opposing arguments as well, although not to the same extent as in the former.

Such figures show clearly enough that Benelux public opinion by the end of the 1960s and the beginning of the 1970s was still strongly favorable to further NATO membership. Whether this attitude will be maintained in the future is still an open question. Recent developments in both Holland and Belgium suggest that some change might occur in this respect.

## PROSPECTS FOR THE 1970s: TOWARD DEALIGNMENT?

Benelux faithfulness during the first two decades of NATO's existence does not mean that membership of the alliance will be problem-free in the years to come. Although none of the allies has followed the French example and although alliance has to some extent been adapted to changing circumstances, urgent problems may at any moment cause new strains.

The first of these concerns American-European economic relations and American uneasiness with the European defense effort. In fact, the Atlantic crisis goes on, and may become more serious than ever in the next few years. Criticism on U.S.-policy in Vietnam and Latin America has grown constantly in Europe; at the same time American preparedness to intervene with nuclear weapons in Europe in case of an armed attack has become less certain. *(67)* New isolationist tendencies in the American Congress and demands for a reduction of U.S. forces in Europe have both contributed to this uncertainty. Europeans fear the shift in American attitudes as a reaction to the country's overcommitment in the world and as a response to Europe's growing economic

---

66 The most valuable arguments opposing the transfer were the following: the transfer of NATO and SHAPE to Belgium involves too many additional expenses (52.1 percent); will import too many foreigners; we will no longer feel at home (24.4 percent); risks to increase prices (32.0 percent); increases the dangers in case of war (37.4 percent); brings our country under the influence of the Americans (26.2 percent); is contrary to our country's role in the European unification (7.7 percent); diminishes the prestige of our country (4.6 percent). Among the arguments in favor of the transfer the most valuable were: will increase the international prestige of our country (36.6 percent); will bring money into Belgium (30.2 percent); will stimulate commerce and tourism (45.5 percent); will increase the influence of our country in international organizations (25.3 percent); will create new jobs (53.0 percent); proves that our country wants to contribute to the security of the Western world (29.1 percent); will contribute to the economic rélance of a disadvantaged region of our country (33.2 percent).

67 See, for example, K.P. Bloema, *Moderne politieke strategieën. Een kritiek op het defensie-en het buitenlands beleid* (The Hague, 1968), pp. 41-50.

power, seen by some Americans as a source of conflict in the U.S. international commercial and financial position. In the meantime, a Eurogroup within NATO has flourished, and Common Market countries regularly meet to discuss foreign policy problems. These developments, together with thoughts about a European Defense Community and even a European nuclear force, cannot be advantageous to U.S.-European relations, including the Atlantic alliance. On its side, the U.S. is urging the European allies to support a larger share of the common defense burden since they, especially those of the EEC, are prospering and the U.S. is experiencing serious balance-of-payments difficulties at the moment. By the end of 1970, Europe was ready to spend a little more on defense through the EDIP, and made an extra effort in the following years. How long such initiative will be able to satisfy American demands is an open question. In my opinion, only for a very short period. Nevertheless, a slight increase in defense expenditure is at this time the only alternative in the Benelux countries, since political reasons do not allow an extension of military service or the recruitment of more men. Although Luxembourg's token force of five hundred soldiers still exceeds Iceland's contribution to the alliance, it seems to be all the country can afford, and to a certain extent Belgium and Holland are also committed to their maximum defense effort. In Belgium there is a strong tendency to further reduce military service, as illustrated by the Socialists and Christian Democrats government's promise of January 1972 to lower service time for the men stationed in Germany to ten months. At the moment most parties aim at a service of six months for everybody, and a reduction of the number of individuals in service can be expected in the near future. *(68)* Since NATO considers Belgium's financial effort as a strict minimum, reductions are almost impossible, and criticism on this point is therefore much weaker. This is not the case in Holland, where the government barely managed to pass its 1972 defense budget through the Second Chamber, and where objections to the country's defense budget originate from several sources. *(69)* The talks on mutual balanced force reductions, further détente, or a greater cooperation among European NATO countries in such areas as defense procurement may open new possibilities for the further reduction of

---

68 The Belgian government's reorganization plan of November 1972 contained these points, and they also figured in the program of the new coalition government composed of Socialists, Christian Democrats, and Liberals and formed in late January 1973. See *De Standaard* (13 November 1972) and *Volksgazet* (18 January 1973).

69 Nevertheless, a majority of the van Rijckevorsel commission, which has recently been studying Dutch defense policy, recommended in its report the increase of the defense expenditure from 3.94 to 4.25 percent of the country's GNP. *De Telegraaf* (28 March 1972). The new leftist government formed in early 1973 will certainly not follow this advice.

national defense efforts. *(70)* Especially for the smaller Benelux countries, such a development would be most welcome.

A second possible source of new strains upon the Benelux countries' NATO commitments is the opposition to NATO, defense, and the military in general that has grown steadily in recent years among a variety of pressure groups. The sharpest opposition is found among the youth, especially among students, as well as in pacifist circles and left-wing groups in political parties in all three countries. To them, NATO is a typically capitalist weapon for the defense of the interests of big industry and banking. They urge détente, the abolition of all military blocs, and even a unilateral disarmament to free energy and money for aid to the Third World and for the internal needs of a modern, more humane society.

Beginning in 1973, the next few years will be crucial to the Benelux nations' continued membership in NATO. In both Holland and Belgium, elements for a great public debate on NATO and defense policy seem to be developing. The futility of increased spending in a time of nuclear parity, the growing interest in détente, and pacifism are all factors in the growing disillusion among the population. Strong popular uneasiness over past U.S. policy in Vietnam and over the presence in NATO of undemocratic régimes such as Portugal, Greece, and Turkey are important as well. Especially in Holland, the latter point seems to have had a strong impact on the discussion taking place in most political parties and many other groups. The heavy U.S. bombing of North Vietnam in late December 1972 substantially influenced this debate and led to a sharp reaction in Dutch public opinion. *(71)* Whether European unification and Atlantic cooperation are compatible is also under discussion in Holland at the moment. Moreover, new advocates for a neutral policy have emerged. Such a policy might be, of course, one of the many choices open to all of Western Europe once a process of real détente and dealignment is underway. And one of its ultimate consequences could be a substantial growth of Soviet influence in this part of the European continent, a process known as Finlandization.

In Belgium, demonstrations among young people and school strikes precipitated by the government's new reorganization plan for the army have initiated

70  In May 1972, the Eurogroup reached an agreement on the principles for future cooperation in the procurement of military equipment.
71  This point was formulated well by Mr. van der Louw, president of the Dutch Socialist Party (PvdA): "The tension between the rational consideration to stay in NATO and the immoral behavior of the American allies becomes more and more unbearable". *NRC Handelsblad* (8 January 1973). For the view of the KVP (Catholic People's Party), see de *Volkskrant* (9 January 1973). Of course, the end of the Vietnam war has eased this criticism.

intense public discussion of the country's defense policy. Behind the direct criticism on particular points in the program is an antimilitarist feeling that questions Belgium's defense effort and its NATO obligations. In addition, Belgian political parties are also discussing and reconsidering the country's military options.

This does not mean that these public debates will lead to an immediate change in official Benelux policy. However, growing détente and cooperation in Europe, the possibility of positive results of a European Security Conference, of the talks on MBFR and SALT, plus increasing internal pacifism and anti-militarism may lead to a substantial alteration in the nature of their NATO membership. But the crucial factor in the issue will be the outcome of the U.S.-European negotiations on matters of trade, finance, and military burden-sharing. Finally, the evolution of European integration will influence this whole process. The ultimate result might well be a dissolution of both NATO and the Warsaw Pact. But questions on alternatives to the organizations, as well as on the actual security of Western Europe if such an occurence takes place, can only be speculation at the present time.

# CONCLUSION

Largely because of the failure of both neutrality and of collective security, political leaders from the Low Countries operating in London during World War II advanced regional alliances as a framework for postwar security in Europe. In their minds, such groupings were totally compatible with the new universal organization for peace and security being created toward the end of World War II.

In 1945 and 1946 the emphasis of their policies changed markedly in favor of the UN, however, and in a remarkable show of goodwill they agreed to give it a fair chance. Therefore they tried to avoid alarming the Soviet Union through the creation of a Western European defense organization, which might have harmed cooperation among the superpowers and thus weakened the UN. In addition, U.S. pressure as well as British and French reluctance toward a regional organization certainly influenced the Benelux countries' favorable attitude towards the UN in this period. Understanding among big powers very quickly proved illusory, however, while at the same time the Western European democracies were confronted with serious economic problems. Fear of Soviet expansionism and Communist ideology, plus the need for economic cooperation and aid, were the main factors that drove the weakened Western European democracies to regional alliances in 1948 and 1949.

The role of the Benelux countries in the creation of both the Brussels pact and the North Atlantic alliance has not been unimportant. On the contrary, their influence on the content of the former was decisive, and in this way they facilitated to a certain extent U.S. commitment in a larger Atlantic alliance. From its initiation NATO became the cornerstone of Benelux foreign and defense policies, and the price of the security provided by the alliance from 1949 to the present has been rather low, even very low in the case of Belgium and Luxembourg. Growing demands for welfare policies, promises by political parties to cut the length of military service, growing pacifism, in short, a lack of political will and of a militarist tradition have not favored the maintenance of the military effort the international situation and the evolving NATO strategy demanded. However, defense efforts have been steadily decreasing in many European NATO countries since the mid-fifties, and the Benelux nations are no exception to a pattern which has been a source of uneasiness among U.S. officials. Holland has been part of this downward trend, although its defense expenditure is still a good deal higher than that of Belgium and Luxembourg. Partly for this reason, partly because of its outspoken pro-NATO position, Holland has played an important role in enhancing small powers' possibilities for consultation among the allies in the 1960s. On the other hand, Belgium's less vocal stance and its rather low defense expenditure has undoubtedly facilitated that nation's ability to further NATO's détente policy. On the whole, Belgium operates more on a systemic level, within the East-West system, whereas Holland participates more on a subsystemic level within the alliance.

So far, the Benelux countries have been very faithful allies, and in the late 1960s the alliance apparently still enjoyed the support of a large majority in both their Parliaments and among their populations. Only a few smaller political parties pressed for dissolution of NATO or at least for immediate withdrawal of their country. However, in Belgium the opposition against the transfer of NATO installations was much larger than the traditional opposition to the alliance as a whole. Those who opposed the transfer were afraid for two reasons. NATO presence on their territory would make them more vulnerable to attack in case of war. In addition, Belgium's position as an advocate of détente might be impaired. And although Belgium experienced some difficulty in finding sufficient parliamentary support for the new commitment, Luxembourg's case was worse. In that country all political parties approved the end of the compulsory military service by 1967 and the creation of a very small volunteer army. In terms of defense expenditure Luxembourg is certainly the least faithful of the three countries, although its NATO membership as such has never been seriously questioned. Holland is the most faithful, not only in its political attitude but also through a defense expenditure still considerably higher than that of Belgium and especially that of Luxembourg.

By the end of the 1960s, the motivation for continued NATO membership differed in some respects from that which decided the Benelux countries to enter the alliance in 1949. The main motive, security, was still the same, but in 1969 security was defined in terms of both defense and détente, clearly a change of emphasis, if not of concept, in comparison with 1949. Moreover, attractive prospects for military and economic aid were no longer a factor, and NATO's image as protector of Western civilization and ideology had certainly declined with growing détente. On the other hand, many people saw NATO as providing an opportunity for small powers to expand their role and influence in international politics, and they advanced strong demands for more political consultation and cooperation within the alliance. Yet increasing tensions between Western Europe and the United States, growing East-West détente, further European integration, and spreading popular opposition to NATO and defense expenditure may well lead to changes in Benelux defense policies and alliance membership in the years to come.

# GENERAL CONCLUSIONS

by Omer De Raeymaeker

# MOTIVES FOR ALIGNMENT

Relationships among powers at the close of the second world war made it possible for the Soviet Union to recoup a great deal of territories in Eastern Europe that had formerly been under the domination of the Russian Empire. Estonia, Latvia, Lithuania, and parts of Finland and Poland returned to Russian suzerainty in this manner, and, northeastern Prussia, eastern Czechoslovakia, and Moldavia were annexed to the Soviet state. Moreover, after the German defeat, the power vacuum in Europe and the strength of the Red army presented Soviet leaders with the opportunity to realize another double objective of Soviet foreign policy. By extending and consolidating their influence deep into east central Europe and by establishing Communist régimes in Poland, Hungary, Rumania, and Bulgaria, they furthered the interests of world Communism as well as the traditional, security-based, national interests of the Soviet state. In addition, they were able to exert pressure either directly or indirectly on an area traditionally an objective of Russian penetration, the eastern Mediterranean and northern Iran. This process of power extension and satellization culminated in the Czech coup of 1948.

As a result of these moves, most Western nations came to see the Soviet Union as an aggressive expansionist power, although whether Western Europe was actually threatened by Soviet imperialism is a matter for debate. The fear was omnipresent, however, especially since the U.S.S.R. had the means to use to its advantage powerful and subservient Communist parties, particularly in Italy and France. Difficult economic straits and a resultant social unrest made Western Europe's democratic institutions unusually vulnerable to the kind of threat these parties were seen to be. In his 1948 speech before the U.N. General Assembly, Belgian Foreign Minister Spaak articulated the common feeling: "There is but one Great Power that emerged from the war having conquered other territories, and that Power is the U.S.S.R."

## SECURITY IN RELATION TO THE GEOGRAPHICAL SITUATION

Faced with Soviet expansion, the nations of Europe recognized the need to seek adequate means of guaranteeing their security, and they turned to the U.S., the only country powerful enough to confront Soviet strength. Thus security was the overriding consideration for small nations after the war, and alliance an expedient means to attain it. Yet this motive for becoming members in the North Atlantic Treaty Organization was not equally important to all of them.

In *Greece* and *Turkey* security was crucial. These countries were the first to feel the effects of Communist internal subversion and/or outside pressure. In Greece a civil war raged, and Communist guerrilla forces supported by Bulgaria, Yugoslavia, and Albania were on the verge of a complete takeover. The British inability to continue military and economic support to the Greek government made prospects very bad indeed, and clearly, unless the U.S. intervened Greece would become a Communist state. At this point American and Greek government interests coincided. Greece's strategic geographic situation was too important to allow a gradual absorption of this small Balkan country into the Soviet orbit. Moreover, Greece's political and military ties with the West were a matter of record. On the other hand, Turkey enjoyed a strong tradition of neutrality in foreign and military policy, and would have seriously considered the continuation of Atatürk's nonalignment principles, had the Soviet Union not presented a real and menacing threat. The Turks stood alone for some time, and even without full Western backing they refused to negotiate with the Soviets about the existing régime of the straits and on the territorial status of the Kars-Ardahan districts. The Truman Doctrine was introduced to alleviate the situation, and Greece and Turkey became America's first allies in the containment of Soviet expansion. Although not a formal alliance, the doctrine institutionalized various economic and military ties between the U.S. and the two Mediterranean countries.

World War II had proven to *Scandinavia* that, in a global conflict, its territories -- both the land itself and the waters surrounding it -- were too important to be left unoccupied. When the postwar antagonism between the U.S. and the U.S.S.R. crystallized into the Cold War, the strategic importance of the Scandinavian countries grew in turn, situated as they were between the new land power, Russia, and the leading sea power, America, each with interests projected on the West European mainland. In particular Norway, a traditional maritime and trading nation with a long and vulnerable coast and sharing a common border with the Soviet Union, sought political and military guarantees with the Atlantic powers. But Norway and Denmark were also aware of Soviet needs for security, and they made every attempt to keep the conflict over control of continental Europe from spreading to Scandinavia. They gave as low a profile to their alliance membership as possible by refusing to allow foreign troops and later nuclear warheads on their territory.

To the *Benelux countries* the desillusion about the failure of collective security was very great because they had put all their faith in it. On the other hand, their leaders were realistic enough to understand the necessity for a true balance of power on the European continent. By promoting the idea of a regional defensive grouping within the U.N., they helped turn the Franco-British alliance originating in the Dunkirk Treaty into a West European one realized by the Brussels Pact. From its inception, this Western defense scheme was intended as an invitation to the U.S. to participate in and support the European defense effort. Not surprisingly, therefore, the three Benelux countries wholeheartedly joined the Atlantic alliance.

Although *Portugal* saw security as important, defense was not its major reason for joining the Atlantic alliance. Thousands of miles from Moscow, Lisbon could not perceive the Soviet military build-up in Central Europe as an immediate threat to its own independence and territorial integrity. Yet Prime Minister Salazar shared the view of most European and American statesmen of the period that with the German bulwark dismantled Slavic Communism would spread all over Europe if nothing were done to stop it. The danger was imminent. Europe, still free, could survive only if united, and Portugal would not undermine the collective Western defense effort by refusing to participate in it.

## PRESTIGE OR STATUS IN THE INTERNATIONAL COMMUNITY

Compared with security, prestige or status in the international community is a less tangible motive for a nation to adhere to an alliance or to pursue a policy of alignment. Yet it did influence some small NATO members. *Portugal* is the most obvious of these. Its participation in a great democratic Western alliance gave the country a democratic image abroad. Portugal accepted its invitation into NATO with pride, especially since Spain was not to be a part of the new organization.

For several reasons *Greece and Turkey* were not among NATO's founding members, although the Truman Doctrine had brought both countries within the American defense perimeter even before the North Atlantic Treaty was signed. Prestige definitely played a role in their relentless struggle to be included. This is particularly true for Turkey, which was anxious to promote its image as a European country. Moreover, the unequal power relationship between the Greeks, the Turks, and the U.S. had already created some animosity; in these terms a multilateral organization could provide the psychological satisfaction of equal treatment. For Greece and Turkey belonging to the Atlantic alliance was a matter of honor, and parliamentary ratification was merely routine.

Far from seeing in their NATO membership a means of enhancing their prestige, *Scandinavian leaders* felt that their membership brought with it a loss of status. They abandoned their neutral bridge-building role, they were forced to participate in loathed power politics, and they lost all chance for Nordic unity. Norway from the beginning had urged continued cooperation with the Atlantic powers, however; it saw in its NATO membership a mere continuation of its wartime policies.

Although the *Benelux countries* did not enter the Atlantic pact for reasons of prestige, once members, they made good use of the status membership brought them. It is no accident, for example, that three out of the five NATO secretaries-general have come from a Benelux country.

## DOMESTIC STABILITY

Domestic stability as a motive for alignment was perhaps most important in *Greece*, where the immediate postwar years were characterized by governmental instability. Threatened by Communist guerrilla forces, the ruling elite sought American economic and military assistance, thereby linking the internal situation directly to the alignment process. Moreover, the U.S. viewed Greek government stability as a prerequisite for the successful implementation of its military and economic programs, and various interventions into Greek internal affairs illustrate American concern. Because of its traditional one-party rule the situation in *Turkey* was quite different. Stability played no part in the decision to ally; the entire Turkish population stood united behind the government in its diplomatic war with the Soviet Union. During the Menderes administration, however, it was feared, particularly within the Republican People's party, that NATO and the U.S. would prohibit the ouster of the oppressive Menderes government, and in fact it seems reasonable to assume that Menderes remained in power for almost a decade because he identified his government with America's stake in Turkey.

*Portugal*'s alignment with NATO not only increased its prestige abroad but did much to improve the government's position at home. Admission into the community of democratic nations was an excellent argument against liberal opposition, and gave Salazar virtually unlimited security of tenure without permitting foreign interference with Portuguese sovereignty. Salazar saw clearly that the vagueness of the treaty's preamble would result only in an anti-Communist interpretation of its principles.

396

Internal stability was not overly important in the *Benelux* countries except in the broader framework of West European political, economic, and social stability. In this sense, the Benelux political elite welcomed both Marshall aid and NATO as means to combat possible Communist subversion, since economic recovery and social stability were not possible without simultaneous provisions for external safety.

On the other hand, internal stability had some impact in the three *Scandinavian* NATO countries, although in ways opposite those their partners experienced. There, membership in the Western alliance was contrary to very widespread and deeply-felt commitments to neutrality and noninvolvement with power politics, and provoked strong opposition among broad segments of the population.

## ECONOMIC AID AND MILITARY ASSISTANCE

The prospect of military and economic aid was certainly among the major considerations in the alignment process.

Military aid was crucial for the beleaguered *Greek* government, especially once British assistance ended, and American materiel and supplies were instrumental in the final defeat of the communist forces. Economically, the second world war followed immediately by calamitous civil war had left Greece bankrupt. Material damages reached an astronomical figure, and American aid was crucial in alleviating the situation. American military and economic missions poured into Greece, where they were entrusted with final authority in the reconstruction of the Greek army and the implementation of stringent economic programs. Armed neutrality had saved *Turkey* from severe war damage. However, the maintenance of a 500,000-man army proved too costly for the precarious Turkish economy. As in Greece, American experts were responsible for economic and military rehabilitation programs.

Unlike their allies, who entered the alliance primarily to obtain material help, *Norway, Denmark,* and *Iceland* were motivated by security. Independent plans for a Scandinavian defense pact were forestalled by the American refusal to supply arms of sufficient quality and quantity to modernize and rebuild the Norwegian and Danish armed forces. Once members of NATO, however, both countries received substantial U.S. aid, enabling them to keep the economic strains of rearmament at an absolute minimum. Allied help freed other resources for welfare programs and further growth.

Differing war experiences made the need for economic assistance greater in *Holland* and *Luxemburg* than in *Belgium*. Nevertheless, each country was allotted sizeable amounts of American financial aid. In fact, the Benelux countries as a group ranked second on the list of beneficiaries of U.S. largess in the period between 1949 and 1952. Clearly, their participation in the Marshall Aid Program and their dependence on U.S. military assistance were major incentives to ally within the North Atlantic Treaty.

The significant financial, economic, and military assistance that usually tempts a small country into alignment had little effect in *Portugal* at the end of the forties. At the time Prime Minister Salazar believed that Portugal could develop a viable economy alone. He particularly feared the political consequences of economic dependence, and felt aid should go to those countries most exposed to the Soviet threat.

## IDEOLOGY

Salazar's political philosophy was violently anti-Communist. He saw atheistic Communism as the heresy of the epoch, a worldwide, monolithic conspiracy of evil forces pitted against the political and moral values he believed the West should stand for, and he had no difficulty in supporting anti-Communist movements wholeheartedly. In fact, containing the Communist menace was allowed to override all previous Portuguese efforts at isolation.

Ideology was undoubtedly a factor in the alignment of both *Greece* and *Turkey*. In Turkey traditional hostility toward Russia combined with fervent anti-Communism prompted the move toward alliance. Moreover, Turkey wanted to impress the West about its intentions to be a Western-type democracy. The one-party rule was officially ended and new parties were allowed to compete for political power. In Greece, memories of the civil war and the threat of a final conflict with the Greek Communists produced a political climate favorable to the conservative and rightists parties.

In the *Benelux countries* the spectre of Soviet hegemony in Europe added to fear of Communist ideology. The Benelux leaders hoped that NATO would safeguard the principles of democracy, rule of law, and individual liberty as vital parts of the common western culture.

This was equally true for the *Scandinavian* countries. In these progressive nations, where social-democratic influence is traditionally strong and whose

socialist-oriented or controlled governments have consistently sponsered programs to further public welfare, fear of Communist ideology understandingly
was less great than in, say, Portugal. Yet Marxism infused Soviet behavior
with a vitality that has made the Scandinavians particularly wary in their
relations with the East.

## MOTIVES FOR POSSIBLE DEALIGNMENT

In the late 1940s and early 1950s the world was clearly bipolar, both militarily -- on the nuclear and the conventional level -- as well as politically, and
the monolithic nature of both blocs left little room for maneuverability to the
smaller states. Less powerful nations possessed no viable alternative to almost
total dependence on U.S. leadership. This reduced the theoretical interest in the
Atlantic alliance in its early period. The present international system is bipolar
only at the nuclear level, however, and has become so complex that policy
choices for the small powers are not only possible but necessary. Indeed, the
changed nature of the international situation has led some small NATO
partners to question their participation in the Atlantic organization. Dealignment, while not the obvious policy, was one of the positions the following
factors again made possible:

1) changes in technology and nuclear strategy, from massive retaliation to
   flexible response;
2) a more sophisticated perception by the leaders of small states of the
   significance of nuclear weapons;
3) changes within NATO precipitated by French withdrawal from the
   organization;
4) changes in East-West relations and their bearing on the European security
   issue; and
5) changes in small states' perception of the U.S. commitment to Europe
   and U.S. credibility, damaged by the American involvement in a major
   land war in Southeast Asia.

Many of the small states initiated prolonged debates on the advantages and
disadvantages of their continued membership in the Atlantic alliance. Then in
1968 the Warsaw Pact invasion of Czechoslovakia put an abrupt end to the
growing dealignment tendencies.

## SECURITY IN RELATION TO THE GEOGRAPHICAL SITUATION

The Soviet naval presence in the Mediterranean and the Arab Middle East seemed to indicate that the traditional Russian objectives in these areas have remained unchanged. This and the Soviet invasion of Czechoslovakia stiffed any interest the *Turks* had fostered in a return to neutralism. The suppression of free discussion and parliamentary democracy precluded debate in *Greece*, where military rulers insisted that NATO remained crucial to Greek national security. Yet in this case the Cyprus situation was, and perhaps continues to be, a unique factor in Greece's and Turkey's relationship with NATO. Neutralist tendencies in both countries as well as subsequent anti-American and anti-NATO feelings were at least initially the result of nationalism. Conflict over dominance on the island stirred chauvinistic emotions which were soon almost beyond control. The "neutral" attitude of the other NATO allies, especially the U.S., to the situation created bitterness and resentment among Greeks and Turks alike. Each claimant in the conflict sees NATO and the U.S. as fundamental obstacles to the realization of its goals.

In general, the *Scandinavian* members of NATO felt a loosening of pressure in the 1960s. The confrontation between the Soviets and the Americans was becoming institutionalized and as a result less dangerous. In particular Denmark and Iceland, always the least threatened of the group, felt increasingly secure in that decade. Had it not been for the 1968 invasion of Czechoslovakia, their governments might have felt it more difficult to overcome anti-alliance feelings among the population and to maintain their NATO-membership. Norway's attitude alone was different. As the only nation on NATO's northern flank to face the historical conversion of the Soviet Union from a land to a sea power, and constantly aware of Soviet naval pressure down a long and vulnerable coast, Norway had strong security reasons for remaining in NATO after 1969.

In the *Benelux nations* the hope for further relaxation of tensions also ran high, although the consensus agreed that no lasting détente was possible without a strong defense. They never seriously considered leaving the alliance, and events in Czechoslovakia served to strengthen that position.

Rebellions in its overseas territories threw the whole of *Portugal*'s defense and diplomatic effort toward the preservation of suzerainty in these provinces. The Soviet Union was seen less as a direct menace to Europe than as a dangerous support for rebels against the remains of Europe's colonial empire. As a result, Portugal consistently pleaded for the extension of NATO guarantees to the area south of the Tropic of Cancer.

## PRESTIGE OR STATUS IN THE INTERNATIONAL COMMUNITY

*Greek* and *Turkish* leaders saw continued membership in NATO as a means to increase status in the international community. In *Denmark* and *Norway*, most officials agreed that the amount of goodwill their leaving the alliance would earn them from nonaligned countries would be more than offset by the simultaneous disaffection of Western industrialized countries, where their real economic and political interests lay. Moreover, both countries had committed themselves to the Common Market, and there seemed to be no reason to split from their European partners on the security issue. NATO offered the *Benelux* countries important opportunities for international cooperation and consultation. The Harmel proposal, their presence in the Nuclear Planning Group, their housing of NATO headquarters all served to augment their status in the international community.

The preservation of *Portugal*'s prestige in the international community made that country's continued participation in the Atlantic alliance vital. Consequently, its opposition to NATO policy was never more than vocal. Even if it threatened not to be among the last to leave the alliance, Portugal clearly could not keep up resistance in Africa without the tacit agreement of most of NATO's members. Without NATO Portugal would risk complete isolation in Europe and Afro-Asia, deprived of all support except that of the white régimes in southern Africa.

### DOMESTIC STABILITY

NATO continued to lend strength to the *Portuguese* government, which had managed to forestall liberal opposition by claiming that Portugal's alliance with countries founded on democratic principles was proof that Salazarism was not as reactionary and oppressive as some critics said. Without doubt, Portugal's membership in NATO continued to bolster the security of tenure of the Salazarian elite.

In *Greece and Turkey* partnership in NATO has had a debilitating effect on the position of the ruling elite. Once backed by massive public support, the Atlantic alliance and the U.S. are now criticized intensely by the Turkish population. The growing political instability in Turkey is demonstrated by the intervention of the Turkish military in 1970. Of course, NATO is only one of many variables that have stimulated political unrest in recent years, but the days when the organization was a cohesive element in Turkey's internal politics are gone. Between 1964 and 1967, Greece's internal situation deteriorated, culminating in Papandreou's fall and the apparent failure of democracy. Again NATO was by no means the only factor which created domestic instability; the crisis was far more the result of internal conditions than of foreign policy issues. Yet the present Greek situation offers an excellent example of how the U.S. can be helpful, even decisive, in keeping a ruling elite in power. In the Greek case, Washington's motivations are apparently purely military and strategic, and connected with NATO's southern wing. But whatever its rationale, the American presence definitely strengthens the position of the military junta.

In *Scandinavia* political stability also became an increasingly important factor, albeit a negative one, in the 1960s. Membership in an alliance that also included countries like Greece, a military dictatorship, or Portugal and the United States, perpetrators of imperial wars in Africa and Southeast Asia, colored Norway's and Denmark's continued membership in the alliance with an undercurrent of unrest. In Iceland, the physical presence of American troops and their impact on the identity and cultural homogeneity of the population led directly to strong anti-American and even anti-NATO sentiments.

The *Benelux* countries experienced no serious threats to their internal stability in the sixties. Nevertheless, a small but vocal fraction of public opinion, particularly the youth, became increasingly critical of NATO during that period.

## ECONOMIC AID AND MILITARY ASSISTANCE

Economic and military aid ceased to be among alliance considerations in the *Benelux* and *Scandinavian* countries. As such aid had been stopped almost completely by the midsixties.

Foreign aid remains crucial for the realization of *Turkish* development plans, while in *Greece* economic dependence on the U.S. decreased when the country began experiencing a real economic boom. On the other hand, only continued American military assistance programs prevent Greek defense expenditures from becoming unbearable.

Since the early sixties NATO had become of utmost importance for *Portugal*. Major NATO allies, in particular the U.S., were the sources of economic and financial support as well as military assistance and arms sales that made the

402

costly African wars possible. As could be expected, the situation in the overseas territories had caused a complete reversal in Portugal's anti-foreign aid policy.

## IDEOLOGY

Over the years, the three *Scandinavian* and the *Benelux* members of the Atlantic alliance had become aware that whatever threat still emanates from the Soviet Union springs more from traditional great power interests than from the ideological fervor of a revolutionary régime.
*Portugal, Greece*, and *Turkey* did not depart from their traditional anti-Communist, conservative course. Far from the forefront in the fight for détente, their governments continued to use anti-Marxism to curtail opposition.

\*  \*  \*

In the introduction of this book we stated that the core of the study evolved around the small powers' basic strategic choices in a world which, in part because of alliances, aims at equilibrium. We have assumed that a small power elite making decisions about alignment, nonalignment, and dealignment seeks to maintain or improve its position in the international, regional or domestic arena. To supply reliable guidance in analyzing alignment and nonalignment motives, we set up an unpretentious yet operational framework of analysis based on five motives or determinants. The movement toward or away from alliance was supposed to be a function of these five motives: security, the status of states and régimes in the international community, domestic stability, economic aid and military assistance, and ideology. A small power's basic strategic choice was supposed to be based on the hypothetical gains and liabilities associated with each of the main grounds for alliance or nonalliance. This study confirms the above hypothesis. In each case under investigation we found that most of the motives did play a role, although, it is true, in different ways. Whether interstate or intergroup conflicts determined a small country's position depended on their relative intensity.

# BIBLIOGRAPHY

BIBLIOGRAPHY

I. GENERAL WORKS ON SMALL POWERS AND ALLIANCES

## 1. Books

Aron, R. *Palx et guerre entre les nations*. Paris: Calmann-Lévy, 1962.

Benedict, B. *Problems of Smaller Territories*. London: Athlone Press, 1967.

De Raeymaeker, O. "Betekenis van de alliantie-oplossing voor de kleinere landen". *Eeuw-feest Krijgsschool 1870-1970*. Edited by Krijgsschool. Brussels, 1971.

Fox Baker, A. *The Power of Small States. Diplomacy in World War II*. Chicago: Chicago University Press, 1959.

Liska, G. *Alliances and the Third World*. Baltimore: Johns Hopkins Press, 1968.

Liska, G. *Nations in Alliance*. Baltimore: Johns Hopkins Press, 1962.

Mathisen, T. *The Functions of Small States in the Strategies of the Great Powers*. Oslo: Universitetsforlaget, 1971.

Osgood, R. *Alliances and American Foreign Policy*. Baltimore: Johns Hopkins Press, 1968.

Robinson, E. *Economic Consequences of the Size of Nations*. London: Macmillan, 1960.

Rothstein, R. *Alliances and Small Powers*. New York: Columbia University Press, 1968.

Vital, D. *The Inequality of States*. Oxford: Clarendon Press, 1967.

Vital, D. *The Survival of Small States. Studies in Small Power — Great Power Conflict*. London: Oxford University Press, 1971.

Wright, Q. *A Study of War*. Chicago: Chicago University Press, 1965.

## 2. Articles

Bjøl, E. "The Power of the Weak." *Cooperation and Conflict*, XI, No. 3 (1968), 157-168.

De Raeymaeker, O. "La signification de l'appartenance à une alliance pour les petits états." *Chronique de politique étrangère*, XXIV, No. 1 (1971).

Keohane, R. "Lilliputian Dilemmas: Small States in International Politics." *International Organization*, XXIII, No. 2 (1969), 293-294.

Paterson, E. "The Western European Small States in the Modern World." *Internationale Spectator*, XXV, No. 3 (1971), 333-342.

Van Staden, A. "Opvattingen over het begrip 'kleine staat'." *Internationale Spectator*, XXV, No. 9 (1971), 908-923.

II. PORTUGAL

## 1. Public Documents

Portugal. Ministry of Foreign Affairs. *Dez anos de politica externa, 1936-1947*, Vol. i-v. A collection of diplomatic papers (Lisbon: Ministry of Foreign Affairs, 1961-5).

Portugal. Bank of Portugal. *Report of the Board of Directors Statement of the Audit- Council for the year 1968*. (Lisbon: Printing Works of the Bank of Portugal, 1969).

UN General Assembly. *Official Records* (A/PV 947) December 14, 1960, 21.

UN General Assembly. *Official Records* (A/PV 1097) January 25, 1962, 1279.

UN Security Council. *Official Records* (S/PV 946) March 15, 1961, 21.

UN Secretariat. *Statistical Yearbook of the U.N., 1969*. Twenty First Issue (New York, 1970), 563.

U.S. Congress, House. *U.S. Overseas Loans and Grants from International Organizations -- July 1, 1945 - June 30, 1965)*. Special Report prepared for the House Foreign Affairs Committee (Washington, D.C.: U.S.G.P.O.).

U.S. Congress, Senate. *Foreign Aid Program: Compilation of Studies*. Special Committee to Study the Foreign Aid Program; Compilation of Studies — Survey presented by Theodore Francis Green, Chairman (Washington, D.C.: U.S.G.P.O., 1957).

U.S. Department of State. *Foreign Relations of the United States, 1943. Diplomatic Papers*. Europe vol. II (Washington D.C.: U.S.G.P.O., 1964).

U.S. Department of State. "Importance of Azores Agreement to the U.S.: Summary of Negotiations with Portugal." *Department of State Bulletin*, XVIII, No. 469 (1948), 839.

U.S. Department of State. U.S. Treaties and Other International Agreements. "Mutual Defense Assistance Agreement between the U.S. and Portugal." TIAS No. 2187 (Washington, D.C.: U.S.G.P.O.).

U.S. Department of State. U.S. Treaties and Other International Agreements. "Defense Agreement between Portugal and the U.S.A. signed at Lisbon, Sept. 6, 1951." TIAS No. 3087 (Washington, D.C.: U.S.G.P.O.).

U.S. Department of State. United States Treaties and Other International Agreements. "Exchange of Notes between the Portuguese Minister for Foreign Affairs and the American Ambassador." TIAS No. 3791 (Washington, D.C.: U.S.G.P.O., 1957).

## 2. Books

Ayling, S.E. *Portraits of Power. An Introduction to Twentieth-Century History through the Lives of Seventeen Great Political Leaders*. New York: Barnes and Noble, 1963.

Bosgra, S., and Dijk, A. *De strijd tegen het portugese kolonialisme: Angola, Mozambique, Guinea*. Amsterdam: Paris, 1969.

Churchill, W.S. *The Second World War*. Vols I-IV. London: Cassell, 1948-51.

*Colóquios de Politíca Internacional*. Estudos de ciências políticas e sociais, No. 3. Lisboa: Junta de investigações do Ultramar; Centro de estudos políticos e sociais, 1960.

Crollen, L. *Portugal, the U.S. and NATO*. Leuven: Leuven University Press, 1973.

De Carvalho, H.M. *O Pacto Atlântico e a política mundial*. Lisboa: Editora Gráfica Portuguesa, 1955.

De Carvalho, H.M. *Política externa Portuguesa*. Estudos de ciências políticas e sociais, No 70. Lisboa: Junta de investigações do Ultramar; Centro de estudos políticos e sociais, 1964.

De Carvalho, H.M. *Portugal e o Pacto Atlântico*. Lisboa: Editora Gráfica Portuguesa, 1953.

De Medeiros, C. *Conceitos de Política Atlantica*. Lisboa: A.M. Pereira, 1968.

*Dictionnaire politique de Salazar*. Etabli par Jacques Ploncard d'Assac. Lisbonne: S.N.I.,1964.

Eden, A. *The Reckoning*. London: Casswell, 1965.

Ferro, A. *Salazar: Portugal and her leader*. London: Faber and Faber, 1939.

Fryer, P. and McGowan Pinheiro, P., *Oldest Ally: A Portrait of Salazar's Portugal*. London: D. Dobson, 1961.

*Investments in Portugal*. Lisbon: Banco de Fomento Nacional, 1968.

Kay, H. *Salazar and Modern Portugal*. London: Eyre and Spottiswoode, 1970.

Kennan, G.F. *Memoirs, 1925-1950*. Boston: Little, Brown, and Company, 1967.

Lawrence, L. *Nehru Seizes Goa*. New York: Pageant Press, 1963.

*La Pensée de Salazar*. Lisbonne: Ed. S.P.N., 117.

*Le Portugal et son économie*. Bruxelles: Office belge du commerce extérieur, 1960.

Massis, H. *Salazar face à face: Trois dialogues politiques*. Paris: La Palatine, 1961.

Medlicott, W.N. *The Economic Blockade*. London: Her Majesty's Stationery Office, 1952.

Moreira, A. *Portugals Überseepolitik*. Baden-Baden: Verlag Lutzeyer, 1963.

Ploncard d'Assac, J. *Dictionnaire politique de Salazar*. Lisbonne: S.N.I., 1964.

*Portuguese Foreign Policy. 1965: Extracts from Statements Made by the Portuguese Minister for Foreign Affairs Dr. Franco Nogueira*. Lisbon: Ministry for Foreign Affairs.

*Portuguese Foreign Policy, 1965-1967: Extracts from Statements Made by the Portuguese Minister for Foreign Affairs Dr. Franco Nogueira*. Lisbon: Ministry for Foreign Affairs.

Portugal: *Economic and Commercial Conditions, 1945-1948*. London: His Majesty's Stationery Office, 1949.

Schlesinger, A. *A thousand Days: Kennedy in the White House*. London: André Deutsch, 1965.

Wainhouse, D. *Remnants of Empire: The United Nations and the End of Colonialism*. New York: Harper and Row, 1964.

Whitaker, A.P. *Spain and the Defense of the West*. New York: Harper and Brothers, 1961.

## 3. Articles

"Air Transit Agreement with Portugal." *Department of State Bulletin*, XVIII, No 450 (1948), 231.

"Agreement on Transit Use of Azores Airfields." *Department of State Bulletin*, XIV, No 364 (1946), 1080-1087.

Caetano, M. "L'alliance Anglo-Portugaise: histoire et situation actuelle." *Chronique de politique étrangère*, XX, No 6 (1967), 695-708.

Jenner, P. "Iberian Atlantic Command watches over Crossroads of the Seas." *NATO Review*, XIX (1971), 5-8.

O'Ballance, E. "Portugal's War Potential." *Military Review*, XLIV, No 8 (1964), 84-90.

"The Anglo-Portuguese Alliance." *The British Survey*, No 207 (June, 1966), 1-20.

Wheeler, D.L. "Thaw in Portugal." *Foreign Affairs*, XLVIII, No 4 (July, 1970), 759-781.

III. GREECE AND TURKEY

## 1. Public Documents

U.S. Congress, House. *U.S. Overseas Loans and Grants from International Organizations —* July 1, 1945 - June 30, 1965). Special Report prepared for the House Foreign Affairs Committee (Washington, D.C.: U.S.G.P.O.).

World Peace Foundation. *Documents on American Foreign Relations, 1947.* Vol. IX. Princeton, N.Y.: Princeton University Press, 1949.

Hurewitz, J.C. *Diplomacy in the Near and Middle East. A Documentary Record.* 1914-1956, Vol. II. Princeton, N.Y.: D. Van Nostrand, 1956.

## 2. Books

Acheson, D. *Present at the Creation. My Years at the State Department.* New York: W.W. Norton and Company, 1969.

Adams, T.W. and Cottrell, A.J. *Cyprus between East and West.* Baltimore: The Johns Hopkins Press, 1968.

Campbell, J.C. *Defense of the Middle East. Problems of American Policy.* New York: Frederick A. Praeger, 1960.

Carey, J.P.C. and Carey, A.G. *The Web of Modern Greek Politics.* New York: Columbia University Press, 1968.

Couloumbis, T.A. *Greek Political Reaction to American and Nato Influences.* New Haven: Yale University Press, 1966.

Dendias, M.A. *The Truman Doctrine and the Freedom of Greece.* Athens: National and Capodistrian University of Athens, 1967.

Djilas, M. *Conversations with Stalin.* New York: Harcourt, Brace and World, Inc., 1962.

Erkin, F.C. *Les Relations Turco-Soviétiques et la Question des Détroits.* Ankara, Başnur Matbaasi, 1968.

Giritli, I. *Fifty Years of Turkish Political Development, 1919-1969.* Istanbul: Fakülteler Matbaasi, 1969.

Hammond, P.Y. *The Cold War Years: American Foreign Policy since 1945.* New York: Harcourt, Brace and World, Inc., 1969.

Hurewitz, J.C. *Middle East Politics. The Military Dimension.* New York: Frederick A. Praeger, 1968.

Hurewitz, J.C. *Soviet-American Rivalry in the Middle East.* New York: Capital City Press, 1969.

Jones, J.M. *The Fifteen Weeks.* New York: Harcourt, Brace and World, Inc., 1955.

Kennan, G.F. *Memoirs 1925-1950.* Boston: Little, Brown and Company, 1967.

Lewis, B. *The Emergency of Modern Turkey.* London: Oxford University Press, 1961.

Lewis, G. *La Turquie.* Verviers: Marabout, 1968.

Marceau, M. *La Grèce des Colonels.* Paris, Robert Laffont, 1967.

411

Martin, L.W. "The Changing Military Balance," *Soviet-American Rivalry in the Middle East*. Edited by J.C. Hurewitz, New York: The Academy of Political Science, 1969.

Nato. *Facts and Figures*. Brussels: Nato Information Service, 1969.

Spaak, P.H. *Combats inachevés. De l'espoir aux déception*. Paris: Fayard, 1969.

Spanier, J. *American Foreign Policy since World War II*. New York: Frederick A. Praeger, 1965.

Stavrianos, L.S. *Greece: American Dilemma and Opportunity*. Chicago: Henry Regnery, 1952.

Tansky, L. *U.S. and U.S.S.R. Aid to Developing Countries: A Comparative Study of India, Turkey, and the U.A.R*. New York: Frederick A. Praeger, 1967.

Truman, H.S. *Memoirs*. 2 vols. Garden City: Doubleday and Company, 1956.

Tsoucalas, C. *The Greek Tragedy*. Harmondsworth: Penguin Books Ltd., 1969.

Ulam, A.B. *Expansion and Coexistence. The History of Soviet Foreign Policy 1917-1967*. New York: Frederick A. Praeger, 1968.

Váli, A. *Bridge accross the Bosporus. The Foreign Policy of Turkey*. Baltimore: The Johns Hopkins Press, 1971.

Weiker, F. *The Turkish Revolution, 1960-1961*. Washington, D.C.: The Brookings Institution, 1963.

Xydis, S.G. *Greece and the Great Powers: 1944-47*. Thessaloniki: Institute of Balkan Studies, 1963.

## 3. Yearbooks

Daniel, J. "Turkey's Position in the post-war World." *The Yearbook of World Affairs, 1951*, London: Stevens and Sons Limited, 1952.

## 4. Articles

Cabiaux, M.-P. "Les Relations Turco-Soviétiques." *Chronique de Politique Etrangère*, XIX, No 6 (November, 1966), 619-702.

Campbell, J.C. "The Soviet Union and the United States in the Middle East." *The Annals*, Vol. 401 (May, 1972), 126-135.

Crollen, L. "Les Flancs de l'Alliance sont-ils Menacés?" *Revue Générale Belge*, Special Issue "Pourquoi l'OTAN?" (September, 1969), 79-111.

Eren, N. "Die Internationalen Positionen der Turkei." *Aussenpolitik*, XXVI, No 10 (October, 1965), 704-717.

Giritli, I. "Turkey since the 1965 Elections." *The Middle East Journal*, (Summer, 1969), 351-363.

Mc Ghee, G.C. "Turkey joins the West." *Foreign Affairs*, Vol. 32, No 4 (July, 1954), 617-630.

Rustow, D.A. "Defense of the Near East." *Foreign Affairs*, Vol. 34, No 2 (January, 1956), 271-286.

Sadak, N. "Turkey Faces the Soviets." *Foreign Affairs*, Vol. 27, No 3 (April, 1949), 449-461.

Sattertwaite, J.C. "The Truman Doctrine: Turkey." *The Annals*, Vol. 401, (May, 1972), 74-84.

Sulzberger, G.L. "Greece under the Colonels." *Foreign Affairs*, Vol. 48, No 2 (January, 1970), 300-311.

"The Government Position on Nato and Foreign Policy in General." *International Relations*, (Athens: January-June, 1967), 5-11.

Ulman, A.H. and Dekmejian, R.H. "Changing Patterns in Turkish Foreign Policy, 1959-1967." *Orbis*, XI, No 3 (Fall, 1967), 772-785.


## 5. Newspapers and Periodicals

*De Standaard.* March 10, 1971.

*Department of State Bulletin.* Vol. 17 (November 23, 1947).

*Documentation Française.* Notes et Etudes Documentaires, No 2052.

*International Herald Tribune.* April 17, 1972.

*Keesing Historisch Archief.* 1971-1972.

*Le Monde.* 1961-1972.

*Neue Zürcher Zeitung.* 1971-1972.

*Newsweek.* 1969-1973.

*Nieuwe Rotterdamse Courant.* March 20, 1971.

*Outlook.* August 21, 1968.

*The Jerusalem Post.* April 25, 1972.

*The New York Times.* 1965-1970.

*The Reporter.* September 9, 1965.

*The Times* (London). August 27, 1964.

*Time* (Magazine). 1969-1973.


## 6. Unpublished Materials

Galloway, J.V. "*Nato's Southern Flank.*" Unpublished paper, Harvard University, 1967.

IV. NORWAY, DENMARK AND ICELAND

## 1. Public Documents

U.S. Office of the Assistant Secretary of Defense, *Military Assistance and Foreign Military Sales, Facts*, Washington, D.C.: Government Printing Office, March, 1970.

U.S. Congress, House, *Overseas Loans and Grants and Assistance from International Organizations, July 1, 1945 - June 30, 1965.* Special Report prepared for the House Foreign Affairs Committee. Washington, D.C.: Government Printing Office, 1966.

Norway, Ministry of Defense, *Vårt Forsvar.* Oslo, 1964.

Denmark, Udenrigsministeriet, *Dansk Sikkerhedspolitik, 1948-1966*, I. Fremstilling, II. Bilag Copenhagen, Olsen, 1968.

Denmark, Udenrigsministeriet, *Udviklingen inden for NATO, 1966-1967.* Copenhagen, Olsen, 1968.


## 2. Books

Andersen, S.V. *The Nordic Council. A study of Scandinavian Regionalism.* Seattle: University of Washington Press, 1967.

Andrén, N. *Power-Balance and Non-Alignment. A Perspective on Swedish Foreign Policy.* Stockholm: Almqvist and Wiksell, 1967.

Andrén, N. *Government and Politics in the Nordic Countries; Denmark, Finland, Iceland, Norway, Sweden.* Stockholm: Almqvist and Wiksell, 1964.

Bjerregaard, S., Christensen, I., *et al. 9 om NATO.* Copenhagen: Atlantsammenslutningen, 1969.

Bjøl, E., *et al. Danmark og NATO.* Copenhagen: Gyldendal, 1968.

Borberg, F. *Danmark i NATO.* Copenhagen: Atlantsammenslutningen, 1958.

Brauer, K., Bro, K. *et al., NATO i 1970' erne. Syv unge Politikere for og imod NATO.* Copenhagen: Atlantsammenslutningen, 1968.

Brundtland, A.O. *Sikkerhetspolitisk Omprøving?* Oslo: Norsk Utenrikspolitisk Institutt, 1968.

Burgess, P.M. *Elite Images and Foreign Policy Outcomes. A Study of Norway.* Columbus: Ohio State University Press, 1967.

Carlyle, M. ed. *Documents on International Affairs*, edited under the Auspices of the Royal Institute of International Affairs, vols. II-IV, London: Oxford University Press, 1954.

Greve, T. *Norway and NATO.* Oslo: Press Department, Royal Ministry of Foreign Affairs, 1968.

Gröndal, B. *Iceland, from Neutrality to NATO Membership.* Oslo: Universitetsforlaget, 1971.

Haekkerup, P. *Danmarks Udenrigspolitik.* Aarhus, AOF Fremad, 1965.

Haagerup, N.J. *NATO efter 1969.* Copenhagen, Berlingske Forlag, 1967.

Henningsen, S. "The Foreign Policy of Denmark", *Foreign Policies in a World of Change*, Eds. Joseph E. Black and Kenneth W. Thomsen. New York, Harper and Row, 1963.

Himle, E. *Forsvarsutgiftene og den økonomiske baereevne*. Oslo, Den Norske Atlanterhavs-komité, No 4, 1968.

Holst, J.J. *Norsk Sikkerhetspolitik i Strategisk Perspektiv*. I : Analyse; II : Dokumentasjon. Oslo, Norsk Utenrikspolitisk Institutt, 1967.

Jakobson, M. *Finnish Neutrality*. London, Hugh Evelyn, 1968.

Klenberg, J. *The Cap and the Straits. Problems of Nordic Security*. Occasional Paper No 18, Center for International Affairs, Harvard University. Cambridge, Massachusetts, April 1967.

Kragh, E. *Focus på Danmarks Sikkerhedspolitik*. Copenhagen, Atlantsammenslutningen, 1967.

Loechen, E. *Norway in European and Atlantic Cooperation*. Oslo, Universitetsforlaget, 1964.

Miller, K.E. *Government and Politics in Denmark*. Boston, Houghton Mifflin and Co., 1968.

Neuchterlein, D.E. *Iceland Reluctant Ally*. Ithaca, Cornell University Press, 1961.

Nordal, J. and V. Kristinsson, eds. *Iceland 1966*. Handbook published by the Central Bank of England. Reykjavik, Istafoldarprentsmietja, 1967.

Petersen, K.H. *Debat om Forsvaret*. Copenhagen, Hasselbachs, 1967.

Reske-Nielsen, E. and Kragh, E. *Atlantpagten og Danmark, 1949-1962*. Copenhagen, Atlant-sammenslutningen, 1962.

Schou, A. and A.O. Brundtland. eds., *Small States in International Relations*. Stockholm, Almqvist and Wiksell, 1971.

X., *Danmarks Sikkerhedspolitik*. Copenhagen, Socialdemokratiets Udenrigs- og Forsvars-politiske Udvalg, 1969.

## 3. Articles

Anderssen, T. "The Royal Norwegian Air Force." *The Royal Air Force Quarterly*, VIII, No 2 (Summer, 1968), 97-100.

Bassett, J.A. "The Invasion of Norway. An Example of Extended Strategy." *Military Review*, XXIX, No 7 (October, 1949), 3-16.

Benediktsson, B. "Islands Platz in der Welt." *NATO-Brief*, No 6 (June 1968), 2-7.

Berg, O. "Security Policy Considerations." *Cooperation and Conflict*, X, No 1 (1971), 31-38.

Bindlingmaier, G. von. "Die Bedeutung der Ostsee für die NATO und die Aufgaben der Bundesmarine." *Wehrkunde*, VII, No 12 (December 1958), 674-682.

Biörklund, E. "On NATO's Northern Flanc." *Revue Militaire Générale*, No 6 (June, 1961), 45-57.

Bjøl, E. "NATO and Denmark." *Cooperation and Conflict*, VII, No 2 (1968), 93-107.

Bjøl, E. "A Soviet View of Northern Europe." *Cooperation and Conflict*, VI, No 2 (1967), 112-115.

Bjøl, E. "Le Danemark et l'Europe." *Revue Danoise*, No 37 (1971), 16-19.

Brundtland, A.O. "The Nordic Balance." *Cooperation and Conflict*, I, No 2 (1962), 31-63.

Burbank, L.B. "Scandinavian Integration and Western Defense." *Foreign Affairs*, XXXV, No 1 (October, 1956), 144-150.

415

Campbell, C.S. "The Influence of Domestic Politics on the Defense Policy of Iceland." *Naval War College Review*, (December, 1970), 76-99.

Crollen, L. "Les Flancs de l'Alliance sont-ils menacés?" *Revue Générale Belge*, Special Issue "Pourquoi l'OTAN?" (September, 1969), 79-111.

Dau, M. "The Soviet Union and the Liberation of Denmark." *Survey*, No 76 (1970), 64-81.

Edmonds, M. and Skitt, J. "Die Neue Maritime Strategie der Sowjetunion und die NATO." *Europa-Archiv*, XXIV, No 2 (January, 1969), 47-62.

F.C.U. "De Rol van de Marine in de Noorse Defensie." *Het Leger en de Natie*, XII, No 10 (October, 1957), 21-25.

Frankel, J. "Compairing Foreign Policies. The Case of Norway." *International Affairs* (London), XXXXIV, No 3 (July, 1968), 482-493.

Fritsch, J. "Les Etats Scandinaves à l'heure du Choix." *Revue de Défense Nationale*, XXIV (March, 1968), 450-460 and (April, 1968), 645-657.

Guenther, H.K. "Dänemark und die Verteidigung Westeuropas." *Wehrwissenschaftliche Rundschau*, V, No 5 (May, 1956), 254-265.

Haekkerup, P. "Pourquoi le Danemark doit rester dans l'OTAN." *Nouvelles de l'OTAN*, XVI, No 4 (April, 1968), 2-5.

Hansen, G. "Pourquoi la Norvège doit rester dans l'OTAN." *Nouvelles de l'OTAN*, XVI, No 12 (December, 1968), 2-5.

Haagerup, N.J. "NATO efter Czekoslovakiet." *Fremtiden*, XXIII, No 5 (1968), 5-6.

Haagerup, N.J. "Denmark's Security Policy." *Survival*, XIII, No 5 (May, 1971), 172-178.

Haagerup, N.J. "Nordek and Europe." *Internationale Spectator* (The Hague), XXIV, No 9 (May, 1970), 801-814.

Haagerup, N.J. and Örvik, N. "The Scandinavian Members of NATO." *Adelphi Papers*, No 22 (December, 1965), 1-13.

Haagerup, N.J. "Politische Erwägungen über die Zukunft der dänischen Verteidigung." *Wehrkunde*, XIV, No 10 (October, 1965), 532-537.

Haugan, A. "The Defense of Norway." *Military Review*, XLIV, No 1 (January, 1964), 17-23.

Healey, D. "Les Perspectives de la Politique Militaire Soviétique." *Nouvelles de l'OTAN*, XVII, No 3 (March, 1969), 24-29.

Holst, J.J. "The Soviet Build-up in the North-East Atlantic." *NATO Review*, XIX, No 9-10 (September-October, 1971), 21-23.

Holst, J.J. "A Norwegian Look in the Early 'Seventies'." *International Organization*, XXIV, No 2 (Spring, 1969), 356-366.

Holst, J.J. "The Soviet Union and Nordic Security." *Cooperation and Conflict*, X, No 3-4 (1971), 137-145.

Jansson, J.M. "La Neutralité Finlandaise. Les Perspectives Européennes." *Politique Etrangère*, XXXVI, No 4 (1971), 361-372.

Jouve, G. "La Neutralité Finlandaise." *La Revue Socialiste* (March-April, 1971), 35-46.

Jung, H. "Strategische Probleme um die Ostsee." *Wehrkunde*, VII, No 3 (March, 1958), 121-127.

Krag, J.O. "Europe and Denmark." *Chronique de Politique Etrangère*, XIX, No 4 (1966), 345-354.

Lauesen, M.L. "Die Entwicklung der dänischen Strategie." *Wehrkunde*, XVI, No 9 (September, 1967), 472-476.

Lenormand, Ch. "L'Islande en 1972." *Revue de Défense Nationale*, XXIIX (August-September, 1972), 1267-1278.

Lund, N. "Warum gehört Schweden nicht zum Atlantikpakt?". *Wehrkunde*, IX, No 8 (August, 1960), 389-393.

Nielsson, G.P. "The Nordic and the Continental European Dimensions in Scandinavian Integration: NORDEK as a Case Study." *Cooperation and Conflict*, X, No 3-4 (1971), 173-181.

Örvik, N. "Die strategische Lage Skandinaviens und der NATO." *Wehrkunde*, XVII, No 5 (May, 1968), 256-263.

Örvik, N. "Scandinavia, NATO and Northern Security." *International Organization*, XX, No 3 (Summer, 1966), 380-396.

Örvik, N. "NATO, NAFTA, and the Smaller Allies." *Orbis*, XII, No 2 (Summer, 1968), 455-464.

Padelford N.J. "Regional Cooperation in Scandinavia," *International Organization*, XI, No 4 (autumn 1957), 597-614.

Petersen, H.M. "Maritime Denmark." *Proceedings* (U.S. Naval Institute), XCIV, No 1 (January, 1968), 37-49.

Petersen, N.H. "Alliance-systemernes Opløsning." *Fremtiden*, XXIII, No 5 (1968), 17-21.

Riggert, E. "Norwegische Heimwehr." *Wehrkunde*, VIII, No 2 (February, 1959), 97-99.

Riggert, E. "Grundzüge Skandinavischer Rüstung." *Wehrkunde*, XII, No 1 (January, 1963), 30-36.

Schützsack, A. "Neutralität und Machtbalance in Nordeuropa." *Aussenpolitik*, XXII, No 9 (September, 1971), 553-562.

Stoel, M. van der "Le Flanc Nord de l'Alliance Atlantique." *Nouvelles de l'OTAN*, XVII, No 9 (September, 1969), 16-20.

Wettern, D. "NATO's Northern Flanc." *Proceedings* (U.S. Naval Institute), XCV, No 7 (July, 1969), 52-59.

Wettmore, W.C. "Norwegian Defense Posture gives Key Role to Air Force." *Aviation Week & Space Technology*, XC, No 11 (March, 1969), 40-45.

Wettmore, W.C. "Denmark Unifying top Military Command." *Aviation Week & Space Technology*, XC, No 13 (March, 1969), 55-62.

Wilkinson, J.R. "Denmark and NATO: the Problem of a Small State in a Collective Security System." *International Organization*, X, No 3 (August, 1956) 390-401.

X. "Denmarks New Territorial Army." *Military Review*, XXXII, No 1 (April, 1952), 92-95.

Zitzewitz, H. von. "Die Gesamtverteidigung Dänemarks." *Wehrkunde*, XIV, No 6 (June 1965), 316-322.

Zitzewitz, H. von. "Die Gesamtverteidigung Norwegens." *Wehrkunde*, XIV, No 9 (September, 1965), 459-465.

## 4. Newspapers and Periodicals

Der Spiegel

Time

Berlingske Tidende

The Military Balance, 1960-1972

NATO Review

Jane's Fighting Ships

International Herald Tribune

Fremtiden

Le Monde

Keesing's Historisch Archief

Internasjonal Politikk

## V. BELGIUM, HOLLAND, AND LUXEMBOURG

## 1. Public Documents

Belgium. *Parlementaire Documenten*, Kamer, 1945-1971.

Belgium. *Parlementaire Documenten*, Senaat, 1945-1971.

Belgium. *Parlementaire Handelingen*, Kamer, 1945-1971.

Belgium. *Parlementaire Handelingen*, Senaat, 1945-1971.

Belgium. Ministère des Affaires Economiques et des Classes Moyennes. *L'Economie Belge en 1947*, 1948, 1949, 1950, 1951, 1952. Brussels, 1949-1953.

Belgium. Ministère des Affaires Economiques. *L'Economie Belge en 1953*. Brussels, 1954.

Belgium. Ministerie van Economische Zaken en Energie. Nationaal Instituut voor de Statistiek. *Handel — Toerisme — Verkeer en Vervoer 1900-1961*. Brussels, n.d.

Belgium. Ministerie van Landsverdediging. *De Landsverdediging in Cijfertaal*. Brussels, 1971.

Belgium. Ministerie van Landsverdediging. *Landsverdediging 1961-1965*. Brussels, 1964.

Holland. *Handelingen van de Staten-Generaal, Eerste Kamer*, 1945-1971.

Holland. *Handelingen van de Staten-Generaal, Tweede Kamer*, 1945-1971.

Holland. *Nota inzake het Defensiebeleid 18 mei 1954*. The Hague, 1954.

Holland. *Nota inzake het NAVO- en het Defensiebeleid 1968*. The Hague, 1968.

Holland. Persdienst van het Ministerie van Economische Zaken. *Nederlands Economisch Herstel*. n.p., 1952.

Luxembourg. *Compte Rendu des Séances de la Chambre des Députés du Grand-Duché de Luxembourg*, 1945-1971.

OEEC. *Rapport sur l'amélioration de la situation économique en Europe occidentale*. n.p., June 1949.

United Nations. *Etude sur la situation économique de l'Europe depuis la guerre*. Geneva, 1953.

U.S. Congress. House. *U.S. Overseas Loans and Grants and Assistance from International Organizations, Obligations and Loan Authorizations July 1, 1945 - June 30, 1965*. Special Committee. Washington, D.C.: Government Printing Office.

U.S. Office of the Assistant Secretary of Defense. *Military Assistance and Foreign Military Sales Facts*. Washington, D.C.: Government Printing Office, 1970.

## 2. Books

Acheson, D. *Present at the Creation. My Years in the State Department*. New York: W.W. Norton and Company, Inc., 1969.

Ball, M.M. *Nato and the European Union Movement*. London: Stevens and Sons Ltd., 1959.

Bloema, K.P. *Moderne Politieke Strategieën. Een kritiek op het defensie- en het buitenlands beleid*. The Hague: Nijgh and Ditmar, 1968.

Bloes, R. *Le 'Plan Fouchet' et le problème de l'Europe politique*. Bruges: College of Europe, 1970.

Bodenheimer, S. *Political Union: A Microcosm of European Politics 1960-1966*. Leiden: M. Nijhoff, 1967.

Brakel, W. *De industrialisatie in Nederland gedurende de periode der Marshall-hulp*. Leiden: Stenfert Kroese N.V., 1954.

Burrows, B. and Irwin, C. *The Security of Western Europe. Towards a Common Defence Policy*. London: Charles Knight and Co. Ltd., 1972.

Camu, L. "The Postwar Monetary Policy of the Benelux Countries in its effect on Foreign Trade". *International Banking and Foreign Trade*, (Lectures delivered at: the Eighth International Banking Summer School, Christ Church, Oxford, September 1955). Published for the Institute of Bankers. London, 1955.

De Raeymaeker, O. *België's internationaal beleid 1919-1939*. Brussels: N.V. Standaard Boekhandel, 1945.

Diebold, W., Jr. *Trade and Payments in Western Europe. A study in Economic Cooperation 1947-1951*. New York: Harper and Brothers, 1952.

Goguel, F., and Grosser, A. *La politique en France*. Paris: A. Colin, 1964.

Harlow, C.J.E. *Defence, Technology and the Western Alliance*. London: ISS, 1967.

Hemmer, C. *L'Economie du Grand-Duché de Luxembourg*. 2 vols. Luxembourg: Eds. J. Beffort, 1948-1953.

Jaquet, L.G.M. "The Role of a Small State within Alliance Systems." *Small States in International Relations*. Edited by A. Schou and A.O. Brundland. Stockholm: Almqvist and Wiksell, 1971.

Joint, J.E. *Belgium. Report on economic and financial conditions in Belgium. With an annex on the Grand-Duchy of Luxembourg*. London: H.M.S.O., 1949.

Kennan, G.F. *Memoirs 1925-1950*. New York: Bantam Books Inc., 1969.

Kieft, D.O. *Belgium's Return to Neutrality. An Essay in the frustrations of small power diplomacy*. Oxford: Clarendon Press, 1972.

Kill, J. *1000 jähriges Luxemburg. Woher? — Wohin? Ein Beitrag zum bessern Verständnis der Geschichte des Luxemburger Landes*. Luxembourg: Druck und Verlag, C.O.P.E., 1963.

Kissinger, A. *The Troubled Partnership*. New York: Anchor Books, 1966.

Luyckx, T. *Politieke Geschiedenis van België*. Brussels: Elsevier, 1964.

Miller, J.K. *Belgian Foreign Policy Between Two Wars 1919-1940*. New York: Bookman Associates, 1951.

NATO Information Service. *NATO Facts and Figures*. Brussels, 1969.

Pfaltzgraff, R.L., Jr. *The Atlantic Community. A Complex Imbalance*. New York: Van Nostrand Reinhold Company, 1969.

Royal Institute for International Relations. *La Belgique et les Nations Unies*. New York: Manhattan Publishing Company, 1958.

Russett, B.M. *What Price Vigilance? The Burdens of National Defense*. New Haven: Yale University Press, 1970.

Schaus, L. "Les Fondements du statut international du Luxembourg 1944-1957." *Le Conseil d'Etat du Grand-Duché de Luxembourg Livre jubilaire*. Luxembourg, 1957.

Smit, C. *Diplomatieke Geschiedenis van Nederland*. The Hague: M. Nijhoff, 1950.

Spaak, P.H. *Combats Inachevés. De l'Indépendance à l'Alliance*. Paris: Fayard, 1969.

Spaak, P.H. *Combats Inachevés. De l'espoir aux déceptions*. Paris: Fayard, 1969.

Spanier, J.W. *American Foreign Policy Since World War II*. New York: F.A. Praeger, 1965.

Stikker, D.U. *Men of Responsibility — A Memoir*. New York: Harper and Row, 1965.

Truman, H.S. *Memoirs*. Vol. II. *Years of trial and hope*. New York: Doubleday and Company Inc., 1956.

van B. Cleveland, H. *The Atlantic Idea and its European Rivals*. New York: Mc Graw Hill, 1966.

van Campen, S.I.P. *The Quest for Security — Some Aspects of Netherlands Foreign Policy, 1945-1950*. The Hague: M. Nijhoff, 1958.

Vandenbosch, A. *Dutch Foreign Policy Since 1815. A Study in Small Power Politics*. The Hague: M. Nijhoff, 1959.

Van der Beugel, E.H. "Defensie-Aspecten in het Europa van morgen." *Centenaire Ecole de Guerre — Eeuwfeest Krijgsschool 1870-1970*. Brussels, 1971.

Van der Beugel, E.H. *From Marshall Aid to Atlantic Partnership*. Amsterdam: Elsevier Publishing Company, 1966.

Van Der Mensbrugghe, J. *Les Unions Economiques. Réalisations et Perspectives*. Brussels: Institut des Relations Internationales, 1949.

van Langenhove, F. *La Sécurité de la Belgique. Contribution à l'histoire de la période 1940-1950*. Brussels: Edition de l'Université de Bruxelles, 1971.

Van Meerhaeghe, M.A.G. *Internationale Economische Betrekkingen en Instellingen*. Leiden: Stenfert Kroese, N.V., 1964.

Van Zuylen, P. *Les Mains Libres. Politique extérieure de la Belgique 1914-1940*. Brussels: L'édition universelle, 1950.

Vivario, G. "La défense de la Belgique." *Centenaire Ecole de Guerre — Eeuwfeest Krijgsschool 1870-1970*. Brussels, 1971.

Weil, G.L. *The Benelux Nations. The Politics of Small-Country Democracies*. New York: Holt, Rinehart and Winston Inc., 1970.

Willis, F.R. *Italy chooses Europe*. New York: Oxford University Press, 1971.

Zoetewey, H. *De Dollarschaarste in West-Europa*. Leiden: Stenfert Kroese N.V., 1949.

## 3. Yearbooks

Holland. *Jaarboek van het Ministerie van Buitenlandse Zaken*. The Hague, 1949-1968.

United Nations. *Statistical Yearbook of the United Nations, 1949-1950*. New York, 1950.

## 4. Articles

Anders, J. "L'Evolution économique du Grand-Duché de Luxembourg depuis la libération." Banque Nationale de Belgique. *Bulletin d'Information et de Documentation*, XXIII, Vol. II, No 1 (August, 1948), 1-17, and *Bulletin d'Information et de Documentation*, XXV, Vol. I, No 3 (March, 1950), 113-127.

Boon, H.N. "What is détente?" *Internationale Spectator*, (July 8, 1968), 1045-1079.

CEPESS. "Regeerakkoord van 15 Januari 1972." *Cepess-Dokumenten*, Nos 3-4 (Brussels, 1971), 177-210.

Colot, L. "La politique Belge en matière de détente et de coopération en Europe." *Chronique de Politique Etrangère*, (January, 1969), 53-74.

Coppieters, E. "Economische en sociale gevolgen voor België van een eventuele ontwapening." *Internationale Spectator*, (July 8, 1971), 1277-1296.

Cordemans, M. "België en de Mogendheden." *De Gids op Maatschappelijk Gebied*, Nos 3-4 (March-April, 1949), 493-520.

Damm, C. and Goodhart, Ph. "Die Euro-Gruppe im Atlantischen Bündnis." *Europa-Archiv*, No 4 (1973), 137-146.

De Raeymaeker, O. "Regionale accoorden en wettige zelfverdediging." *Politica*, VII, No 3 (July, 1957), 193-213.

Enkelaar, H.F. "Naar een doelmatig bedrijfseconomisch beheer bij de Koninklijke Lucht-macht." *Militaire Spectator*, No 9 (September, 1968), 425-431.

Fens, M.J.J. "L'Organisation de la défense aux Pays-Bas." *La Revue Politique*, No 2 (July, 1957), 191-195.

Harmel, P. "België, Europa en de NAVO." *NAVO-Maandblad*, (June, 1966), 2-8.

Hayoul, M. "L'Europe de l'Est, le groupe des 'neuf' et M.P. Harmel." *La Revue Nouvelle*, No 6 (June 15, 1967), 633-641.

Howard, G.B. "The Role of Belgium in Nato." *The Military Review*, (July, 1971), 17-22.

Keesing, F.A.G. "Le Développement économique des Pays-Bas depuis la Libération." Banque Nationale de Belgique. *Bulletin d'Information et de Documentation*, XXIV, Vol. I, No 6 (June, 1949), 269-275.

Leurdijk, J.H. "De Nederlandse buitenlandse politiek en de nucleaire bewapening." *Internationale Spectator*, (January 8, 1972), 21-41.

Luns, J.M.A.H. "Independence or interdependence." *International Affairs*, (January, 1964), 1-40.

Marmol, A. Baron del "Belgische opvattingen over het Europees nucleaire afschrikkings-wapen." *Internationale Spectator*, (January 8, 1965), 39-48.

M.T. "The Benelux Countries and NATO." *The World Today*, XV, No 5 (May, 1959), 195-204.

O'Ballance, E. "The Armed Forces of Belgium." *Revue Militaire Générale*, (January, 1967), 54-71.

O'Ballance, E. "In Defense of Holland." *Arms Quaterly*, No 2 (July, 1961), 182-191.

Patijn, C.L. "Nederlands Buitenlands Beleid." *Internationale Spectator*, (January 8, 1970), 14-23.

Russell, R.W. "The Atlantic Alliance in Dutch Foreign Policy." *Internationale Spectator*, (July 8, 1969), 1189-1208.

Samkalden, I. "A Dutch Retrospective View on European and Atlantic Co-operation." *Internationale Spectator*, (April 8, 1965), 626-642.

Savorning Lohman, W.H. de "Quelques Aspects de la Défense néerlandaise." *Revue Militaire générale*, No 10 (December, 1969), 611-627.

Schipper, R.A.H., van Staden, A., Tazelaar, C.A., Wassen, W.J., and Wesseldijk, J.W. "Rol-opvattingen in de naoorlogse buitenlandse politiek van Nederland." *Internationale Spectator*, (January 8, 1973), 21-30.

Servais, A. "L'Effort militaire belge et la dissuasion." *Revue Militaire générale*, (May, 1968), 575-587.

Spits, F.C. "Nederlandse gedachten over vrede en veiligheid, ontspanning en neutraliteit." *Militaire Spectator*, (December, 1969), 545-553.

Tindemans, L. "De toekomst van de NAVO." *Le Monde Atlantique -- De Atlantische Wereld*, (December, 1969), 19-25.

Van Staden, A. "Oordelen over het Nederlands buitenlands beleid." *Acta Politica*, (January, 1972), 10-153.

Van Eekelen, W.F. "Nucleaire wapenen en de Westelijke verdediging." *Internationale Spectator*, (July 8, 1970), 1211-1230.

Vincineau, M. "Le Parlement Belge devant la crise de l'alliance atlantique." *Chronique de Politique Etrangère*, (Janvier, 1968), 89-164.

von Zitzewitz, H. "Der NATO Beitrag und die nationale Verteidigung der Niederlande." *Wehrkunde*, XIV, (November, 1965), 580-586.

Werner, V. "La défense nationale." *Pallas*, (September, 1962), 14-27.

Werner, V. "La défense nationale." *Pallas*, (November, 1962), 14-26.

## 5. Newspapers and Periodicals

*De Standaard*. April 24, June 22, November 13, December 5, 6, 7, 29, 1972.

*De Telegraaf*. March 28, 1972; April 24, 1973.

*De Volksgazet*. January 18, July 6, 1973.

*Elsevier Magazine*. November 8, 1969; October 24, 1970; and May 29, 1971.

*Keesing's Contemporary Archives*, 1946-1971.

*Keesing's Historisch Archief*, 1948-1972.

*La Libre Belgique*. May 9, 10, 11, and June 27, 1966.

*Le Soir*. March 16, 1966.

*NAVO Kroniek*. November-December, 1972.

*NRC Handelsblad*. January 8, 1973.

*The Military Balance*, 1963-1972.

## 6. Unpublished materials and other sources

Brasseur, G. *"La Politique militaire de la Belgique depuis la fin de la seconde guerre mondiale."* Brussels: Krijgsschool, March, 1968. (Mimeo.).

Brauers, W.K. *"Effekt van de Belgische Militaire Uitgaven op de Belgische Economie en Landsverdediging."* Brussels, March, 1972.

International Research Associates. *"L'implantation de l'OTAN et du SHAPE en Belgique. Rapport des résultats d'une enquête concernant les attitudes du public belge à l'égard de l'implantation de l'OTAN et du SHAPE en Belgique.* Brussels, May 19, 1967.

NIPO. *"Bericht nr. 1285."* Amsterdam, May 1, 1969.

VanDepoele, L. *"De eerste vormen van organisatorische samenwerking in West-Europa, in de periode 1947-1949, als gevolg van de Marshallrede. De Belgische Houding* (Regering en Parlement)." Louvain, July 1964. (Mimeo.).

Wolter, J.C. *"Le Luxembourg et l'OTAN."* Luxembourg, 1963. (Mimeo.).

*Previously published in the same series:*

STUDIES IN INTERNATIONAL RELATIONS NUMBER 1

# PORTUGAL, THE U.S. AND NATO

by LUC CROLLEN

**Contents**

1973. 163 pages.      (ISBN 90 6186 006 7)      Guilders 25.–

MARTINUS NIJHOFF - PUBLISHER - P.O.B. 269 - THE HAGUE